Essential Clinical S

MW00823978

Series editor

Carol Tosone, New York, USA

More information about this series at http://www.springer.com/series/8115

Barbara Probst

Editor

Critical Thinking in Clinical Assessment and Diagnosis

 Springer

Editor
Barbara Probst
School for Social Work
Smith College
Northampton, MA, USA

Essential Clinical Social Work Series
ISBN 978-3-319-38311-8   ISBN 978-3-319-17774-8   (eBook)
DOI 10.1007/978-3-319-17774-8

Springer International Publishing AG Switzerland is part of Springer Science+Business Media (www.springer.com)

In Loving Memory of My Parents
Lillian S. Hawthorne, MSW
Edward I. Hawthorne, PhD

Foreword

The book you are now holding in your hand, *Critical Thinking in Clinical Assessment and Diagnosis*, should unsettle you. And for that, you should be thankful. Let me explain why.

For several centuries, those who attended to people in the United States who seemed very disturbed or disturbing to others believed that they knew what was wrong and what needed to be done. The medieval view was that the disturbed were possessed by the devil and needed to be burned at the stake to save their souls persisted into Colonial times. In the mid-nineteenth century, the belief was that they were suffering from the stresses of the new urban environments and needed to be sequestered in quiet, well-structured, small asylums in rural environments that would restore their spirits so that they could be returned cured to their home communities. By the turn of the twentieth century, those small asylums had become massive institutions, mislabeled as state hospitals, where the disturbed were in involuntary confinement as incurable and where they would spend the rest of their lives. By the mid-twentieth century, encouraged by psychoanalysis, the troubled were understood to be suffering from a cauldron of unconscious tensions about which they needed to gain insight through the talking cure. By the turn of the twenty-first century, the disturbed—their numbers now expansively defined from a rare few to the majority of the population—are understood to have bad genes, chemical imbalances, or faulty electrical circuits in their brains—and are encouraged and at times coerced to ingest an array of expensive proprietary drugs manufactured by huge corporations, sanctioned by the FDA, and dispensed by a sales force of physicians.

For none of this history is there any reasonable evidence of the veracity of the helpers' beliefs or the effectiveness of their interventions. And there is no evidence that the proportion of the disturbed or disturbing in the country has declined. It is likely that interventions in the name of promoting mental health may have harmed more people than they helped. It is not enough for us to simply recognize our past failures. In this book, Barbara Probst and her eminent co-authors attempt to make it less likely that in 25 or 50 years from now, we have merely continued the errors of previous generations.

As social work students entering the field of mental health, you may be baffled by much of this history. You will wonder how prior generations could concoct such simple-minded explanations for personal troubles, adopt such brutal interventions, and proceed for decades without critically assessing the effects of these purported explanations or treatments. Although you may be told by some "experts" that the confusions and mistakes of the past are far behind us, that we now really understand what causes unhappiness, anxiety, and troublesome behavior, and that we now know how to effectively cure it, this book should help you more critically assess the complexities of our ignorance and the ways we can guard against false assumptions.

The field of mental health and clinical practice is *not* an arena of serenity, certainty, and self-assurance. Currently, the field is struggling with many fundamental questions about the nature of mental disorders, how they should be assessed, understood, and treated, and how and what services should be provided. For example, there are profound debates about whether the behaviors defined as symptoms of mental illness in the *Diagnostic and Statistical Manual of Mental Disorders* (DSM) and the classification system based on those definitions, which for 35 years has served as the foundational document in psychiatry, are scientifically valid. In fact, in an unprecedented action, the Director of the National Institute of Mental Health (NIMH) rejected the latest edition of DSM-5 for not being scientifically valid and stated that DSM would no longer be used in NIMH research. This was a massive earthquake.

This development is relevant to you and to social work because our profession has had a romance with the profession of psychiatry for nearly a century. The allure of psychiatry to social work has been, in part, because of psychiatry's proximity to medicine with its well-established record of scientific advances in understanding physical diseases, treating illnesses, and discovering cures. Most psychiatrists eagerly and understandably adopted the same medical language and assumptions of medicine, although psychiatry never achieved anything similar to medicine's scientific grounding. Clinical social work, itself not well grounded scientifically either, has always had some doubts and ambivalence about psychiatry, revolving around whether disturbing behavior and psychological turmoil could be fully understood or ameliorated without serious attention to the social environment and social justice, a focus that psychiatry has steadily abandoned as it has morphed into bio-psychiatry.

This volume organized and framed by Barbara Probst contains essays written by an outstanding group of critical thinkers. They counter the simplistic thinking and reductionist propaganda that are easily found in the mental health field. Their observations and arguments may challenge your beliefs; they do not want you to be seduced into the false certitude that blinded prior generations. You will not be offered a simple, one-dimensional view of client problems, assessment, and intervention. This book will encourage you to have a much more nuanced and respectful understanding of your clients and their troubles and will enhance the effectiveness of your professional practice.

Stuart A. Kirk
Luskin School of Public Affairs
University of California
Los Angeles, CA, USA

Contents

1 Why This Book Is Needed 1
Barbara Probst

2 Epistemological Issues in Diagnosis and Assessment 15
Barbara Probst

**3 The DSM-5 Definition of Mental Disorder: Critique
and Alternatives** 45
Bruce A. Thyer

**4 Making Assessment Decisions: Macro, Mezzo,
and Micro Perspectives** 69
Jeffrey R. Lacasse and Eileen Gambrill

5 Situating Disorder: Mental Disorder in Context 85
Barbara Probst

**6 Neuroscience, Resilience, and the Embodiment
of "Mental" Disorder** 111
Eric L. Garland and Elizabeth Thomas

**7 The Role of Temperament in Conceptualizations
of Mental Disorder** 133
Mary K. Rothbart

**8 A Psychodynamic Perspective on Assessment
and Formulation** 151
Brian Rasmussen

9 Narratives of Illness, Difference, and Personhood 171
John P. McTighe

**10   Person-Centered and Contextualized Diagnosis
      in Mental Health**   189
      Juan E. Mezzich and Ada M. Mezzich

11   Integrating Practice and Research on Mental Disorder   205
      Mark Hardy

12   Meeting the Challenge of Teaching Integrated Assessment   229
      Howard Robinson

13   Assessment and Diagnosis in Action.   247
      Barbara Probst

14   Supplementary Materials   267

      Appendix A: Case Study: The Case of Ray.   268

      Appendix B: Historical Overview of the DSM.   272

      Appendix C: Challenging the Narrative of Chemical Imbalance:
                    A Look at the Evidence.   275
                    Jeffrey Lacasse and Jonathan Leo

      Appendix D: Results of a Survey: MSW Students' Views
                    About Mental Disorder   283
                    Barbara Probst, Catherine Balletto
                    and Nichole Wofford

      Appendix E: Special Issues in the Assessment of Children
                    and Families.   288
                    Barbara Probst

      Appendix F: Sample Assignments and Exercises for Students   290
                    Fordham University, Graduate School
                    of Social Service

      Appendix G: Sample Syllabus Using This Book
                    as a Course Text.   298

Index   301

Editor and Contributors

About the Editor

Barbara Probst, Ph.D. teaches advanced clinical practice, clinical assessment and diagnosis, and qualitative research methods in the graduate schools of social work at Fordham University and Smith College. She has published extensively in numerous scholarly journals, where she is also a peer reviewer, and is the author of a book on depathologizing difference in children, *When the Labels Don't Fit* (2008). Throughout her career, she has given dozens of presentations to public and professional organizations across the country. Her research focuses on the experience of receiving and living with a mental health diagnosis.

Contributors

Catherine Balletto, MSW is a licensed clinical social worker with extensive experience providing direct service and leadership in innovative programs serving diverse at-risk populations. She received her psychodynamic training at the Women's Therapy Center Institute in New York City, and is now a doctoral student at the Smith College School for Social Work.

Eileen Gambrill, Ph.D. is professor at the Graduate School and Hutto Patterson Charitable Foundation Professor Emerita in Child and Family Studies at the School of Social Welfare, University of California at Berkeley. Her research interests include evidence-based practice, professional decision-making, social learning theory, and evaluation of practice. Recent publications include *Propaganda in the Helping Professions* (2012), *Critical Thinking in Clinical Practice: Improving the quality of judgments and decisions* (3rd edition, 2012), and *Social Work Practice: A critical thinker's guide* (3rd edition, 2013).

Eric L. Garland, Ph.D. is associate director of Integrative Medicine in Supportive Oncology at Huntsman Cancer Institute and associate professor at University of Utah College of Social Work. He has published extensively on the role of mindfulness in cognitive reappraisal, psychological well-being, and pain management, and has received funding from NIH to develop and test *Mindfulness-Oriented Recovery Enhancement*, an intervention targeting transdiagnostic mechanisms underpinning addiction, stress, and pain.

Mark Hardy, Ph.D. is lecturer in social work at the University of York, UK. He is co-author of *Evidence and Knowledge for Practice* (Polity Press 2010) and *Governing Risk: Care and control in contemporary social work* (Palgrave Macmillan 2015). He is currently co-editing a new volume entitled *Mental Health Social Work: The art and science of practice* (Routledge).

Stuart A. Kirk, DSW is distinguished professor emeritus at the Luskin School of Public Affairs, University of California, Los Angeles. His research critically examines the conventional wisdom of the helping professions, focusing on the interplay of science, values, policy, and politics. He has authored numerous articles and co-authored several books including *Science and Social Work: A Critical Appraisal*, (2002), *The Selling of DSM: The Rhetoric of Science in Psychiatry* (1992); *Making Us Crazy: DSM—The Psychiatric Bible and the Creation of Mental Disorders* (1997), and *Mad Science: Psychiatric Coercion, Diagnosis and Drugs* (2013).

Jeffrey R. Lacasse, Ph.D. is assistant professor, College of Social Work, Florida State University. His research agenda examines psychiatric diagnosis and treatment within the biomedical industrial complex. Publications address barriers to evidence-based mental health practice, including articles on critical thinking in mental health, clinical treatment of children, publication bias, data manipulation, and the use of psychiatric medications. He was also guest editor for a special issue of *Research on Social Work Practice* on the implications of DSM-5.

Jonathan Leo, Ph.D. is a professor of Neuroanatomy at Lincoln Memorial University–DeBusk College of Osteopathic Medicine. His research examines the biological basis of mental disorders such as ADHD, schizophrenia, and clinical depression. His articles have appeared in *The Journal of Mind and Behavior, Society, Psychiatric Times, and PLOS Medicine.* He is the past editor in chief of *Ethical Human Psychology and Psychiatry, and is co-editor* of the recently released book *Rethinking ADHD,* published by Palgrave.

John P. McTighe, Ph.D. is assistant professor at the School of Social Work, Ramapo College of New Jersey, holding graduate degrees in both Divinity and Social Work. Dr. McTighe's research focuses on the development of narrative theory and practice, including its relationship to resilience; other areas of specialization include clinical supervision, multicultural social work, and spirituality in clinical practice. He has published in the areas of narrative, shared traumatic stress, and the use of self in clinical process, and has presented his work both nationally and internationally.

Juan E. Mezzich MD, Ph.D. served as chair of the World Psychiatric Association (WPA) Section on Classification, member of the ICD-10 Mental Disorders Workgroup and the DSM-IV Task Force, and chair of the NIMH Group on Diagnosis and Culture. He has authored over 200 scientific journal articles and book chapters and 25 books. Former President of the World Psychiatric Association and Founding President of the International College of Person-centered Medicine, he is currently professor of Psychiatry at Mount Sinai and editor in chief of the *International Journal of Person Centered Medicine.*

Ada M. Mezzich MSW, MPIA holds graduate degrees in both social work and public and international affairs. She has spent the last two decades working to protect, empower, and treat those who suffer from abuse, neglect, and injustice. She has also worked as a mental health disaster coordinator at the American Red Cross, child advocate specialist, and assisted with a book entitled *Participatory Dialogue: Towards a Stable, Safe and Just Society* for the Economic and Social Affairs Council of the United Nations.

Brian Rasmussen, Ph.D. is associate professor in the School of Social Work at the University of British Columbia, Okanagan, and is also an adjunct associate professor at Smith College School for Social Work. He teaches clinical theory and clinical social work practice. He has published over 25 peer review articles and chapters, with much of his recent research and writing focused on integrating critical social theory with psychodynamic ideas. Dr. Rasmussen is also an international editor for several scholarly journals.

Howard Robinson, DSW is a clinical associate professor of social service at Fordham University's Graduate School of Social Service. Dr. Robinson taught at the Tel Hai College of Social Work, Israel, in 2012–2013, as a Fulbright Teaching Scholar. He has worked professionally for more than 25 years treating traumatized children, youth, and families in therapeutic preschools, foster care settings, preventive services, mental health clinics, and in private practice, and is a former director of postgraduate certificate training in child and adolescent treatment at Fordham University.

Mary K. Rothbart, Ph.D. is distinguished Professor Emerita of Psychology at the University of Oregon. She has received numerous awards for her work on individual differences in temperament, including the 2009 Gold Medal for Life Achievement in the Science of Psychology from the American Psychological Foundation and the 2014 *Block Award* from the Society of Personality and Social Psychology for research accomplishment in the field of personality psychology. Her recent book on temperament is *Becoming Who We Are: Temperament and Personality in Development* (2012).

Elizabeth Thomas, MSW is a doctoral student at the University of Utah College of Social Work. She currently works at the Center for Change, a residential and inpatient hospital specializing in the treatment of eating disorders, and is also a captain on active duty in the United States Army, serving as commander of a civil affairs company.

Bruce A. Thyer, Ph.D. is a professor and former dean with the College of Social Work at Florida State University. His research interests involve the promotion of evidence-based practice, evaluation research, applied behavior analysis, and social work theory. Dr. Thyer has produced over 260 articles, 80 chapters, and 30 books in the fields of social work, behavior analysis, psychology, and psychiatry including the *Handbook of Social Work Research Methods* (2010) and *Social Work in Mental Health: An evidence-based approach* (2007). For the past 25 years he has edited the peer-reviewed journal *Research on Social Work Practice.*

Nichole Wofford, MSW is a licensed marriage and family therapist who manages the Connect Center, a comprehensive youth and family resource center in Sacramento, California. She has worked in the mental health field for over 20 years, providing direct service, clinical supervision, program development and management, and is now a doctoral student at the Smith College School for Social Work.

Chapter 1
Why This Book Is Needed

Barbara Probst

Abstract A conceptual introduction sets forth the book's aim: to guide clinical social work students (and practicing clinicians) to explore assessment from a range of theoretical frameworks, each with its own emphasis, limitations, and form of evidence, and to think critically about what each perspective has to offer, takes for granted, omits, and counts as knowledge. It begins by exploring the meaning of the key terms "critical thinking," "diagnosis," and "assessment" and draws on both theory and research to trace how these concepts have been addressed in social work education and practice. Following an overview of the book's structure and content, including introduction to the case of Ray (a case that will be used throughout the chapters and analyzed from each clinical perspective), the introduction concludes with specific suggestions for educators about ways to use the book to develop complex, reflexive, and critical thinking in their students.

Introduction

A fundamental tenet of clinical practice is that it begins with assessment. Without a sound grasp of what is going on, interventions cannot be meaningful or effective.

An assessment, in general usage, means an appraisal of something's nature, authenticity, or worth. In psychiatry, it refers to the examination of symptoms and collection of information in order to identify the underlying disease or difficulty. For social workers, the term tends to be understood more broadly as exploration of the biological, psychological, interpersonal, environmental, cultural, and spiritual factors that affect a person's situation. It includes strengths, resources, and protective elements as well as deficits and stressors and takes place incrementally throughout the clinical relationship.

Assessment is thus both a process and the result of that process—the art of gathering relevant information and the formulation of conclusions based on that

B. Probst (✉)
School for Social Work, Smith College, Northampton, MA, USA
e-mail: Barbara.H.Probst@gmail.com

© Springer International Publishing Switzerland 2015
B. Probst (ed.), *Critical Thinking in Clinical Assessment and Diagnosis*,
Essential Clinical Social Work Series, DOI 10.1007/978-3-319-17774-8_1

information. The latter depends on the former. If a particular question is not asked, the knowledge that question might have provided will not be included in the analysis and will not play a role in determining the nature of the problem or the selection of appropriate actions. The clinician's perception of a situation is therefore shaped—and limited—by the questions that are asked. More is not always better. On the one hand, *asking only a few questions* can lead to an incomplete and biased view of the client's situation; at the same time, *asking many questions* simply for the sake of quantity can produce a "laundry list" of disconnected facts that lacks meaning or clinical utility. Learning how to ask useful questions is thus a key for skilled practice.

Many templates have been developed to help clinicians gather the information they need. Intake forms, interview protocols, symptom checklists, inventories, diagnostic rubrics, and a host of other tools have been created to facilitate the complex task of trying to understand another human being—to address the profound question of who is this person in front of me, what is going on here, and what do I need to know in order to be of help?

The clinician is faced with two tasks. The first task is to determine which elements among the vast amount of information that *might* be attended to, both objective data and subjective impressions, are truly important in a particular instance: Which are salient cues and which are of relatively minor significance? That is the task of discrimination and *de*construction. The second task is to discover how these elements are connected and what they mean or point to. That is the task of *re*construction. It is not a matter of gathering facts and *then* trying to put them together, like steps in a linear process. The two inquiries are simultaneous and recursive, each progressively illuminating the other. As new information becomes available, it is seen in the light of existing information, consciously or unconsciously, while also reflecting back on that information to suggest new ways of understanding the very structures that frame its meaning. This iterative process allows the clinician to explore patterns and relationships, including contradictions, and to note areas where knowledge may be thin or missing.

The process is complicated because information is rarely given in a logical order, no matter how well organized the intake form, but revealed bit by bit through association, sidebars, hints, and the development of trust. Initial notions may need to be reconsidered as more becomes known. Ambiguous or misleading information may be offered first, either because trust has not been established or because that is the way the client remembers it; the distortion is itself a kind of data. Features that seem striking early in a clinical relationship may mask issues that are actually far more significant. The client's situation may also change during the course of treatment, prompting re-assessment. Assessment is thus provisional and ongoing.

As the person doing the assessment works to make sense of all this emergent information, new material is inevitably compared to previous experience and existing mental schemas to see where it fits and what it signifies or suggests. All information is not given the same clinical weight. Deciding that certain facts (e.g., irritability or difficulty waiting one's turn) are clinically significant while others (e.g., a slow tempo or a tendency toward irony) are not is a judgment based on reference, whether tacit or explicit, to an underlying conceptual system. Conceptual systems set forth categories and their criteria; by delineating what "counts" as a criterion, they determine what is relevant and what is not, and which features ought to be attended to and which can be ignored.

For example, in the system for sorting color in contemporary Western culture, hue counts but intensity does not. Pale blue and navy blue are placed in the same category and given the same label, while pale blue and pale green are placed in different categories. There is no intrinsic reason for hue to be the sorting mechanism; color terms could just as easily be based on intensity. But as long as everyone in the culture accepts the rules and agrees on where category lines are drawn, communication is possible and the system works.

In the USA, the system for conceptualizing and classifying mental, emotional, and behavioral conditions is the *Diagnostic and Statistical Manual of Mental Disorders* (DSM), now in its fifth edition. Most other countries use the *International Classification of Diseases* (ICD). Developed and managed by the World Health Organization to monitor a wide range of public health issues, translated into 43 languages, and endorsed by 117 member nations, ICD covers both infectious medical diseases and mental disorders, with a special section on the classification of mental and behavioral disorders providing both clinical descriptions and diagnostic guidelines (http://www.who.int/classifications/icd/en/bluebook.pdf?ua=1). While conversion to ICD-10 codes will shortly be required by most insurance providers in the USA, there appears to be little effort thus far to phase out the DSM or to replace its terms and categories with ICD nomenclature for practice, research, or education.

Overall, the two systems are quite similar, however, and have the same underlying premise: provision of a common framework for diagnosis and communication. Regardless of which system is used, the principle is the same: Once clinicians understand the structure and division into taxonomic categories, they can spot information that "matters," match this clinical data against an agreed-upon template, and make judgments about the category to which a client or a problem belongs that other professionals will accept. Certainly, this is important—otherwise clinical judgment would be entirely subjective and communication difficult. Mastery of the prevailing template—in the USA, that means mastery of the DSM—has thus become the hallmark of professional expertise: the organizing principle for clinical assessment courses and textbooks, client evaluation, insurance reimbursement, empirical research, and clinical licensure.

But that is only part of the story.

Purpose, Organization, and Use of This Book

Clearly, it is important for social work students to master the dominant taxonomic system, and there are many books to help them do that. But this book has a different aim: to help students explore assessment from a *range* of conceptual frameworks, each with its own emphasis, limitation, and form of evidence; to wonder what questions they may have forgotten to ask, or assumed had no useful response, or did not know *could* be asked; to ask different questions, new questions, and questions from seemingly incompatible perspectives; and to think critically about what each perspective has to offer, takes for granted, omits, and counts as knowledge—for whom it was developed and whom it serves.

There is a well-known fable about the blind men and the elephant. In this tale, six blind men are asked to determine what an elephant looks like by feeling different parts of its body. One reaches out, touches the elephant's leg, and proclaims that an elephant is like a pillar; another feels the tail and declares that an elephant is like a rope; the third, feeling the trunk, is certain that an elephant is long and flexible like a swaying tree branch; the fourth feels the ear and proclaims that an elephant is broad and flat like a fan; the fifth, feeling the belly, says an elephant is solid like a wall; and the sixth, feeling only the tusk, declares that elephant is hard and sharp like a spear. All, of course, are partly right, yet none knows the whole elephant.

So too, no book can convey the entire elephant—everything one might want to know about a topic. Rather, this volume presents and critically examines an array of approaches to knowledge, each offering its partial truth. Its goal is to promote meaningful inquiry *across* perspectives and thus to invite a shift in the reader, away from the assumption that the psychiatric paradigm of the DSM must "obviously" be at the center of clinical assessment, and toward a flexible and dynamic approach more consonant with social work values and theory.

The first chapter begins by exploring the epistemological assumptions that underlie the ways we think about mental disorder. Epistemology is the theory of knowledge—beliefs about *what* can be known and *how* that knowledge can be acquired. Which kinds of information do we consider credible, based on which assumptions about the nature of individual and social reality? Which means of verifying and communicating do we trust and which do we devalue and discard? Before speaking about "evidence-based practice," we need to examine what we count as "evidence" (Mullen and Streiner 2004; Thyer 2004).

Chapters 2 and 3 address the current diagnostic system, including the validity and reliability of DSM categories, the process of clinical decision making, and barriers at macro-, mezzo-, and micro-levels. Chapter 4 situates disorder in socio-cultural and relational context, examining the transactional nature of distress and dysfunction. The next five chapters explore mental disorder from a range of perspectives: psychodynamic theory, temperament, illness narratives, behavioral neurobiology, and person-centered integrative diagnosis. Chapter 10 connects assessment with practice-based research; Chap. 11 offers practical suggestions for teaching and learning that foster students' capacity to hold and shift among multiple viewpoints; and a final chapter integrates key themes and applies them to real-world practice within a framework of professional ethics and social justice.

Chapters follow a common format, beginning with key terms and guiding questions to orient the reader, and concluding with application to a case study and practical exercises for further exploration. While the focus is on assessment and diagnosis of individuals, suggestions are incorporated for extending the inquiry to families and relationships. Similarly, the emphasis is on assessment of adults, but principles can be applied equally well to children. Historical considerations, empirical evidence, application to diverse populations, and ethical quandaries are also addressed.

Appendices provide supplemental information including a history of the DSM, a summary of research on how social work students think about mental disorder, and examples of classroom exercises and assignments. A final appendix offers an outline for a syllabus to show how the book can be used as a primary course text. While that is not its only possible use—indeed, the book can be used in a range of ways to promote critical inquiry—it is worth reflecting on the role of the course text in shaping the way students think about mental disorder.

Typically, texts for clinical assessment courses are organized by disorders, with chapters on anxiety, depression, trauma, substance abuse, autism, and so on, corresponding to the structure of the syllabus. Chapters usually begin with a discussion of diagnostic criteria, often with information about instruments and scales that can assist the diagnostic process, and go on to discuss differential diagnosis, pathogenesis, and the impact of factors such as gender, developmental stage, and culture on presentation and trajectory. Mental disorders (as defined by the DSM) are the organizing principle, the hub around which other considerations are arranged. This approach to assessment texts—and to the entire course—is so taken-for-granted that we scarcely question it.

There is no reason it has to be this way, however. Rather than passively allowing the DSM's table of contents to dictate the structure of the syllabus, social work educators can begin *proactively*, from the core question—professional and pedagogical—of what clinical students need to know, and need to know how to do, in order to be skilled diagnosticians:

- How to spot material of potential clinical significance.
- How to discover what this material means for the client's life.
- How to reliably rule out what is *not* going on—that is, how to avoid diagnostic errors.

The next question follows naturally: What educational material and approach to learning can foster the development of these skills? *Critical Thinking in Clinical Assessment and Diagnosi*s is a response to that question. There are, in fact, two ways this book can be used: within the "traditional" framework organized around DSM categories or as the basis for an alternative approach.

If the standard disorder-based structure is retained, chapters can be incorporated into the various units to show how understanding of each disorder is enhanced by the use of additional conceptual lenses. For example, Chap. 6 on temperament can be used as part of a unit on anxiety disorders to show how constitutional traits such as intensity, soothability, and reactivity can exacerbate, interact with, or be mistaken for an anxiety disorder. Similarly, Chap. 5 on neuroscience and transdiagnostic processes can be used as part of a unit on depression to show how the downward spiral of memory and interpretation bias, negative appraisal, and negative coping can lead to and/or perpetuate depressive states. Any chapter, in fact, can be used to illuminate any of the major categories of disorder. In this way, chapters can be woven into the curriculum to deepen and broaden students' understanding of the "standard" disorders.

Alternatively, rather than using this book as a supplement to a primary text that is organized by DSM categories, instructors can develop a *different kind of syllabus*, organized instead by conceptual lenses, and use the book as the core text. In this approach, the roles are switched. It is now the DSM disorders that are used as examples, incorporated into each chapter to show how the assessment perspective being explored might be applied to a psychiatric category. Each instructional unit is thus devoted to one of the book's chapters, with DSM material on a specific disorder incorporated into the syllabus as a vehicle for illustrating the use of that lens. The DSM can still be "covered" and mastered, but need not be the primary focus or organizing principle for the syllabus. Appendix F offers an example of such a syllabus.

Setting the Stage

Since the title of this book is *Critical Thinking in Clinical Assessment and Diagnosis*, it may be helpful to begin by examining each of its key terms.

What is Critical Thinking? The National Council for Excellence in Critical Thinking defines critical thinking as the self-guided, intellectually disciplined process of actively and skillfully conceptualizing, applying, analyzing, synthesizing, and/or evaluating information gathered by observation, experience, reflection, reasoning, or communication (http://www.criticalthinking.org/pages/defining-critical-thinking/766). It is rational, reflective, open-minded, and informed by evidence. When we think critically, we examine the quality of our reasoning related to a claim or position. "Critical thinking involves clearly describing and taking responsibility for claims and arguments, critically evaluating our views (no matter how cherished), and considering alternative news and related evidence … It prompts questions such as 'Could I be wrong?' and 'Have I considered alternative views?'" (Gambrill 2005, p. 248).

Critical thinking demands an awareness of *how* we think, as well as *what* we think. It asks us to identify the assumptions, preferences, and mental habits that can foreclose the opportunity to see something in a new way—to recognize the biases, "implied obviousness," and circular reasoning that lead to dismissal of information that does not conform to what we already believe or expect to find. Critical thinkers consider the context, consequences, and challenges to their viewpoints. They continually ask themselves: How do I know something is "true"? What have I counted as evidence and what have I ignored or discarded? On what assumptions or investments is this "evidence" based? What else could this be? Is there another way to look at this? How can I find out?

Critical thinking does *not*, however, mean endless introspection and "analysis paralysis." Taking a step back to reflect and widen one's view does not mean freezing in place, too unsure to ever step forward. Clinicians need to make decisions; the purpose of critical thinking is to help them make better decisions.

What is the Difference Between "Diagnosis" and "Assessment"? While the two words are often used interchangeably, they have different emphases and implications. One way to describe the difference, although it is an over-simplification, is to think of *diagnosis* as determining the category to which a person belongs (where the person fits within a taxonomic system like the DSM) through identification of features that are shared with others, and *assessment* as collecting information, not only about what is shared, but also about what is particular or specific to that person (what else may be important to know, including how the person differs from an ideal instance of the category). It may sound as if diagnosis is simpler and more straightforward, easier to master than assessment because it has fewer elements, yet it is considered a more sophisticated skill. Only experienced social workers at a more advanced level of licensure are permitted to diagnose independently, without supervision by a psychiatrist, while all social workers are permitted to assess (http://www.socialworklicensure.org/articles/social-work-license-requirements.html).

Diagnosis Although diagnosis tends to be thought of as the identification of disease, it has had a broader meaning in social work. Mary Richmond's *Social Diagnosis*, written nearly a century ago, defined diagnosis as a highly structured method "to arrive at as exact a definition as possible of the situation and personality of the client" (as cited in Turner 2002, p. 8). Richmond's "social" diagnosis consisted of three interacting elements: the social situation, the personality of the client, and the problem. It was not a matter of placing the person's difficulty into a generic category but of understanding the interplay between dysfunction, context, and temperament. "This process of diagnosis did not result in the affixing of a label, but rather in an accurate assessment of the dynamics of the problem in its life context" (Kirk et al. 1989, p. 296). Diagnosis was thus a matter of the whole person, rather than considering the person in relation to a diagnostic type.

Interestingly, Richmond did not reject the medical model but sought to translate its presumed scientific precision into the psychosocial arena, even suggesting that social workers consider themselves "social physicians" providing "social therapeutics." Her hope was that "we shall in time be able to classify and to name our various social diagnoses with a precision comparable to that of diagnosis in medicine" (Sheffield 1924, p. 149, as quoted in Kirk et al. 1989, p. 298).

As time went on, however, diagnosis became synonymous with the identification of internal pathology, and the idea of matching an individual's experience to a list of symptoms replaced the idea of analyzing forces in dynamic interaction. By abandoning Richmond's vision of diagnosis as the relationship among three dimensions, social work has—according to many—lost an important and powerful tool. Diagnosis, Turner (2002) asserts, needs to be reclaimed and re-conceptualized as an essential part of social work practice. In its true sense, diagnosis is the creation of a comprehensive psychosocial portrait, "the process in which a professional opinion is formed stemming from the assessment of a situation as it emerges in our interaction with clients and their significant environments" (p. 51).

Turner goes on to offer a template for what a "social work diagnosis" ought to include: internal structure (mental health status, intelligence, safety, values, personality, communication skills, credibility); overall physical condition, medication; significant roles (including adequacy and comfort in role performance); cultural, gender, racial, ethnic, and religious factors and their significance to the person; strength, quality, and availability of significant relationships and social networks; significant impinging history; substance use; major strengths and major problem areas in relation to people, environment, and resources; and client factors (perceived needs, wishes, expectations, motivation, and prognosis).

This does not necessarily mean that categorical labels are to be avoided. It would be, Turner believes, "just as dangerous to attempt to practice social work without a labeling process as it could be to overuse labels with all their perils" (p. 68). Avoiding reference to a category from fear of its misuse can deprive a client of needed services; social workers have an ethical responsibility to diagnose because of the harm, through inaction, that can ensue when a legitimate diagnosis is overlooked. Similarly, Epple (2007) cautions against the tendency to confuse *thinking diagnostically* with the DSM; doing so creates a "straw man," a false basis for rejecting the useful principle of trying to understand a problem through analysis and linkage to previous similar cases.

It is the DSM system, rather than the notion of diagnosis per se, that has been a source of controversy among social workers. On the one hand, whether they work in mental health agencies or in private practice, clinical social workers can scarcely avoid using DSM terminology (Probst 2012). A diagnostic label is the entrée to mental health treatment—the way to legitimize a client's need, obtain insurance coverage, and communicate with other professionals. It can offer an explanation, a way to make sense of what has been experienced (McQuaide 1999), and a link to treatment. It enables the clinician to draw on prior experience and research, select interventions that have been effective for others with similar challenges, make predictions, and offer realistic hope.

Unless the client is wealthy enough to self-pay, withholding diagnosis can mean withholding help (Probst 2013), thus fostering a two-tiered mental health system that reinforces power inequity and social injustice. At the same time, an emphasis on problems, deficits, and pathology can be seen as undermining social work's core belief in client dignity and worth (Reamer 2005), and endorsement of the diagnostic system as betrayal of the very ethic that sets social workers apart from other helping professionals (Ishibashi 2005). This is a serious dilemma for social workers, discussed at length in the chapters that follow.

Assessment Assessment tends to be seen as a more flexible and open-ended process, the endeavor to understand "*what is happening* in the client's transactional world, *why* what is happening may be happening, what the client and others *want to construct*, and *what resources* are available for that work" (Mattaini 2005, p. 63; italics in the original). This is a broad definition, linked to context and goals.

Mattaini groups assessment systems into categorical, dimensional, and contextual models. Categorical systems separate phenomena into mutually exclusive classes based on particular criteria, focusing on information that can be used to place the individual in one category rather than another and discarding other information. Dimensional approaches focus on severity and can be used to determine whether a problem is getting better or worse. Contextual systems look at the person within relationships and environments in order to understand contributing factors (stressors), mitigating factors (resources), and impact on the person's life course and identity (meaning).

The nature and scope of an assessment depends on its purpose. In some instances — for example, to determine if a person is at risk of self-harm or if there is evidence of abuse—the assessment may be brief and tightly focused. At other times, it may be more open, and the clinician will have to decide how much time to take and how much information to include; this can be challenging when there is agency or insurance pressure to come up with a problem formulation and treatment goals.

The process can be daunting. Should *all* dimensions of potential significance be considered—defense mechanisms, attachment style, personality traits, cognitive functioning, family dynamics, cultural background, social support, and spiritual beliefs and practices, to name just a few? Should all these elements be given equal significance, or are some more important than others? While assessment takes place at a particular moment in time, how can the person's history be taken into account —prior trauma or loss, cumulative stress, the success or failure of previous attempts to cope? How can these vertical (developmental) and horizontal (environmental) elements be integrated so they are not simply a collection of disconnected facts? Is there, or should there be, an organizing principle, a hub, a central theme that gives shape and meaning to these diverse elements? How can that theme be known?

Clinical assessment also includes a review of the person's motivation and readiness for change. How great is the distress caused by the present situation? How strong is the hope and expectation that change is possible? Has the person faced similar challenges in the past? What helped or hindered? What capacities, inner and outer, can be mobilized and are they sufficient? What is needed to help the person reach a point where change is possible? What is meant by "change," anyway? Who decides what needs to change and how that change can be measured? What if the goal is acceptance or stability, rather than change?

Clearly, there is no single lens with sufficient breadth and flexibility to account for everything about every case. A more practical approach may be to make use of *several* lenses, with a critical eye for what each can offer—to examine the elephant's legs, trunk, tail, and flank, while understanding that the elephant is also a living whole that exists in a particular place and time. Hippocrates, the founder of modern medicine, said it well: "It is more important to know what sort of person has the disease than to know what sort of disease a person has."

Social Work's Role Social workers help to improve the well-being of individuals, families, and communities and are the nation's largest group of mental health service providers (Kirk 2005). There are, in fact, more clinically trained social workers than psychiatrists, psychologists, and psychiatric nurses combined: 60 % of mental health professionals are clinically trained social workers, as compared to 10 % of psychiatrists and 23 % of psychologists; in addition, nearly every social work job has a mental health component (http://www.socialworkers.org/pressroom/features/general/profession.asp). With a dramatic rise in the number of people diagnosed with mental disorders, now estimated at one of every four American adults (http://www.nami.org/factsheets/mentalillness_factsheet.pdf), there is a growing need for social workers who can provide clinical services across a range of settings and populations. The challenge is for a level of preparation that includes state-of-the-art psychiatric knowledge as well as skilled integration of a uniquely "social work" perspective that can understand human suffering within a relational, socioeconomic, and cultural context. It is a far more complex preparation than simply mastering DSM categories, although that is certainly part of professional education, yet social work courses are dominated by the DSM's psychiatric framework.

The trend has been well documented. The earliest survey of the role of the DSM in social work education, conducted by Raffoul and Holmes in 1986, examined the extent to which MSW programs included content from DSM-III (the edition in use at the time) and how social work educators perceived its advantages and disadvantages. Newman et al. (2007) replicated the study 20 years later, using a questionnaire based on items measured in the 1986 study and following similar recruitment procedures, in order to see if use and attitudes had changed. With similar response rates (67 and 59 %, respectively), the authors of the 2007 study found a dramatic increase in the percentage of curricula offering and/or requiring a DSM-based course. In the earlier study, while only one-third of the schools had a specific DSM course and only 16 % required students to take it, two-thirds of the students *did* take the DSM course and 91 % believed that graduate schools of social work should provide specific instruction in the DSM, stating that social workers needed to be knowledgeable about its use in order to "take their rightful places next to, rather than behind, clinical psychologists and psychiatrists" (Raffoul and Holmes 1986, p. 30). In the later survey, 74 % of the sample offered a DSM-specific course, with 48 % requiring it and three-fourths of the students taking the course whether required or not.

Keenly aware of a growing emphasis on the DSM in real-world clinical practice, particularly for reimbursement by third-party providers, social work educators are often torn. Social work students entering the professional arena need to be proficient in the manual's use, yet many educators feel strongly that a psychiatric taxonomy should not be the organizing principle for teaching social work practice. A well-known debate in the *Journal of Social Word Education* captured the two sides of this controversy.

On the one hand, Kutchins and Kirk (1995) argue that the DSM was never intended as a social work text, does not help students to critically review a range of theoretical approaches, ignores vast areas of theory and research, and contradicts the tenets of social work ethics and practice including the crucial role of families and culture, client strengths and empowerment, and individualization of the client seen in developmental perspective. Selecting a DSM label does little, they say, to help social workers understand the complex issues of clients in crisis, under acute or chronic stress, in dysfunctional relationships, or lacking resources or skills to negotiate social service systems. As they point out, Virginia Woolf and the bag lady who sleeps in the alley may receive the same diagnosis, but the problems they confront and the help they might need are quite different. Agreeing that social workers should be able to use the manual competently is not the same as saying it should be the basis for teaching clinical practice.

Williams and Spitzer (1995) counter that the DSM is the best available system and a necessary component of a comprehensive psychosocial assessment, faulting Kirk and Kutchins for condemning the entire system without highlighting portions that could be useful or proposing an alternative approach to standardizing the identification and classification of mental distress, noting that it is "far easier to knock down a barn than to build one" (p. 152). The DSM, they assert, can be effective for communicating information and helping with management and prognosis. Refusing to name a condition can trivialize conditions that may evolve into more serious disorders and become risk factors for other problems. It also undermines public support for funding of mental health research.

Lacasse and Gomory (2003) posed a broader question. In a survey of 80 top-ranked graduate schools of social work, they sought to determine the extent to which *differing* viewpoints about mental health were taught. That is, were social work students being taught to critically consider the empirical evidence for a range of theoretical and practice approaches to mental health? Reviewing the syllabi, they found that 88.7 % followed the structure of the DSM-IV, with 74.6 % of courses requiring purchase of the manual; for 63.4 % of the courses, DSM was the only text required. Reviewing assigned readings, they discovered that only 39.4 % of the courses included an alternative perspective (the psychodynamic in nearly one-third of the cases, with ecosystems a distant second). Overall, they found little evidence that graduate social work courses in mental health covered viewpoints other than the biomedical.

> Social work's lack of critical content in mental health has much to do with the profession's inability to set itself apart ideologically from psychiatry … In order to survive as a 'player' in the personal problems jurisdiction in the new scientific age, social work had to look 'scientific' and in this domain the only 'science' in town was psychiatric … We do not appear to have the professional self-confidence to forge our own separate perspective, even based on the existent well-tested science that often contradicts much that is asserted to be factual by institutional psychiatry (Lacasse and Gomory 2003, p. 398-400).

This is deeply troubling. Given the complexity of factors that contribute to both "mental health" and "mental illness," it seems doubtful that a single viewpoint can adequately explain the range of problems a clinician might encounter. If clinical social workers are truly committed to providing the best possible service to our clients, we must be able to draw skillfully, resourcefully, and flexibly on a range of models. For that, a foundational guide is needed that can help students understand, critique, compare, and make intelligent use of multiple perspectives.

That is the aim of this book.

A Note for Instructors

A detailed discussion of teaching strategies is provided in Chap. 12. Several key questions are also offered here that can be carried by both students and instructors as they explore each chapter:

1. How can content and self-reflection be taught simultaneously? Courses tend to be content-driven, yet the two dimensions are inseparable in practice. Indeed, can reflexivity be taught? What can foster its development?
2. We understand, in theory, that multiple lenses are always needed in order to understand another human being. But how, practically, can we increase the capacity of the learner to "hold" or contain complexity? How can we teach fluid thinking and nurture the ability to shift skillfully among frames of reference in a way that can incorporate what is new or contradictory?
3. At the same time, too much complexity can produce a disorganized over-abundance of information that is not clinically useful. All information is not salient for all clients or at all times. How to help students learn to select from the vast amount of information and determine what is salient? Salient for whom, the client or the clinician? For the client, salience may depend on cultural values; for the clinician, it may depend on theoretical orientation. If that occurs, how to negotiate two sets of criteria for clinical salience?
4. These "multiple lenses" cannot be a list of disconnected aspects; they must be integrated into a new whole for each client. What can facilitate the transformation of knowledge into a meaningful and clinically useful whole?

Many students will not welcome and, indeed, are not ready for an approach to clinical knowledge that emphasizes continual self-questioning. Before they can question what they know, they first need to know it—to become competent and secure in their grasp of a single paradigm before daring to set it aside in favor of a more fluid, uncertain, and reflexive approach. Mastering one framework at a time may seem difficult enough! Students may resist the critical, multi-lensed model of practice presented in this book because it threatens their still-tentative sense of professional mastery. It may seem overwhelming and confusing, a distraction from the task of acquiring clinical skills, especially for those who like definite answers and are uncomfortable with vulnerability.

Students have different temperaments and levels of readiness; they mature at different rates. One of the challenges for the instructor, as discussed in the final chapter, is to adjust to individual student needs. "Beginning where the student is" needs to parallel "beginning where the client is."

Use of the Case Study Each chapter includes application to a common case study (found in Appendix A). As preparation, students are encouraged to try the following exercise after an initial reading of the case:

- Take the point of view that Ray's core problem stems from childhood sexual abuse and provide an argument for why this is the key to understanding his difficulties.
- Then argue the *opposite* position—that this is not the core issue at all because Ray's difficulties began much earlier.
- Take another angle on the case and do the same thing. For instance, argue that adoption (feeling abandoned or out of place) is the core theme.
- Then argue *against* this position.

Each student can also take a case from his or her own field experience and examine it through the perspectives of the various chapters. This ongoing assessment and re-assessment of a case, selected by the student, can parallel the assessment and re-assessment of the case of Ray undertaken by the class as a whole.

References

Epple, D. M. (2007). Inter and intra professional social work differences: Social Work's challenge. *Clinical Social Work Journal, 35*, 267–276.

Gambrill, E. (2005). Critical thinking, evidence-based practice, and mental health. In S. A. Kirk (Ed.), *Mental disorders in the social environment: Critical perspectives* (pp. 247–269). New York: Columbia University Press.

Ishibashi, N. (2005). Barrier or bridge? The language of diagnosis in clinical social work. *Smith College Studies in Social Work, 75*(1), 65–80.

Kirk, S. A., Siporin, M. & Kutchins, H. (1989). The prognosis for social work diagnosis. *Social Casework: The Journal of Contemporary Social Work.* 295–304.

Kirk, S. A. (2005). Critical perspectives. In S. A. Kirk (Ed.), *Mental disorders in the social environment: Critical perspectives* (pp. 1–22). New York: Columbia University Press.

Kutchins, H. & Kirk, S.A. (1995). Should DSM be the basis for teaching social work practice in mental health? No! *Journal of Social Work Education, 31*(2), 159–165.

Lacasse, J. R. & Gomory, T. (2003). Is graduate social work education promoting a critical approach to mental health practice? *Journal of Social Work Education, 39*(3), 383–408.

Mattaini, M. A. (2005). Mapping practice: Assessment, context, and social justice. In S. A. Kirk (Ed.), *Mental disorders in the social environment: Critical perspectives* (pp. 62–82). New York: Columbia University Press.

McQuaide, S. (1999). A social worker's use of the diagnostic and statistical manual. *Families in Society, 80*(4), 410–417.

Mullen, E. J. & Streiner, D. L. (2004). The evidence for and against evidence-based practice. *Brief Treatment and Crisis Intervention, 4*(2). 111–121.

Newman, B. S., Clemmons, V. & Dannenfelser, P. L. (2007). The diagnostic and statistical manual of mental disorders in graduate social work education: Then and now. *Journal of Social Work Education, 43*(2), 297–307.

Probst, B. (2012). Diagnosing, diagnoses, and the DSM in clinical social work. *Families in Society, 93*(4), 255–263.

Probst, B. (2013) Walking the tightrope: Clinical social workers' use of diagnostic and environmental perspectives. *Clinical Social Work Journal, 41*(2), 184–191.

Raffoul, P. R. & Holmes, K. A. (1986). DSM-III content in social work curricula: Results of a national survey. *Journal of Social Work Education, 22*(1): 24–31.

Reamer, F. G. (2005). Social work, mental health, and mental disorders. In S. A. Kirk (Ed.), *Mental disorders in the social environment: The ethical dimensions* (pp. 411–429). New York: Columbia University Press.

Thyer, B. A. (2004). What is evidence-based practice? *Brief Treatment and Crisis Intervention*, (2). 167–176.

Turner, F. J. (2002). *Diagnosis in social work: New imperatives*. Binghamton, NY: Haworth Press.

Williams, J. B. W. & Spitzer, R. L. (1995). Should DSM be the basis for teaching social work practice in mental health? Yes! *Journal of Social Work Education, 31*(2), 148–153.

Chapter 2
Epistemological Issues in Diagnosis and Assessment

Barbara Probst

Abstract This book begins with a thoughtful exploration of two fundamental questions that underlie all clinical decisions. First, what exactly is a "mental disorder," as opposed to other kinds of suffering or maladaptive behavior that we would call *non*-mental disorders? What makes a disorder specifically *mental*? And second, on what do we base these definitions and distinctions? What do we consider reliable (and unreliable) sources of knowledge, and what are some of the pitfalls in our assumptions about what we "know" and how we've come to "know" it? Common cognitive errors are explored, along with their consequences. These include circular reasoning, the difficulty of determining threshold or cut-off point, assumptions about causality, and the problems inherent in mental heuristics such as anchoring and availability. The chapter then explores the role of labels and labeling theory, the aims and limitations of classification systems such as the DSM, and the challenge of trying to develop a way to think about mental disorder that is useful for both general purposes (to make predictions based on shared characteristics) and specific aims (to understand and help particular individuals).

Keywords Anchoring · Availability · Continuum · Correlation · Deviance · Dysfunction · Heuristic · Nomothetic and idiographic · Reification · Sensitivity · Specificity · Syndrome · Threshold

Introduction: Why This Matters

What exactly *is* a mental disorder, and how can we know if someone has one?

The first question is ontological (what kinds of things exist) and the second is epistemological (how can we know them). These may seem like abstract inquiries, far removed from the real-world challenges that social work clients face, but they

B. Probst (✉)
School for Social Work, Smith College, Northampton, MA, USA
e-mail: Barbara.H.Probst@gmail.com

© Springer International Publishing Switzerland 2015
B. Probst (ed.), *Critical Thinking in Clinical Assessment and Diagnosis*,
Essential Clinical Social Work Series, DOI 10.1007/978-3-319-17774-8_2

are deeply practical questions that lie at the heart of all clinical work. They may not be easily or entirely answerable, but that does not mean that they are not worth asking. To *not* ask is to assume that the answers are obvious and the presumed definitions sufficient—hardly the route to ethical practice.

One reason these questions seldom get asked is that mental illness categories are usually taken for granted in intervention studies, counting as part of the "given" for testing other kinds of hypotheses. This gives a false impression of what is actually known and thus capable of serving as a basis for testing what is *un*known (Banzato et al. 2005). In order to test or compare interventions for anxiety, for example, we need to be clear about what we are calling "anxiety"; that is the only way for anxiety to serve as a stable background against which other factors can be varied and examined. But reference to a common term does not mean that everyone agrees on what the term signifies. Surprisingly, this fundamental point is often overlooked in discussions about empirically supported treatments. When we fail to attend to these basic conceptual issues, we risk arriving at—and promoting—misleading and potentially harmful conclusions about the best way to help our clients.

Thus, it is important for anyone embarking on clinical practice to investigate two fundamental questions. First, what are the underlying notions about mental disorder that serve as the basis for clinical decisions? And second, what do we consider reliable (and unreliable) sources of knowledge? That is, how did we arrive at these notions? How do we know what we know about the phenomena we call "mental disorder"? How does our "way of knowing" affect our belief about who is disordered and who is not? Are there flaws, traps, or errors that might cast doubt on what we claim to know?

Guiding Questions

1. What are some definitions of "mental disorder" and what is each based on?
2. What is a symptom? By definition, it indicates the existence of something else. How can a symptom establish the existence of a more complex entity, like an illness?
3. How do cognitive habits affect the way diagnostic decisions are made?
4. How do words, labels, and narratives affect the way that difference, distress, and disorder are understood?

What Makes a Disorder "Mental"?

Terms like "mental disorder" and "mental illness" are used to denote problems of the mind or psyche, as differentiated from problems of the body. This mind–body split is becoming increasingly problematic, however, as more is understood about the mutuality of mental and physical experience. The benefits of physical exercise for mental health and cognitive functioning; the impact of mental conditions such as depression on weight, somatic pain, and fatigue; the way anxiety, purported to be a "mental" state, is experienced through the body as a pounding heart and knotted stomach; and the well-documented power of neuroplasticity—the way life experience shapes the brain as a physical organ, rather than the other way around (Garland and Howard 2009)—are examples of the interconnection between these two realms.

This creates a thorny definitional problem. If, as Berganza et al. (2005) point out, both mental and physical disorders are based on some kind of central nervous system anomaly or malfunction, then where is the crucial difference? Or is there one?

Some authors, like Thyer (see also Chap. 2), take a somewhat different approach in challenging the notion that there are distinctly "mental" disorders. A mental disorder would, presumably, originate and reside in the mind, yet "there are many viable approaches to understanding unusual behavior besides contending that they are manifestations of mental phenomena" (Thyer 2006, p. 65). There is no real reason, Thyer asserts, to account for what a person does or reports by reference to mental processes that cannot be directly observed. A better approach, in his view, is to re-name these phenomena *behavioral* disorders, as long as behavior is broadly defined as "actions, reactions, and interactions in response to external or internal stimuli, including objectively observable activities, introspectively observable activities, and unconscious processes" (Corsini 2002, p. 99, as cited in Thyer 2006, p. 65). A behavioral disorder could thus include disordered thought, feeling, affect, and action.

Behavior, body, brain, nervous system—what, then, is a "mental" disorder?

This is a troubling situation. There is an entire "mental health" industry—more than half a million people in professional practice (according to the US Department of Labor's Bureau of Labor Statistics); an infrastructure composed of insurance companies, regulations, and an ever-expanding database; a growing body of research, funded by public and private dollars—yet it is not clear if this industry is based on something real. Clearly, people "really" suffer. But is this suffering distinctly mental? Can it be separated from its context, the person-within-a-body and the person-within-an-environment?

On the one hand, many researchers believe that each psychiatric diagnosis will eventually be linked to, and understood as, an underlying neurological dysfunction —that is, that variation among psyches will be explainable by variation among brains. In their view, there is no split: A brain disease is no different from a disease of the liver or kidneys, so we should be able to map psychological problems onto structural or neurochemical anomalies, just as we do for so-called "medical" problems. Yet even if we can do this—that is, find clear correlations between behavioral and neurological differences—there is a snag, since there is no way to know which is cause and which is result. The brain of a child diagnosed with ADHD may appear different from the brain of a child who does not carry this diagnosis, but we do not and cannot know which came first. Because brains are plastic, any observed difference might be the result of the chronic experience of being criticized for not sitting still, not listening, never feeling accepted or good enough or in control of one's actions—a neurological portrait of shame and anger, real but *secondary* phenomena, distinct from the *primary* features of the disorder.

It is appealing to think we can use a scientific tool such as an MRI to identify brain differences and conclude that these differences are the source of a disorder such as ADHD. However, that only works if *all* children with ADHD display this particular brain difference, *only* children with ADHD have it, and the brain difference was clearly there prior to the appearance of the behavior. That would require a formidable research design: scanning the brains of every newborn, following up with repeated scans until adulthood, identifying clear patterns within and between individuals, and then ruling out other factors that might account for any difference in behavior.

Perhaps the most ambitious undertaking in the quest for a brain-based theory of mental disorder is the Research Domain Criteria Project (RDoC), launched in 2009 by the National Institute of Mental Health. The goal of the RDoC is "to create a framework for research on pathophysiology, especially for genomics and neuroscience, which ultimately will inform future classification schemes" (Insel et al. 2010, p. 748). The project begins from several assumptions:

> First, the RDoC framework conceptualizes mental illnesses as brain disorders … [that] can be addressed as disorders of brain circuits. Second, RDoC classification assumes that the dysfunction in neural circuits can be identified with the tools of clinical neuroscience, including electrophysiology [and] functional neuroimaging … Third, the RDoC framework assumes that data from genetics and clinical neuroscience will yield biosignatures that will augment clinical symptoms (p. 749).

Neuroanatomy is not the first explanatory principle that is been suggested, of course, simply the most recent. Across cultures and epochs, mental disorder has been linked to punishment for sins in present or past lives, sorcery, curses, spirit possession, misaligned organs, and repressed sexual desire. "From capture by evil spirits to the wages of sin, from the loss of soul to breaches of sacred taboos, to conflicts and tensions in our internal psychological dynamics to dysfunctional families and parents" (Saleebey 2001, pp. 151–152), people have sought an explanation for human suffering. Less than a century ago, much of the emotional distress and maladaptive behavior that we now explain as neurochemical failure was seen as the consequence of moral failure—a weakness of character or a lack of will. In an epoch that idealized the self-made pioneer, this idea was culturally syntonic, neatly tying happiness to merit and suffering to a lack of moral fiber.

By mid-century, this was supplanted by a psychodynamic explanation in which mental illness was due, instead, to poor parenting—coldness, inconsistency, inadequate discipline, and lack of maternal bonding. Kanner's theory of the "refrigerator mother" who caused schizophrenia and the evils of "permissive parenting," leading to hyperactivity and conduct disorder, were the examples of this kind of thinking. Bad parents replaced bad character. Then, in the 1990s, the "decade of the brain" (per President Bush's 1989 declaration), bad brains replaced bad parents. Some people were simply born with unfortunate neural wiring, an organic mechanism that was treatable medically, like any other organic flaw. The idea of a no-fault, brain-based explanation had wide appeal, offering the hope of cure and control (Saleebey 2001). Reinforced by the pharmaceutical industry and a new wave of psychotropic medications, led by *Prozac* as it hit the U.S. market in 1987, this notion revolutionized the way Americans thought about mental disorder. Neurosis and repression were out; neurochemistry was in.

As Leo and Lacasse discuss later in this book, however, research does not support the idea of mental disorder as chemical imbalance; it is simply the most recent idea to capture popular imagination, fitting into the prevailing cultural narrative just as the notion of disorder as moral weakness fit into the cultural narrative of our predecessors.

In short, different notions of causality have shaped the beliefs about mental disorder that have been embraced in different epochs and by different groups—as if knowing what *causes* something is equivalent to understanding what it *is*. This is odd, since we know that many causes can lead to the same result. Childhood hyperactivity, for example, can be affected by diet, allergy, lack of sleep, exposure to lead paint, sensory overload, undiagnosed learning disability, giftedness, trauma, and a host of other factors. So too, a particular event or anomaly can lead to a range of different consequences. Yet the search for a causal definition of mental disorder has persisted.

In general, there are three ways that people try to explain mental dysfunction. One is to seek a fundamental "first principle"; currently, this is the brain, its structure and chemistry, although there could be and have been other principles. This approach rests on what Brown (2002) calls a *mechanistic* epistemology. In a mechanistic epistemology, we look for ways to show that A causes B or depends on B; the metaphor is a chain, with links that connect one event to another. Connections are linear, and the temporal order is clear. Another approach is transactional. Here, mental disorder is seen as the inability to handle the cumulative or intersecting stressors in one's life. In this *contextual* or *contingent* epistemology, disorder would not exist if not for the presence of these external stressors, exacerbated by a lack of adequate supports and coping strategies. In a contextual epistemology, we seek to understand the relationship between A and B; the metaphor is a tapestry or web, a net of connections. A third approach views mental disorder as a social construction as the way those in power label people who do not conform to their notions of normalcy (a *constructivist* epistemology). Its source lies in the power of the dominant group to define who is normal and who is not.

Each way of thinking about mental disorder rests on a different approach to knowledge. It is not a question of which is best, since epistemology is untestable (Banzato et al. 2005). That is, epistemology is conceptual, not empirical. There is no way to compare the "evidence base" for each theoretical framework and demonstrate that one is superior or inferior to another, just as one value system cannot be shown to be better or worse than another value system. The terms, premises, arguments, and forms of evidence of one conceptual system may seem inadequate, irrelevant, or just plain wrong to those operating under a different system (Brown 2002). Debates about clinical methods and effectiveness are, in many cases, really debates about epistemology.

Thinking About Thinking

Given the elusive nature of mental disorder, it can be tempting to escape from what may seem like an endless hall of mirrors by saying that it simply does not exist (the "denialism" discussed in the next two chapters) or by taking refuge in cognitive shortcuts that seem to make this Gordian knot more manageable. These habits of thought are so common, so invisible, and—often—so misleading that it is important to begin by taking a careful look at *how* we think, as well as *what* we think.

Circular Reasoning As noted above, there is a tendency to define mental illness by its cause—to say, for example, that mental disorder "is" a malfunctioning of the brain. This replaces one challenge with another, however. Demonstrating causality would require a controlled prospective experiment, isolating two groups of human beings who are identical except for a core feature, hypothesized to be causal, in order to see if one group develops a mental disorder and the other does not. In a curious twist, cause is often inferred *retro*spectively by "explaining" an illness through its "cure": if medication alleviates the symptoms, the symptoms must have had a biomedical origin and hence the condition itself must be biomedical. Yet that would be just as absurd as stating that because Advil relieves a headache, the headache must have been due to insufficient Advil (Erikson and Kress 2005). In medical practice, no physician would define a skin rash as the disorder and its disappearance as the explanation (McWilliams 2011).

Unfortunately, the tail often wags the dog when "tests" are used to demonstrate the existence of the very condition the person is presumably being "tested" for. Diagnostic terms are assumed to represent internal entities, which are then assumed to explain the dysfunctional thoughts or actions—the label thus explaining the very events from which it is inferred (Brown 2002). In this kind of circular definition, conclusions and premises "prove" each other. If the child scores high on a checklist for ADHD, indicating that he or she "has" the condition, this is taken as proof that the checklist is an accurate way to establish the presence of the disorder!

If you think about it, this makes no sense. It stands to reason that a child who scores high on a checklist of ADHD symptoms will also meet DSM criteria for the disorder, since the checklist is based on those symptoms. But this does not prove that these particular items (parts) are the best way to determine the presence of ADHD (the greater whole)—no more than a person's SAT score has proven to be the best way to determine intellectual aptitude.

Thyer (2014) makes a similar point. "The existence of most of the conditions labeled by the DSM-5 are inferences made on the basis of the very behaviors these so-called mental illnesses are said to cause," he writes. "If the only evidence for the disorder is the behavior the disorder is said to cause, then there is no genuine explanation" (p. 165). We decide that someone has ADHD if he or she displays the behaviors that constitute the definition of ADHD, but that does not explain what ADHD *is*, other than a collection of behaviors. Calling the behaviors a syndrome and assuming that they are linked to a common etiology, presumed to lie in brain chemistry or genetics, does not explain anything unless it can be shown how specific anomalies of brain anatomy precede, predict, or at the least correlate consistently with these behaviors. But we cannot do that. In the absence of independent biomarkers, the assumption is made that symptom clusters are (somehow) sufficient to identify the distinct forms of pathology of which they are presumed to be either a part or a result (Kirmayer 2005). But without independent evidence, the reasoning is circular.

The problem is not new. It was noted nearly a half century ago by Temerlin (1968), reflecting on the challenge of "separating *diagnoses* [italics in the original] of mental illness from mental illness itself, if it exists, because there is no operational criterion of mental illness which is independent of psychiatric diagnosis and with which psychiatric diagnosis might be correlated in a validity study" (p. 353). In other words, criteria are not independent operational markers—even if checklists give the impression that they are.

Mixing Levels and Frames of Reference Other cognitive errors occur when we try to explain one level of organization by reference to another. Reference to a higher, more abstract level is *reification*: Assuming that something like depression has an independent existence, above and beyond its manifestations, even though we cannot ever know it. Reference to a lower, more concrete level is *reductionism*: "explaining" experience by reference to one of its components, like equating depression with a decrease in serotonin levels. Low serotonin may be part of depression, but it is unclear if it is a cause, result, or correlate. While mental processes may have biological underpinnings, "they [still] require other levels of conceptualization, since biology does not directly translate into overt behavior, normal or otherwise" (Berganza et al. 2005, p. 168). Reification of notions like depression has become so commonplace that it is scarcely questioned, especially when "authority figures such as psychiatrists use the term and act as if it is unproblematic" (Gambrill 2005, p. 256). Yet even Thomas Insel, director of the National Institute of Mental Heath, has said that DSM categories do not refer to real entities that actually exist "out there" in the world (Insel 2013, as quoted in Jacobs 2014).

What *do* DSM categories refer to, then? If diagnostic terms are not indicative of discrete conditions, does it mean they are useless? Not necessarily. It depends, as Brown (2002) points out, on what we require of our terms. Terms may refer to "natural kinds," classes of objects bounded by underlying, defining properties: this is an essentialist or naturalist approach. They may also be linguistic conventions: a pragmatist approach. In this case, categories are simply useful ways of sorting phenomena into groups in order to promote a shared understanding (Haslam 2000; Markova and Berrios 2009). Here again, the point is to make sure we know which approach we are using and not to mistake a pragmatist approach for an essentialist one.

Confusion can also occur when observational and experiential phenomena are assumed to be mutually referential, each serving as a proxy for the other—that is, when we assume that externally observed criteria map onto internal experience. They might not. A person might be *acting* depressed yet not report *feeling* depressed. In that case, which do we trust? Does *being* depressed depend on acting or feeling? There is no rule, so it is up to the clinician's judgment. As Berganza et al. (2005) point out, diagnostic assessment often requires a double interpretation: The clinician's interpretation of the patient's interpretation of his/her own experience. There are now two layers between the symptom and the entity to which it is presumed to refer.

A similar difficulty occurs when "hardware," the organic structure of the brain, is confused with "software," the psychological mechanisms through which a person experiences and participates in life. Dysfunctional behavior does not necessarily mean that something is wrong with the organic structure of the brain. "Just as computer software can malfunction even when the underlying hardware is functioning flawlessly, so, in principle, the mind's 'programming' might become dysfunctional for reasons other than that there is a malfunction of underlying brain mechanisms" (Wakefield 2005, p. 85). Since those "other reasons" may be difficult to pin down, it can be tempting to conclude that the fault must lie in the neurological "hardware"—especially since brain activity is easier to observe, measure, and document. But that does not prove the conclusion is correct.

The Problem of Reference, or "What is a Symptom?" In clinical assessment, we use manifestations (symptoms) to make inferences about conditions at a more complex level of organization (diagnoses). The inference is sound if it can be established that the symptom reliably points to a specific referent—that is, signals or emanates from an underlying disordered mechanism and not from other sources. This is tricky, as noted above, because symptoms such as difficulty sleeping can indicate many different problems ranging from anxiety to caffeine, from a disrupted circadian rhythm to a noisy apartment. Again, it is a matter of ontology and epistemology. What sort of "objects" are symptoms, how can we know them, and what kind of knowledge can they provide?

DSM nosology is based on the idea that symptoms are observable behaviors, yet there are symptoms that are not actually "observable," such as delusions or feelings of worthlessness. We can (and do) use what people say as a proxy for internal states and events, although we cannot necessarily be certain that someone is a reliable reporter of his or her inner life. Markova and Berrios (2009) address this dilemma by dividing symptoms into subjective complaints and observable signs.

Subjective complaints are reported changes in a person's internal state, typically undesirable changes. To describe the experience, the person must turn to available categories or images, determined by sociocultural constructs, personal experience, education, and imagination. Complaints are shaped by "personal participation in their construction" (p. 344): whether one calls something sadness, fatigue, pain, hollowness, or a sense of dread depends on personal inclination and the available pool of words and meanings. These are limited in number, varying by epoch, culture, region, class, and gender. As Watters (2010) and others have noted, different cultures have different "symptom pools" that rise and fade over time.

Speaking about the "hysteria" and "hysterical paralysis" common in Victorian times, Watters comments:

> This was not a matter of anyone faking those symptoms, but rather that this was the unconscious mind striving to speak the language of suffering for its given moment in history. Suffering, when it comes out in a symptom, is a form of communication. The unconscious mind searches out the expression of the symptoms that would be understood as suffering in that moment in history (www.international.gc.ca/cfsi-icse/cil-cai/magazine/v06n02/1-1-eng.asp).

Emotional distress is thus expressed in the words, metaphors, and somatic manifestations available at a particular time and place. Hearing voices, "running amok," refusing to eat, pulling out one's hair, cutting one's arms, and abusing alcohol may all be expressions or externalizations (that is, symptoms) of the same internal state.

In order for something to be a subjective complaint, according to Markova and Berrios, the internal experience needs to be perceived as a *change for the worse,* and for that the individual must have had sufficient awareness of *another* inner state, perceived to be more typical or positive. Without a baseline, the sense that something is wrong may be less clear. Distance from the baseline determines the perceived severity of the experience, yet subjective descriptors of severity cannot be matched against some sort of objective grid since the same experience may be felt as devastating depression by one person and as feeling a bit blue by another, depending on where they started. Thus, the relationship between an experience and an individual's judgment and the subsequent naming of that experience can vary.

Observable signs, on the other hand, are behaviors deemed pathological by others. They require a judgment that the behavior is abnormal rather than normal, weighed against an external rule. This raises questions of values and authority: who decides if something indicates abnormality? The American Psychiatric Association, DSM committee members, researchers, therapists, popular opinion, friends, and relatives?

There are additional challenges. For example, even if symptoms *do* represent an underlying mental problem, not all symptoms "behave" in the same way. Some arise gradually, others suddenly and acutely; some fluctuate, others are constant. What if a person has two or three symptoms of a disorder, but fewer than the minimum required by the DSM? What if those two symptoms are especially intense? Do all symptoms have the same weight and significance? DSM symptoms are unweighted, so we don't know whether five symptoms is the "right" number for admission into a category, if six or seven or four might be more or less valid (Paris 2013). They are simply a part of the diagnostic algorithm. As Paris argues, a *syndrome* is a group of symptoms while a *disease* is the result of a pathological process. Unless the symptoms on a DSM list share a clear pathogenesis or specific pathway from cause to illness, mental disorders are actually syndromes, not diseases. Without evidence that a group of symptoms inherently cohere into a pathological entity, DSM terms are simply *labels.*

The Problem of Threshold Unless it can be established that mental disorders are discrete entities with sharp borders ("natural kinds"), there will always be the question of demarcation between categories—the line between one disorder and another, and the line between disordered and non-disordered. What is the threshold, the minimum level of pathology, that marks entrance into a category?

Many authors maintain that there is no sound empirical evidence for natural boundaries between clinical syndromes (Jablensky 2005), since conditions described in the DSM are not mutually exclusive and share many features. People also tend to have partial membership in more than one category, with some features of one disorder and some features of another; others have "sub-threshold" or non-specific complaints. Overlap, partial membership, and variation within each category mean that neither *within*-group similarities nor *between*-group differences are as clear as they should be for a good taxonomy. Because of variation and heterogeneity within diagnostic categories, people receiving the same diagnosis may actually be *less* like each other overall, and *more* like people receiving other diagnoses or no diagnosis at all.

Distinguishing between disordered and non-disordered conditions is equally difficult. On what basis do we determine that someone has crossed the line dividing normal life variation or transient response to stress from true "mental disorder"? Listing symptoms does not resolve the question (Jacobs 2014). Is it a matter of severity? That only works if severity is a reliable indicator of clinical significance. Here again, the question is: significant to whom? For some people, even mild symptoms may carry profound distress and impairment.

At the same time, the idea of mental disorder as shading imperceptibly into normalcy can trivialize the experience of those who are truly suffering (First 2005). Even if the point of demarcation along a continuum is arbitrary, that does not mean that the disorder itself is illusory, invalid, or trivial. While dimensional or continuum models allow for a graded transition between normality and pathology, they do not solve the problem of understanding mental illness. At some point on the continuum, the line still has to be drawn. Regardless of the number of gradations, dimensional approaches will always end up being categorical at some point, as differences in degree become differences in kind (Paris 2013).

One solution might be to think of the mental illness–mental health spectrum as a moveable continuum along which an individual shifts from greater to lesser symptomatology, within his or her individual range, depending on what else is occurring. Thus, a graded or continuum model may be more useful for comparing people with *themselves* at various points in time (to assess if a condition is getting better or worse) than for deciding whether a particular individual is disordered.

One-dimensional Thinking When considering complex topics such as illness and well-being, it is risky to rely on just one dimension or domain of knowledge. It is not so much that psychiatric concepts are "wrong" as it is that they represent only one kind of data and one way of thinking; additional forms of data and knowledge may be needed. Clinicians who operate from psychodynamic, humanistic, behavioral, and family systems perspectives are often troubled by the widespread reliance on descriptive psychiatry to define disorder (McWilliams 2011). Because psychiatry has acquired the status of "expert" knowledge, its language dominates; other terms, metaphors, and narratives that might be used to describe human problems are assumed to be less useful or significant. This affects how problems are perceived, as well as the solutions that are proposed, adopted, and paid for (Gambrill 2005).

Yet there are other forms of clinical knowledge based on temperament, affect, defenses, attachment style, developmental tasks, interpersonal relations, and ful-fillment of social roles that can shed equal light on human distress. When the focus is simply on observable behavior, other factors that may be crucial for treatment choices can be overlooked, leading to treatment goals defined by reduction or elimination of the criteria that defined the disorder in the first place. Important personal goals may be excluded that have to do with resilience, flexibility of coping strategies, affect tolerance, sense of agency, healthy attachment, stability of self-esteem, expansion of black-and-white thinking, and other aims that are not nec-essarily tied to the reduction of target symptoms.

As McWilliams (2011) reminds us, most clients' suffering cannot be adequately captured by diagnostic categories, nor can their sense of improved well-being be as easily measured as symptom reduction. Equating mental disorder with the presence of symptoms, and mental health as the lessening of those symptoms, trivializes the depth and complexity of our clients' lives. Yet, this is the approach endorsed in many practice settings, prompted and maintained by third-party payers. Going beyond its narrow focus requires additional effort that may not be recognized by agency personnel—and may even be discouraged because it does not match the computerized treatment plans and billing systems.

One-dimensional assessment can mean looking at only one *type* of information, like behavioral symptoms, or looking at only one *direction* of influence rather than trying to understand the reciprocal transactions between individuals and their sur-roundings. Most elements of human experience flow in two directions, from inside to outside and from outside to inside. Attributing the locus of a problem solely to individual characteristics that "produce" dysfunctional behavior is as much of an over-simplification as attributing the locus of a problem solely to environmental factors. Even in genetics, an area previously believed to be wholly deterministic and one-directional, we now understand from the study of epigenetics that gene expression is profoundly shaped by environment and experience.

For example, a psychological difficulty like an unstable sense of self might be due to identity conflict from forces such as acculturation following immigration, rapid social mobility, or intergenerational expectations. Assuming that it represents internal pathology such as borderline personality disorder—and should be addressed as such —can lead to ineffective and potentially harmful treatment decisions. Over-simpli-fication can also proceed in the opposite direction. Discounting a person's claim that dysfunctional behavior is due to external factors—as if that were a mere defensive projection, a way to deflect responsibility—may be equally wrong. It would be like treating a woman for depression without addressing the abusive domestic relationship that led to and sustains the depressive behavior. Helping someone to function or feel better in an unjust situation is not the aim of social work.

The Power of Cognitive Heuristics

While it may be comforting to imagine a therapist consulting DSM symptom lists, comparing each set of diagnostic criteria with carefully gathered notes on a client's particular troubles, and then deciding which category is the correct match—it does not often happen that way. In the busy world of clinical practice, the choice of DSM label may depend more on the associations in the therapist's mind *at the moment the diagnostic choice is made* than on diagnostic acuity or the scientific evidence behind the various categories.

If that sounds like an alarming statement, think about how we make decisions in daily life. Suppose, for instance, that you want to select a restaurant for dinner. The choices that come to mind are the ones that are most readily accessible, either because you have heard about the place or have been there before. As options, they are more vivid and easier to retrieve, and thus have an edge of credibility—or seem to. In other words, you are more likely to go to a restaurant that is *already been activated in your mind* than to one that has not.

That shows cognitive heuristics work. Cognitive heuristics is the study of the information-selecting and information-processing mechanisms through which decisions are made. Given the overwhelming amount of information available when considering a client's situation, clinicians make choices about what to focus on by using subconscious heuristics, or information-processing shortcuts. Beliefs and the cognitive structures that support them, including prior therapeutic orientation, "have a powerful influence on the information we attend to and how we interpret it. This is particularly true when there is some ambiguity in the cues, as is almost always the case in a helping situation" (Berlin and Marsh 1993, p. 56).

There is considerable research (e.g., Tversky and Kahneman 1973, whose work earned the Nobel Prize) indicating that initial conceptions tend to be formed quickly with minimal information and then act as self-fulfilling prophecies. When faced with difficult decisions, people tend to employ a limited number of cognitive strategies that reduce complex judgment tasks to simpler ones based on comparison and classification. Sometimes the initial classification is valid, but it can lead to errors when the similarity is superficial and results in dismissal of other relevant considerations.

Many diagnostic errors are due to the set of mental heuristics collectively called "cognitive dispositions to respond" (Croskerry 2003). These cognitive shortcuts rely on pattern recognition as a means for placing new information into familiar categories.

> The clinician quickly forms a working hypothesis about the nature and cause of the client's dilemma and proceeds to probe for the kind of evidence that will make it seem true. Snap

judgments about what is wrong are aided both by referral information that contains previous diagnoses and by the general ease with which certain 'preferred' diagnostic classifications come to mind (Berlin & Marsh, 1993, p. 57).

One powerful heuristic is *availability*, the tendency to judge the likelihood of an
event by the ease with which similar instances come to mind due to recent exposure
(Berlin and Marsh 1993; Groopman 2007). In a series of experiments, Tversky and
Kahneman (1973) found compelling evidence that judgments about the likelihood
of an event taking place or someone's membership in a particular category are
affected by the ease with which related instances are recalled. Berlin and Marsh
(1993) made a similar point: information that is most accessible tends to be more
vivid, specific, personally relevant, and familiar. A clinician who has recently
encountered a particular disorder "is more likely to classify ambiguous clusters of
symptoms as representing that disorder rather than employing other equally plausible
diagnostic categories. Due to recency, frequency, and familiarity … the diagnostic category is cognitively readily accessible" (Berlin and Marsh 1993, p. 19).
If you can think of it more easily, then—because of the power of *availability*—you
assume it is more important, correct, and real than alternatives that would require a
bit of mental searching and stretching.

The same thing happens in diagnosis. Particularly when a clinician is pressed for
time, clients may be more likely to receive one of the popular diagnoses *du jour*—to
be placed in a category the clinician has heard about, utilized, and discussed—than
they are to be placed in a category the clinician has not encountered or thought
about as recently or frequently. If the therapist has several other patients diagnosed
with OCD, just read a journal article on OCD, or attended a special workshop about
treatment for OCD, it is more likely that a diagnosis of OCD will be considered if it
is at all relevant. Popular diagnoses can thus become self-fulfilling prophecies,
capturing the interest of mental health professionals who "see" the disorder in
ambiguous cases and thus unconsciously contribute to an increase in reported
prevalence (Overholser 2014).

Since symptom lists have considerable overlap, flexibility, and room for interpretation, clinical judgments frequently involve a choice between plausible alternatives. It is not simply that having a hammer makes everything looks like a nail.
The availability heuristic might suggest something a bit more subtle: if the hammer
is easier to reach or worked well last time, then that is the tool you will reach for—
though you will never know what might have happened if you had picked up the
pliers or wrench instead.

Pattern recognition is the heuristic used to assess the fit between new information and familiar categories in order to determine where a new instance belongs.
More weight is given to how the new instance resembles the category than to how it
differs: in other words, we look for matches and, once the match has been made,
ignore evidence that does not support our choice. Once someone as been diagnosed
with ADHD, for example, we tend to focus on ways the person resembles an
ADHD prototype rather than the ways the person is unique or deviates from the
stereotype. People with the same label may seem to be the *same* in some essential

way, and essentially different from everyone outside the category, even if they are actually more different than alike in other ways such as talent, sense of humor, and spirituality.

Another powerful heuristic is *anchoring*, the tendency to lock into salient features early in assessment and then fail to adjust one's thinking in light of subsequent information about other features (Croskerry 2003)—that is, to selectively notice only those features that we expect to see. Like an anchor that sets the position, the first piece of information becomes the reference point for evaluating whatever comes next. "Anchoring" on the fact that the Sunset Café has an outdoor patio can lead a prospective diner to evaluate all other restaurants by the same criterion instead of by other criteria that might be equally important such as price or location. By setting a baseline, anchoring can shape choices and predictions. In one of their early studies, Tversky and Kahneman demonstrated that when asked to guess the percentage of African countries in the United Nations, people who were asked if it was more or less than 10 %—the anchored figure—guessed lower values, on average (that is, closer to 10 %), than those who were asked if it was more or less than 65 %. The percentage that was "anchored" in their minds, just by being uttered, influenced their response.

In the same way, clinicians who have recently diagnosed several people with bipolar disorder are likely to classify new patients as having bipolar disorder if they fall within a general zone of similarity, *even if symptoms are less severe*. Thus, it takes fewer cues to make the category seem plausible because the therapist's "bipolar radar" is already activated. Through availability and anchoring, new cases are judged by less rigorous criteria, inflating the number of people who seem to belong in the category and causing diagnostic rates to soar. This is reinforced, Overholser (2014) points out, by the research process itself. As investigators seek to recruit enough eligible participants, they may soften and expand the diagnostic criteria used for inclusion in the study. This loosening then becomes the new standard. With more people eligible for the label, there is an apparent surge in incidence, creating the impression of an "epidemic" that benefits both service providers and service recipients. Using the example of autism, Overholser notes that "when diagnostic criteria are 'softened,' they capture a larger market for professional services, allowing parents to pursue early intervention or special educational services" (p. 55).

In this way, epistemological assumptions and cognitive heuristics contribute to "epidemics." It is not necessarily that more people are being *born* with autism nowadays, for example; it may also be that more people are being *diagnosed* with autism. Because of public awareness, parents are more inclined to look for signs and to seek help, and clinicians to spot the hallmarks more readily. As diagnostic thresholds become relaxed, there is an increase in cases at the milder end of the spectrum. Because of softened borders and "diagnostic creep," it is easier to gain entrance into the category.

Several heuristics contribute to this process. One is *confirmation bias*, the tendency to dismiss alternative or disconfirming information because of how satisfying it is to re-affirm a decision already made or something already believed to be true. This is reinforced by *satisfaction of search* or *premature closure*, when one stops searching as soon as something has been found, even though there may be more left to find (Croskerry 2003). "Once an uncertain situation has been perceived or interpreted in a particular fashion, it is quite difficult to view it in any other way" (Tversky and Kahneman 1973, p. 230). *Diagnosis momentum* then sets in, the tendency for a label to get "stickier" over time; once made, the diagnostic decision gains momentum until it becomes solidified and other possibilities are quickly excluded.

Another heuristic that can affect clinical assessment is *dispositional bias* or *fundamental attribution error,* the tendency to attribute the source of the problem to something within the person rather than to factors within the ecological situation— i.e., to overestimate the influence of individual factors and underestimate the influence of situational factors. There is substantial evidence, Berlin and Marsh (1993) maintain, that clinicians unconsciously try to correct for the sense that clients tend to blame their troubles on external factors or project blame onto other people; as a counterweight, they may minimize or simply dismiss client assertions about external causes for their difficulties. If, for example, a client reports feeling unjustly treated and rejected, dispositional bias can cause a clinician to attribute that feeling to an internal problem such as low self-esteem rather than to factors in the client's ecological situation. This dispositional bias may be reinforced by institutional expectations and the requirement of insurance companies that an internal mental disorder must be cited if services are to be covered.

Other heuristics include *order effects*, the tendency to focus more on what was heard or experienced at the beginning or end of an encounter, and *commission bias*, the tendency to do something rather than nothing, to want to act and be "helpful" (Croskerry 2003). Decisions about how to help are also influenced by the kinds of resources that are easily available or familiar from prior use. Empirical research indicates that any intervention "tends to do better in comparison with other interventions when it is conducted by people who are expert in its use" (Chambless and Hollon 1998, p. 12) and when it corresponds to, rather than conflicts with, the clinician's own beliefs about how change takes place.

Priming or "Readiness to Respond"

These mental shortcuts are set in motion by a phenomenon called *priming*. In the same way that priming a wall makes it ready to accept a coat of paint, cognitive priming occurs when recent exposure, leading to mental "readiness to accept," makes certain aspects of a situation more salient and available than they would normally be.

> When an individual is asked to evaluate a novel stimulus, such as a questionnaire item, he or she will generate a response by scanning whatever information is available at that moment. The information that is most salient and relevant at the time of the question will be used to formulate a response (Moss and Lawrence 1997, p. 394).

In Moss and Lawrence's experiment, priming theory was used to show how recent information about stress led participants to report higher levels of stress than in the absence of priming. Some participants were given pamphlets to read about stress before taking a survey, others were not; those who had read the pamphlet reported higher levels of stress on the questionnaire than those who had not been primed. In another study by Milich et al. (1992), recent information about diagnostic labels led children and adolescents to judge their "misbehaving" peers more harshly and to give them more negative labels.

The mechanisms through which priming operates are category accessibility and confirmatory bias, the unconscious selective search for information that confirms information previously received (Moss and Lawrence 1997). Ledgerwood and Chaiken's study (2007) further demonstrates how information falling within a person's "latitude of acceptance" is perceived as *more* similar to the original reference point than it really is, and information falling within the "latitude of rejection" is perceived as *less* similar. A person primed to expect similarity is more likely to find similarity. In the same way, being primed to expect disorder makes a person more likely to find disorder.

Another way that priming occurs is through the suggestion of someone perceived to be an expert or of higher status. Temerlin's (1968) experimental study offers a vivid example of how this can occur. In his study, a professional actor trained to portray a "normal" mentally healthy man was interviewed as if he were a prospective patient. Five groups listened to the taped interview, each group stratified to represent the same distribution of psychiatrists, clinical psychologists, and psychology graduate students. All were instructed to diagnose the man by drawing from a list of categories in use at the time: psychoses, neuroses, and personality types including "normal" or "healthy." In order to isolate the influence of clinical setting, two of the groups were told that the interview was either part of a new procedure for conducting judicial sanity hearings or for selecting scientists to work on a new research project. Just before listening to the interview, a "prestige confederate" remarked to the fourth group that the patient on the tape seemed neurotic but was actually psychotic. A fifth group received the "prestige suggestion" reversed. A control group was given no special instruction.

The "prestige suggestion" had the most effect upon psychiatrists—members of the same profession as the "prestige confederate"—biasing them in the direction of psychosis. While no one in the control group diagnosed psychosis, 60 % of psychiatrists in the "prestige suggestion" group did so. Temerlin further notes: "It is doubtful that prestige suggestion could bias medical diagnosis so dramatically, on the theory that the substantive reality of physical illness would counter-balance the distorting effects of prestige suggestion" (p. 353), implying that mental illness is not "substantively real" in the way that physical illness is real.

The diagnostic system of the DSM is a potent vehicle for priming. It is a set of officially sanctioned categories that can predispose its users to "see" clients according to, and limited by, the categories it offers. A number of studies have shown how this happens. Ravotas and Berkenkotter (1998) found that therapists tend to interpret what a client says in a way that supports the DSM diagnosis *they already gave* to that person. In a self-perpetuating circle, the therapist reprocesses whatever the patient says and does in a way that "justifies the therapist's particular diagnosis of mental disorder which, in turn, supports the therapist's treatment choice" (p. 211). Client actions and statements that do not fit into the definition of the disorder *already diagnosed* are minimized or ignored, while actions and statements that seem to fit are inquired about more often and in more detail, described in clinical notes, and accorded more importance in case discussions. This tendency is supported by the heuristic of confirmation bias and by the assumption that diagnoses are essentialist categories. As Kirmayer (2005) notes:

> Unfamiliar symptoms or problems are reinterpreted to fit a specific prototype or discounted and ignored as minor and irrelevant. Insofar as the patient's experience does not fit the template, the discrepancies are viewed as irrelevant ... This stripping down of illness experience to fit the diagnostic paradigm is justified on the basis of the notion that diagnostic entities have essential characteristics and that what is crucial about the patient's condition can be typified by these core features (p. 195).

Overholser (2014) notes that a clinician's personal interest in a particular disorder can influence what is attended to and how that information is interpreted. "When intake workers have a diagnosis they find intriguing, they are more likely to notice potential symptoms, interpret symptoms as part of the disorder, and assign the label" (p. 54). Use of ready-made diagnostic constructs thus "functions to *black box* many of the dissonances, contradictions, power relations, and situational asymmetries that exist in any institutional context" (Ravotas and Berkenkotter 1998, p. 217).

Cognitive signals that tell you to stop looking can exert a powerful influence, especially when there is pressure to come to a diagnostic decision, often within the first 45-min encounter, since treatment plans and insurance claims cannot be filed without it. Berlin and Marsh (1993) sum up the interplay of these forces in their book on clinical decision-making:

> The clinician quickly forms a working hypothesis about the nature and cause of the client's dilemma and proceeds to probe for the kind of evidence that will make it seem true. Snap judgments about what is wrong are aided both by referral information that contains previous diagnoses and by the general ease with which certain 'preferred' diagnostic classifications come to mind (p. 57).
> In other words, *believing is seeing* and not the other way around.

Related to priming and the disposition to *respond* is "selective attention," an attentional bias that affects our disposition to *notice*. In their well-known "invisible gorilla" experiment, Harvard researchers Christopher Chabris and Daniel Simons offer a deceptively simple demonstration of how much we miss of what is going on right in front of us—without even suspecting how much we are missing. One of the reasons that we fail to register seemingly obvious elements like the gorilla is that *we're not looking for gorillas*. When we are intent on a predetermined task, whether it is counting basketball passes or counting DSM symptoms, we tend to focus only on information that seems pertinent to our aim and unconsciously filter out information that we do not believe is relevant. As the experiment shows, it is not just that we put this information to the side; we simply do not see it. In clinical assessment, this means there we may fail to perceive—and thus fail to include—information that is "not on the list" of elements that we've decided in advance may be clinically significant.

The process of diagnosing medical conditions is similar to the process of diagnosing mental health conditions—leading to similar errors. Reviewing the literature on diagnostic error among medical doctors, Berner and Graber (2008) point out that there are two general ways of coming to clinical decisions. One is through *hypothetico-deductive reasoning* in which physicians gather initial data and, often within seconds, formulate diagnostic hypotheses; they then gather additional data in order to evaluate these hypotheses and arrive at a diagnostic conclusion. Errors can occur from failure to elicit complete and accurate information from the patient, failure to recognize the significance of that information or, most commonly, failure to integrate facts about a specific patient with general medical knowledge—that is, to synthesize and apply nomothetic principles to an individual case.

As physicians gain experience and expertise, they are more likely to use the more intuitive and subconscious process of *pattern-recognition* (Berner and Graber 2008). As noted above, pattern-recognition works by recalling cases similar to the one under review, attending to what seem to be protypical features, and matching them to familiar patterns. Other elements, which might be equally or even more significant, may be overlooked or dismissed as irrelevant. Even if more information is sought, it is likely to be information that confirms the initial hypothesis rather than information that opens up new possibilities: the physician does not even realize that anything has been left out. This reflects a failure of metacognition, "the willingness and ability to reflect on one's own thinking processes and to critically examine one's own assumptions, beliefs, and conclusions" (Berner and Graber 2008, p. S7). One of the marks of an expert is having "the ability to recognize when one's initial impression is wrong and having back-up strategies readily available when the initial strategy does not work" (p. S9). If that is true, then insisting that one's initial judgment must be right is the mark of a *non*-expert.

Berner and Graber go on to explore *overconfidence* as a contributing factor for diagnostic error: underestimating the degree and likelihood of error, believing that error rates only pertain to others, minimizing and dismissing one's own errors when they do occur, and rationalizing that errors are inevitable. Overconfidence leads to complacency, self-deception, and an inflated sense of one's own accuracy. This is fostered by inadequate feedback from patients combined with the use of patient outcome as a proxy for diagnostic acumen. If patients state that they feel better, get better regardless of whether the diagnosis was correct, or do not return with additional complaints, the physician may assume that the diagnosis was correct. "In the absence of information that the diagnosis is wrong, it is assumed to be correct" (p. S10). When the diagnosis is incorrect, the physician may never know.

Labels as Agents of Perception

Labeling theory, also called "societal reaction theory," focuses on the linguistic tendency of majorities to negatively label minorities or those seen as "deviant," and asserts that society's *reaction* to certain behavior, more than the behavior itself, is a key factor in an individual's defining himself as disordered. The theory has two roots, one in symbolic interaction theory, developed by George Mead in the 1930s, and the other in conflict theory, derived from the writings of Marx and Foucault. Symbolic interaction theory maintains that during socialization people learn and internalize the meanings and attitudes attached to certain behaviors; conflict theory focuses on how those in power determine what and who is labeled as deviant in order to maintain a social order that promotes their interests. Both are sociological theories concerned with the human behavior in social groups, in contrast to theories that focus on individual psychology.

Although others had written about deviance and labeling as a societal response to rule breaking, it was sociologist Thomas Scheff who offered the first complete articulation of the theory in his 1966 book *Being Mentally Ill*. Scheff proposed the radical idea that the *act of being labeled* by those in power creates the "disordered" status, not the behavior itself. His ideas had a wide appeal, fitting well with the anti-diagnosis and anti-authoritarian movement of the 1960s and 1970s.

In Scheff's model, the effects of labeling are direct. Negative concepts of mental illness are independent of a person's actual behavior, due instead to the label imposed on that behavior. Societal conceptions of mental illness lead to labeling, which produces responses that cause the labeled person to adopt the role of a "mentally ill person," thus internalizing a definition of himself as disordered and forming an identity around that role that acquires master status. Behavior gradually conforms to the expectations and cultural stereotypes of the deviant role (such as being dangerous or incompetent), and it becomes increasingly difficult for the labelled person to inhabit any other role. As illness behavior becomes crystallized, the mental illness persona becomes self-fulfilling and appears to justify the label's validity. In this way, mental illness is a social role, with societal reaction the determinant of entry into that role.

By the 1980s, labeling theory had come under attack. The proposed causal chain could not be demonstrated, making it difficult to test the validity of the theory to explain and predict. In addition, there was no way to measure concepts such as "identification with a deviant label." Research tended to rely on proxy measures such as self-esteem, yet one can adopt a "deviant" identity with either high or low self-esteem. Critics asserted that the evidence for labeling effects was so overwhelmingly negative that the theory should be dismissed, simply a fad of the radical 1960s and 1970s.

Meanwhile, however, Bruce Link and his colleagues were conducting empirical studies and developing a new model for a *modified* labeling theory (1987, 1989) that proposed a more complex and indirect route between label and disorder. The act of labeling does not produce the mental disorder, they said, but leads to negative outcomes that exacerbate and maintain disordered behavior. Socialization leads people to develop a set of beliefs about mental illness, with expectations that the mentally ill will be devalued and discriminated against. When a person enters treatment, these beliefs become personally relevant; he or she is now subject to a response from others based on notions of mental illness that are contained in and conveyed by the label. Believing that he himself will be devalued and discriminated against, the labeled individual avoids social contact that he fears will lead to judgment and rejection. Withdrawal and concealment, in turn, lead to further negative consequences—reduction in social support, access to employment, and self-esteem—causing additional isolation and demoralization. In a self-perpetuating cycle, stigma is experienced through others' responses and reinforced through internalization of a defective identity (Corrigan 2007).

Research also suggests that a label's effects may vary by social context and by the status of both the labeled and the labeler. When symptoms are more visible, disruptive, or severe, categorization is likely regardless of social status. But when symptoms are moderate or mild, those with more social power and resources may be able to resist being labeled or to substitute less pejorative terms like "eccentric millionaire." The more negative labels a person receives (homeless, delinquent, dropout, mentally ill, etc.), the more power and status are diminished. At a certain point, however, effects may level off and become redundant for who have received so many or such serious labels that they have already been deemed "non-members" of society.

While few people believe that labeling effects provide a complete explanation for mental disorder, it is clear that labels play a powerful role. The label defines the problem—alcoholic, unemployed, on probation, bipolar—and affects those being labeled as well as those who interact with them, turning people into "clients" and "clinicians." Resistance to being labeled can affect willingness to enter treatment, transformation of identity, and trajectories following treatment (Corrigan 2007). Consideration of the labeling process is thus an important part of assessment. That does not mean all labels should be avoided, but that the client's response to a proposed label—or to receiving *any* label—needs to be taken into account. For some, the label can feel like a loss of identity and efficacy. For others, the label may bring a sense of relief, legitimacy, and connection with others who have struggled in similar ways (McQuaide 1999; Probst 2013).

Difference, Distress, and Impairment

Definitions of mental disorder tend to include three elements—distance from "normal" experience, a sense of personal distress, and impairment in daily functioning—although with varying emphases. How "different" or "deviant" from prevailing social norms does a person need to be? How much does this difference have to trouble the person, leading to pain and suffering? How much impairment does it have to cause, in the person's own ability to live a satisfying life and in potential harm to others?

Some authors, concerned about the constructed nature of illness labels and the values on which they are based, prefer to sidestep the first question about degree of deviance and to focus on the experience of distress and dysfunction. One such attempt is Wakefield's notion of "harmful dysfunction." A hybrid approach, the "harmful dysfunction" hypothesis seeks to bridge the sociological notion of mental disorder as a social construction, primarily for the enforcement of social norms, and the biomedical notion of mental disorder as the failure or malfunctioning of part of the brain. The former, Wakefield says, is value-based while the latter is factual and thus value-free. Rather than taking sides, he attempts to include both. "Dysfunction," in his definition, refers to the failure of an internal biological mechanism to carry out the function for which it was designed; "harmful" means that this failure is or leads to conditions judged as negative by sociological standards, such as social impairment and/or psychological distress. "Dysfunction" is rooted in the evolutionary biology; "harmful" is rooted in the sociocultural context (Wakefield 2007).

Wakefield is attempting to answer the question of how we can know that something is "not merely a form of normal, albeit undesirable and painful human functioning, but indicative of psychiatric disorder" (Wakefield 2007, p. 149). Yet this definition has its own pitfalls. What exactly are these alleged functions and mechanisms of the mind, and how can we know if they are working "properly" or improperly (Jacobs 2014)? What would "proper functioning" look like, and who gets to decide? What about non-pathological eccentricity, such as the unusual but not necessarily disordered way that visual–spatial thinkers and other creative individuals think in associative spirals? The same question can be asked about "harm." Harmful to whom? Harmful, as compared to what? On whose authority is the consequence or experience deemed harmful?

In fact, neither distress nor impairment is necessary for mental disorder. Personality disorders, for instance, are by definition ego-syntonic and are not experienced as personally distressing. Other individuals, who may suffer deeply from chronic anxiety or depression, may nonetheless continue to function adequately in the world, either because they have to do so in order to survive or because these actions provide some relief from their pain. To say that they fail to meet the criteria for mental disorder, simply because they have managed to cope, would be to invalidate their suffering. The disordered condition thus needs to be decoupled with the disability that it might (or might not) lead to (Berganza et al. 2005).

Even when disability is present, that *still* cannot tell us for certain whether the condition is a true disorder of the brain and/or psyche or an adaptive response to challenging life circumstances. The problem of defining symptom or disorder has simply been replaced with the problem of defining function and harm, and we are back to the same question.

Perhaps there is another way to approach this dilemma. If we cannot decide what mental disorder *is*, perhaps we can decide what it *isn't*. By determining what lies *out*side its borders, we may have a better idea of what lies *in*side. Valid exclusionary criteria should help to distinguish a true mental disorder from other kinds of human problems. Certainly, disorders that are fundamentally physical in nature ought to be excluded, even if they lead to emotional distress. So too, we ought to eliminate forms of suffering or dysfunction that represent a transient or adaptive response to the stresses of life, as well as what we might call non-pathological quirkiness. What else is left, once we have ruled these out? Surely *that* will indicate a trustworthy definition of mental disorder.

Unfortunately, however, the same difficulties arise when attempting to remove criteria presumed to be irrelevant—under the assumption that what remains is a valid core—as arise when attempting to isolate criteria presumed to be essential. Nearly anything can be relevant, depending on the person and situation. The problem remains.

Cataloging Disorder

While some theorists have concentrated on the question of distinguishing mental disorder *from* other kinds of difficulty, others have focused on ways to distinguish *among* the various forms of disorder—that is, on developing classification systems or taxonomies. Creating a good taxonomy is no small task. First, there is the matter of determining what constitutes a "category." What is the defining feature? Where should lines be drawn, and how to handle cases that do not fit into any of the available categories? Is it better to have *more* categories, each with precise features, or *fewer* categories that indicate essential sub-types?

The classification system for mental disorder used in the US, as noted earlier, is the DSM, a system developed (and periodically changed) by the American Psychiatric Association. Its taxonomic principle is the grouping of psychiatric conditions into various families according to common features and "known similarities" based on "new scientific understanding of their principal features" and "advancements in our understanding of the underlying vulnerabilities as well as symptom characteristics of disorders" (American Psychiatric Association 2013). The goal of the diagnostic process is to determine which psychiatric category is the best match for a client's presenting symptoms. The client might, of course, *also* belong to other categories if viewed against templates organized around criteria such as demographic variables, blood type, and political affiliation. Membership in these categories is not considered relevant for clinical diagnosis, which is presumed to rely on stand-alone criteria that cut across demographic and other lines. Many have questioned this assumption, however, citing evidence that the choice of diagnostic label is influenced by factors external to psychiatric criteria such as race, class, age, and gender.

Mental health classification systems are not inherent in nature, but created; they are devised, *re*vised, and revised again according to historically and geographically embedded notions of what constitutes normalcy, deviance, well-being, and appropriate social functioning. DSM-5, for example, is organized quite differently from its predecessors. As the next chapter will indicate, there is no basis for assuming that recent revisions of the system are more accurate than earlier ones. In general, the trend has been toward finer and finer distinctions, but "finer" does not necessarily mean "more accurate." Distinguishing sub-types of disorder is only helpful if the differences are clinically important; otherwise, it is just a matter of semantics. The first system for classifying mental disorders, the 1840 census, used a single category of idiocy/insanity; a report compiled in 1888 listed seven types of mental illness (dementia, alcoholism, epilepsy, mania, melancholia, monomania, and paresis). The American Psychiatric Association's 1917 manual included 22 diagnoses. The most recent edition of the DSM, published in 2013, lists more than 300 (see Appendix B: Historical Overview of the DSM).

When there are *too few* categories, important distinctions can be overlooked that affect treatment decisions, while *too many* categories can confuse and distract the clinician by diverting attention to minor points. What makes a classification system both practical and conceptually coherent is not the number of categories it proposes but how well it addresses questions of sensitivity and specificity.

Suppose, for instance, that a friend comes up to you and says, "Look at my new pet! Isn't he adorable?" How can you tell if the pet is a cat or a dog?

The answer may seem obvious: How could anyone mistake a cat for a dog? But if you jot down the key features you would use to *describe* each animal, you may find that many of them do not actually *differentiate* the two species. A cat's fur, four legs, whiskers, and tail are all significant to the cat and to anyone who seeks to understand the cat, but they have no significance when it comes to distinguishing a cat from a dog. Nor can you use behavior since not all cats climb trees and not all dogs like to swim. What, then, guides you so you know for certain that you have placed the pet in the right category?

That is what diagnostic *specificity* is about. When a feature is specific to membership in a particular category, it serves as a reliable sorting mechanism and helps to place someone in one category rather than another. Unfortunately, criteria for specificity are hard to come by in the world of human behavior and experience. The same feature can be interpreted in more than one way (ambiguity) or point to more than one category (overlap). Studies have shown, for example, that two-thirds of the children diagnosed with bipolar disorder also meet criteria for ADHD (imagine if two-thirds of your pets could be classified equally well as cats or dogs). Many people have features that seem to belong to one category and features that belong to another, or meet some but not all the criteria for a particular disorder.

The other important issue is *sensitivity*, or how accurately you can spot an instance of the category. Do you miss a lot of cases (under sensitivity)? Do you put people into the category who do not really belong (over sensitivity)? Without good sensitivity, prevalence figures don't really mean anything. Sensitivity depends on *threshold*, the point where someone enters the category. Here again, it is not so easy since many disorders exist on a continuum. There are people with milder and more severe versions of the illness, even though they may receive the same label, and people who seem to fit into the category at some moments but not at others since they move along a continuum, depending on what is going on in their lives. If every symptom is equally important and it is a matter of having a sufficient number in order to enter the category, then these "sub-threshold" people are excluded from a classification that might actually be appropriate. DSM-5 does include a way to indicate severity for many disorders; while helpful, these severity ratings tend to remain static once entered into a chart and rarely capture the dynamic nature of most people's experience.

An intriguing alternative was proposed by Oldham and Morris in 1995, in their theory of personality types. They suggest that each psychiatric disorder represents a type of adaptive functioning and exists along a situationally embedded continuum. At times of low stress, a trait may manifest in a mild and functional way (for example, checking everything carefully, a behavior called "conscientiousness"), while at times of high stress, the same trait may become more intense and thus dysfunctional (checking everything so much that it interferes with your life, a behavior called "compulsiveness"). In the first instance, at the low end of the continuum, the behavior helps people cope with stress or uncertainty, providing a sense of order and control that allows them to function. At the high end, it becomes maladaptive. Same person, different situations—should the person receive a DSM label? Or should the label have a time limit, subject to renewal at intervals? That creates other creates difficulties, of course. People could claim mental illness when if suited them, mental health when it did not—who would determine when the person entered and left the category?

A good classification system allows people to make reliable and meaningful distinctions between categories. But distinguishing between categories is not the same thing as determining clinical significance. A rough tongue helps you to know that your pet is a cat rather than a dog (taxonomic significance); whiskers do not help to do that, yet are equally important to the animal itself, especially if they are not working properly (clinical significance). It is the same with features like loss of appetite or inability to concentrate: They may be clinically significant without necessarily helping to place someone in one group rather than another. The problem, for students, is when taxonomic and clinical significance are not taught in an integrated manner and they learn taxonomic specificity in one course, clinical sensitivity in another.

The merit of a taxonomic system rests on its sorting mechanism, the criteria used to define its categories. With a few exceptions such as Post Traumatic Stress Disorder and Reactive Attachment Disorder, the DSM uses behavior; the origin of the problem does not really matter, only the way you feel and behave. That is the rationale for elimination of the bereavement exclusion from DSM-5: in the past, depression due to bereavement did not qualify as "true" depression since it could be explained by an external event without requiring the presence of internal dysfunction.

The bereavement exclusion was, perhaps, a sensible way to avoid pathologizing human grief. It also helped to differentiate treatment for grief from treatment for other kinds of depression. With most forms of depression, the goal was to reduce the depressive thoughts, feelings, and behaviors; with grief work, feelings of loss and sadness need to be fully experienced and run their course. At the same time, the bereavement exclusion created other problems. If death of a loved one meant that a person was not "truly" depressed, then what about depression due to loss of home or job, to serious illness, infidelity, or a host of other stressful events? Cause cannot matter in one case but not in others.

One could, of course, imagine an alternative classification based *entirely* on cause—problems stemming from impaired attachment, identity diffusion, shame, lack of agency, and so on—rather than on behavior. History would matter in that case, not observed behavior. In fact, clinicians consider both. They look at patterns and events over a client's life course, current symptoms, and the contexts in which those symptoms occur—the details of a person's life story and the meaning of those details to that specific individual (Phillips 2005). That is, they take an *idiographic* approach. The term "*idiographic*," from the Greek word "idios" meaning "own" or "private," refers to the unique, subjective, individual phenomena that comprise a person's self-narrative (see Chap. 8).

Theorists and researchers, on the other hand, take a *nomothetic* approach. The word "nomothetic" comes from the Greek word "nomos," meaning "law." A nomothetic orientation is concerned with broad categories and characteristics of populations; it seeks to formulate laws or generalizations. In nomothetic inquiry, between-group differences are significant; in *idiographic* inquiry, within-group differences are just as important (Corrigan 2007). A taxonomic system such as the DSM uses a nomothetic approach to describe ideal, prototypical, or essentialist types.

The clinical encounter, in contrast, utilizes a two-step process. The initial act of diagnosis serves to map a person's individual story and clinical presentation onto a general set of categories. Once the client has been diagnosed, the clinician moves in the opposite direction to particularize, qualify, and contextualize (Kirmayer 2005). Each approach has its emphasis and purpose; both are important for clinical understanding. Difficulty arises when categorical formulations are presumed to capture the information needed for individual assessment—when what is required for nomothetic inquiry is taken to represent what is required for idiographic practice (Phillips 2005). "The simplifying assumptions build into a model (or theory) that give the model normative value also distance it from actual descriptions of clinical reality" (Henry 2006, p. 193).

In real-world clinical practice, the diagnostic lens widens. Client problems are viewed in an "expanded explanatory context of vulnerabilities, life circumstances and stresses, personality dispositions, ways of thinking, social influences, and developmental pathways" (Haslam 2000, p. 1035). To this list, one might add cultural values and forms of expression, available outlets and supports, genetics, and overall physical health. Some disorders might have a stronger genetic component, others a stronger cognitive or cultural influence. Thus, the template for understanding the meaning and trajectory of a condition will not be the same for all diagnoses or individuals. As indicated in a recent study of clinical social workers, many consider the psychiatric paradigm to be important for more severe disorders but less so for milder ones (Probst 2012, 2013).

Conclusions

We return to the epistemological question of how we "know" someone has a mental disorder. Which kinds of knowledge are used to inform clinical decisions, how are they ranked or valued, and by what means was each kind of knowledge acquired? When we decide if someone has a legitimate reason to seek (and receive) help, who defines the terms, who benefits, and who is left out?

Discussion of mental disorder must include issues of power, access, and control. Despite the fact that most clinical services are provided by social workers, control—the way mental disorder is thought about, treated, and paid for—rests with the authors of the DSM. Defenders of the DSM have stated that its categories and criteria are merely "scientific hypothesis," open to testing and modification if evidence is not found to support them. While that may sound reasonable, it is next to impossible for a researcher to obtain funding to test alternative criteria. DSM criteria themselves are not really "tested" either, or "re-tested" once they have appeared in print. There is no feedback system whereby clinicians can report that criteria were not accurate or helpful after all and can propose other criteria that might be considered.

It is a circular and troubling situation: We adopt certain criteria, knowing they are only hypotheses, yet alternative interpretations are never studied because there is no funding to test anything that is not already legitimized by inclusion in the DSM! Nor does research attend very much to issues outside the DSM taxonomy such as relational problems, identity conflict, and existential dilemmas. Even though these issues are important for clinical practice, affecting the trajectory of a disorder as well as the way an intervention will be understood and utilized (Kirmayer 2005), they tend to receive little scientific attention.

Social workers, committed to working with the whole person, need to look beyond the limited epistemology of the DSM—at other kinds of knowledge and other ways of accessing that knowledge. This may be especially important when working with clients whose cultural or spiritual backgrounds rely on different ways of conceptualizing illness, health, personhood, and help. Clinicians unused to examining and thinking critically about their own cognitive assumptions will not have the acuity or flexibility necessary for serving their clients. That is why a candid, thoughtful exploration of epistemology is essential for ethical practice.

Application to the Case of Ray

Subsequent chapters will offer various perspectives or ways to think about the Case of Ray (see Appendix A: The Case of Ray for a complete description of the case). Before considering these interpretations, however, it may be useful to *think about the way you think* by undertaking the following set of exercises:

First, take stock of your assumptions about the kinds of evidence that will be sought, found, and considered. Which forms of evidence do you presume are most trustworthy—Ray's self-report, hospital records, clinician observation and intuition, practice wisdom, correspondence to DSM categories? This will provide insight into your epistemology. You might want to list the pertinent facts about the case and consider how you "know" each is true. Which facts seem most important? Why do you feel that way?

Next, consider your assumptions about the various groups that Ray belongs to. What assumptions do you have about police officers, 911 responders, Irish Catholics, victims of sexual abuse, men who admit to violence against women, people who have been hospitalized? That does not mean all your assumptions are false, only that they need to be illuminated. Listing them explicitly can help to mitigate the effects of priming and other cognitive errors.

Each of these categories is a label, evoking stereotypes and judgments. How do you think Ray felt about these labels? Which made him feel proud, ashamed, or uneasy because his inner sense of himself did not correspond to others' perceptions about members of that group? Which labels did he choose, and which were given to him by others? Are there any contradictions among these labels?

Certainly, membership in a group like the police force implies power, while other groups that Ray belongs to imply powerlessness. How do these dissonant experiences affect his sense of identity and ego integrity? Which identities has he embraced and which has he denied?

Third, take note of Ray's salient traits—for instance, his anger at perceived "disloyalty," self-blame, and attempts to escape or avoid. Which of these are symptoms—that is, criteria for a DSM diagnosis? Remember that a symptom can be an observable behavior or a subjective complaint; internal experiences are not observable so we tend to use external signs, including verbal descriptions, as "evidence" of internal states. Clearly, Ray appears to have both: outer behavior such as violence, including violence toward his partner, and self-medication; he also reports subjective complaints including guilt, remorse, rage, loss, and feeling overwhelmed. Which diagnostic categories, if any, might these features point to?

Ray has, in fact, received two different diagnoses. The first was major depression, the second bipolar disorder II. Depression may have been selected because of the Tylenol overdose that led to hospitalization, his reports of ongoing difficulty sleeping, and the way he presented to hospital staff. We assume that they made the best diagnosis they could, given the information they had available at the time. After the second overdose, the diagnosis was changed, perhaps because the second depressive episode was seen as part of a cycle. Since Ray had been relatively stable in between the two episodes, the depression was not continuous; in the absence of a true manic episode, the diagnosis of Bipolar II probably seemed reasonable. It is important to remember that hospital staff had no knowledge of Ray's prior trauma; thus, a diagnosis of PTSD was unlikely to have occurred to them

Fourth, review your overall impressions and initial judgments. What was your first hunch about what is going on? What made you think so? What if you are wrong? What else could it be? Again, there may be merit in your initial formulation, but the best way to guard against the effects of anchoring, confirmation bias, and satisfaction of search is to *keep looking*. Brainstorm as many possibilities as you can about the nature of Ray's core struggle, no matter how unlikely they seem, as well as their sources and implications. Share the case with a colleague to get another brainstormed list.

It can also be useful to examine the cognitive heuristics that others may have used in assessing Ray. What did hospital staff "anchor onto," based on the kinds of cases they may have seen before and on Ray's most dramatic symptom? Did they stop looking once a seemingly reasonable diagnosis had been made?

Finally, consider what you do not yet know about the case. What's missing? How might you find out? To which sources of knowledge are you most likely to turn?

Different people in Ray's life are likely to have different perceptions of him. What do you think would be a major difference in how Ray's father and Leslie, his ex-wife, would describe him? Which aspects might each highlight or ignore? What questions would you like to ask each of them? What might happen if you brought them into the room at the same time? What do you imagine each might say to Ray or ask him?

Practical Exercises

1. What are Ray's symptoms? Describe each one in terms of observable behavior. Are these symptoms severe and consistent enough to add up to a diagnosis? Why or why not? Do they represent a change from a previous level of functioning? If you had to give Ray a diagnosis, which one would you select? Why? What would be a disadvantage of selecting that diagnosis?
2. Think of client you have recently met for the first time, and review the intake form or your initial notes. What are some possible "anchors" that might have influenced the diagnosis given? How might you guard against or correct for the influence of these anchors?
3. Carlo, an 8-year-old boy, has just received a diagnosis of ADHD. What are some ways that this label might negatively affect him and acquire "master status"? What are some ways that it might be helpful to him and his family? What questions might you have about the meaning of his symptoms and his diagnosis? How would you be able to know the label's effects?

References

American Psychiatric Association. (2013). *Diagnostic and Statistical Manual of Mental Disorders* (5th ed.). Arlington, VA.
Banzato, C. E. M., Mezzich, J. E., & Berganza, C. E. (2005). Introduction. *Psychopathology, 38*(4), 159–161.

Berganza, C. E., Mezzich, J. E., & Pouncey, C. (2005). Concepts of disease: Their relevance for psychiatric diagnosis and classification. *Psychopathology, 38*(4), 166–170.

Berner, E. S., & Graber, M. L. (2008). Overconfidence as a cause of diagnostic error in medicine. *The American Journal of Medicine, 121*(5A), S2–S23.

Berlin, S. B., & Marsh, J. C. (1993). *Informing practice decisions*. New York: MacMillan.

Brown, J. F. (2002). Epistemological differences within psychological science: A philosophical perspective on the validity of psychiatric diagnoses. *Psychology and Psychotherapy: Theory, Research and Practice, 75*, 239–250.

Chambless, D. L., & Hollon, S. D. (1998). Defining empirically supported therapies. *Journal of Consulting and Clinical Psychology, 66*(1), 7–18.

Corrigan, P. W. (2007). How clinical diagnosis might exacerbate the stigma of mental illness. *Social Work, 52*(1), 31–39.

Croskerry, P. (2003). The importance of cognitive errors in diagnosis and strategies to minimize them. *Academic Medicine, 78*(8), 775–781.

Deleuze, G., & Guattari, F. (1996). *What is philosophy?* New York: Columbia University Press.

Erikson, K., & Kress, V.E. (2005). *Beyond the DSM Story: Ethical quandaries, challenges, and best practices*. Sage: Thousand Oaks, CA.

First, M. B. (2005). Mutually exclusive versus co-occurring diagnostic categories: The challenge of diagnostic comorbidity. *Psychopathology, 38*(4), 206–210.

First, M. B. (2010). Paradigm shifts and the development of the diagnostic and statistical manual of mental disorders: Past experiences and future aspirations. *The Canadian Journal of Psychiatry, 55*, 692–700.

Gambrill, E. (2005). Critical thinking, evidence-based practice, and mental health. In S. A. Kirk (Ed.), *Mental disorders in the social environment: Critical perspectives* (pp. 247–269). New York: Columbia University Press.

Garland, E. L., & Howard, M. O. (2009). Neuroplasticity, psychosocial genomics, and the biopsychosocial paradigm in the 21st century. *Health and Social Work, 34*(3), 191–199.

Groopman, J. (2007). *How doctors think*. New York: Houghton Mifflin.

Haslam, N. (2000). Psychiatric categories as natural kinds: Essentialist thinking about mental disorder. *Social Research, 67*, 1031–1058.

Henry, S. G. (2006). Recognizing tacit knowledge in medical epistemology. *Theoretical Medicine and Bioethics, 27*, 187–213.

Insel, T., Cuthbert, B., Garvey, M., Heinssen, R., Pine, D. S., Quinn, K., et al. (2010). Research domain criteria (RDoC): Toward a new classification framework for research on mental disorders. *American Journal of Psychiatry, 167*, 748–751.

Jablensky, A. (2005). Categories, dimensions, and prototypes: Critical issues for psychiatric classification. *Psychopathology, 38*(4), 201–205.

Jacobs, D. H. (2014). Mental disorder or "normal life variation?" Why it matters. *Research on Social Work Practice, 24*, 152–157.

Kirmayer, L. J. (2005). Culture, context and experience in psychiatric diagnosis. *Psychopathology, 38*, 192–196.

Ledgerwood, A., & Chaiken, S. (2007). Priming us and them: Automatic assimilation and contrast in group attitudes. *Journal of Personality and Social Psychology, 93*(6), 940–956.

Link, B. G., Cullen, F. T., Struening, E. L., & Strout, P. E. (1989). A modified labeling theory approach to mental disorders: An empirical assessment. *American Sociological Review, 54*(3), 400–423.

Markova, I. S., & Berrios, G. E. (2009). Epistemology of mental symptoms. *Psychopathology, 42*, 343–349.

McQuaide, S. (1999). A social worker's use of the diagnostic and statistical manual. *Families in Society, 80*(4), 410–417.

McWilliams, N. (2011). The psychodynamic diagnostic manual: An effort to compensate for the limitations of descriptive psychiatric diagnosis. *Journal of Personality Assessment, 93,* 112–122.

Mezzich, J. E., & Berganza, C. E. (2005). Purposes and models of diagnostic systems. *Psychopathology, 38*(4), 162–165.

Milich, R., McAninch, C. B., & Harris, M. J. (1992). Effects of stigmatizing information on children's peer relations: Believing is seeing. *School Psychology Review, 21*(3), 400–409.

Moss, S. E., & Lawrence, K. G. (1997). The effects of priming on the self-reporting of perceived stressors and strains. *Journal of Organizational Behavior, 18,* 393–403.

Overholser, J. C. (2014). Chasing the latest fad: Confronting recent and historical innovations in mental illness. *Journal of Contemporary Psychotherapy, 44*(1), 53–61.

Paris, J. (2013). *The intelligent clinician's guide to the DSM-5.* Oxford: New York.

Phillips, J. (2005). Idiographic formulations, symbols, narratives, context, and meaning. *Psychopathology, 38*(4), 180–184.

Probst, B. (2012). Diagnosing, diagnoses, and the DSM in clinical social work. *Families in Society, 93*(4), 255–263.

Probst, B. (2013). "Walking the tightrope:" Clinical social workers' use of diagnostic and environmental perspectives. *Clinical Social Work Journal, 41*(2), 184–191.

Ravotas, D., & Berkenkotter, C. (1998). Voices in the text: the uses of reported speech in a psychotherapist's notes and initial assessment. *Text, 18*(2), 211–239.

Saleebey, D. (2001). Nature and nurture, neurons and narratives: Putting it all together (Chap. 5). In D. Saleebey (Ed.), *Human behavior and social environments: A biopsychosocial approach.* New York: Columbia University Press.

Scheff, T. A. (1966). *Being mentally Ill: A sociological theory.* Chicago: Aldine.

Temerlin, M. K. (1968). Suggestion effects of psychiatric diagnosis. *Journal of Nervous and Mental Disease, 147*(4), 349–353.

Thyer, B. A. (2006). It is time to rename the DSM. *Ethical Human Psychiatry and Psychology, 1,* 61–67.

Thyer, B. A. (2014). Review of Alan Francis' essentials of psychiatric diagnosis: Responding to the challenge of DSM-5. In *Research on Social Work Practice, 24*(1), 164–168.

Tversky, A., & Kahneman, D. (1973). Availability: A heuristic for judging frequency and probability. *Cognitive Psychology, 5,* 207–232.

Wakefield, J. C. (2005). Disorders versus problems of living in DSM: Rethinking social work's relationship to psychiatry. In S. A. Kirk (Ed.), *Mental disorders in the social environment: Critical perspectives* (pp. 83–95). New York: Columbia University Press.

Wakefield, J. C. (2007). The concept of mental disorder: Diagnostic implications of the harmful dysfunction analysis. *World Psychiatry, 6,* 149–156.

Watters, E. (2010). *Crazy like us: The globalization of the American psyche.* Free Press: New York.

Chapter 3
The DSM-5 Definition of Mental Disorder: Critique and Alternatives

Bruce A. Thyer

Abstract The chapter begins by dissecting the definition of mental disorder offered in the latest edition of the diagnostic manual, incisively pointing out its flaws and shortcomings. These flaws are of two kinds. First, there is the DSM's overreach in what it "counts" as a mental disorder—e.g., enduring conditions with a clear biological etiology such as Down's syndrome; temporary states caused by events such as alcohol intoxication, dehydration, or fever-induced delirium; and reactions to adverse environmental stressors. For a condition to be categorized as a mental disorder, its etiology ought to be mentally related, not simply represent a condition that adversely effects mental functioning; indeed, distress and dysfunction can be caused by a wide range of factors, not all of which constitute "mental disorders." Second, there are fundamental errors in logical reasoning found throughout the manual—e.g., the assumption that diagnoses represent natural and coherent syndromes, as well as the pervasive reification and tautological reasoning in how mental disorder is "explained" by the very elements that comprise its definition. Alternatives to the DSM are explored including various forms of "denialism," symptomatic treatment, and functional behavioral assessment. The chapter concludes with a reflection on the consequences for clinical assessment and treatment of the DSM's vision of mental disorder and a call for social workers to critically examine its tenets and decide for themselves the model(s) they wish to use.

Keywords Denialism · Etiology · Syndrome · Reification · Circular reasoning · Symptomatic treatment · Functional assessment of behavior

Portions of this chapter previously appeared in Thyer (2014).

B.A. Thyer (✉)
College of Social Work, Florida State University, 296 Champions Way,
Tallahassee, FL 32317, USA
e-mail: bthyer@fsu.edu

© Springer International Publishing Switzerland 2015
B. Probst (ed.), *Critical Thinking in Clinical Assessment and Diagnosis*,
Essential Clinical Social Work Series, DOI 10.1007/978-3-319-17774-8_3

Introduction: Why This Matters

The *Diagnostic and Statistical Manual of Mental Disorders*, 5th edition (DSM), promises to be even more influential than its predecessors. Widely used within the USA, the DSM is the mental health field's predominant method of categorizing supposedly psychopathological conditions. Apart from its international influence, the DSM plays an important role in the education of social workers in the USA (McLendon 2014; Robbins 2014) and many other countries, with most master's programs including an entire course in the use of this manual. Such an influential document has not gone without its criticisms, and the purpose of this paper is to describe how, in some very fundamental ways, the DSM is a scientifically flawed document. From the very definition of mental disorder provided in the DSM to its pervasive errors in logical reasoning, the manual is a conceptually problematic set of diagnostic guidelines. While pragmatic reasons may dictate the DSM's continued use in many practice settings, social work students, faculty, and practitioners need to understand the manual's limitations, and not confuse its unsupported assertions with nature's reality.

Social workers and other mental health professionals have long contributed to the critical literature related to the process of psychiatric diagnosis (e.g., First and Wakefield 2010; Horowitz and Wakefield 2012; Thyer 2006, 2014a, b; Wakefield 1992), but the publication of the new edition of the DSM presents fresh opportunities for a review and analysis of the concept of mental disorder, and of some of the specific changes found in the DSM-5.

Guiding Questions

1. Do the mental disorders found within the DSM-5 reflect diseases, in the medical sense?
2. How does the DSM-5 definition of "mental disorder" differ from that of previous versions of the DSM?
3. Does it make sense to call conditions caused by a clear biological etiology a "mental" disorder, when the origin of the problem is not psychological?
4. How does the heterogeneous nature of the syndromes described in the DSM-5 impact the usefulness of this classification scheme?
5. This chapter describes some alternatives to the DSM-5, when assessing clients. Which of these seem most useful to you?

The Definition of Mental Disorder

Let us begin with the definition of mental disorder now included in the DSM-5:

A mental disorder is a syndrome characterized by clinically significant disturbance in an individual's cognition, emotion regulation, or behavior that reflects a dysfunction in the psychological, biological, or developmental processes underlying mental functioning. Mental disorders are usually associated with significant distress or disability in social, occupational or other important activities. An expectable or culturally approved response to a common stressor or loss, such as the death of a loved one, is not a mental disorder. Socially deviant behavior (e.g., political, religious, or sexual) and conflicts that are primarily between the individual and society are not mental disorders unless the deviance or conflict results from a dysfunction in the individual, as described above (American Psychiatric Association, APA 2013, p. 20).

The beginning and ending of this first definitional sentence reads: "A mental disorder is a syndrome characterized by clinically significant disturbance in... processes underlying mental functioning." By itself this is tautological, repeating the same sense in different words, and hence is unsatisfactory from a scientific standpoint, akin to saying that a particular type of rock is easily broken because it is brittle, or that sleeping pills work because they possess soporific qualities. Saying that a mental disorder is caused by a disturbance in mental functioning is no different.

Leaving aside the question of how behavioral and psychological manifestations differ from each other, it is clear that the DSM-5 definition of mental disorder significantly expands beyond the definition found in the four previous versions of this manual. Here is the definition of mental disorder as presented in the DSM-III, DSM-IIIR, DSM-IV, and DSM-IVR:

...a clinically significant behavioral or psychological syndrome or pattern that occurs in an individual and that is associated with present distress (e.g., a painful symptom) or disability (e.g., impairment in one or more important areas of functioning) or with a significantly increased risk of suffering, pain, disability, or an important loss of freedom (APA 2000, p. xxxi).

The DSM-5 definition greatly expands upon that of its predecessors by creating nine different pathways for mental disorder, with three potential sources of disturbance or etiology (psychological processes, biological processes, and developmental processes) causing dysfunction in three domains of functioning (cognitions, emotional regulation, and behavior). Yet I am aware of no scientific breakthroughs that have transpired in the past decade to justify this considerable expansion of the causes of mental illness and its impacts.

The DSM is perhaps on more solid ground when it contends that mental disorders have their origins in psychological processes (although the tautology remains) and much less so by arguing that conditions caused by biological processes represent mental illnesses. For example, the DSM-5 contains a chapter titled *Medication-induced movement disorders and other adverse effects of medications* (e.g., Parkinsonism), but these are explicitly said *not* to be mental disorders (APA 2013, p. 20). This is good. Yet the DSM-5 does contain other, very long sections describing conditions with well-established drug-induced or other biological etiologies, and it seems difficult to construe these as supposed mental disorders in any coherent sense. Down's syndrome, a known genetic disorder, is listed among the

Intellectual Disabilities currently found in the DSM. The DSM-5 contains the new mental disorder called *obstructive sleep apnea–hypopnea* (OSAH). This condition is clearly said to be caused by repeated episodes of upper airway obstruction during sleep (APA 2013, p. 379), related to some physical issue such as obesity, enlarged tonsils or adenoids, deviated septum, and dental issues. Treatment usually includes changes in sleeping position or use of a positive pressure sleep mask. Actual "cures" may follow weight loss, surgery on the upper palate, or procedures to correct dental malocclusions or a deviated septum. Is it realistic to contend that OSAH is a genuine mental illness, when the cause is clearly physical? Or that a psychiatrist is particularly well trained to treat people with this condition? The American Board of Sleep Medicine may disagree.

The question may be asked as to why organically mediated conditions such as Down's syndrome or OSAH are included in manual of supposed mental disorders? True, such individuals may have dysfunctions in their biology, behavior, and development, but these can in no reasonable manner be construed as mental illnesses. The etiology of Down's syndrome does not reside in the person's mind, but in genes, brain, and indeed the entire body, and in the same way that the etiology of OSAH resides in the person's throat, nose, or allergic reaction. To imply that Down's syndrome or OSAH is form of "mental" disturbance opens up all biologically caused conditions as potential mental illnesses, and indeed this is close to what is found in the DSM-5.

For example, we find listed *Substance/medication-induced psychotic disorder; Catatonia due to another medical condition; Substance/medication-induced depressive disorder; Substance/medication-induced sexual dysfunction*; and even *Alcohol intoxication* all listed as mental disorders! Does it make any scientific sense to label someone who has recently consumed a large amount of vodka as mentally ill? If *Medication-induced movement disorders and other adverse effects of medications* are excluded as mental disorders, why should *Alcohol intoxication* be included? I think it should not be and believe this exemplifies psychiatric overreach, trying to pathologize an ever-expanding array of human phenomena beyond the realm of legitimate psychopathology, as vividly described by Horwitz and Wakefield (2012).

There are thus two types of overreach contained within the DSM-5. Classifying enduring conditions with a clear biological etiology (e.g., Huntington's disease, sleep apnea, Alzheimer's disease) as mental disorders is one, and classifying temporary conditions caused by brief abnormal states (alcohol intoxication, delirium induced by high fever) as mental disorders is a second one. For a condition to be categorized as a mental disorder, it would seem that its etiology must be mentally related, not simply represent a condition that adversely effects mental functioning. Many biological and environmental conditions impact supposed mental functions, and it makes no sense to define impaired mental state as a mental disorder, unless the *cause* of the impairment is clearly related to psychological processes. And when we have a compelling non-mental cause established (e.g., dehydration, recent ingestion of psychedelic drugs), we have an admittedly toxic state but it is not *caused* by a disturbance in the person's mental functioning.

Rather, disturbances in mental function, behavior, affect, and intellect are all caused by a common factor (recent drug use, high fever, tumor, etc.), and there is no reason to give primacy to the person's mind as the etiological agent. It would be more legitimate to *exclude all* conditions with a clear and compelling drug, medical, or other biological etiology as among the mental disorders (Thyer 2006). This would dramatically reduce the size of this ever-expanding manual with its 947 pages and almost 300 diagnoses, reduce the stigma associated with the label of mental disorder being applied to biologically caused conditions, and curtail the scope of psychiatry to a more manageable and justifiable domain.

Contrast the current perspective on mental disorders, embracing every aspect of dysfunctional cognition, behavior and affect, with that of the enormously influential early psychiatrist Wilhelm Greisinger who asserted that

> Although...every mental disease proceeds from an affection of the brain, every disease of the brain does not, on that account, belong to the class of mental diseases...(and that)...The ordinary diseases of the brain...are not termed mental diseases, even although in these affections the mental faculties are usually more or less deranged...(Greisinger 1867, pp. 7, 8)

Thus, almost 150 years ago in the history of mental disorders, psychiatrists were content to limit their scope of practice to human dysfunction *not* caused by conspicuous brain diseases. Consider this syllogistic reasoning sequence:

Major Premise   Brain diseases can cause human dysfunction.
Minor Premise   This person displays dysfunction of thought, affect, or behavior.
Conclusion   This person has a brain disease.

This is a logical error, known as affirming the consequent. There can be many reasons causing dysfunction, not simply brain disease. The reasoning error is illustrated similarly here as follows:

Major Premise   All social workers have ethical standards.
Minor Premise   Bruce has ethical standards.
Conclusion   Bruce is a social worker.

Because many people have ethical standards yet are not social workers, the error in logical inference occurs. Here is another example:

Major Premise   Epilepsy causes seizures.
Minor Premise   Caesar had a seizure.
Conclusion   Caesar has epilepsy.

Because seizures can be caused by many conditions apart from epilepsy (e.g., high fever, drug withdrawal, stroke, tumors, metabolic disturbances), the conclusion is logically incorrect.

Major Premise   People with social anxiety disorder avoid crowds.
Minor Premise   Bruce avoids crowds.
Conclusion   Bruce has social anxiety disorder.

Perhaps Bruce simply has the flu and is trying to avoid infecting other people. There are many reasons for aberrant behavior. That this sometimes occurs because of psychological disturbance is undoubtedly true. However, it does not follow that all aberrant behavior is caused by psychological disturbance and hence a mental disorder.

Years ago, it was ultimately found that some supposedly mental illnesses had demonstrable causes in brain disease (e.g., the general paresis associated with syphilis, epilepsy caused by visible brain lesions, emotional dysfunction caused by endocrine disorders), and these findings led Greisinger and other somaticists of the late 1800s to confidently assert that all mental illnesses were caused by underlying brain pathology, which, if not detected yet, would someday, in the fullness of time, be located. This has not happened. There are now far more instances of supposed mental disorder lacking a demonstrable organic etiology that there were in Greisinger's time, and so long as frenetic attempts are made to increase the reliability of the diagnostic process via increasingly miniscule nosological subdivisions, the absolute numbers of mental illnesses will likely increase.

Corresponding advances in discovering genetic causes, biomarkers, or other organic causes continue to elude incredibly intensive research efforts. Recognition of the flaws in the DSM has resulted in the US National Institute for Mental Health announcing a move away from using the DSM-5 categories to an alternative system called the Research Domain Criteria (Insell 2014) which will, it is hoped, promote more progress than the more purely descriptive-syndromal approach of the DSM-5. This latter approach is akin to saying that symptomatically similar problems are essentially the same thing. Hallucinations are all said to be the forms of a mental disorder called psychosis, and little attention is given to differential diagnosis, and excluding non-mental causes of hallucinations. It is also an overbroad approach akin to saying that all instances of fever are examples of a single underlying disease. Fever can be caused by many different things such as bacterial infection, viral illness, heat exhaustion, extreme sunburn, or a tumor. To assert that fever is a single type of disease—when in reality it is the body's adaptation to a variety of potentially causes, each of which is its own distinct condition, would be a serious conceptual error. It is equally erroneous to group together supposed clusters of signs and symptoms and assert the existence of a mental disorder as the origin of these problems.

When a Syndrome Is not a Syndrome

The description of a mental disorder in the DSM states that these conditions are syndromes, a syndrome defined as "A grouping of signs and symptoms, based on their frequent co-occurrence, that may suggest a common underlying pathogenesis, course, familial pattern or treatment selection" (APA 2013, p. 830). However, the DSM-5 recognizes "…that the current diagnostic criteria for any single disorder will not necessarily identify a homogenous group of patients who can be characterized reliably with all of these validators" (DSM-5, 2013, p. 20). So mental disorders are syndromes, which may not be homogenous clusters of signs and symptoms; hence, they are either syndromes or they are not.

The diagnostic criteria for major depressive disorder are illustrative of the DSM syndromal approach. Criterion A (APA 2013, pp. 160–161) states that a patient must have five or more of nine specific symptoms present during the same two-week period. Now, five is slightly more than half of the possible symptoms; thus, one client could meet the criteria for major depressive disorder and display, for example, depressed mood, anhedonia, weight loss, insomnia, and psychomotor agitation. Another person could experience psychomotor retardation, fatigue, inappropriate guilt, indecisiveness, and recurrent thoughts of death, literally *none* of the symptoms of the first client, yet be given the identical diagnosis. Similarly, Criterion A for Panic disorder requires four or more of 13 discrete symptoms (APA 2013, p. 208). Thus, three different people could be given the diagnosis of panic disorder and have no overlapping symptoms. Such heterogeneous constellations of symptoms cannot reasonably be labeled as syndromes, in the sense that they possess a similar grouping of features.

Fundamental Errors in Reasoning

The DSM-5, as did its predecessors, exemplifies two forms of errors in reasoning. The first is the error of *reification*, of attributing reality status to a hypothetical construct, absent credible evidence of the genuine existence of the construct (Hyman 2010). This occurs when a theorist/clinician/nosologist invents or hypothesizes some energy, force, or structural mental apparatus. Examples include Freud's id, ego or superego, Jung's introverted and extroverted personalities, the Greco-Roman humors or temperaments, Wilhelm Reich's orgone energy, the acupuncturist's energy meridians, Julian Rotter's locus of control, and Alfred Adler's will to power. Initially written and spoken about as hypothetical constructs, with time there is a natural tendency to refer to the psychological concepts as a real things. Many of the DSM-5 diagnoses are examples of reified constructs. A specific phobia is asserted to be something that exists in the person's mind (as do all the DSM-5 conditions). Patients may refer to *their* phobia, as something distinct from the way the person feels, thinks, or acts.

Once reification occurs, a second logical error often arises, the mistake of *circular reasoning*, which most often occurs in mental health when behavior is used to explain behavior. An observer sees that a person runs away when they encounter dogs. When asked why the person runs away, the observer says it is because the person has a specific phobia of dogs and that this causes fear and avoidance. Now, the only evidence for the phobia is the person's fear and avoidance. When asked for the causes of the fear and avoidance, the phobia is given as the reason. In this instance, cause and effect are indistinguishable, and hence, no real explanation is provided. Similar examples can be given for depression and most other diagnoses found in the DSM-5. Why does the person have this behavioral problem? Because of a particular diagnosis. How do you know they have that diagnosis? Because of their behavioral problem. Circular reasoning does not occur when there is independent evidence for the existence of a diagnosis, as in some biological test or clinical indicator. However, very few of the DSM-5 diagnoses possess such benchmarks, and those that do are those with a demonstrable biological etiology, such as Down's syndrome or Alzheimer's disorder. As previously stated, it makes no sense to call these mental illnesses since their etiology does not arise through psychological processes. Allen Francis, the editor of the DSM-IV-TR and fierce critic of the DSM-5, supports this, saying "The DSM mental disorders are no more than descriptive syndromes; they are not necessarily discrete diseases...There are no biological tests in psychiatry, and (with the exception of tests for dementia) none are in the pipeline for at least the next decade" (Francis 2013, pp. 9, 11).

Behavior requires more than other behavior in order to be explained. A phobia may arise from being badly bitten by a dog. If the person had no fear or avoidance to dogs prior to being bitten, only displayed fear after being bitten and they themselves say something like "Yes, my phobia arose from being bitten," then the clinician has a non-circular accounting for the etiology of the phobia, an accounting that is potentially verifiable by checking medical records, parental recollections, etc., for the occurrence of the dog bite and the subsequent emergence of phobia reactions. Depression is not caused by behavior. Rather, the causes of depressed behavior, cognitions, and affective reactions are more plausibly sought among biological conditions (e.g., lack of sleep, medication reactions) or the experience of adverse psychosocial or environmentally based experiences (e.g., unemployment, loss, ill-health, failure, personal humiliation). The latter type of account is much more congruent with social work's traditional person-in-environment perspective than presumptive inner mental states or theories of biological causation and much more amenable to change and intervention.

Some psychiatrists are promoting a more medical model of mental illness in an effort to create what they believe would be a more valid system of classifying so-called mental disorders (e.g., Insell 2014; Nesse and Stein 2012). While this would more fully integrate psychiatry within the discipline of medicine, it would likely result in more of these conditions being treated by non-psychiatric medical doctors. Attention to situational context and to surrounding environments is also largely ignored in the DSM-5. As Nesse and Stein note

> In psychiatry, emotions sufficient in duration and intensity are categorized as disorders irrespective of the situation. This encourages treatment without investigating possible causes, on the assumption that anxiety and depression are abnormal...For instance, a man who is laid off from a job might feel anxiety about possibly losing his home, anger about the employer's broken promises that may be excessive because it stirs childhood memories, and low mood because he sees no way to find a new job. *These responses are not diseases* (2012, p. 4, emphasis added).

The DSM-IV-TR advised that in the instance of an adolescent who otherwise meets the criteria for a diagnosis of conduct disorder, the psychiatric label should not be applied if the disruptive behavior could be reasonably attributed to the client being exposed to a pathological environment or otherwise high-risk living circumstance (American Psychiatric Association 2000, pp. 96–97). This situational awareness is much less conspicuous in the DSM-5, which merely states "...the context in which the undesirable behaviors have occurred should be considered" (American Psychiatric Association 2013, p. 474). Thus, in the DSM-IV-TR environmental context and situational circumstances may properly (in my opinion) be used to rule out a formal diagnosis of mental disorder. However, the DSM-5 merely says these should be considered. This too is an illustration of diagnostic overreach. Where learning history, long-term environmental contexts, and situational circumstances can be used to justifiably exclude arriving at diagnoses of mental illness, the scope of practice of contemporary psychiatry would dramatically shrink. If much of aberrant behavior can be attributed in a direct causal manner to environmental forces, the hypothesis that the dysfunction is caused by problems *within* the individual (e.g., psychological, or located in the mind) rapidly becomes less tenable. If, say, depression is seen more as a reaction to aversive repetitive and chronic experiences, the locus of the problem is *environmental,* not *mental.*

This was experimentally demonstrated by Kirk and Hsieh (2004) in a vignette study wherein clinicians read case histories with varying amounts of environmental context being presented. Where the client's behavioral, affective, and cognitive problems could be plausibly attributed to their real-world experiences, the likelihood of the client being given a formal diagnosis of a mental disorder was much less likely. Also, less likely would be the possibility that the client would be prescribed medications for their problems. Instead, the focus of therapy would more fundamentally deal with person-in-environment transactions, which of course would imply a greater role for social work services, not medical ones (see Chap. 4 for additional discussion of this study).

Early in American psychiatry, many conditions were labeled as reactions (e.g., affective reactions, psychoneurotic reactions), which at least recognized that the disorders were not purely psychological conditions, but a response to some experience of the individual. The psychiatrist Adolph Meyer heavily stressed a psychobiological approach to understanding disordered behavior, resisting the somaticists' a priori, and usually unsubstantiated, claims of organic pathology and the psychoanalysts' equally unsubstantiated assertions as to the underlying purely psychological causes of mental disorder (see Lamb 2014)

Alternatives to the DSM-5

Although not widely discussed in the professional social work literature, there are a number of viable alternatives to assessing clients, apart from the DSM. Here are several, each with its merits and worth considering.

Denialism This approach simply denies the existence of mental disorders entirely. It is exemplified by Thomas Szasz, the author of *The Myth of Mental Illness* (Szasz

1961) and numerous other influential books and articles. His arguments have some parallels with those outlined earlier in this chapter. Absent clear organic causation, it is inappropriate to label disordered behavior as a medical disease. When biological causal factors are found, then the condition segues from the world of psychiatric illness to the wider field of medicine, where it is usually more appropriately treated by suitable specialists, such as neurologists, endocrinologists, and surgeons. Behavioral problems correctly attributable to person-in-environmental factors, a chaotic upbringing, abuse, trauma, malignant peer influences, external contingencies of reinforcement or punishment, etc., fall outside the scope of medicine, and more into the world of behavioral and social science. More elastic definitions of medicine obscure the almost exclusive focus of medical training on physiological causative factors and the minimal attention given to psychosocial factors.

Szasz' critique went beyond simply denying the existence of *mental* illness and extended to viewing psychiatric care as a form of coercive social control whereby the government co-opts medicine and the patient–doctor relationship and, via involuntary psychiatric hospitalization and treatment, succeeds in curtailing the behaviors of those citizens deemed socially unacceptable. He advocated a broad tolerance for aberrant behavior, until someone commits a crime. Although a psychiatrist himself, Szasz was an unflinching critic of many psychiatric practices, including the use of nonscience-based diagnostic systems such as the DSM. Readers can keep in mind that persons with behavioral disorders were cared for, sometimes surprisingly effectively, for centuries before the advent of the DSM. Diagnosis, accurate or not, need not be a perquisite for properly caring for persons with a supposed mental disorder. Szasz would simply decline to evaluate patients using the DSM, and many of his followers similarly make no use of psychiatric diagnosis.

Carl Rogers, the founder of client-centered (later called person-centered) therapy, made no use of DSM-categorization systems, and the humanistic psychology movement he founded similarly avoids providing clients with formal diagnoses. As described by Rowe (1996, p. 82) "Person-centered theory has been fundamentally opposed to diagnostic classification." The thriving field of marital and family therapy has an influential group of practitioners known as family systems therapists. For this group, there is essentially no such thing as individual psychopathology, inasmuch as all interpersonal problems and behavioral disorders are theorized to have their origins in past and present intra-familial dynamics. It is seen as impossible to understand a person in isolation from their family of origin and the current family structure. So-called psychopathology is often seen as transmitted across multiple generations and impossible to grasp via clinical interviews with the identified client alone. Meeting with the larger family is seen as essential. Graduate programs in marriage and family therapy often contain no training in learning to use the DSM, and these professionals seem to practice quite well without the use of psychiatric nomenclature.

Similarly, the influential approach to practice developed by social workers Steve de Shazer and Insoo Kim Berg, solution-focused brief therapy, completely avoids making a psychiatric diagnosis in favor of looking at clients' strengths and potential solutions, not problems (see, for example, Franklin 2012; Berg 1994). There is a large professional organization devoted to this approach (see http://www.sfbta.org/about_sfbt.html). So too, several models developed in the late 1990s—including Martin Seligman's positive psychology, the strength-based perspective of social worker Dennis Saleebey, and the narrative approach of Michael White (discussed in Chap. 8)—offer approaches to assessment and practice that focus on mental well-being rather than mental disorder. These approaches, all of which continue to flourish, further suggest that denying the value of a formal DSM-5 diagnosis and focusing instead on promoting healthy functioning can be a pragmatically viable and responsible approach to social work practice.

Each of the above approaches—client-centered, solution-focused, family systems models, etc.—offers its own theoretically based practice alternative. Space limits do not permit describing these alternatives in depth, each of which could easily require one or more complete books. The point is that large segments of the practice community simply ignore the DSM and the whole psychiatric diagnostic enterprise, and apparently thrive.

Symptomatic Treatment This alternative approach views the problems presented by a client as not necessarily reflective of an underlying disease entity with a comprehensive psychiatric label. Rather, absent credible evidence that the client meeting the criteria for a given primary DSM-5 diagnosis actually has a biologically caused condition (e.g., a client apparently meeting the DSM-5 criteria for generalized anxiety disorder has a thyroid problem), and the social worker helps the client operationally define the nature of the various supposed signs and symptoms that are creating distress.

As an example, take a client meeting DSM-5 criteria for post-traumatic stress disorder (PTSD) who complains of recurrent involuntary and distressing memories of the traumatic event, recurrent distressing dreams related to the traumatic event, intense anxiety when exposed to cures related to the traumatic event, and active avoidance of situations resembling the traumatic event. Rather than arranging for the client to be given anti-anxiety medication or providing non-specific psychotherapy (e.g., psychodynamic, client-centered) which is eventually expected to ameliorate the entire condition labeled as PTSD, the social worker aligns with the client to pick the aspect of the condition that seems most troubling, such as dreams or avoidance. Consulting the contemporary research literature, the social worker learns about psychosocial treatments that have been shown to be useful to alleviate nightmares, the behavioral avoidance associated with PTSD, and so on. Client-friendly and professional articles are obtained and shared with the client. Options are discussed and an agreement is arrived at regarding what therapy will be used, for what specific problem. A search of the literature will reveal that a cognitive-behavioral therapy known as imagery rehearsal has been shown to be helpful for the treatment of nightmares associated with PTSD (Casement and Germain 2014; Casement and Swanson 2012; Sloan et al. 2013). Another behavioral therapy, prolonged exposure therapy, has good evidence that it is helpful in overcoming both behavioral avoidance to trauma-related cues and to the anxiety elicited by such stimuli (Morkved et al. 2014). After discussion with the client, discussing the pros and cons of treatment options suggested by the credible research literature, the social worker provides one of the therapies for one of the client's presenting issues, say, nightmares. If these are resolved, then discussion ensues about selecting a treatment for a different problem presented by the client, such as avoidance. If the initial problem is not resolved, then the research literature is further consulted, and the client is presented with other options. Treatment proceeds by tackling one major issue at a time, and as each is resolved, at some point the client no longer meets the criteria for so-called PTSD, and he or she is essentially cured. But a good therapist is not content with helping the client achieve a sub-syndromal level of functioning and continues treatment beyond ameliorating major symptoms to the point that minor ones are resolved as well.

This form of symptomatic treatment does not assume the existence of a disease entity called PTSD. The constellation of signs and symptoms found in the DSM-5 may or may not reflect such a singular entity. If, in the fullness of time, this is demonstrated, well and good. Science marches on. But one need not accept the theory found in the DSM-5 that the disorders contained therein reflect disease states that must be treated as a whole. One can proceed in a purely symptomatic and empirical fashion, addressing each problem one at a time, until the diagnosis no longer exists and client functioning is restored.

A similar approach may be used with clients who meet the DSM-5 criteria for schizophrenia and other non-biologically caused diagnoses. A client may present with delusions, hallucinations, have problems working because of these behaviors, with the condition having lasted over six months and not attributable to medication or another medical condition. One need not posit the existence of an underlying brain disease that needs to be treated via medications prescribed by psychiatrists. Rather, one takes a purely empirical and symptomatic approach, dealing with various aspects of the behavioral, affective, and cognitive disorders that comprise the DSM-5 construct labeled as schizophrenia.

Informed social workers are aware of the degree to which the pharmaceutical industry has exaggerated the effects of so-called anti-psychotic medications, and suppressed or underreported their side effects and lack of efficacy (see Whitaker 2010; Wong 2014); they are also aware of the burgeoning scientific literature demonstrating the positive effects of psychosocial treatments for persons with supposedly psychotic conditions. Again, one may review this contemporary research with clients and find treatments that have been effective in the past for reducing hallucinations or delusions, and for developing the kinds of social skills needed to function independently in the community (see for example, Hagen et al. 2013; Turkington et al. 2014; Favod et al. 2013; Van der Gaag et al. 2014). Rather than providing powerful drugs to treat a presumptive underlying disease, the clinician collaborates with clients in applying psychosocial treatments to minimize the effects of hallucination and delusions, to reduce their frequency and intensity, in some cases to make them go away, or to more effectively cope with them and maintain high functioning. Again, by whittling away at the individual's presenting problems, these problems are improved, reduced, or eliminated, and the diagnosis simply evaporates. This should not come as a surprise. In the natural history of the life course of so-called mental disorders, many conditions go away on their own, even psychotic conditions, sometimes never to return. If this can happen naturally, why be surprised that effective psychosocial treatments have the potential to hasten the process?

In this model, "...the symptoms" are taken as the problem to be explained, not some presumed underlying illness. "When the symptoms are removed, the psychoses or neuroses by definition are removed" (Akers 1977, p. 329). Indeed, absent demonstrable organic pathology, the behavioral, cognitive, and affective "signs and symptoms" of the various DSM-5 categories are not signs and symptoms at all, in the sense of being reflective of centrally causative disease state (like fever can be a symptom of an underlying infection). The notion that the constellation of signs and symptoms are not by themselves of "real" significance, but rather merely epiphenomena of an underlying problem is a holdover of psychodynamic theory. To be superficial, the signs and symptoms of someone with a fear of snakes actually are caused by from a neurotic conflict related to phalluses. The features of depression reflected unconscious intrapsychic conflicts related to "anger-turned-inward." This of course required prolonged insight-oriented therapy to resolve. The continuing use of the phrase "signs and symptoms" perpetuates the notion that clients' presenting problems are somehow not genuinely significant (at least in the field of mental health). This may be appropriate in the case of biologically caused illnesses but in the field of mental health, it now seems unjustifiable. Whether a presenting problem (e.g., nail biting) is an autonomous behavior or reflective of some underlying disorder should be an empirical question to be investigated with each client, not determined a priori by one's preferred theoretical framework.

One caveat, of course, is that there are few guarantees in therapy. Even the best research-supported psychosocial treatments, when applied to specific clients in a specific setting, may not work as well as they did in published trials. This is to be expected and discussed with clients. But as practitioners, we have to make a choice in what services to provide, and the increasingly influential evidence-based approach to practice states that research-supported treatments, which are ethical, acceptable to clients, and practical to carry out, should be the first-choice treatments that are offered. Not necessarily the treatments we were trained in, nor the ones based on our favorite theoretical orientation, or those promoted by our personal therapeutic idol. Rather, we should offer services that have a strong backing in well-crafted clinical outcomes research, where this is known to exist. And increasingly, for most psychosocial problems presented by clients to social workers, such supported interventions do exist. We just need to look for them (see Thyer and Wodarski 2007). In the case of schizophrenia, the *International Society for Psychological and Social Approaches to Psychosis* is one good place to start. They

provide a comprehensive bibliography of such methods on their Website (see http://
www.isps-us.org/).

It is important to note that the decision to *not* make use of the DSM-5 does not
absolve the social worker from undertaking a comprehensive diagnostic evaluation,
in the broader sense of the term (see Franklin and Jordan 2011). Imagine a client
presenting severe anxiety symptoms, insomnia, generalized anxiousness, an exaggerated startle response, nightmares, and reclusiveness. It would be borderline
malpractice to treat this client symptomatically if, for example, she was an ongoing
victim of domestic violence. In this instance, the initial focus of care would be on
ensuring the safety of the client. Symptomatic treatment would provide little benefits so long as she remained in an abusive relationship and could potentially be
quite harmful. Similarly, if a client presented with problems reflective of being
depressed, symptomatic treatment would not be indicated if the client was
continuing to lead a life filled with ongoing aversive experiences.

Functional Behavioral Assessment The approach known as functional behavioral
assessment (Functional Assessment of Behavior, or FAB) shares some features with
the symptomatic approach described in the previous section. FAB is empirical,
pragmatic, and based in contemporary research findings, but unlike the purely
symptomatic approach, FAB is thoroughly grounded in a specific conceptual
framework—that of social learning theory. Social learning theory consists of
experimentally supported principles demonstrating how people learn and is comprised of three main elements, responding learning theory (Thyer 2012), operant
learning theory (Wong 2012), and observational learning theory (Deguchi 1984;
Fryling et al. 2011). While there is no assumption that these three aspects of
learning can account for the etiologies for *all* behavioral disorders, it is assumed
that they are often important and are worth considering in developing hypotheses as
to how a given client's problems emerged and are maintained. Social learning
theory is also the conceptual framework for the approach to practice known as
Applied Behavior Analysis (ABA).

In FAB, the social worker need not make use of any DSM-5 diagnosis. Instead,
he or she works collaboratively with the client (or designated caregivers) to develop
operational descriptions of specific problem behaviors experienced by the client.
This is done via clinical interviews and direct observations of the client's behavior,
preferably in the client's natural environments (Wilder and Wong 2007). Efforts are
made to develop measures of the behaviors in question that lend themselves to
quantification of their frequency, duration, intensity, or other measurable dimensions. Baseline measures are made of one or more target behaviors the client wishes
to alter, of the conditions under which they occur, generally, and also of the
circumstances wherein they are more or less likely to be displayed, and, ideally,
conditions during which the behaviors are absent. Hypotheses are made, based on
these observations and derived from social learning theory, as to the *function* the
behavior is serving. For example, is the behavior usually followed by something
reinforcing? Is the behavior usually followed by relief from something aversive?

Is the behavior more likely when the client has gone without sufficient sleep, food, or liquids (e.g., may be tired, hungry, or thirsty)? Are there certain times of the day when the behavior is more or less likely (e.g., just before lunch, or later in the evening)? Is the behavior associated with the client being uncomfortable or in pain? From such observations and client reports, a hypothesis can be derived, stipulating the possible causes of the behavior, based on consequences that usually have followed the behavior in the past, or of the other environmental conditions associated with the behavior. With an etiological hypothesis in place, this is empirically tested by providing new consequences, removing aversive ones, or altering the client's physical or psychosocial environmental conditions. The behavior continues to be monitored and recorded, and the data usually portrayed in the form of line graphs, with the element of time on the horizontal axis and the outcome measure on the vertical axis. If the behavior improves following the intervention, then one has possible evidence that the etiological hypothesis was correct. The apparently successful intervention can then be maintained, strengthened, otherwise altered, and perhaps over time, faded out. Below is a simple example of the FAB process, described by a social worker over 40 years ago:

> During the initial phases of a project integrating orthopedically handicapped children into groups of non-handicapped children, no specific instructions were given to the group leaders regarding the degree of "special attention" they were to provide the handicapped children. After a few sessions, it was noticed that one leader appeared especially over-protective; every time the handicapped child approached this leader, he was treated with excessive warmth and openness. At the direction of his supervisor, the leader observed the results of this interaction carefully. It became apparent that the leader was, in effect, rewarding passive, dependent behavior and that this was detrimental to the integrative attempts. On the basis of this observation, the leader predicted that if he were to respond more critically to this behavior, that is, to redirect the handicapped child whenever feasible and realistic, the child would become less passive and more independent and would interact more with his peers (at this point a hypothesis has been developed and a "prediction" made wherewith to test the hypothesis). The leader adopted this approach, and his prediction was borne out, namely, that a more objective response did affect the specific elements of behavior under consideration in a desired fashion (Holmes 1967, pp. 95–96).

If a client refuses to bathe, and it is determined that he finds the process of getting into a bathtub and being immersed in water aversive, perhaps showers should be substituted and extra reinforcers provided for completing showers. This approach was successfully described by Schock et al. (1998). If a client displays increased delusional speech when caregivers make demands of the client (e.g., perform some chore), with the result that the requests are withdrawn "so as to not upset the client," it may be hypothesized that delusional speech is at least under partial control by the client and in being inadvertently maintained by the caregivers' removal of unpleasant demands when the client acts more delusional. Are problems greater when the client is left alone and is apparently bored? Provide more social engagement or interesting activities for the client.

While there is an extensive literature on the process of FAB in the behavior analytic literature, it has not penetrated the profession of social work to a great extent. Filter and Alvarez (2012), Filter and Horner (2009) and Cipani (2014) are some laudable exceptions. This is unfortunate since FAB is the prototypical person-in-environment perspective that is said to characterize our field. Observing the apparent functions which a behavior serves as the person interacts with his or her environment, developing an etiological hypothesis, empirically testing this hypothesis in the context of employing a single-system research design (Thyer and Myers 2007), and adjusting the intervention based on the results would greatly strengthen the effectiveness of social work practice by integrating the conceptual foundation of social learning theory, contemporary intervention research findings, and the empirical evaluation of practice, into one model. The functional analysis of behavior is a highly viable alternative to using the DSM-5 diagnostic system. FAB possesses the advantages of being theoretically based, provides etiological implications, and provides obvious guidance for treatment (see also Harrison and Harrison 2009; School Social Work Association of America 2001). These are all features the DSM-5 lacks.

International Classification of Diseases The International Classification of Diseases, 10th Edition (ICD-10), is a comprehensive system of medical diagnosis that includes sections on mental and behavioral disorders. It is widely used internationally (see http://www.who.int/classifications/icd/en/), but unfortunately it mirrors many of the difficulties included in the DSM-5, such as including known organically caused disorders (e.g., Alzheimer's and mental retardation), and has relatively poor inter-rater reliability. It also uses outmoded labels, such as hebephrenic schizophrenia, and terms that are of dubious validity (e.g., anankastic personality disorder). Most health care providers, agencies, insurance firms, and other third-party vendors in the USA use the DSM-5, not the ICD-10. Because of these problems, the ICD-10 is not usually recommended as a viable alternative to the DSM-5.

The World Health Organization also produces an *International Classification of Functioning, Disability and Health* (ICF, see http://www.who.int/classifications/drafticfpracticalmanual2.pdf?ua=1). It is intended for clinical and research purposes and for use as an outcome measure in evaluation studies. It also contains ways to categorize the environmental contexts of clients but does so from a decidedly medical orientation (e.g., air quality within the home of persons suffering from asthma) and is primarily intended for use with clients who have clear health-related problems found in the ICD-10. Its system of categorizing disability and functioning is primitive, and virtually nothing is known about the inter-rater reliabilities of the various groupings. Thus, it too is not a viable alternative to the DSM-5. Another international model is the Latin American Guide of Psychiatric Diagnosis (GLADP), an application of the person-centered integrative diagnosis (PID) model described in Chap. 9 of this book.

The Psychodynamic Diagnostic Manual The Psychodynamic Diagnostic Manual or PDM (Etnyre 2008) is another proposed alternative to the DSM, created by a psychoanalytically oriented interdisciplinary group of practitioners and researchers who were dissatisfied with the atheoretical orientation of the DSM and its general omission of traditional psychiatric nomenclature (e.g., neurosis). Unlike the ICD-10 and ICF, the PDM is a commercial proprietary product (see https://sites.google. com/a/icdl.com/pdm/table-of-contents). It has some superficial similarity to the DSM, and bears an obvious and heavy imprint of psychodynamic theory. It appears to have had little impact in the mental health field, however, and is largely absent from the training of clinical social workers. Its scheme of nosology is virtually untested, and in the writer's opinion, is not suitable for clinical use, lacking any evidence of reliability or validity, and being largely clinically constructed as opposed to research based. (see Chap. 7 for another perspective on the PDM.)

Person-in-Environment System   Yet another proposed alternative approach is the person-in-environment system or PIE, commissioned and supported by the National Association of Social Workers (NASW) and suggested for use in classifying common life problems of adult social work clients (see Karls and O'Keefe 2009). In one sense, it has served a DSM-like function for the profession of social work, namely to carve out a classificatory scheme that would somehow be unique to the practice of social workers and help to elevate the profession's stature. However, it was not intended to replace the DSM as a means of categorizing mental disorders, since its focus is more on problems of living and social functioning. It was hoped to provide a unifying perspective for the assessment process useful for social workers. It allows for the appraisal of four "operationalizing factors," with Factor I describing the client's social role and functioning, Factor II addressing the client's current environment, Factor III being used to provide a DSM diagnosis, if appropriate, and Factor IV provides for describing one or more ICD-10-defined medical diagnoses, if known. Since a PIE assessment includes a DSM diagnosis, this tool was seen as an extended form of evaluation, designed to expand upon the DSM, not replace it (see Chap. 4 for further discussion).

Judging by the professional literature, there has been little uptake of PIE in the practice or research communities. Following initial publications describing the development and possible uses of PIE (Karls and Wandrei 1994a, b), there appear to be no published studies pertaining to the reliability and validity of this approach, and none demonstrating its clinical value. At best, it seems to be a conceptual model, yet one that has failed to impact practice. A few studies describe how it has been used (Nilsson et al. 2013; Karls et al. 1997; Karls and O'Keefe 2009), but apart from having obvious face validity, its inter-rater and test–retest reliability, as well as its concurrent and predictive validity, are uncertain. Curiously, the NASW continues to sell the manual despite this lack of evidence (Karls and O'Keefe 2008).

Conclusions

The DSM-5 perpetuates some of the problems of previous editions and creates some new ones. The new definition of mental disorder is tautological, encourages reification and circular reasoning, and creates nine new distinct pathways whereby a client can be diagnosed with a mental illness, absent any scientific breakthroughs that would justify this new definition. Conditions with clearly established organic etiologies continue to be labeled as mental disorders, when the reality is that disturbances in a person's cognition, affect, or behavior are not properly attributable to psychological functioning. Fundamental errors in logical reasoning appear to form the manual's conceptual foundation. The DSM-5 unjustifiably expands to scope of practice of psychiatry by pathologizing normative reactions to environmental stresses and one's personal learning history. Heterogeneously presenting conditions are collapsed into singular categories of mental disorder, which confuses the assessment and diagnostic process, and deflects attention away from demonstrable person-in-environment variables to hypothetical inner causes. One consequence of these problems is an unwarranted focus on treating mental disorders via medications and other somatic therapies said to impact the client's mind, as opposed to improving the client's ability to effectively engage the environment reducing the level of stressful and aversive encounters.

A clinician's etiological formulations are crucial in structuring treatment. The DSM-5, while seemingly an atheoretical nosological system, has been created by a discipline, psychiatry, (a discipline largely influenced by the pharmaceutical industry) that strongly favors biological perspectives. After all, that is the strength of their medical training. The contemporary narrative is that mental disorders are caused by irregular brain chemistry. The somaticists of Greisinger's day have seemingly triumphed. But we have seen this before. After the American civil war, Robert Battey hypothesized that women's emotional and behavioral disorders were caused by diseased ovaries and he popularized the practice of ovarectories, resulting in with many thousands of women having healthy gonads removed surgically (Wood 1973). The young Sigmund Freud and his colleague Wilhelm Fleiss thought that the etiology of mental disorders resided in a "nasal reflex neurosis," to be treated surgically (Masson 1986). The focal infection theory of schizophrenia and bipolar disorder claimed that these illnesses were caused by diseased teeth, and thousands of mental patients had healthy teeth extracted by zealous practitioners (Wessely 2009). Lobotomies were widely practiced in the 1940s and 1950s, based upon a theory of disturbed brain functioning, resulting in serious injuries to thousands and deaths to many. And now, we have the various neurotransmitter etiological theories, calling for the promiscuous dispensing of psychotropic medications, often absent credible evidence of their effectiveness, much less of the validity of the underlying theory their use is based on (see Whitaker 2010). With time, we may look back on the current mania for psychotropic treatment, aided and abetted by the DSM-5, with the same sense of incredulity and horror that we now read about ovariectomies, nasal cauterizations, teeth extractions, and lobotomics.

Social workers need not use the DSM-5. There are a number of viable and ethical alternatives to participating in this flawed classification scheme, including simply avoiding use of the DSM-5 (denialism), providing purely symptomatic but research-informed treatment of client's presenting problems, and the functional assessment of behavior (FAB). It is up to each individual social worker to decide how they wish to practice. DSM-5 content does appear on the licensed examinations used by all states to qualify as a clinical social worker, and most states require a graduate-level course in psychopathology in order to be licensed. In practice, this translates to teaching clinicians to use the DSM-5, not in providing actual content on the causes of supposed psychopathological behavior (recalling that the DSM-5 deliberately contains virtually no information on the causation of mental disorders). Many public and private agencies require that clients be given a DSM-5 diagnosis, and to some extent, clients have come to expect receiving a diagnosis. These factors all conspire to perpetuate the DSM-5 system. Most practitioners reluctantly use it for these pragmatic reasons, while holding their noses. Like it or not, the DSM-5 will likely remain the dominant approach to the diagnosis of mental disorders. Perhaps, in the fullness of time, we can dispense with the entire concept of mental illness, in favor of a more empirically grounded system of biologically based conditions, and those seen as the result of a person's learning history, upbringing, past and current environmental contexts, and present experience of reinforcing and aversive experiences. The former would fit solidly within the profession of medicine. The latter approach would be very suitable for the profession of social work, as it has worked so well for the discipline of behavior analysis.

Application to the Case of Ray

Ray has had some tough experiences in this life. The theme of betrayal is evident. His biological mother abandoned him. His priest repeated sexually assaulted him. His wife Cecilia was unfaithful. He has had two suicide attempts and a number of horrific experiences that were undoubtedly severely traumatic. His problems have been said to meet the DSM criteria for major depression, and later for bipolar disorder, Type II. Treatment has been two different medications (Zoloft, Depakote), individual therapy (apparently of a nonspecific variety), psychiatric hospitalizations, and, briefly, couples counseling. Given the information regarding Ray's background, I would conduct a careful evaluation to see whether he currently meets the DSM-5 criteria for post-traumatic stress disorder (PTSD), a diagnosis not mentioned in the case history. Here are some of the diagnostic criteria for PTSD:

"A. Exposure to actual or threatened death, serious injury, or sexual violence in one (or more) of the following ways:

1. Directly experiencing the traumatic event(s).
2. Witnessing, in person, the event(s) as it occurred to others….
3. Experiencing repeated or extreme exposure to aversive details of the traumatic event(s) (e.g., first responders collecting human remains; police officers repeatedly exposed to details of child abuse)….

B. Presence of one (or more) of the following intrusion symptoms associated with the traumatic event(s), beginning after the traumatic events occurred:

1. Recurrent, involuntary, and intrusive distressing memories of the traumatic event(s).
2. Recurrent distressing dreams in which the content and/or affect of the dream are related to the traumatic event(s).

E. …Irritable behavior and angry outbursts (with little or no provocation), typically expressed as verbal or physical aggression toward people or objects reckless or self-destructive behavior,,,sleep disturbance." (American Psychiatric Association 2013, pp. 271). These are just a few of the criteria associated with the diagnosis of PTSD, and Ray displays many more. My review of the DSM-5, and Ray's case material, lead me to believe that PTSD is the most appropriate diagnosis in this case. Given that depression can be a consequence of PTSD, the latter would seem to be the more appropriate diagnosis. The apparent absence of any history of prior depressive or manic episodes would also seem to render the diagnosis of bipolar II disorder inappropriate, also perhaps subsumed by PTSD. Conspicuously absent from the case description is any mention made of the use of standardized assessment measures for PTSD, depression, nightmares, and mania, measures that could be used to quantify and monitor these problems, not just at initial assessment, but repeatedly over time. Absent this, it can be difficult to assess whether or not Ray is improving or deteriorating over the course of treatment.

Determining that Ray meets the DSM-5 criteria for a diagnosis of PTSD is not the same thing as saying that Ray suffers from a disease called PTSD, or even actual mental disorder. Ray's exposure to repeated severe traumas (9/11, firefighting and witnessing death, stairway violence) may have given rise to many of Ray's behavioral, cognitive, and affective difficulties. Although there are effective treatments for some of these, there is little evidence that Ray has been provided with them. Zoloft is approved for the treatment of PTSD, but absent quantified measures of his supposed signs and symptoms, it is impossible to tell whether the Zoloft has been helpful. Judging from Ray's continuing complaints it has not been. Dosage is of course important and we have no information on this. Sub-optimal dosing can be completely ineffective. Depakote is usually used to treat seizure disorders (no evidence of this in Ray's case) and mania (but not depression). True episodes of mania are not a part of Ray's history, although impulsive and risky behavior certainly is; hence, the Depakote seems a questionable prescription.

Several research-supported treatments have been shown to be effective for PTSD's many features, including exposure-based interventions provided with or without medications such as Zoloft (Pull and Pull 2013; Lee et al. 2014; Jun et al. 2013; Watts et al. 2013). In fact, these treatments, prolonged exposure therapy and Zoloft, have been specifically evaluated with adult survivors of the World Trade Center attack of 9/11 and shown to be helpful with this population (Schneier et al. 2012). I would most certainly explore this combination of treatments with Ray.

I would continue to encourage Ray's attending the support group for survivors of priest abuse, and as a social worker, I would possibly offer to attend the first session or two with him, to encourage him to come into contact with this resource. I would also connect him the *Project Liberty*, a peer-based mental health assistance program for New York City police officers who worked the 9/11 attack (Dowling et al. 2006; Donahue et al. 2006). All these activities would be undertaken in the context of an ongoing single-client research design, wherein several of the more prominent behavioral and affective problems experienced by Ray were regularly assessed and plotted on a graph (see Thyer and Myers 2007), to provide triangulated information to go along with information obtained by our ongoing clinical interviews. Other specific treatments might be added, such as the behavioral therapies for nightmares cited earlier in this chapter, or anger control training (e.g., Deschner and McNeil 1986). All of this could be undertaken *without* assuming that Ray is mentally ill or suffers from some underlying disease state reflected in Ray's many problems.

Practical Exercises

(1) Pick one diagnosis found in the DSM-5 that is not known to have a clear biological etiology, and search recent research literature online to see if you can locate one or more references to a well-supported psychosocial treatment for that condition.
(2) Describe how a functional assessment of behavior might be undertaken with a client who meets the criteria for one of the diagnoses found in the DSM-5. Speculate on how these behaviors associated with the condition might result in reinforcing consequents for the client.
(3) One position taken in this chapter is that disorders that are biologically caused but negatively impact a client's overt behavior, thoughts, or feelings, should not be construed as a mental disorder. React to this position. Does it seem justifiable to you, or too limiting?

References

Akers, R. L. (1977). *Deviant behavior: A social learning approach*. Belmont, CA: Wadsworth.
American Psychiatric Association. (2000). *Diagnostic and statistical manual of mental disorders* (4th ed.). Washington, DC: Author.
American Psychiatric Association. (2013). *Diagnostic and statistical manual of mental disorders* (5th ed.). Washington, DC: Author.
Berg, I. K. (1994). *Family-based services: A solution-focused approach*. New York: W. W. Norton.
Casement, M. D., & Germain, A. (2014). Is group imagery rehearsal for posttraumatic nightmares as good at reducing PTSD symptoms as group treatment for PTSD? *Psychological Trauma, 6*, 259–260.

Casement, M. D., & Swanson, L. M. (2012). A meta-analysis of imagery rehearsal for post-trauma nightmares: Effects on nightmare frequency, sleep quality, and posttraumatic stress. *Clinical Psychology Review, 32,* 566–574.

Cipani, E. (2014). Comorbidity in DSM childhood mental disorders: A functional perspective. *Research on Social Work Practice, 24,* 78–85.

Deguchi, H. (1984). Observational learning from a radical-behaviorist viewpoint. *The Behavior Analyst, 7,* 83–95.

Deschner, J. P., & McNeil, J. S. (1986). Resulting of anger control training for battering couples. *Journal of Family Violence, 1,* 111–120.

Donahue, S. A., Jackson, C. T., Shear, K. M., Felton, C. J., & Essock, S. M. (2006). Outcomes of enhanced counseling services provided to adults through Project Liberty. *Psychiatric Services, 57,* 1298–1303.

Dowling, F. G., Moynihan, G., Genet, B., & Lewis, J. (2006). A peer-based assistance program for officers with the New York City Police Department: Report of the effects of Sept. 11, 2001. *Psychiatric Services, 163,* 151–153.

Etnyre, W. (2008). Psychodynamic diagnostic manual. *Clinical Social Work Journal, 36,* 403–406.

Favod, J., Rexhaj, S., Bardy, S., Ferrari, P., Hayoz, C., & Moritz, S. (2013). Sustained antipsychotic effect of metacognitive training in psychosis: A randomized controlled study. *European Psychiatry, 29,* 275–281.

Filter, K. J., & Alvarez, M. E. (2012). *Functional behavioral assessment.* New York: Oxford University Press.

Filter, K. J., & Horner, R. H. (2009). Function-based academic interventions for problem behavior. *Education and Treatment of Children, 31*(2), 1–19.

First, M. B., & Wakefield, J. C. (2010). Defining 'mental disorder' in DSM-V. *Psychological Medicine, 40,* 1779–1782.

Francis, A. (2013). *Essentials of psychiatric diagnosis: Responding to the challenge of DSM-5.* New York: Guilford.

Franklin, C. S. (Ed.). (2012). *Solution-focused brief therapy: A handbook of evidence-based practice.* New York: Oxford University Press.

Franklin, C. S., & Jordan, C. (Eds.). (2011). *Clinical assessment for social workers* (3rd ed.). Chicago: Lyceum Books.

Fryling, M. J., Johnston, C., & Hayes, L. J. (2011). Understanding observational learning. *The Analysis of Verbal Behavior, 27,* 191–203.

Greisinger, W. (1867). *Mental pathology and therapeutics.* New York: Hafner (1965 reprinted facsimile).

Hagen, R., Turkington, D., Berge, T., & Grawe, R. W. (2013). *CBT for psychosis: A symptom-based approach.* New York: Routledge/Taylor & Francis.

Harrison, K., & Harrison, R. (2009). The school social worker's role in the tertiary support of functional assessment. *Child and Schools, 31,* 119–127.

Holmes, D. (1967). Bridging the gap between research and practice in social work. In National Conference on Social Welfare (Ed.), *Social work practice,* (pp. 94–108). New York: Columbia University Press.

Horwtiz, A. V., & Wakefield, J. C. (2012). *All we have to fear: Psychiatry's transformation of natural anxieties into mental disorders.* New York: Oxford University Press.

Hyman, S. W. (2010). The diagnosis of mental disorders: The problem of reification. *Annual Review of Clinical Psychology, 6,* 155–179.

Insell, T. (2014). The NIMH Research Domain Criteria (RDoC) Project: Precision medicine for psychiatry. *American Journal of Psychiatry, 171,* 395–397.

Jun, J. J., Zoellner, L. A., & Feeny, N. C. (2013). Sudden gains in prolonged exposure and sertraline for chronic PTSD. *Depression and Anxiety, 30,* 607–613.

Karls, J. M., Lowery, C. T., Mattaini, M. A., & Wandrei, K. E. (1997). The use of the person-in-environment system in social work education. *Journal of Social Work Education, 33,* 48–58.

Karls, J. M., & O'Keefe, M. (2008). *Person-in-environment system manual* (2nd ed.). Washington, DC: NASW Press.

Karls, J. M., & O'Keefe, M. (2009). Person-in-environment system. In A. R. Roberts (Ed.), *Social worker's desk reference* (2nd ed., pp. 371–376). New York: Oxford University Press.

Karls, J. M., & Wandrei, K. E. (1994a). *Person-in-environment system: The PIE classification system for social functioning problems*. Washington, DC: NASW Press.

Karls, J. M., & Wandrei, K. E. (1994b). *The PIE manual*. Washington, DC: NASW Press.

Kirk, S. A., & Hsieh, D. K. (2004). Diagnostic consistency in assessing conduct disorder: An experiment on the effect of social context. *American Journal of Orthopsychiatry, 74*, 43–55.

Lamb, S. D. (2014). *Pathologist of the mind: Adolph Meyer and the origins of American psychiatry*. Baltimore: Johns Hopkins University Press.

Lee, Q. A., Doctor, J. N., Zoellner, L. A., & Feeny, N. C. (2014). Cost-effectiveness of prolonged exposure therapy versus pharmacotherapy and treatment choice in posttraumatic stress disorder (the Optimizing PTSD Treatment Trial): A doubling randomized preference trial. *Journal of Clinical Psychiatry, 75*, 222–230.

Masson, J. M. (1986). *The assault on truth: Freud's suppression of the seduction theory*. New York: Farra, Straus and Giroux.

McLendon, T. (2014). Social work perspectives regarding the DSM: Implications for social work education. *Journal of Social Work Education, 50*, 454–471.

Morkved, N., Hartman, K., Aarsheim, L. M., Holen, D., Milde, A. M., Bomyea, J., & Thorp, S. R. (2014). A comparison of narrative exposure therapy and prolonged exposure therapy for PTSD. *Clinical Psychology Review, 34*, 453–467.

Nesse, R. M., & Stein, D. J. (2012). Towards a genuinely medical model for psychiatric nosology. *BMC Medicine, 10*, 5. http://biomedcentral.com/1741-7015/10/5.

Nilsson, D., Joubert, L., Holland, L., & Posenelli, S. (2013). The why of practice: Using PIE to analyze social work practice in Australian hospitals. *Social Work in Health Care, 52*, 280–295.

Pull, C. N., & Pull, C. B. (2013). Current status of treatment for posttraumatic stress disorder: Focus on treatments combining pharmacotherapy and cognitive-behavioral therapy. *International Journal of Cognitive Therapy, 7*, 149–161.

Robbins, S. P. (2014). From the editor—the DSM-5 and its role in social work assessment and research. *Journal of Social Work Education, 50*, 201–205.

Rowe, W. R. (1996). Client-centered theory: A person-centered approach. In F. Turner (Ed.), *Social work treatment* (pp. 69–93). New York: Free Press.

Schneier, F. R., Neria, Y., Pavlicova, M., Hembree, E., Suh, E. J., Amsel, L., & Marshall, R. D. (2012). Combined prolonged exposure therapy and Paroxetine for PTSD related to the World Trade Center attack: A randomized controlled trial. *American Journal of Psychiatry, 169*, 80–88.

Schock, K., Clay, C., & Cipani, E. (1998). Making sense of schizophrenic symptoms: Delusional statements and behavior may be functional in purpose. *Journal of Behavior Therapy and Experimental Psychiatry, 29*, 131–141.

School Social Work Association of America. (2001). *Functional behavioral assessments and behavior intervention plans*. Indianapolis, IN: Author.

Sloan, D. M., Feinstein, B. A., Gallagher, M. W., Beck, J. G., & Keane, T. M. (2013). Efficacy of group treatment for posttraumatic stress disorder symptoms: A meta-analysis. *Psychological Trauma: Theory, Research, Practice, and Policy, 5*, 176–183.

Szasz, T. (1961). *The myth of mental illness*. New York: Hoeber-Harper.

Thyer, B. A. (2006). It is time to rename the DSM. *Ethical Human Psychology and Psychiatry, 8*, 61–67.

Thyer, B. A. (2012). Respondent learning theory. In B. A. Thyer, C. N. Dulmus, & K. M. Sowers (Eds.), *Human behavior in the social environment: Theories for social work practice* (pp. 47–81). New York: Wiley.

Thyer, B. A. (2014a). A review of *Essentials of psychiatric diagnosis: Responding to the challenge of DSM-5* by Allen Frances. *Research on Social Work Practice, 24*, 165–169. doi:10.1177/1049731513505000.

Thyer, B. A., & Myers, L. L. (2007). *A social worker's guide to evaluating practice outcomes*. Alexandria, VA: Council on Social Work Education.

Thyer, B. A., & Wodarski, J. S. (Eds.). (2007). *Social work in mental health: An evidence-based approach*. New York: Wiley.

Turkington, D., Munetz, M., Pelton, J., Montesana, V., Sivec, H., Nausheen, B., & Kingdon, D. (2014). High-yield cognitive behavioral techniques for psychosis delivered by case managers to their clients with persistent psychotic symptoms. *Journal of Nervous and Mental Disease, 202*, 30–34.

Van der Gaag, M., Valmiggia, L. R., & Smith, F. (2014). The effects of individually tailored formulation-based cognitive behavioural therapy in auditory hallucinations and delusions: A meta-analysis. *Schizophrenia Research, 156*, 30–36.

Wakefield, J. C. (1992). Disorder as harmful dysfunction: A conceptual critique of DSM-III-R's definition of mental disorder. *Psychological Review, 99*, 232–247.

Watts, B. V., Schnurr, P. P., Mayo, L., Young, Y., Weeks, W. B., & Friedman, M. J. (2013). Meta-analysis of the efficacy of treatments for posttraumatic stress disorder. *Journal of Clinical Psychiatry, 74*, E541–E550.

Wessely, S. (2009). Surgery for the treatment of psychiatric illness: The need to test untested theories. *Journal of the Royal Society of Medicine, 102*, 445–451.

Whitaker, R. (2010). *Anatomy of an epidemic*. New York: Crown Publishing Group.

Wilder, D. A., & Wong, S. E. (2007). Schizophrenia and other psychotic disorders. In P. Sturmey (Ed.), *The handbook of functional analysis and clinical psychology* (pp. 283–305). Philadelphia, PA: Elsevier.

Wong, S. E. (2012). Operant learning theory. In B. A. Thyer, C. N. Dulmus, & K. M. Sowers (Eds.), *Human behavior in the social environment: Theories for social work practice* (pp. 83–123). New York: Wiley.

Wong, S. E. (2014). A critique of the diagnostic construct Schizophrenia. *Research on Social Work Practice, 24*, 132–141.

Thyer, B. A. (2014b). The definition of mental disorder found in the DSM-5: Too much and too little. *Mental Health and Social Work, 42*(4), 21–33.

Wood, A. D. (1973). "The fashionable diseases": Women's complaints and their treatment in nineteenth-century America. *Journal of Interdisciplinary History, 4*, 25–52. doi:10.2307/202356.

Chapter 4
Making Assessment Decisions:
Macro, Mezzo, and Micro Perspectives

Jeffrey R. Lacasse and Eileen Gambrill

Abstract This chapter addresses potential barriers to good clinical decision-making, found at all levels of practice. It begins with decision-making at the *micro*-level—that is, at the level of the individual clinician, who faces a series of decisions with each new case: how to frame problems, what outcomes to pursue, when to stop collecting information, what risks to take, what criteria to use to select practice methods, and how to evaluate progress. The flexible and diverse nature of clinical practice, while allowing for consideration of specific client needs, also leaves room for many kinds of error. These errors can be avoided, or at least minimized, by the use of evidence-informed assessment practices as outlined in the chapter. At the *mezzo*-level, requirements of the practice setting (such as mission and funding source) can shape and constrain the way assessment takes place; the media, professional literature, and structure of professional training also exert a powerful influence. *Macro*-level influences include the widespread medicalization of human behavior; the pharmaceutical companies and managed care institutions comprising the "biomedical industrial complex;" and entities such as the National Institute of Mental Health, the American Psychiatric Association, and the welfare and legal systems. The chapter concludes by urging students to consider the biases that may be inherent in the information on which they base their decisions, as well as how the environment they work in may affect their ability to make sound clinical decisions.

Keywords Accountability · Astro-turfing · Biomedical industrial complex · Constructional versus eliminative · Crazy checks · Ghostwriting · Medicalization · Selective reporting

---

Note: Some of the material in this chapter has been adapted from Gambrill, E. (2013). *Social work practice: A critical thinker's guide*. New York: Oxford University Press.

J.R. Lacasse (✉)
College of Social Work, Florida State University, Tallahassee, FL, USA
e-mail: jlacasse@fsu.edu

E. Gambrill
School of Social Welfare, University of California, Berkeley, CA, USA

© Springer International Publishing Switzerland 2015
B. Probst (ed.), *Critical Thinking in Clinical Assessment and Diagnosis*,
Essential Clinical Social Work Series, DOI 10.1007/978-3-319-17774-8_4

Introduction: Why This Matters

The decisions that social workers make have significant impact on their clients. When these decisions are inaccurate—whether due to faulty assumptions or to a lack of evidence-based information—clients can be affected in serious ways. Thus, in order to deliver effective and ethical services, social workers need to be aware of potential pitfalls in the decision-making process and strive to avoid them. These potential barriers to good decision-making can be found at all levels of practice: micro, mezzo, and macro. While social workers may have less control over the incentives and constraints that exist in mezzo- and macro-environments than they do at the micro-level, they can nevertheless benefit from examining the mezzo- and macro-environments in which they practice and examining how their assessment and decision-making process is affected by these factors.

In this chapter, we discuss factors related to decision-making at all three levels. We begin by discussing clinical decision-making at the micro-level—that is, at the level of the individual clinician. We then discuss other issues that may impact decision-making, such as the widespread medicalization of human behavior and the influence of pharmaceutical companies. Making good clinical decisions in social work practice is challenging, but may be improved through increased awareness of the issues described here.

Guiding Questions

1. What are the steps in clinical decision-making?
2. What macro-level factors shape and constrain clinical decisions? Through what layers, visible, and invisible, does this influence travel?
3. What macro- and mezzo-level factors can contribute to errors in clinical judgment?
4. Who holds power? How is this power sustained?

The Central Role of Decision-Making

Decision-making is at the heart of every step in clinical practice. Decisions must be made about what information to collect, how to gather and organize it, and what to do with it. What sources of information will be drawn on, and what criteria will be used to evaluate their accuracy? In assessing a client who presents with depressive symptoms, for example, is it better to have the client complete a standardized measurement instrument like the Beck Depression Inventory and/or to talk to family members and take a careful history? Will giving a DSM diagnosis help to understand the client's depression? On what basis are these decisions made?

Assessment lays the groundwork for selecting plans and indicating how likely it is that hoped-for-outcomes can be attained. Assessment frameworks differ in their scope, purpose, and the degree to which they can be and have been critically tested. In other words, they differ in how compatible they are with empirical data regarding how behavior develops, changes, and is maintained, and how successful they have been in helping clients. The history of the helping professions is replete with the identification of false causes for personal troubles and social problems (Gambrill 2012). Complex classification systems with no empirical status such as those based on physiognomy (facial type) and phrenology (skull formation) were popular in past epochs, leading to the creation of metal phrenological hats to aid in diagnosis (Gamwell and Tomes 1995; McCoy 2000). Classificatory labels have also been devised and used for social control rather than as a guide to alleviating suffering—for example, conditions such as drapetomania (an irresistible propensity to run away), a "disease" that was allegedly common among slaves in the southern United States. Some authors (e.g., Moncrieff 2008) suggest that a psychiatric framing of problems supports conservative political views by framing "discontents" such as depression and anxiety as caused by individual deficiencies, overlooking the political and economic factors such as unemployment and inadequate housing that contribute to these conditions.

Decision-making in clinical practice allows a wide range of individual discretion. Each clinician must determine how to frame problems, what outcomes to pursue, when to stop collecting information, what risks to take, what criteria to use to select practice methods, and how to evaluate progress. This can differ from clinician to clinician, and from case to case. Problems differ in their prospects for resolution, which are influenced by the accuracy of assessment. The flexible and diverse nature of clinical practice, while allowing for consideration of specific client needs and contexts, also leaves room for many kinds of error. Among the assessment errors that may occur are:

- Errors in description: For example, stating that Mrs. V. was abused as a child, when she was not.
- Errors in presuming the extent of covariation or causality: For example, assuming that people who are abused as children will abuse their own children.
- Errors of omission: For example, overlooking the strengths and resources that a person has because one is focusing entirely on the maladaptive behavior.
- Errors in prediction: For example, predicting that insight therapy will prevent a particular woman from abusing her child again when this does not prove to be true.

These errors may result in failing to offer help that could be provided and is desired, offering help that is *not* needed or desired, forcing clients to accept "help" they do not want, or using procedures that aggravate rather than alleviate client concerns (that is, procedures that result in iatrogenic effects, the creation of new and avoidable problems). Errors may occur during assessment by overlooking important data, using invalid measures, or attending to irrelevant data. Errors may occur during intervention by using ineffective methods or during evaluation by using inaccurate measures of progress.

Evidence-Informed Assessment Errors can be reduced by the use of evidence-informed assessment. An evidence-based assessment means:

- Selecting assessment frameworks that reflect research findings
- Using reliable, valid assessment measures including those designed to assess risk
- Avoiding common errors in collecting and integrating data
- Involving clients as informed participants and considering their values and preferences

An evidence-informed assessment includes a clear description of areas of concern; a description of what the person can and cannot do, can or cannot learn to do; what the person wants, prefers, expects, and is expected to be able to do, as well as contextual factors that influence and contribute to the behaviors of concern (Gambrill 2013). It encourages the description of processes rather than of conditions. For example, rather than describing a client as anxious, assessment requires a description of the contexts in which the anxiety occurs and the patterns of related behaviors, thoughts, and feelings. As in other phases of the helping relationship, specialized knowledge and critical thinking skills may be needed to appraise the accuracy of claims and to integrate diverse sources of information including findings from practice- and policy-related research and the unique circumstances and characteristics of a client, including cultural differences in problem-solving styles.

Assessment should also identify "leverage points" for pursuing desired outcomes. It should suggest objectives that, if attained, would resolve problems as well as suggestions for how they can be pursued most effectively and the probability of attaining them, given current resources and options. Interrelated goals of assessment (sometimes referred to as a "case formulation") include identifying hoped-for-outcomes, detecting related characteristics of clients and their environments, and interpreting and integrating the data that has been collected.

A multilevel, individualized, contingency analysis—that is, an assessment that spans multiple domains and focuses on the individual—informed by relevant research findings is vital for understanding presenting concerns and selecting effective intervention plans (e.g., Gambrill 2013; Layng 2009). Unfortunately, such analyses are not always carried out due to a lack of time in a resource-scarce climate and/or a lack of required knowledge and skills for seeking out competing alternative repertoires.

Constructional Assessment Many assessment models focus on the alleged pathologies of clients and may overlook valuable resources including both internal and external client assets. A contextual–constructional approach, in contrast, attends to client characteristics and circumstances including alternative behaviors that may be able to replace less desired behaviors, client strengths, environmental resources such as sources of social support, and policies and related legislation that influence resources available such as health care and financial aid. It focuses on strengths and resources that can help in the achievement of client aims, as well as on personal and environmental obstacles. The aim is to discover and create positive "repertoires" that can be used to attain hoped-for-outcomes, rather than merely eliminating negative repertoires (e.g., Gambrill 2013; Layng 2009; Goldiamond 1974; Schwartz and Goldiamond 1975).

Learning how to make sound, evidence-based assessment decisions takes time and practice. But it is something that an ethically competent professional can, and should, learn to do. The social worker's skill and willingness to engage in evidence-based practice thus constitutes the *micro*-context in which clinical decision-making takes place.

Clinical Decision-Making in the Biomedical Industrial Complex

There is a larger context to clinical decision-making, of course, one that is strongly impacted by social policy and other macro-level factors. Which services are funded or reimbursable has a significant impact on what services clients receive; as has been noted in previous chapters, psychiatric diagnosis may be driven not by clinical necessity, but by reimbursement requirements (Frazer et al. 2009; Greenberg 2013; Probst 2013). Thus, if we are to apply critical thinking to clinical decision-making, it is important to identify contextual influences that likely impact the way we perceive and respond to the problems that clients bring.

The Context of Clinical Decision-Making: Macro Level Factors

The current mental health system has been called the "biomedical industrial complex" (Gomory et al. 2011). Similar to the "military-industrial complex," it consists of related interlocking and mutually supportive entities. These include the pharmaceutical industry, federal agencies such as the National Institute of Mental Health and the Food and Drug Administration, the American Psychiatric Association, advocacy organizations such as the National Alliance for the Mentally Ill (NAMI), and medical insurance, both public, and private. The term "biomedical industrial complex" is not meant to convey a conspiratorial explanation. However, it does capture where power and influence lies in the mental health system, and it is important for clinicians to be aware of the impact these macro-level influences can have on decisions they make.

The Pharmaceutical Industry (Big Pharma) It is difficult to overstate the influence of pharmaceutical companies (Big Pharma), especially in mental health (Cosgrove et al. 2006). Their goal is transparent—to sell their products (psychiatric drugs) in order to earn as high a profit for their shareholders as possible. They use a variety of well-documented tactics to accomplish this. First, they generously fund both psychiatric research and influential researchers called key opinion leaders. It is difficult to find a well-respected academic psychiatrist who does not have at least some financial conflict of interest with a pharmaceutical company. Second, they also fund advocacy organizations such as NAMI; this is called "astro turfing" because these advocacy efforts may look like a "grass-roots movement" when in fact they largely reflect corporate interests. Third, they flood the offices of general practitioners (who diagnose and treat a great deal of mental health conditions) with "detailers" (salespeople). And fourth, they flood the television airwaves, the internet, and the pages of popular magazines with advertisements for their products in the form of paid direct-to-consumer advertising (DTCA). These messages, bombarding the public through multiple channels, have an enormous impact.

The Federal Drug Administration (FDA) FDA is charged with regulating the ubiquitous DTCA by Big Pharma. This is an important role because such advertisements can shape how clients and clinicians see their problems (Moynihan and Cassels 2005). Many of these advertising campaigns have been noted to be inaccurate from a scientific point of view—for instance, claiming that serotonin imbalance causes depression (Lacasse and Leo 2006) and that antidepressants re-balance brain chemistry back to normal (Lacasse 2005). The FDA also has the authority to approve psychiatric drugs and regulate what appears on the product label, including warnings. Unfortunately, the FDA has often been criticized for being more a partner of Big Pharma than a critical regulator, perhaps due to the rotating door between employment at the FDA and at the various drug companies (Angell 2005).

The National Institute of Mental Health (NIMH) NIMH is the largest funder of mental health research in the world, and as such is very influential. The organization tends to take a biomedical point of view toward human problems. This makes sense, since NIMH is a subsidiary of the National Institutes of Health, yet emphasizing the biomedical model promotes the idea that mental health treatment is merely a branch or type of *medical* treatment. For instance, the NIMH website that explains various mental disorders explicitly states that these disorders are due to brain malfunction, even though the Surgeon's General report notes—equally explicitly—that the cause of mental disorders remains unknown (U.S. Department of Health and Human Services 1999, as cited in Gomory et al. 2011). In addition, many NIMH studies are carried out by academics who also receive funding from Big Pharma, raising the question of how objective such research really is.

The American Psychiatric Association (APA) The American Psychiatric Association (APA) writes and publishes the DSM, which defines who is viewed as "mentally ill." As such, the APA is a powerful and influential private guild, mated with the pharmaceutical industry. Each year, there are fewer and fewer psychiatrists who are trained in and offer psychotherapy, with most psychiatrists now working as applied pharmacologists (Carlat 2010). This creates multiple conflict of interest issues—financial, intellectual, and ideological. The DSM is the APA's primary product and profit maker, and the release of DSM-5 may have had more to do with the APA's finances than with a real need for a new version of the manual (Greenberg 2013). There is a significant body of literature critiquing the APA and the DSM; among the critiques is the omission of social workers in the development of the new manual, despite the fact that social workers provide most of the nation's mental health services and outnumber psychiatrists. The removal of Axis IV attending to environmental factors (the "social work axis"), discussed at length in Chapter Four, is one example of the APA making major decisions without consulting its constituencies.

Insurance Companies (Managed Care) As noted in numerous places throughout this book, psychiatric diagnoses are required by insurance companies in order for treatment to be covered. Reimbursement, even for psychotherapy, thus requires diagnosis of a putative brain disease (Greenberg 2010). Third-party payers such as Medicaid will pay for antipsychotics more readily than for long-term psychosocial interventions.

NAMI and Other Advocacy Groups NAMI is often thought of as an advocacy organization for the families of those diagnosed with severe mental disorders such as schizophrenia. However, NAMI has a close relationship with the pharmaceutical industry and may be an example of "astro-turfing," described above. NAMI's perspective is almost purely the medical model of mental disorder, with drug treatment often described in its literature as essential. Bias is indicated, for example, in Hess et al's analysis (2014) of educational materials provided by NAMI, which found that the claims made were not reflective of the data on recovery in mental health or neuroplasticity. To put it bluntly, most of NAMI's claims are indistinguishable from those of the pharmaceutical industry and the American Psychiatric Association, entities with vested interests in the medical model.

"Downstream" but equally influenced by the biomedical industrial complex are other entities including the social welfare system and the legal system:

The Social Welfare System There are significant financial incentives for clients who receive mental health diagnoses. Mental health disability rates have been rising rapidly (Whitaker 2010), and one hypothesis is that disability payments for mental disorder serve as a *de facto* welfare system for those in poverty. The Social Security Administration reported that as of 2011, 19.2 % of disability payments were paid for mental disorders or developmental disabilities, and a recent analysis of a self-directed care program for clients labeled SMI (Seriously Mentally Ill) found that they spent a large proportion of their funds on basic needs (Spaulding-Givens and Lacasse 2015). Parents of children can receive payments if their children are diagnosed with a mental disorder such as ADHD; this is known as receiving "crazy checks" (Kubik 1999). For those in poverty, this may incentivize defining children's behavioral problems as a medical disease. Once diagnosed with a mental disorder and put on Medicaid, clients who attain functional recovery may lose their livelihood and health insurance as a result, constituting a penalty for recovery. Clearly, such incentives can impact how a client's problems are framed.

The Legal System The court system also plays a significant role, as conveyed by the statement that "it's better to be crazy than criminal." If clients are diagnosed with a mental disorder and commit a crime, they may be deemed "not responsible" and subject to forced inpatient or outpatient psychiatric treatment rather than to incarceration or another form of punishment; confinement, medication and therapy can thus be court-ordered. As a result, it is often in the best interest of the person accused of a crime to accept or even pursue a diagnosis of mental disorder.

The Context of Clinical Decision-Making: Mezzo Level Factors

Clinical social workers also practice within mezzo-settings that affect the choices available to them and how those choices are made. Mezzo factors include host settings, the media, professional education programs, and the professional literature.

Host Settings Many social workers practice in "host settings" (that is, settings that are not organized around a social work mission or run by social workers) such as hospitals and schools, each with own agenda and priorities. Mental health agencies and clinics, even if social work based, also have their own hierarchies, bureaucratic procedures, reimbursement requirements, and constraints that limit the clinician's options. This will vary; for instance, a clinician at a college counseling center may not be required to enter a DSM diagnosis in a client's chart, but in other settings this may be an eligibility requirement.

In practice settings where social workers are working for or under physicians, the issue of required deference to medical authority often arises. There is a clear power imbalance between medical prescribers (i.e., psychiatrists) and psychosocial helping professionals, such as social workers (Gomory et al. 2011; Probst 2012). By virtue of their medical authority, the decisions of prescribers are more highly valued than those of their social work colleagues. Discharge or involuntary commitment decisions are often made unilaterally by psychiatrists, for example, as well as decisions to medicate clients. This power imbalance is troublesome, given that many social workers are not impressed or pleased with the level of care that clients receive from prescribers (McMillen et al. 2007). Navigating such hierarchies while advocating for clients is often one of the more challenging aspects of working in a host setting. Private practice, while more autonomous in some ways, still requires interaction with private insurance companies for reimbursement; this may not be true when practitioners require payment directly from clients, although typically only a small number of social work clients are able to self-pay.

In short, there are constraints on the availability of certain kinds of interventions in every setting and form of practice. In many settings, psychotropic medication is standard practice, utilized more readily and frequently than psychosocial intervention. The influence of the biomedical industrial complex is clearly evident, with many consumers having come to trust and even expect pharmacological intervention—accepting and internalizing the current cultural notion of human problems as medical illnesses that are curable through medication. Medication may be cheaper in the short run, but may have a greater long-term cost (Whitaker 2010).

Unfortunately, agencies may discourage rather than encourage critical reflection about the assessment methods and frameworks being used. A distinction between what a clinician knows is needed, and what is offered or available, may contribute to burnout, job turnover, and worker dissatisfaction.

The Media The mainstream media (including print, film, television, and internet websites) is a major source of information on mental health for the general public. Information put forward in such sources is often highly misleading. For example, the notion of a "chemical imbalance" underlying mental disorders has been widely disseminated by the media (Leo and Lacasse 2008; see also Appendix C of this book). Critics have noted that the viewpoint expressed in the media is often that of pharmaceutical companies or the American Psychiatric Association, rather than the voices of clients or the general public.

The ways in which "mental disorder" is portrayed, described, and discussed in news reporting and films also affect public perceptions. When people who commit crimes are described in news stories as "mentally ill," readers may quickly conclude that the illness caused the crime and thus all people with mental disorders are likely to commit criminal acts, reinforcing notions of fundamental difference and dangerousness that lead to stigma, misunderstanding, and isolation. Similarly, movies and television often portray those with mental disorders as frightening, helpless, pitiful, or miraculously able to overcome all challenges. People who read, listen to, and watch these portrayals—and then search the internet for further "information" about the disorder—may come away with highly distorted perceptions, especially since there is little regulation or guidance to help the reader know which films or websites offer reliable information. (See Wedding and Niemiec's *Movies and Mental Illness* for a comprehensive review of how more than 1500 films portray psychopathology. The authors also catalog and rate these films and provide critical thinking questions, links to related websites, and other useful resources.)

Professional Education It has been argued that there is pervasive bias in the way clinical social workers (as well as some other helping professionals) are educated and trained. It is therefore useful to consider the biases inherent in a conventional mental health education. This may seem odd, since students attend graduate school to develop expertise, which would presumably mean that they acquire a broad exposure to issues and perspectives on mental health. However, there is evidence that this is not the case. A study of syllabi in social work psychopathology courses (Lacasse and Gomory 2003) revealed most of these courses promoted a biomedical/psychiatric model and did *not* expose students to well-argued empirically tested alternative points of view. Such courses were largely focused on teaching students about the DSM—necessary knowledge for mental health practice, but one requiring robust critique as well as coverage of alternative views such as those discussed in other chapters of this book. This is but one example of the unfortunate promotion of "avoidable ignorance" (Gambrill 2014) in social work education programs.

The Professional Literature Increasingly, it is acknowledged that much of the psychiatric literature is highly biased and that a great deal of it meets the definition of propaganda. This is often a shocking (and daunting) issue for students to face, as they have been taught to go to the peer-reviewed literature for answers. To be sure, it is important for students and practicing social workers to be familiar with the peer-reviewed literature. But it is also important for them to realize the limitations of this literature and how it may be shaped by those with power and authority.

A relevant example is the DSM-5 field trials published in the *American Journal of Psychiatry*. As the publication date for DSM-5 drew near, field trials became very important: if they had good results, this would lend scientific legitimacy to the controversial new manual. However, the articles reporting the DSM field trials—authored by the DSM-5 investigators from the American Psychiatric Association—used classic propagandistic techniques to shape the way the reader interpreted the results. For instance, they simply decided that any kappa value above 20 (20 % agreement between two clinicians) was acceptable and that 21–40 was "good." They then reported the results using the term "good" as a descriptor, but without quotation marks, so that a reader who had not read all the articles would be led to believe that these results were actually "good." They were not, as academic psychiatrists Allen Frances (Chair of DSM-IV) and Robert Spitzer (Chair of DSM III and III-R) pointed out (Frances 2012; Spitzer and Endicott 2012, as cited in Jones 2012). The field trials reported a very high kappa value for PTSD, for example, trumpeting the results. However, these field trials took place at VA hospitals at a time when many recent veterans have been deployed and seen combat—a setting, point in time, and population sample likely to skew the results. Whether clinicians can agree on who has PTSD in the civilian population is an equally important question, but was not explored in these field trials.

Bias in the psychiatric literature is also prevalent in the related issue of diagnosis and psychiatric medications. For example, an article in the *Wall Street Journal* about the plans of a drug company to market their new medication revealed that an important part of that plan was to promote the condition, OCD, that the medication was purported to "cure," simultaneously increasing awareness of the "problem" and its "solution" (see Albee 2002).

In addition, it is now well known that many published studies of psychiatric drugs were ghostwritten by staff in (or contracted by) pharmaceutical companies (Lacasse and Leo 2010). Such studies list academic authors with impressive credentials on the byline, but the real authors are staff in the marketing departments of pharmaceutical companies and subcontracted medical writers. Strangely, this is permitted in the medical literature as long as the medical writer (the real author) is listed in the acknowledgements section. Healy (2012) has compared these published randomized controlled trials of psychiatric drugs in the peer-reviewed literature to "infomercials" because of the clear corporate interests pushing their agendas in ostensibly scientific journals.

The psychiatric literature underlying much of contemporary mental health practice suffers from other problems as well, including the selective reporting of data. For example, studies of psychiatric drugs alleging positive findings are published, sometimes repeatedly (such as in the case of Zyprexa; see Healy 2012), while data showing that the medications are ineffective or harmful are suppressed and not published. Sometimes pharmaceutical companies will launch a campaign within peer-reviewed journals in order to further their interests when their product is under attack. For instance, the antipsychotic drug Zyprexa is known to cause metabolic problems such as weight gain and can lead to diabetes. Eli Lilly suppressed this information for years and supported a series of articles, published in the professional literature, that argued that schizophrenia, not Zyprexa, caused diabetes. Eventually, researchers published results showing that there were no cases of diabetes upon admission among psychotics admitted to a mental hospital in the pre-antipsychotic era (Le Noury et al. 2008). The "blame the disease, not the drug" strategy did buy Eli Lilly some time, confusing clinicians and the general public in a way that favored their interests.

Similarly, SSRI drugs have long been promoted as being highly effective. One can find hundreds of seemingly rigorous studies in peer-reviewed sources attesting to their efficacy and utility in the treatment of many conditions. In 2008, Eric Turner, a former FDA employee, published an analysis in the *New England Journal of Medicine* showing that clinicians, clients, and the general public were overestimating the effectiveness of antidepressants because the drug companies had been publishing positive studies and hiding the rest (see Appendix C).

These issues obviously present a serious dilemma for clinicians who earnestly search the literature in order to engage in evidence-informed practice. However, although the peer-reviewed psychiatric literature is marred with bias and selective reporting, there are excellent scholarly books that present a more balanced review. Books such as *The Truth About the Drug Companies, Blaming the Brain, Pharmageddon, Anatomy of an Epidemic, Mad Science, Propaganda in the Helping Professions,* and others have contributed to an excellent critical scholarly literature that gives insight and context to our current zeitgeist regarding mental health diagnosis and treatment. It is possible for students and clinicians to familiarize themselves with these issues. It does require being skeptical of authorities and the conventional wisdom, but if one is interested, the literature is there. Becoming familiar with this literature is a partial remedy for some of the problems discussed above and can in fact help social workers to be more helpful to their clients.

The Context of Clinical Decision-Making:
Micro Level Factors

The micro context—the personal situation of the individual clinician—also influences the quality of assessment, as discussed in the first part of this chapter. Characteristics of the social worker such as conscientiousness and critical thinking skills influence the way decisions are made. Evidence-based practice emphasizes "conscientious, explicit and judicious use of best current evidence in making decisions about the care of individual [clients]" (Sackett et al. 1997, p. 2). Like members of any large group, individual social workers differ in these characteristics. Inflated self-assessments are common (Dunning et al. 2004), encouraging an overconfidence that is not warranted and interferes with critical reflection. Social workers also differ in the quality of common factors such as warmth and empathy that can affect the degree to which clients share vital assessment information (Wampold 2010). The role of other factors in decision-making, such as susceptibility to cognitive biases and the unconscious use of cognitive heuristics or shortcuts, are discussed in detail in Chap. 1.

Conclusions

This chapter has described the process of making good assessment decisions within the larger context of a biomedical industrial complex in which powerful entities shape how we see clients and their problems, just as mezzo-level incentives and constraints guide clinical decisions. Depending on the practice setting, mezzo and macro level factors may make good decision-making more or less possible.

Improving practice and clinical decision-making requires constantly learning about these issues and testing one's ideas. Evidence-based or evidence-informed practice is rooted in this ideal. Unfortunately, getting rigorous, well-tested information on mental health issues can often be a challenge, even in venues that are often thought of as committed to rigorous science such as graduate school curricula and peer-reviewed medical journals. Social workers should thus consider where they are getting the information they are using and the veracity and biases that may be inherent in that information.

One issue that aspiring social workers should consider is the congruence between how they view these issues and how the organization where they are employed sees them. In nursing, there is a literature on "moral distress," the angst created in a clinician when there is a difference between what they know they should do, and what they are pragmatically able or allowed to do. As graduate students in social work think about their career plans, they would be wise to consider how the environment they work in will affect their ability to make sound clinical decisions that promote the involvement of clients as informed participants. They can also advocate for systems where clinicians are able to make sound clinical decisions, where sound clinical decisions are facilitated (not blocked) by the existing incentives and constraints.

Application to the Case of Ray

Ray has had a complicated life, filled with events that would impact any person who experienced them. He was discharged from the hospital after a short stay with the diagnosis of a major mental disorder, Bipolar disorder, and placed on Depakote, a mood stabilizer. A thoughtful social worker might well question the validity of applying this diagnosis to Ray so quickly, given the short amount of time that the hospital's clinical staff had to gather the information on which the diagnosis was based. Certainly, the events that precipitated his hospitalization point to the presence of significant symptoms; at the same time, other factors that might help to explain his essential difficulties (e.g., previous trauma and abuse) may not have been disclosed to hospital clinicians during this short time frame. The circumstances in which the diagnosis was given—in a hospital, quickly, immediately following a crisis situation, and without a therapeutic alliance that could create a safe environment for full disclosure of his history—must be taken into account before accepting the diagnosis.

Rather than uncritically accepting such a hospital-based diagnosis, other factors should be considered. The diagnosis of Bipolar disorder has been skyrocketing in recent years. Was Ray diagnosed with Bipolar II because this is now a popular diagnosis? What evidence is there that Ray has demonstrated symptoms of hypomania as required by the DSM? Is there evidence that Ray finds his current diagnosis and psychiatric medication helpful? If one examines the DSM-5 criteria for Bipolar Disorder II, it does not seem likely that Ray meets the criteria. This is not unusual in clinical practice; research has shown that many clients diagnosed as depressed do not actually meet DSM criteria, for instance. The label of Bipolar disorder can be quite stigmatizing, and we might wonder about its effect on Ray's sense of self and his hope for recovery, as well as its effect on his friends, family, and potential employers. Additionally, anticonvulsants like Depakote can have adverse effects, especially when taken long term. To what extent was medication simply assumed to be part of his ongoing treatment, especially given the fact that the treatment plan was developed in a medical setting? If a treatment team was meeting about Ray, one would hope that the social worker would consider the validity of the assessment and treatment decisions, viewing them within a more holistic life context.

Following his discharge from the hospital, the setting for his outpatient treatment is unclear. Is the therapist in private practice, or working under the auspices of an agency or clinic? What requirements, protocols, agendas, and funding sources are involved? Are medication and/or case management services a required or optional part of the services Ray can receive? These mezzo-level factors also need to be considered.

Clearly, Ray has suffered multiple traumas. While he does not meet all the classic criteria for post-traumatic stress disorder (e.g., he has no flashbacks), it would be naïve to think that these events have not affected him. The overlap in criteria between PTSD, Depression, and Bipolar II is significant; many clients diagnosed with depression also have a history of trauma. Is treatment within the conventional psychiatric paradigm the best thing for Ray? What about Trauma-Informed Care, or peer support, or any number of other options?

The most striking aspect of the case study of Ray is that he seems to be getting worse rather than better. In part, this may be due to the inaccurate diagnosis of Bipolar disorder. However, it is also worthwhile to consider whether his lack of progress is possibly the result of a misguided therapeutic approach. As a vignette-based case example, we cannot know the details of what therapy consisted of. Nonetheless, based on what is related, some questions come to mind. He has had months of therapy, much of which seems to have focused on encouraging Ray to recapture a history of abuse. Does the literature support this kind of digging up of past abuse? Did his helpers clearly identify exactly what Ray would like to be different in his life and then systematically pursue these outcomes informed by a contextual assessment and intervention, carefully tracking progress on each? Were his therapists skilled in contextual, strength-based assessment, and intervention? Did they identify alternative competing repertoires that could be increased?

It is also worrisome that he has not been coached to seek legal representation concerning his "formal hearing." What attention has been devoted to how he is going to make a living? There is a vagueness regarding many key areas [e.g., he "spends as much time with (his children) as he can"]. How much time is this? What is the quality of interaction? How often does he see his children? There also seems to be no attention to helping him deal with regret (e.g., intense guilt about the abortions). Was his counselor skilled in effective cognitive-behavioral methods for handling "shoulds"? How has his capacity been supported to form new healthy relationships? Was his history of violence, including violence toward women, give sufficient attention including referral to relevant support services?

One might also want to consider the impact of the macro context on Ray's perception of his situation. What has he read or heard about 9/11, about sexual abuse by priests, about people who are hospitalized, and about mental disorder in general? These are topics that have had widespread media coverage. How does he compare his own experience to the heroic tales of other first responders during 9/11? What has it been like for him to read stories in the press about others who were sexually abused by clergy? Has he searched the internet for websites, testimonies, and solutions? What images or projections have influenced his self-perception, and in what ways might these have contributed to his internal experience and external actions?

Practical Exercises

1. Consider your field placement. What view of unusual or disliked behavior does your agency promote? What sources are appealed to in this promotion? What assessment frameworks are favored?

2. Go online to find a recent article in a reputable publication (such as *The New York Times)* about the results of a study pertaining to a "mental health" concern. Critique the report using your skills in critical appraisal to develop a list of questions about potential concerns such as behind-the-scenes stakeholders, methods, hidden aims, limitations, selective reporting, and misuse of findings.
3. Think about a client you have in your current placement or had in the past. What are presenting concerns? Have they been clearly described? What are hoped-for-outcomes? What sources of assessment information did you use? Did you use observation in real-life settings if relevant and possible (e.g., in a classroom)? If not, why not? Was some assessment data missing? Were there any pressures to use assessment methods because of agency reimbursement process? How did you cope with these pressures? What steps did you take, or could take, to minimize avoidable errors in assessment? What were the barriers, if any, to taking these steps?

References

Albee, G. W. (2002). Just say no to psychotropic drugs! *Journal of Clinical Psychology, 58*(6), 635–648.

Angell, M. (2005). *The truth about the drug companies: How they deceive us and what to do about it.* New York: Random House Trade Paperbacks.

Carlat, D. (2010). *Unhinged: The trouble with psychiatry-a doctor's revelations about a profession in crisis.* New York: Simon and Schuster.

Cosgrove, L., Krimsky, S., Vijayaraghaven, M., & Schneider, L. (2006). Financial ties between DSM-IV panel members and the pharmaceutical industry. *Psychotherapy and Psychosomatics, 75*, 154–160.

Dunning, D., Heath, C., & Suls, J. M. (2004). Flawed self-assessment: Implications for health, education, and the work place. *Psychological Science and the Public Interest, 5*, 69–106.

Frazer, P., Westhuis, D., Daley, J. G., & Phillips, I. (2009). How clinical social workers are using the DSM-IV: A national study. *Social Work in Mental Health, 7*(4), 325–339.

Gambrill, E. (2012). *Propaganda in the helping professions.* New York: Oxford.

Gambrill, E. (2013). *Social work practice: A critical thinker's guide* (3rd ed.). New York: Oxford.

Gambrill, E. (2014). Social work education and avoidable ignorance. *Journal of Social Work Education, 50*, 391–413.

Gamwell, L., & Tomes, N. (1995). *Madness in America: Cultural and medical perceptions of mental illness before 1914.* Birmingham, NY: Cornell University Press.

Goldiamond, I. (1974). Toward a constructional approach to social problems: Ethical and constitutional issues raised by applied behavior analysis. *Behaviorism, 2*, 1–84.

Gomory, T., Wong, S. E., Cohen, D., & Lacasse, J. R. (2011). Clinical social work and the biomedical industrial complex. *Journal of Sociology and Social Welfare, 38*(4), 135–165.

Greenberg, G. (2010). *Manufacturing depression: The secret history of a modern disease.* New York: Simon and Schuster.

Greenberg, G. (2013). *The book of woe: The DSM and the unmaking of psychiatry.* New York: Blue Rider.

Healy, D. (2012). *Pharmageddon.* California: University of California Press.

Hess, J. Z., Lacasse, J. R., Harmon, J., Williams, D., & Vierling-Claasen, N. (2014). 'Is there a getting better from this, or not?' Examining the meaning and possibility of recovery from mental disorder. *Child and Youth Services, 35*(2), 116–136.

Jones K D (2012). A critique of DSM-5 field trials. *Journal of Nervous and Mental Disease, 200*(6). 517–519.

Kubik, J. D. (1999). Incentives for the identification and treatment of children with disabilities: The supplemental security income program. *Journal of Public Economics, 73*(2), 187–215.

Lacasse, J. R. (2005). Consumer advertising of psychiatric medications biases the public against non-pharmacological treatment. *Ethical Human Psychology and Psychiatry, 7*(3), 175–179.

Lacasse, J. R., & Gomory, T. (2003). Is graduate social work education promoting a critical approach to mental health practice? *Journal of Social Work Education, 39*(3), 383–408.

Lacasse, J. R., & Leo, J. (2006). Questionable advertising of psychotropic medications and disease mongering. *PLoS Medicine, 3*(7), 1192.

Lacasse, J. R., & Leo, J. (2010). Ghostwriting at elite academic medical centers in the United States. *PLoS Medicine, 7*(2), e1000230. doi:10.1371/journal.pmed.1000230.

Layng, T. V. J. (2009). The search for effective clinical behavior analysis: The nonlinear thinking of Israel Goldiamond. *Behavior Analyst, 32*, 163–184.

Le Noury, J., Khan, A., Harris, M., Wong, W., Williams, D., Roberts, T., & Healy, D. (2008). The incidence and prevalence of diabetes in patients with serious mental illness in North West Wales: Two cohorts, 1875–1924 and 1994–2006 compared. *BMC Psychiatry, 8*(1), 67.

Leo, J., & Lacasse, J. R. (2008). The media and the chemical imbalance theory of depression. *Society, 45*, 35–45.

McCoy, R. (2000). *Quack! Tales of medical fraud from the museum of questionable medical devices*. Santa Monica, CA: Santa Monica Press.

McMillen, J. C., Fedoravicius, N., Rowe, J., Zima, B. T., & Ware, N. (2007). A crisis of credibility: Professionals' concerns about the psychiatric care provided to clients of the child welfare system. *Administration and Policy in Mental Health and Mental Health Services Research, 34*(3), 203–212.

Moncrieff, J. (2008). Neoliberalism and biopsychiatry: A marriage of convenience. In C. I. Cohen & S. Timimi (Eds.), *Liberatory psychiatry: Philosophy, politics and mental health* (pp. 235–256). New York: Cambridge University Press.

Moynihan, R., & Cassels, A. (2005). *Selling sickness: How the world's biggest pharmaceutical companies are turning us all into patients*. New York: Nation Books.

Probst, B. (2012). Not quite colleagues: Issues of power and purview between social work and psychiatry. *Social Work in Mental Health, 10*, 367–383.

Probst, B. (2013). "Walking the Tightrope:" Clinical social workers' use of diagnostic and environmental perspectives. *Clinical Social Work Journal, 41*(2), 184–191.

Sackett, D. L., Richardson, W. S., Rosenberg, W., & Haynes, R. B. (1997). *Evidence-based medicine: How to practice and teach EBM*. New York: Churchill Livingstone.

Schwartz, A., & Goldiamond, I. (1975). *Social casework: A behavioral approach*. New York: Columbia University Press.

Spaulding-Givens, J., & Lacasse, J.R. (in-press; forthcoming 2015). Self-directed care: Participants' service utilization and outcomes. Psychiatric Rehabilitation Journal.

Wampold, B. E. (2010). The research evidence for the common factors models: A historically situated perspective. In B. M. Duncan, S. D. Miller, M. A. Hubble, & B. E. Wampold (Eds.), *The heart and soul of therapy* (pp. 49–82). Washington, DC: Psychological Association.

Whitaker, R. (2010). *Anatomy of an epidemic: Magic bullets, psychiatric drugs, and the astonishing rise of mental illness in America*. New York: Crown.

Chapter 5
Situating Disorder: Mental Disorder in Context

Barbara Probst

Abstract This chapter addresses the various contexts—cultural, historical, socio-logical, and individual—in which "mental disorder" exists and is understood. Clearly, notions of normalcy (the baseline against which "abnormal" is measured) vary by cultural values and historical era: what is "disorder" in one place or at one time may not be "disorder" in another, as the chapter illustrates through well-documented examples. Thus, assessment protocols based on a dominant Eurocentric paradigm may not capture the experience, meaning, or impact of a particular client's distress. Clinicians are urged to consider the influence of environment, social context, cultural values and beliefs, class, race, and gender in how client problems are viewed. A detailed review is provided of social work theory and research pertaining to each of these issues, including proposed models for better addressing cultural and environmental factors. The role of relationships—another kind of context—is also considered, together with an overview of the debate about including "relational disorders" in the DSM, the connection between relational and attachment issues, and suggestions for assessing attachment.

Keywords Afrocentric · Analogue studies · Bias · Equifinality · Eurocentric · Intersectionality · Minimization · Multi-axial · Paradigm · Protocol · Relational disorders · Transactionality · V codes

Introduction: Why This Matters

Like any condition, "mental disorder" is always personal and idiographic, its meaning and impact affected by individual history, resources, social location, values, and beliefs about what "mental health" can and ought to be. As Loring and Powell cautioned over a quarter century ago, reflecting on the new behavioral

B. Probst (✉)
School for Social Work, Smith College, Northampton, MA, USA
e-mail: Barbara.H.Probst@gmail.com

© Springer International Publishing Switzerland 2015
B. Probst (ed.), *Critical Thinking in Clinical Assessment and Diagnosis*,
Essential Clinical Social Work Series, DOI 10.1007/978-3-319-17774-8_5

criteria of DSM-III that seemed to offer a longed-for solution to the subjectivity of the diagnostic process, "a false sense of confidence in objective measures can be dangerous" (Loring and Powell 1988, p. 19).

While examining symptoms to see how they match generic criteria, a clinician must also identify specific elements in the client's environment, culture, and developmental history that shape the experience and trajectory of the disorder *for that individual*. Unfortunately, there is no consistent, standardized way to do this. While most social workers *do* include context in their assessment, they do so without the benefit of a validated instrument, typically through informal inventories provided by their agencies or developed through personal experience.

In the third and fourth editions of the DSM, there was an attempt to promote comprehensive bio-psycho-social assessment through a five-part diagnostic framework known as the multiaxial system. Five dimensions or "axes" provided a format for recording aspects of physical health and environment that might contribute to the genesis, persistence, or exacerbation of a disorder. Axis IV, the so-called social work axis, was a place where environmental risk factors and psychosocial stressors could be noted. Multiaxial assessment quickly became optional rather than mandatory, however, since only the first two axes (primary mental health disorder and underlying personality disorder) could be used for insurance reimbursement. Axis IV, irrelevant for billing, was relegated to the periphery. The multiaxial system was eventually dropped from DSM-5, and social work's hope that context would have a formal role in assessment across disciplines was never realized (Probst 2014).

Like its predecessors, DSM-5 includes an extensive list of V codes for conditions other than disease or disorder that may warrant clinical attention. These V codes cover relational, academic, occupational, and acculturation problems as well as factors that can influence care such as malingering and noncompliance with treatment. While the list is useful for highlighting issues to consider in formulating a clinical portrait, it is little more than Axis IV in a new format since a V code is still not reimbursable. A "real" mental health problem residing in the individual must be cited, or the client will have to pay out-of-pocket. Only those with sufficient financial means to bypass insurance can rely solely on V codes—an ironic situation, since it is often those with limited finances whose distress is more closely linked to, and conveyed by, V codes related to ecological stressors of poverty, oppression, isolation, and marginalization.

This is a serious problem for social workers, committed to social justice and a transactional approach that focuses on the interface between people and their environments (Buchbinder et al. 2004). Hippocrates' observation, cited in the Introduction to this book, underscores the profession's emphasis on situating disorder in the experience of specific people in specific contexts: "It is more important to know what sort of person has the disease than to know what sort of disease a person has."

This chapter will explore that challenge.

Guiding Questions

1. How do cultural and historical paradigms affect notions of what constitutes a problem?
2. How do social environment and socioeconomic class affect the diagnostic process? How do they affect the way a condition is seen, interpreted, and named?
3. What do we mean by "environment" and what is its relationship to disorder?
4. Is there such a thing as a relational disorder, where the problem lies in the relationship rather than within either individual? How can this dimension be included in assessment?

Person-in-Paradigm

Few people would argue for a strictly universal definition of what it means to be mentally ill, since notions of normalcy—the baseline against which "abnormal" is measured—vary by worldview, geography, and historical era. In order to understand a client's distress, the clinician must first understand the worldview in which that distress is experienced—the client's assumptions about the nature of self and group, the construction of knowledge, and the nature, causes, and cures for suffering. These paradigms or models of reality shape the way people think about causality and attribution, motivation, agency, authority, self and personhood, modes of coping, styles of expression, and ways of seeking help. They "tell people what to attend to, what to ignore, what things mean, and what should be done about them" (Saint Arnault and Shimabukuru 2011, p. 305). They are maps, charters of the social world (Kirmayer 2005), templates for interpreting the significance of events and experiences.

Clinicians embedded in a Western, Eurocentric worldview may have to set aside their most basic assumptions about life, knowledge, and personhood in order to understand clients from non-Western backgrounds. In the Afrocentric paradigm, for example, the spiritual dimension is central and all things are interconnected. Human identity is social identity; community, harmony, mutual aid, and collective well-being are more important than competition or individual achievement; affective, intuitive ways of knowing are just as valid as rational means; and help takes place through mutual immersion and interdependence rather than by the intervention of experts (Schiele 1996; Mazama 2001).

These principles suggest an approach to health care radically different from that of Western psychiatry. Because of life's collectivist nature, a person does not become ill or heal in isolation. The very notion of *individual* diagnosis or treatment may be completely alien, and it can seem inappropriate or meaningless to talk about personal symptoms. If asked to frame an illness experience in personal terms, Afrocentric clients may respond with statements that do not make sense to Eurocentric clinicians, who are likely to misinterpret or dismiss the statements as insignificant to the diagnostic task. Lacking a relevant context, they may adopt an unconscious position of "paradigmatic privilege" and rely on ethnocentric explanations that use their own group as the standard for interpreting client behavior (Dadlani et al. 2012).

The assessment protocol itself can be a source of miscommunication when—as most are—it is based on Eurocentric, hetero-normative, or classist notions of the kinds of questions that ought to be asked. The questions that would have actually gotten to the heart of the client's experience may not have been raised. Thus, information that is most important about the experience, in that person's worldview, such as somatic pain or spiritual imbalance, may never be disclosed.

Paradigms vary by era as well as by culture. As noted in Chap. 1, beliefs about mental disorder have changed over the years. Diagnostic fads have come and gone; disorders have been added or dropped from the DSM; and age parameters for conditions such as separation anxiety or bipolar disorder have been revised both up and down. There are no more "neurotics," but hoarding and gambling, previously considered character flaws, have become mental disorders. In some cases, political agendas have helped to shape what counts as a disorder, who qualifies for it, and what the category is called. An example is the removal of self-defeating personality disorder from DSM-IV. As chronicled by Tosone (1998), the DSM-IV Personality Disorders Work Group was concerned that the diagnosis, as it existed in DSM-III, could harm women who were victims of abuse or marginalization by making it seem as if their internal pathology was the actual cause of their suffering—"blaming the victim"—and thus further disempowering women who were, in fact, either victims of someone else's pathology or simply choosing to put the needs of others ahead of their own, a gendered and socially reinforced trait that "became distorted as a sickness" (p. 415). In an effort to be politically correct, the authors of DSM-IV decided to eliminate the disorder from the new edition of the manual, in much the same way as homosexuality was eliminated from DSM-III in 1973. In both cases, the decision was political rather than scientific. That is not to say that either condition is or is not a mental disorder—certainly, few would call sexual orientation an "illness" nowadays—but that the decision was made in response to political pressure rather than to new evidence.

It is rarely a matter of new evidence correcting previous errors, but of new social attitudes that shape which human variations are construed as disorders, which labels are deemed more or less pejorative. For example, when autism and Asperger's syndrome were added to the list of conditions entitling a child to special accommodation under the Individuals with Disabilities Educational Act (IDEA), diagnostic rates for these conditions soared while rates for other disorders, such as mental retardation, plummeted (Shattuck 2006). The change was not in children's brains but in clinicians' choices. It is certainly possible that more children were being born or reaching school age with Asperger's syndrome and fewer with cognitive impairment. However, it seems more likely that they were simply being given a different label.

In fact, there may have always been more than one plausible label for many of these children. The label selected at a particular moment in time may reflect public awareness and perceptions about services, social acceptance, and relative stigma, rather than precise diagnostic criteria. What Shattuck calls "diagnostic substitution"—replacing one label with another because the latter yields greater benefits or simply seems preferable—may be less of a conscious choice than an unconscious reflection of diagnostic popularity, fostered by the availability and anchoring heuristics discussed in Chap. 1. Through priming, a clinician who has heard again and again about the autism "epidemic" may be more likely to interpret a child's behavior as autistic rather than indicative of a different condition—thus reinforcing autism's reported prevalence.

In a related study of whether children who had previously received other diagnoses might now be diagnosed with autism, Bishop (2008) applied diagnostic criteria for autism to adults with a history of developmental language disorder and found that many would "unambiguously" meet criteria for autistic disorder if assessed now. Again, it is a matter of timing. When these adults were children struggling with communication problems, learning disabilities had just captured public attention. People now understood that a learning disability, rather than a lack of intelligence or effort, might account for a child's difficulty. Autism, on the other hand, was seen as a rare and extreme condition. It was not until several decades later that autism began to seem so widespread, although much of the increase appears to have been at the milder end of the spectrum: the same children who might, a generation earlier, have been diagnosed with mild mental retardation or a language disorder were now being diagnosed with Asperger's syndrome or high-functioning autism.

The sharp increase in autism rates has been well documented. The Centers for Disease Control and Prevention (CDC) reported a prevalence of autism spectrum disorder in the USA of 14.7 per 1000 children in 2014, or one in 68. That represents a 30 % increase in only two years; the rate in 2012 was one in 88 (http://www.cdc.gov/mmwr/preview/mmwrhtml/ss6302a1.htm). In the 1980s, the prevalence of autism was 1 in 10,000; in the 1990s, it was 1 in 2500 and then 1 in 1000 (http://www.autismsciencefoundation.org/). The CDC also notes:

> The global prevalence of autism has increased 20-fold to 30-fold since the earliest epidemiologic studies were conducted in the late 1960s and early 1970s … Although the underlying reasons for the apparent prevalence changes are difficult to study empirically, select studies suggest that much of the recent prevalence increase is likely attributable to extrinsic factors such as improved awareness and recognition and changes in diagnostic practice or service availability.

Determining prevalence, or counting cases of a particular disorder, depends on how the condition is defined—how easy or difficult it is to get into the club. In certain cultures or eras, when there is greater tolerance for those who deviate from social norms, a condition may need to be more severe to earn a diagnostic label. That is, thresholds for mental illness categories are higher and fewer people are placed in those categories. At other times or in other places, there is less tolerance, milder cases "count," thresholds drop, and prevalence rates go up.

This is true on both large and small scales, for cultural epochs and for periods in individual lives. Someone who was not diagnosable at one point in his or her life may be diagnosable at another time, partly because symptoms may have intensified, and partly because standards may have tightened or relaxed for macro or mezzo level reasons that have nothing to do with the individual's level of distress or impairment, such as a change in agency standards or media awareness. Someone's coping skills may be adequate when ecological pressures are low, but when new demands are added or familiar supports are taken away, the adaptive balance may tilt. Symptoms intensify and criteria for a disorder will be met   at least for a while. Disorders are not always stable, in their presentation or in the way they are viewed by others. Under certain conditions, it may be beneficial for the client, family members, or service providers if a label can be assigned that will open the door to needed services. At other times, avoidance of a label may be preferred.

Thus, when a client arrives with an existing diagnosis, it is important to know *when* and *where* the diagnosis was given, as well as *by whom*. The location and purpose of a diagnosis—e.g., as part of a legal judgment, to qualify for services or exemptions—and the orientation of the person who made the assessment affect the clinical formulation the client carries and may have internalized, even if it is no longer appropriate. Previous diagnoses can nonetheless be useful indicators of chronicity, cyclical patterns, or responses to episodic stress.

Person-in-Environment

When asked what distinguishes social work from other helping professions, most people would cite the notion of person-in-environment, yet there has been no clear or enduring agreement about the term "environment" actually means. Is environment literal, referring to buildings and streets, noise, sanitation, roads, stores, the use of space? Or does it have a broader meaning—the experience of community, membership, social networks, resources, and barriers? Is it broader still, extending to the political and economic milieu, the impact of large-scale events such as war and oppression? What about climatic conditions, the media, cultural myths and heroes—are these also part of "environment?"

In its early years, social work emphasized the need to understand people within their life contexts and sought to intervene at points of interface. A split arose in the profession, however, with some social workers viewing human suffering as stemming from internal difficulty, indicating psychological intervention, and others viewing it as stemming from problems in living, indicating ecological intervention. In a radical departure from the reformist approach of Jane Addams and other social work pioneers, Mary Jarrett, in her 1919 speech to the National Conference of Social Work, proposed that *internal* factors were just as legitimate a focus of social work as *external* ones.

For many, Jarrett's proposition struck a chord. New psychiatric methods seemed more advanced than casework, since "even when caseworkers were able to successfully manipulate their clients' environments, their clients frequently continued to remain unhappy and maladjusted" (Alperin and Hollman 1992, p. 90). Freudian theory seemed to provide the missing answer. Mary Richmond's formulation that growth occurs through adjustment *between* person and environment was rapidly eclipsed by psychoanalytic theory that emphasized forces *within* the psyche, shifting social work's focus away from its historic ecological framework (Janchill 1969). Environmental manipulation was replaced by exploration of the unconscious.

In the decades that followed, internal processes became the focus of work, and it was not unusual for a social work client to receive no environmental intervention at all. Hollis and Woods (1981) even advised that, for many, intervening in the environment would be counterproductive of psychotherapeutic aims. "Environmental manipulation practiced unnecessarily can undermine treatment and can have a negative effect upon the client's self-esteem and autonomy" (Alperin and Hollman 1992, p. 95). Improving the environment would, in other words, simply mask the underlying psychopathology and deprive an individual of the opportunity for the internal change that was actually needed.

Since then, the pendulum has continued to shift, with ecological and intrapsychic factors varying in importance by both practitioner and era (Probst 2012). Still, person-in-environment has always been social work's conceptual heart, the defining base from which the profession has steadily evolved. "There is not a contemporary theory of personality that does not take the effects of the social environment into account" (Goldstein 2009, pp. 11–12). At the same time, the definition, scope, and operationalization of this (presumably) central notion have been inconsistent and poorly conceptualized. "Ambivalence, disagreement and confusion over what person-in-environment means, what it should mean, and how it is implemented in practice are at the heart of contention over whether this elusive concept is, or should be, a central tenet of the social work profession" (Rogge and Cox 2001, p. 48). Those in favor of person-in-environment as social work's signature concept assert that it promotes holistic assessment; those opposed say it is too broad to guide practice, lacking the precision needed for explanation, prediction, or intervention planning (Wakefield 1996).

"Either the perspective is so ingrained in social work practice that there is no need to name it, or it is much less a guiding perspective than the profession may claim or believe" (Rogge and Cox 2001, p. 64). Its very flexibility, Rogge and Cox suggest, is "one of the construct's most important beneficial attributes or serious limitations, depending on one's point of view" (p. 64). Findings from Probst's (2012) qualitative study of how social workers think about environment support these conclusions. For the 30 participants in that study, environment was seen as background, not foreground—crucial for promoting a deeper understanding of the client, but lacking clinical power as a guide to treatment.

While person-in-environment is clearly a defining feature of social work practice, it remains an orientation rather than a theory since it offers no explanation for *why* or *how* person and environment affect each other or how specific elements of environment contribute to problems or to the process of change. As a perspective, it helps social workers attune to the importance of context and provides an important counterweight to the medical model that locates problems within the individual; yet its utility is limited since it fails to specify the activities, experiences, or mechanisms that enable change to take place (Wakefield 1996). For person-in-environment to be clinically useful, pathways would need to be isolated to indicate how specific aspects of the environment can be harnessed to address problems or improve functioning. Without being grounded in a theory of change, "environment" cannot provide a basis for intervention decisions; as a result, social workers find themselves embracing theories of change from other professions such as psychology and psychiatry (Probst 2012).

Social work's signature attempt to develop its own model of assessment, rooted in environmental transactions, was the Person-in-Environment System or PIE. PIE grew out of an National Association of Social Workers (NASW) task force charged with developing a "new method unique to social work that describes, classifies, and codes the problems of clients" (Karls and Wandrei 1992, p. 80). Task force members determined that "social well-being" and "social performance" were an appropriate basis on which to build a social work classification system and common professional language (Williams et al. 1989). The ensuing system relied heavily on social role theory, with role fulfillment serving as a unifying construct for cataloguing problems in psychosocial functioning (Karls and Wandrei 1992).

In a PIE formulation, a four-factor system delineates interpersonal, environmental, mental, and physical issues. Factor I concerns problems in social role functioning, Factor II notes problems emanating directly from the environment, Factor III refers to mental health, and Factor IV addresses physical health. Unlike the DSM, Factors I and II are the primary focus, although a problem need not be identified for every factor and each factor need not be limited to one core problem. Factor I problems in social role functioning are specified by type of relationship (e.g., control/power, conflict/ambivalence, responsibility, dependence, loss, victimization), severity, duration, and ability to cope. Factor II problems emanating from the environment and affecting social role functioning include difficulties with employment, education, legal/judicial systems, health/welfare, community participation, and social networks (see Chap. 2 for additional discussion of PIE).

PIE has never been widely used, however. Most practitioners found it cumbersome and difficult to master; moreover, insurance companies have never recognized its categories—despite Karls and Wandrei's optimistic prediction that "in the future, when the third party reimbursement system is less oriented toward the disease model, it is hoped that practitioners will be reimbursed for services provided to ameliorate social role and environmental problems" (Karls and Wandrei 1992, p. 85).

Environmental and relational problems have never been billable, whether coded under the PIE system, Axis IV, or as V codes. That does not mean there are no ways to get help for problems in living. People whose difficulties come to the attention of the school system, justice system, or welfare system may be able to receive services through those avenues, since they are supported by funding sources that do not require the "medical necessity" of a psychiatric label.

The dilemma that clinical social workers face is not about problems that are clearly environmental, such as inadequate housing, nor about problems that are clearly neuropsychiatric, such as traumatic brain injury. It lies in the "gray zone" when ecological stressors are *precipitants* of mental or emotional dysfunction: The problem is environmental in origin, and psychological in manifestation. How, then, should the situation be conceptualized: Is a client's shame, dread, and hopelessness about poverty, abuse, isolation, or unemployment a *mental* disorder or an *environmental* problem? While social workers may prefer to say it is both, the system in which they do their work may compel them to say it is one or the other.

The Role of Social Context

As noted in previous chapters, a classification system is useful only insofar as it is valid and reliable. The *principles* used to establish its categories need to be sound and the *categories* need to be clear, with minimal overlap or ambiguity, so people will use them in the same way. Otherwise, the system is not much help for structuring decisions and improving the accuracy of clinical judgment.

Classification of mental disorder can be compromised several ways. If people with different problems are placed in the same category, the meaning of membership in that category is undermined and there is low *validity*. Someone might be erroneously given a diagnostic label when something other than mental dysfunction can account for the observed symptoms (a false positive), or be denied membership in an appropriate category for a trivial reason or because of missed information (a false negative). There is low *reliability* when experts cannot agree on which people qualify for a particular disorder or on the category to which a particular individual belongs. Sources of error can lie in the clinician (e.g., bias or lack of training), the client (e.g., withholding information), the assessment "event" (e.g., constraints of time or location that lead to the collection of misleading or incomplete information), or the categories themselves (e.g., ambivalent criteria).

The whole point of a *psychiatric* diagnosis rests on the ability to distinguish behavior that is genuinely pathological, stemming from internal dysfunction, from behavior representing a reaction to an adverse environment. Otherwise, problems in living can be incorrectly classified as mental disorder (Wakefield 2005). But how can one tell? The notion of equifinality (many causes can lead to same effect) means that a symptom might be a result of mental dysfunction *or* a reasonable reaction to, or perhaps a way to cope with, an adverse environment. With its emphasis on observation (*what*—the symptoms) and eschewal of interpretation (*why*—the cause), the DSM, as a system, does not offer a clear way to distinguish between true mental disorders and problematic person–environment interactions.

Adhering to DSM principles, if factors other than internal pathology can account for the person's behavior, then mental disorder must be ruled out. It is not so easy to isolate the effect of environmental factors, however, since people do not live in experimental conditions. We cannot take two equivalent groups of people and deliberately vary their environmental stressors! We can, however, vary the *infor-mation* about environment that is available to the clinician in order to see whether having more information changes the diagnostic decision. Kirk and Hsieh's (2004) study sought to do just that to see whether knowing about ecological stressors enables clinicians to disconfirm the presence of authentic mental disorder or, when disorder is present, to distinguish among plausible alternatives.

Kirk and Hsieh mailed a case vignette to a nationally representative sample of 1500 mental health clinicians, systematically varying the amount of information provided. Responses to the vignette clearly indicated that experienced clinicians reached different conclusions about the presence of a DSM diagnosis depending on the information they had about the social context of the person's behavior. Those who read the symptoms-only version of the case were more likely to give a diagnosis of conduct disorder, while those who read the environmental-reaction vignette were more likely to use adjustment disorder or no disorder at all.

Kirk and Hsieh's findings suggest that the likelihood of experienced clinicians reaching a similar diagnostic decision (reliability) is significantly altered when the social context of the behavior changes. This underscores the importance of obtaining information about a client's circumstances in addition to simply noting symptomatology, and "shatters the illusion that diagnostic judgment can simply be a matter of matching presenting symptoms with DSM criteria without the need to account for the social context" (p. 51).

The assessing clinician must continue to ask: What information is missing about the source and context of this problem? What don't I know about this case? What else might be happening? How can I find out?

Note: "Social context" is used above to refer to problematic aspects of the environment that can lead to negative responses such as hostility or withdrawal. Clearly, there are also positive aspects of the environment that can serve as pro-tective factors, foster resilience, provide a sense of belonging, and offer hope.

The Role of Culture

In order for an emotion, perception, sensation, or experience to be translated into a "symptom," it has to be culturally interpreted. Once a sensation has been noticed, it must be evaluated in terms of its *normalcy* (whether it is typical for the individual, based on prior experience, and/or for members of the person's social or cultural group) and its *severity* (its impact on comfort and functioning) to see whether it signifies deviance (Saint Arnault and Shimabukuru 2011). The evaluation will differ, depending on sociocultural expectations.

Given the degree to which behavioral dysfunction and mental distress are cul-turally shaped, as well as the increasing diversity of contemporary society, it is important for clinical assessment to be culturally sensitive. Cultural sensitivity includes awareness of a group's history and relationship to the dominant culture along with awareness of its customs and values. A "culture" can refer to a location, historical tradition, or set of shared beliefs, as in religious cultures that may be geographically dispersed.

Many authors (e.g., Barrera and Jordan 2011) have questioned the DSM's capacity to correctly diagnose clients from cultural groups that were not included in the research on which the validity of DSM criteria rests—for instance, when women from poor, non-Western, and racial minority populations are diagnosed with eating disorders using criteria developed from studies of middle-class Anglo-European women (Walcott et al. 2003). People from non-Western cultures may interpret what the Eurocentric perspective calls "mental health problems" in spiritual, somatic, relational, or other culturally sanctioned terms. Behavior that is normative for one population is then wrongly conceptualized into the psychiatric criteria of another population, leading to misdiagnosis.

The same is true for conclusions about willingness to enter and adhere to treatment. Some cultural groups may prefer coping strategies that stress reliance on family and indigenous sources of support, consider mental health terminology so stigmatizing that it is only applied to the most extreme cases, or seek treatment only if behavior disrupts social harmony (Snowden 2003). Barrera and Jordan thus urge a rewording of the DSM statement about the *importance* of taking cultural context into account into a *requirement* to do so.

Various methods have been proposed to support and structure culturally based assessment. DSM-IV, for example, included a "Cultural Formulation Outline" that encouraged clinicians to inquire about a client's cultural identity, differences between client and therapist, cultural variation in the expression of affect, and cultural explanations for the causes of mental illness. Like Axis IV, however, there was no requirement to use the outline, so it is unclear how widely it was actually utilized. In DSM-5, the outline was expanded into a 16-question protocol, the "Cultural Formulation Interview." Specific questions are suggested to guide the clinician in eliciting the client's cultural definition of the problem; perceptions of cause, context, stressors, and supports; cultural factors affecting past experience of coping and seeking help; and factors affecting current help-seeking including barriers, preferences, and concerns about the clinician–patient relationship. Twelve supplementary modules are also offered (Explanatory Model; Level of Functioning; Psychosocial Stressors; Social Network; Cultural Identity; Spirituality, Religion, and Moral Traditions; Coping and Help-Seeking; Patient–Clinician Relationship; Immigrants and Refugees; School-Age Children and Adolescents; Older Adults; and Caregivers) (see http://www.psychiatry.org/practice/dsm/dsm5/online-assessment-measures).

In both editions of the manual, these cultural guides are placed in an appendix, a location that "may cause practitioners to overlook these important tools, especially if practitioners are not trained to take ethnicity and culture into consideration when diagnosing" (Barrera and Jordan 2011, p. 276). When diagnostic criteria and cultural considerations are presented separately—one in the main body of the manual, the other in an appendix—rather than integrated into a single system, cultural meanings may seem to be a secondary add-on, the mere tweaking of Eurocentric categories. This is reflected, Barrera and Johnson suggest, in the way students are taught. Surveying the syllabi and course descriptions of 200 MSW programs accredited by the Council on Social Work Education, they found that only 11 % offered a DSM course that explicitly addressed culture or diversity. While diversity may be highlighted in other courses focusing on policy or social justice, it was not integrated into courses on clinical diagnosis.

Other authors have critiqued the DSM's glossary of culture-bound syndromes, intended to "describe the psychopathology typical in non-dominant-culture ethnic groups" (Dadlani et al. 2012, p. 176). While they agree that cultures have different ways of thinking and talking about mental distress, they object to the "othering" and ethnic stereotyping promoted by a glossary. Suite et al. (2007) use the "culture-bound" condition of *ataque de nervios* as an example of what they call the "superficial stereotyping of an entire national group" and the transformation of a "customary experience into a serious mental health problem with an eccentric location" (p. 881).

Proclaiming that particular cultures have particular mental illnesses can foster an erroneous assumption of cultural homogeneity—the presumption that one has adequately understood an individual simply by learning about his or her group. This can also mask important distinctions between cultural categories. Barrera and Jordan (2011) offer the example of *susto*, *espanto*, and *miedo* in Mexican-American communities, three distinct conditions that are often conflated by outsiders. Although sharing a common origin, each term represents a specific experience of increasing intensity and level of suffering.

Another difficulty, as Saint Arnault and Shimabukuru (2011) note, is that most studies of mental disorder have relied on Western-derived measures that fail to capture the relevant indicators and meanings for people of other cultures. Flexible protocols are needed, they urge, that can elicit various forms of culturally relevant information from people with a range of backgrounds. Their Clinical Ethnographic Interview (CEI) is an effort to convert the DSM topic list into a structured yet flexible and ethnographically sensitive protocol. A unique feature of the CEI is the inclusion of nonverbal assessment tools since, its authors maintain, "the full and subtle exploration of the social, emotional, and physical experiences of people from vastly different cultures requires methods that do not rely on abstractions and verbal analysis" (Saint Arnault and Shimabukuro 2011, p. 303).

The CEI provides opportunities for interviewees to describe their emotional and somatic experience in culturally relevant nonverbal terms. "The interview style used in most mental health clinical encounters in the United States, which is based on cultural values of explicit verbal expression, abstract concepts, and logical expla-nation, is not typical for many cultural groups" (p. 310). A word-based protocol cannot convey what the illness experience means to someone from a culture that does not rely on abstraction, logic, and language. Instead, the CEI situates assessment in local context by using culturally meaningful referents and exercises. Nonverbal assessment methods such as creation of a social network map, a body map to show where and how symptoms are experienced, or a lifeline allow for concrete embodied description that may be more syntonic with cultural forms of expression.

Dadlani et al. (2012) offer several additional tools. Arguing for inclusion of social identity as part of the DSM-5 cultural protocol, they provide Patient and Clinician Social Identity Assessments. These instruments include questions about the experience of discrimination, stigma, systemic oppression, and exposure to social structures based on implicit privilege. An Intersectionality and Diagnosis Worksheet highlights the influence of membership in more than one marginalized social identity. Suite et al. (2007) suggest adding a historical dimension to assessment, especially for clients who are members of oppressed groups, in order to understand the temporal context that shapes ideas about distress, illness, and help. Historically sensitive mental health assessment can "decrease patient-clinician misunderstanding and yield greater precision in diagnostic and prognostic judgments" (Suite et al. 2007, p. 879).

Like Barrera and Jordan, Dadlani et al. call for the repositioning of culture as central to the diagnostic process. Clinicians as well as clients need to reflect on their cultural identities, they maintain, since this affects what they notice about their clients, how they communicate, and how they understand and interpret clients' experience. Culturally competent assessment includes the client, the clinician, and the therapeutic dyad itself. To this end, they offer several principles for enhancing culturally sensitive diagnosis.

First, all patients, even those belonging to the dominant culture, have social identities and are affected by cultural positioning, not merely a subset of clients who are members of marginalized groups. Second, multiple social identities are experienced simultaneously and intersectionally so that no one belongs to only one group; the clinician must endeavor to understand which identities are most significant for each client and how these identities relate to each other. Third, clinicians also have cultural and social identities that influence diagnostic choices; self-assessment is critical for identification of ethnocentric bias. Fourth, clinicians must facilitate open discussion with clients including experiences of privilege and oppression in the therapeutic relationship itself.

The Role of Race, Class, and Gender Bias

The Nature of Bias Bias is an unwarranted opinion or reaction on the basis of perceived membership in a single category, ignoring other attributes and categories to which the person may belong; biased views can be held knowingly or unknowingly. In diagnosis, bias exists when clinical judgment varies as a function of factors extrinsic to the diagnostic criteria themselves, such as gender or race.

As Garb (1997) is careful to point out, bias occurs when the *accuracy* of clinical judgment varies, not when prevalence varies. It is possible that certain conditions may, in fact, be more likely among certain groups; that is variation, not bias. It is an unfortunate fact, for example, that an incarcerated male in the USA is likely to be a person of color, but that does not mean there is an intrinsic or direct relationship between skin color and criminal behavior. Bias occurs when intermediate links such as poverty or racism are omitted and a nonexistent direct relationship is presumed. Nor is bias the same as awareness of cultural differences.

> Taking account of racial and ethnic differences does not in itself constitute bias. Indeed, some critics argue that … appropriate treatment necessitates awareness of critical differences between minority individuals and others in beliefs and sensitivities related to mental health, in expression of symptoms, and in treatment preferences. From this perspective, to ignore racial and ethnic differences reflects a kind of bias (Snowden 2003, p. 239).

Citing the work of Lopez, Snowden (2003) notes that there are two kinds of bias, with opposite effects. *Overpathologizing* occurs when unfamiliar behavior is incorrectly interpreted as a manifestation of mental illness, while *minimization* occurs when real mental illness symptoms are ignored and attributed to cultural beliefs—typically by those who do not understand those beliefs. While disparities in diagnostic labels, access to treatment, continuity, completion, and quality of care are well documented, it is difficult to know the extent to which these disparities are due to bias nor the impact of bias in specific cases. Most of what we know comes from examining trends and patterns.

Bias can accrue through multiple layers of public policy, program administration, and individual practitioner. The effect of cumulative bias is clearly depicted, for example, in a 2014 report examining over 200,000 court cases in New York City from 2010 to 2011. The Vera Institute of Justice found a pattern of racial disparity at multiple stages of the criminal justice process. Reasons for this disparity are cumulative and complex. When prosecutors offer a plea bargain, they consider prior arrests, a standard practice that is seemingly race-neutral. Yet black men are more likely to come from heavily policed neighborhoods where even minor arrests are commonplace. A judge, seeing a previous arrest on the defendant's record, may be "primed" to regard him as a lawbreaker and a poor candidate for a plea bargain, thus falling prey to the confirmation bias that perpetuates racial injustice (http://www.vera.org/sites/default/files/resources/downloads/race-and-prosecution-manhattan-summary.pdf).

Studies of the impact of bias on clinical judgment are of two kinds. In field studies, therapists' decisions are analyzed as they go about their work in order to identify variance in diagnosis that is not accounted for by actual measures of psychopathology in their clients (i.e., the degree of psychopathology is controlled for). In analogue studies, a case vignette is given to different groups of clinicians but systematically varied along a dimension of interest in order to isolate its effect. For example, when gender is being studied, some clinicians will be told that the client to be diagnosed is male, others that the client is female. That way, the impact of gender on clinical judgment can be isolated, since everything else about the case is the same. While an analogue approach can yield elegant designs, as in Loring and Powell's (1988) five-group study of the effects of gender and race, this does not necessarily reflect real-world practice where a host of interlocking factors, rather than isolated demographic variables, can reinforce or mitigate the impact of the others.

As noted previously, bias can arise from a variety of sources. *Diagnostic* bias occurs when criteria are more valid for one group of clients than another, leading to misdiagnosis among groups for whom criteria were never tested or validated. *Clinician* bias occurs when clinicians attend only to information that supports the ideas they already have about a person or group, or assume that certain clients are more credible than others—for example, when the reports of clients who are male or middle-class are presumed to be more trustworthy than the reports of other clients. *Clients* themselves may foster bias by exaggerating or withholding information because of distrust, a desire to appear "sicker" or "healthier," or a wish to please the therapist by saying what they believe the therapist wants to hear.

Race Bias A recent *The New York Times* review (January 3, 2015) offers a wealth of empirical evidence for the independent effect of racial bias in areas such as employment, housing, and health care. One example is provided by Bertrand and Mullainathan's (2004) experimental study of discrimination in the labor market. In this study, researchers mailed fictitious resumes to "help-wanted" ads in Boston and Chicago newspapers. To isolate the effect of perceived race from other factors such as education and economic status, resumes were randomly assigned African-American- or White-sounding names but were equivalent in all other respects. Resumes with "white" names were 50 % more likely to result in callback for an interview than resumes with African-American names, a clear indication of the effect of race whether conscious or unconscious.

Neighbors et al. (1989) provide an insightful overview of how race can influence the diagnostic process with regard to mental disorder, noting that racial bias can operate in contradictory ways. Some studies in their meta-review indicate that black clients and white clients exhibit symptoms in *similar* ways, but diagnosticians interpret these symptoms differently. In these instances, clinicians assign different diagnoses to each group, typically assigning more serious diagnoses to clients of color. Epidemiological studies indicate, for example, that clients of color are more likely to receive diagnoses of schizophrenia and less likely to receive diagnoses of affective disorders than white clients (Garb 1997; Snowden 2003). Refusal to respond is interpreted as a sign of psychosis in one client, a sign of depressed mood in another.

Other studies indicate the opposite pattern—the two groups are expressing the same internal pathology but doing so in *different* ways, with clinicians failing to realize their common origin. For example, a person of color experiencing deep anxiety may externalize that anxiety through boasting and bravado; to a white clinician, this may not "look like" anxiety. The behavior is, incorrectly, taken as a sign of a narcissistic or antisocial personality disorder, justifying the negative stereotype that led to the racially-based error in the first place.

Empirical studies have also found that clients of color disclose significantly less to white therapists than to therapists of similar backgrounds. Because of their experience being stereotyped, marginalized, silenced, and coerced, many clients of color distrust the mental health system and those who represent it (Suite et al.

2007), thus withholding important information and inadvertently contributing to misdiagnosis.

Class Bias Many studies have examined the impact of economic stress and intergenerational poverty on mental disorder. It is no surprise that the deprivation and hopelessness of chronic poverty can affect mental and emotional well-being. Socioeconomic status can also affect the way a condition is *named*. This is especially true when there is "social distance" or privilege disparity between the person giving the label and the person receiving it. When the "disordered" individual occupies a lower social status than the person observing and naming the behavior, the probability of a negative interpretation increases; conversely, those with higher social status are more likely to be protected from negative responses by alternative labels such as "eccentric millionaire" (Avison et al. 2007).

Interestingly, Temerlin made the same observation nearly half a century ago. Citing a 1958 study by Hollingshead and Redlich, Temerlin commented: "The same behavior may be considered evidence of mental illness when it occurs in a member of the lower socio-economic classes and personal idiosyncracy in a member of the upper class" (Temerlin 1968, p. 352).

Gender Bias Diagnostic rates also vary by gender, particularly in the selection of specific personality and affective disorders (Garb 1997). Women are more likely to receive diagnoses of internalizing conditions such as depression and eating disorders, and men more likely to receive diagnoses of externalizing conditions such as conduct disorder and antisocial personality disorder (Eriksen and Kress 2005). As noted above, however, not all variation represents bias. It is only bias if factors other than the diagnostic criteria themselves are used to place someone in a particular category—that is, if men and women with the same symptoms are given different labels. If women express emotional pain differently than men because of different sociocultural conditioning, that is gendered learning, not bias.

An example of gender bias, although it has now been reconceptualized in DSM-5, is the unequal way that diagnostic criteria were formulated and applied for Gender Identity Disorder in DSM-IV. As Zucker (2006) points out, boys are more likely to be referred for gender incongruence than girls due to greater social acceptance of gender-nonconforming behavior in females. A girl who prefers stereotypical "boy's" clothing and games is less likely to be flagged for evaluation than a boy who prefers "girl's" clothing and toys; girls must also display a higher threshold of cross-gender behavior than boys before they meet diagnostic criteria. Zucker notes that this is the *only* diagnosis in DSM-IV for which criteria are differentiated by biological sex. For boys cross-dressing only needs to be a "preference," while for girls it must entail "insistence on wearing only stereotypical masculine clothing" with "marked aversion toward normative feminine clothing." Boys must also express an "aversion toward rough-and-tumble play and rejection of male stereotypical toys, games, and activities," but there is no similar requirement for girls to conform to this kind of socially constructed stereotype. (This disorder has been reconceptualized in DSM-5, as noted, and thus the disparity in entry criteria by gender may not persist.)

Interactional Effects More than one form of bias may be present, each augmenting the others through their intersectionality—that is, the mutual relationships among social identities. Identities that carry status and privilege tend to reinforce each other, as do identities that decrease status and privilege. For example, in their analysis of eight epidemiological surveys encompassing over 22,000 respondents, Kessler and Neighbors (1986) found that the impact of race and class on diagnoses is interactive as well as additive. In other words, in addition to the distinct effect of each factor, there is a third effect produced by their interaction. At the time their research was conducted, it was widely believed that race was not an independent determinant of psychological distress or the way it was named but, rather, served as a proxy for socioeconomic status. People assumed that poverty rather than skin color accounted for bias; equalize economic status, they believed, and race would have no effect. Kessler and Neighbors saw it differently, arguing that the "attempt to pit race and social class against each other as alternative predictors of distress" (p. 107) masked the true effects of racism. Race is important even when social class is held constant, they pointed out, although effects are especially pronounced among people of low income. That is, class exacerbates the impact of race. In other instances, gender and class may intersect, or gender and race.

(For a more comprehensive analysis of the role of bias in clinical decisions, see Caplan and Cosgrove's *Bias in Psychiatric Diagnosis* 2004.)

The Role of Relationships: Are There "Relational Disorders"?

A family or couple may be struggling, as a system, with dysfunctional patterns that impair the fulfillment of life tasks and goals. Is the relationship disordered, or are the individuals disordered? Can individuals be mentally healthy while the relationship, as an entity, is disordered?

"Relational disorders" are persistent and painful patterns of interaction and emotional response involving two or more individuals in an important personal relationship (Denton 2007). They can occur between partners or siblings, between parents and children, among all members of an intergenerational family system, and among members of other systems such as employer and employees. Past or ongoing relational dysfunction can be the primary presenting problem; it can also be important for understanding the dynamics or management of another condition. For instance, other people can become incorporated into the reinforcement of depression or anxiety, thus becoming part of a self-perpetuating cycle that sustains the disorder. Many clinicians who might hesitate to endorse "relational disorders" as distinct diagnostic categories nonetheless agree that a diagnostic system that provided guidance about when to address relationship-based difficulties, or when to use relational interventions to improve outcome for individual disorders, would have great clinical benefit (Beach et al. 2006).

Relational problems such as conflict, rejection, abandonment, betrayal, and abuse are often the very issues that prompt people to seek help, and thus offer a potent target of intervention (Lebow and Gordon 2006). These issues can be listed as V codes, but V codes are not billable—as noted many times in this book—so some other condition, located in the individual, must be cited if insurance coverage is sought. Ironically, as Lebow and Gordon point out, the DSM allows for difficulty *forming* relationships to be a marker of disorder (as in social anxiety disorder or autism) but not for difficulty *occurring* in relationships, even if those relationship patterns are quite pathological (as in inter-partner violence). Again, in the dominant diagnostic system, the problem needs to lie within the individual. This has led to the formulation of categories such as Masochistic or Self-Defeating Personality Disorder—eliminated from DSM-5, but present in earlier editions—that shifted responsibility for dysfunctional interactions onto the victim whose "disordered" personality was at fault for attracting, choosing, and tolerating the negative relationship.

The absence of a category for "relational disorders" creates a dilemma for social workers. While there is a strong body of family theory research and family therapists *do* treat all members of a relational system, someone must still be "the sick one." This may seem a technicality, a matter of paperwork, yet the person carrying the patient role is at a clear disadvantage. Having a psychiatric diagnosis on record can become significant later during custody battles, applying for a job, or seeking security clearance.

As Kaslow noted as early as 1993 and as more recent research has confirmed (e.g., Probst 2013), therapists' inability to cite a relational diagnosis, at least if insurance coverage is sought, can place them in an ethically difficult position. They may feel pressured to skew their understanding of the problem in order to serve those who seek help but are not wealthy enough to forgo a DSM diagnosis and self-pay. Some may try to circumvent the problem by billing first under one person and then under the other, yet this may misrepresent the clinical situation.

> If the therapist submits one or several different diagnoses for individual family members, he or she experiences great discomfort over misrepresenting what the problems being addressed and the treatment methodology really are—perhaps also committing insurance fraud and violation of his or her own professional code of ethics (Kaslow 1993, p. 196).

While there may be compelling reasons to legitimize relational disorders, there may be equally compelling reasons *not* to do so. One difficulty, as Lebow and Gordon (2006) note, is that there is no empirically validated conceptual framework for relational disturbance. Given the complexity of *all* relationships, establishing valid and reliable criteria for "disordered" relationships is a daunting task. According to what measures and by what means would a relationship be deemed "disordered"? If assessed by self-report, do all involved have to agree on the presence, nature, and severity of the disorder? What if they don't? If assessed by behavioral measures, what would those be, and who would determine the cutoff point where a relationship becomes dysfunctional?

The challenge of expanding the notion of mental disorder to include "relational disorder" is not easily resolved. Interpersonal difficulties, no matter how bad, are not illnesses, even though their effects can be at least as devastating and pervasive as disorders said to reside in the individual. As Wakefield, Kirk, and others have argued, the notion of "mental disorder" should not be applied to conditions that are due to social or environmental factors. We cannot have it both ways. If it is inappropriate to pathologize problems in living, then it is also inappropriate to pathologize problems in relating.

Including Relational Disorders in the DSM As early as the 1970s, when DSM-III was in preparation, family therapists have advocated for inclusion of relational diagnoses as stand-alone disorders, viewing them as real and useful ways to conceptualize the problems of many of their clients (Kaslow 1993; Kaslow and Patterson 2006). When work groups were being formed for DSM-IV, family therapists hoped their time had finally come. A coalition of 15 family therapy organizations joined together in a coordinated effort to convince the American Psychiatric Association to include relational disorders in the new manual. As the coalition noted in its 1988 statement, by excluding problems stemming from disturbed relational patterns, the DSM was embracing an a priori theoretical assumption that these are not "real" disorders, even though they represent clinically significant syndromes associated with distress, disability, or dysfunction—just as individual diagnoses do. The whole aim of the third and fourth editions of the manual was to create an atheoretical system, in contrast to the psychoanalytic nature of DSM-II; why, then, adopt the rigid theoretical position that disorder must be an individual condition?

Frances et al. (1984) proposed a different solution, arguing for an independent Axis VI to capture family classification and family pathology when problems of the family system are the appropriate unit of analysis. This new axis, Frances maintained, could measure dimensions of family interaction such as communication, negotiation, conflict, affectivity, control, boundaries, and expressed emotion, as well as charting family patterns and disturbances across generations. Research has shown that factors such as "expressed emotion" in family interactions are predictive of relapse in patients with schizophrenia—a clinically important feature that could not have been captured by individually oriented criteria. After all, Frances pointed out, there is "no reason to believe that the particular five axes chosen for DSM-III are the most useful ones or that additional axes will not find their way into future systems" (p. 407). Why not add an axis to account for family functioning, if that can enrich clinical understanding?

Nonetheless, the DSM-IV task force rejected the coalition's request for inclusion of relational disorders, stating that research on relational problems was insufficient to support reliable guidelines for assessment or to tie relational processes to diagnostic outcomes (Beach et al. 2006). Empirical research, the task force members concluded, "had not yet reached the point of being able to set thresholds for severity that would enable practitioners to identify 'cases'" (Kaslow and Patterson 2006, p. 429)—although the same could be said for most individual disorders. When a subsequent work group, commissioned to evaluate gaps in DSM-IV in preparation for the manual's fifth edition, cited the limited provision for relational disorders as one of the two most important gaps that needed to be addressed (Denton 2007), many hoped that DSM-5 would correct this deficiency. That did not happen, however; the editors of DSM-5 took a different turn.

Meanwhile, considerable research has been conducted on relational disorders, yielding a substantial empirical foundation to connect relational processes to specific mental disorders and diagnostic outcomes (Kaslow and Patterson 2006; Beach ct al. 2006). Validated instruments have been developed for assessing the presence and degree of various kinds of relational dysfunction, together with a comprehensive handbook. In an effort to create a more systematic way of describing relational diagnoses, Beach et al. propose a matrix of relational issues organized along two core dimensions, each implying a different means of inclusion in a diagnostic system. *General* relational processes can be defined without reference to other disorders, in their own section or on their own axis. In contrast, *specific* relational processes may be relevant for some disorders or in certain instances, and thus would be better noted in the context of "standard" disorders as a specifier or modifier, much as specifiers for severity or degree of insight are already used in DSM-5.

Impaired Attachment as a Relational Disorder Many believe that people "are hardwired to seek out attachment, and relational processes will always be an essential part of the human experience" (Denton 2007, p. 1146). Early attachment theorists such as Bowlby and Mahler were interested in understanding how children attach to their caregivers. More recently, research has focused on the consequences of missing or damaged attachment. Authors from diverse backgrounds, writing about children in a range of settings where they lacked selective attachment from a consistent caregiver, have identified similar patterns of behavior. There is now "sufficient evidence that the attachment disorder concept describes 'real' and distinct clinical entities severe enough to warrant clinical attention" (O'Connor and Zeahnah 2003, p. 225).

The hallmark of an attachment disorder is its etiology—a curious departure from the DSM principle that cause does not matter. In the description of Disinhibited Social Engagement Disorder, "pathogenic care" (the behavior of *other* people) is specifically cited as the cause of the disturbed behavior that constitutes the symptoms of the disorder, present in the *child*. Examples of pathogenic care include persistent failure to meet the child's basic emotional needs for comfort, stimulation, and affection; persistent harsh punishment or other types of grossly inept parenting; and repeated changes of primary caregiver that limit opportunities to form stable attachment. The disorder is defined by its cause, yet the unfortunate victim of someone else's "pathogenic" behavior is the one receiving the psychiatric diagnosis. As noted in previous chapters, it is bad science to "include the existence of a putative cause in the list of diagnostic requirements" (O'Connor and Zeahnah 2003, p. 226).

Other features of attachment disorder include its manifestation across situations and relationships; it cannot be relationship specific and thus may be seen in a child's difficulty attaching to peers as well as to caregivers. To avoid false positives, it is important to distinguish between attachment disorder and other conditions, such as an attempt to preserve ego-integrity in the face of trauma and abuse, or normal temperamental variation in sociability that can manifest as reticence or shyness (see Chap. 6).

Assessing for Attachment Disorder O'Connor and Zeahnah review several methods for determining whether an attachment disorder is present. One method is observation, such as the use of Ainsworth's "strange situation" to assess attachment in young children. However, there is no protocol for children at various stages of development, nor is there consensus about how severe or pervasive the behavior needs to be in order to constitute impairment. For observation to be a useful tool for assessment, reliable measures are needed for evaluating parent–child interactions in more naturalistic settings. Other methods include parent interviews and written questionnaires, helpful for determining the history and consistency of behavior, and the study of children's representational models through doll play or other projective techniques. Little information is available, however, on the convergence of information from these various methods. Because we do not know whether information gathered through different channels is consistent, we cannot know whether the assessment tools are reliable or valid.

An additional concern is that attachment disorder is usually assessed by asking *other* people, not the person experiencing the disorder; this is the case with many childhood disorders, defined in terms of relationship dysfunction *as perceived by adults*. For example, there is a new disorder in DSM-5 called disruptive mood dysregulation disorder. "Disruptive" prompts the question: disruptive to whom? Is the child the one with the problem? Or is the problem transactional, a poor fit with the caregiver's temperament or an environment that is temperamentally inappropriate for that particular child? If attachment disorder is a form of relational disorder, it cannot be one-sided.

A parallel question might be posed about assessing attachment disorder in adults; in this case, they would be the ones providing direct answers about their own experience, yet the criteria in use pertain only to children. Is it possible to develop additional criteria that would be valid for adults with impaired attachment? Presumably the effects of insufficient or ruptured attachment persist into adulthood. Would they constitute an adult version of a distinct "attachment disorder," or are they captured in the symptomatology of other conditions that develop out of this crucial missing experience? Certainly, a client's attachment patterns—such as avoidance, ambivalence, neediness, and self-sabotage—could be a fruitful area of investigation.

Conclusions

This chapter has explored the many ways in which the *experience* of disorder—in contrast to the more generic *concept* of disorder—is always situated and local. An assessment cannot simply be the comparison of a person with a prototype to see whether classification is warranted. It must also encompass all the contexts in which the person is embedded: cultural, historical, socioeconomic, and relational. These intersecting contexts shape the meaning and impact of the disordered condition, as well as the whole notion of what mental "illness" or mental "wellness" entails and depends on. Some of these contexts are specific to the individual, while others reflect broad sociocultural forces such as racism and ethnocentrism. Taken together, they offer the possibility of a deeper, richer understanding of our clients' lives and a corresponding possibility of multiple avenues for intervention.

Application to the Case of Ray

Like every client, Ray's story is situated in a particular place, time, and social context. A white heterosexual male, Ray is a member of several privileged groups; his upbringing in an intact, middle-class, English-speaking family offered protection from stressors due to poverty and oppression. At the same time, there seems to have been an underlying sense of being different from those around him: adopted, the only child of quiet older parents, Irish in an Italian neighborhood, the only one of his peers—as far as he knew at the time—to be singled out by the priest. Aware of his privileged status but not *feeling* privileged, Ray was beset with doubt and insecurity from an early age.

While not a victim of race, class, or gender bias, he was nonetheless affected by gender stereotypes. Messages from multiple social systems, both tacit and overt, told him what it meant (or ought to mean) to be male. His story can be seen as a response to the cultural narrative of male strength and invulnerability. Clearly, his childhood experience of being bullied and sexually abused did not fit this portrait of maleness; so too, Ray could not reconcile abuse by a priest with the beloved Church that formed such an important part of his family life. These irreconcilable contradictions led to secrecy, self-blame, and defenses such as overcompensation. His disclosure of the abuse, first to the therapist and then to his father, was a significant moment, yet his rejection of a support group can be seen as a continuing reluctance to expose this vulnerable self to male peers.

The theme of contradiction permeates Ray's life. On the one hand, as a police officer he belongs to a group embodying power and authority. On the other hand, he does not experience himself as powerful. The motto of the police force "to protect and to serve" seems to suit him, yet he feels unable to protect, rescue, or save others—just as no one protected him when he was a child. This sense of failure is devastating, partly because of his childhood history but also because of social expectations that first responders should and *can* save the helpless. The events of 9/11 only exacerbated these micro and macro pressures, reactivating Ray's prior trauma (not being protected) and reinforcing the feeling of having failed his occupational duty (not protecting others). It is likely that he is also experiencing doubt and conflict among his social roles. As a father, he wants to protect his children yet has "abandoned" them by leaving the family; he has also "requested" Cecelia's three abortions while being aware that his own existence, as an adopted child, was the result of a different choice. Father, son, partner, wage earner—none of these social roles seem completely fulfilling or "right" to him.

The events in Ray's life also need to be viewed in regional, historical, and political context. It is striking, for instance, that his disclosure of childhood abuse came at a time when media attention was revealing, for the first time, the scope of sexual abuse by priests. There is no way to know, of course, when or how or whether his disclosure might have taken place if the social context were different, but certainly the timing is significant. So too, the "selection" of symptoms can be seen as culturally constructed. Aggression and violence were "safe" symptoms that did not challenge the narrative of maleness. It is possible that Ray, like many victims of traumatic abuse, also experienced a degree of dissociation—a splitting-off of the unacceptable (weak) aspects from the preferred identity (strong). It was only when this split could no longer be maintained that the barrier crumbled, feelings "overwhelmed" him, and he sought escape.

There is still much we do not know about Ray's situation. We are told that he serves as a volunteer firefighter and belongs to a softball team, so it appears that he has found replacements for the male camaraderie that he formerly found among members of his precinct. However, as a police officer on medical leave, we know little about his occupational or financial situation. Are his disability benefits sufficient, or is he experiencing economic stress? How long can he expect to receive support? Will he be terminated, reinstated, or will he be able to seek other employment? Nor do we know where he lives, how he relates to his community, his current relationship to the Catholic Church, his relationship with his children, or how he feels about the possibility of finding another romantic partner. Ecological resources, social capital, and other components of person-in-environment are also important aspects of assessment.

Practical Exercises

1. Imagine you are a client meeting a new therapist. What would you want the clinician to know about your social location and cultural positioning in order to understand you better? Identify at least one aspect of your socioeconomic, ethnic, or cultural/geographic context that, if overlooked or misunderstood, might lead to an incorrect assessment. How might that take place?
2. What are your beliefs about why people become sick and what is necessary for healing to occur? What kinds of knowledge do you base your views on? What

forms of knowledge do you believe have little worth? How might your views be disproven?

3. Think about a relationship that you would consider "disordered." This can be a relationship you have personally experienced or witnessed, or a relationship depicted in a book or film. If you could create a "relational diagnosis" for this kind of disorder, what would you call it? What would the criteria be?

References

Alperin, R. M., & Hollman, B. C. (1992). The social worker as psychoanalyst. *Clinical Social Work Journal, 20*(1), 89–98.

Avison, W. R., McLeod, J. D., & Pescosolido, B. A. (Eds.). (2007). *Mental health, social mirror*. New York: Springer.

Barrera, I., & Jordan, C. (2011). Potentially harmful practices: Using the DSM with people of color. *Social Work in Mental Health, 9*, 272–286.

Beach, S. R. H., Wambolt, M. Z., Kaslow, N. J., Heyman, R. E., & Reiss, D. (2006). Describing relationship problems in DSM-V: Toward better guidance for research and clinical practice. *Journal of Family Psychology, 20*(3), 359–368.

Bertrand, M., & Mullainathan, S. (2004). Are Emily and Greg more employable than Lakisha and Jamal? A field experiment on labor market discrimination. *American Economic Review, 94*(4), 991–1013.

Bishop, D. V. M. (2008). Autism and diagnostic substitution: Evidence from a study of adults with a history of developmental language disorder. *Developmental Medicine and Child Neurology, 50*(5), 341–345.

Buchbinder, E., Eisikovits, Z., & Karnieli-Miller, O. (2004). Social workers' perceptions of the balance between the psychological and the social. *Social Service Review, 78*(4), 531–552.

Caplan, P. J., & Cosgrove, L. (Eds.). (2004). *Bias in psychiatric diagnosis*. Lanham MD: Jason Aronson.

Dadlani, M. B., Overtree, C., & Perry-Jenkins, M. (2012). Culture at the center: A reformulation of diagnostic assessment. *Professional Psychology: Research and Practice, 43*(3), 175–182.

Denton, W. H. (2007). Issues for DSM-V. Relational diagnosis: An essential component of biopsychosocial assessment. *American Journal of Psychiatry, 164*(8), 11146–11147.

Erikson, K., & Kress, V. E. (2005). *Beyond the DSM story: Ethical quandaries, challenges, and best practices*. Thousand Oaks CA: Sage.

Frances, A., Klarkin, J. F., & Perry, S. (1984). DSM-III and family therapy. *American Journal of Psychiatry, 141*, 406–409.

Garb, H. N. (1997). Race bias, social class bias, and gender bias in clinical judgment. *Clinical Psychology, Science and Practice, 4*(2), 99–120.

Goldstein, E. (2009). The relationship between social work and psychoanalysis: The future impact of social workers. *Clinical Social Work Journal, 37*, 7–13.

Hollis, F., & Woods, M.E. (1981). *Casework: A psychosocial therapy*. McGraw-Hill: New York.

Janchill, M. P. (1969). Systems concepts in casework theory and practice. *Social Casework, 15*(2), 74–82.

Karls, J. M., & Wandrei, K. E. (1992). PIE: A new language for social work. *Social Work, 37*(1), 80–85.

Kaslow, F. (1993). Relational diagnosis: Past, present, and future. *American Journal of Family Therapy, 21*(3), 195–204.

Kaslow, F., & Patterson, T. (2006). Relational diagnosis—a brief historical overview. *Journal of Family Psychology, 20*(3), 428–431.

Kessler, R. C., & Neighbors, H. W. (1986). A new perspective on the relationships among race, social class, and psychological distress. *Journal of Health and Social Behavior, 27*, 107–115.

Kirk, S. A., & Hsieh, D. K. (2004). Diagnostic consistency in assessing conduct disorder: An experiment on the effect of social context. *American Journal of Orthopsychiatry, 74*(1), 43–55.

Kirmayer, L. J. (2005). Culture, context and experience in psychiatric diagnosis. *Psychopathology, 38*, 192–196.

Lebow, J., & Gordon, K. C. (2006). You cannot choose what is not on the menu—obstacles to and reasons for the inclusion of relational processes in the DSM-V. *Journal of Family Psychology, 20*(3), 432–437.

Loring, M., & Powell, B. (1988). Gender, race, and DSM-III: A study of the objectivity of psychiatric diagnostic behavior. *Journal of Health and Social Behavior, 29*, 1–22.

Mazama, A. (2001). The Afrocentric paradigm: Contours and definitions. *Journal of Black Studies, 31*(4), 387–405.

Neighbors, H. W., Jackson, H. S., Campbell, L., & Williams, D. (1989). The influence of racial factors on psychiatric diagnosis: A review and suggestions for research. *Community Mental Health Journal, 25*(4), 301–311.

O'Connor, T. G., & Zeanah, C. H. (2003). Attachment disorders: Assessment strategies and treatment approaches. *Attachment and Human Development, 5*(3), 223–244.

Probst, B. (2012). Living with and living within: Visions of "environment" in contemporary social work. *Qualitative Social Work, 12*(5), 689–704.

Probst, B. (2013). "Walking the tightrope:" Clinical social workers' use of diagnostic and environmental perspectives. *Clinical Social Work Journal, 41*(2), 184–191.

Probst, B. (2014). The life and death of axis IV: Caught in the quest for a theory of mental disorder. *Research on Social Work Practice, 24*(1), 123–131.

Rogge, M. E., & Cox, M. E. (2001). The person-in-environment perspective in social work journals: A computer-assisted content analysis. *Journal of Social Service Research, 28*(2), 47–68.

Saint Arnault, D., & Shimabukuru, S. (2011). The clinical ethnographic interview: A user-friendly guide to the cultural formulation of distress and help seeking. *Transcultural Psychiatry, 49*(2), 302–322.

Schiele, J. H. (1996). Afrocentricity: An emerging paradigm in social work practice. *Social Work, 41*(3), 284–294.

Shattuck, P. T. (2006). The contribution of diagnostic substitution to the growing administrative prevalence of autism in U.S. special education. *Pediatrics, 117*(4), 1028–1037.

Snowden, L. R. (2003). Bias in mental health assessment and intervention: Theory and evidence. *American Journal of Public Health, 93*(2), 239–243.

Suite, D. H., La Bril, R., Primm, A., & Harrison-Ross, P. (2007). Beyond misdiagnosis, misunderstanding, and mistrust: Relevance of the historical perspective in the medical and mental health treatment of people of color. *Journal of the National Medical Association, 99*(8), 879–885.

Temerlin, M. K. (1968). Suggestion effects of psychiatric diagnosis. *Journal of Nervous and Mental Disease, 147*(4), 349–353.

Tosone, T. (1998). Revisiting the "myth" of feminine masochism. *Clinical Social Work Journal, 26*(4), 413–426.

Walcott, D. D., Pratt, H. D., & Patel, D. R. (2003). Adolescents and eating disorders: Gender, racial, ethnic, sociocultural, and socioeconomic issues. *Journal of Adolescent Research, 18*(3), 223–243.

Wakefield, J. C. (1996). Does social work need the eco-systems perspective? *Social Service Review, 70*, 1–30.

Wakefield, J. C. (2005). Disorders versus problems of living in DSM: Rethinking social work's relationship to psychiatry. In S. A. Kirk (Ed.), *Mental disorders in the social environment: critical perspectives* (pp. 83–95). New York: Columbia University Press.

Williams, J. B. W., Karls, J. M., & Wandrei, K. (1989). The person-in-environment (PIE) system for describing problems of social functioning. *Hospital & Community Psychiatry, 40*(11), 1125–1127.

Zucker, K. J. (2006). Commentary on Langer and Martin's (2004) how dresses can make you mentally ill: Examining gender identity disorder in children. *Child and Adolescent Social Work Journal, 23*(5–6), 533–555.

Chapter 6
Neuroscience, Resilience, and the Embodiment of "Mental" Disorder

Eric L. Garland and Elizabeth Thomas

Abstract The transdiagnostic perspective described in this chapter focuses on the core neurocognitive processes that underpin and cut across a broad array of psychosocial disorders. Beginning with a discussion of stress, cognitive appraisal, and adaptation, chapter authors demonstrate how a downward spiral of stress, negative emotion, biased cognition, and maladaptive coping can disrupt the normal healthy functioning of brain and body and result in the maladaptive patterns that underlie a range of mental disorders. Each of the processes that contribute to this downward spiral is explored in depth: automaticity, attentional bias, memory bias, interpretation bias, and thought suppression. An analysis of resilience follows, indicating a pathway for a corrective "upward spiral" that draws on the broaden-and-build theory in which positive emotions broaden individuals' repertoires of cognition, affective response, and behavior through adaptive neuroplasticity and thereby build lasting internal resources. The chapter then explores the neurobiological evidence for the role of mindfulness in enabling individuals to extricate themselves from the stress reaction by facilitating cognitive reappraisal and responding with less emotional distortion and cognitive bias. It concludes by suggesting that a transdiagnostic approach can offer an effective means of case conceptualization and selection of targeted, actionable, and effective interventions.

Keywords Allostasis · Allostatic load · Attentional bias · Automaticity · Bio-psycho-social · Broaden-and-build theory · Cognitive bias · Eustress · Interpretation bias · Memory bias · Mindfulness · Neuroplasticity · Psychosocial genomics · Reappraisal · Resilience · Transdiagnostic

E.L. Garland (✉) · E. Thomas
College of Social Work, University of Utah, Salt Lake City, UT, USA
e-mail: eric.garland@socwk.utah.edu

© Springer International Publishing Switzerland 2015
B. Probst (ed.), *Critical Thinking in Clinical Assessment and Diagnosis*,
Essential Clinical Social Work Series, DOI 10.1007/978-3-319-17774-8_6

Introduction: Why This Matters

The bio-psycho-social model remains a core foundation of social work theory and practice, providing a framework with which to understand the factors that contribute to functional impairment and the development and maintenance of psychological suffering (hereafter in this chapter termed as *disorder*[1]). First articulated by physician George Engel, this model implies that health and illness arise from interdependent relations between biological, psychological, and social factors (Engel 1977). The bio-psycho-social model therefore informs etiological understanding, while also providing the clinician with a broader understanding of the course, prognosis, and clinical outcome of a disorder. This model was a significant advance from the reductionism of the dominant biomedical model of Engel's era, which posited that mental disorders were the result of brain abnormalities stemming from a fundamentally flawed genetic structure. In contrast, Engel's model facilitated a much more nuanced, holistic clinical perspective that acknowledged the enormous variability in the expression of disorders within the larger population and the role of learning, culture, and psychosocial factors in the genesis and course of a given disorder for particular individuals. Despite the precision, utility, and integrative focus of the bio-psycho-social model, diagnosis within the field of mental health has been focused primarily on gross taxonomic categorizations of illness (implicitly grounded in the biomedical model) based on myopic descriptions of the differences between symptomatic expressions of disorders.

In contrast, recent advances in neuroscience indicate that a transdiagnostic perspective (explicitly grounded in the bio-psycho-social model) that focuses on the processes underpinning a broad array of psychosocial disorders may not only be possible, but may also be a more effective means of case conceptualization and selection of targeted, actionable, and effective interventions (Garland and Howard 2014). Further, scientific discoveries in neuroplasticity and psychosocial genomics over the last decade have provided empirical evidence that both validate and elaborate upon the bio-psycho-social paradigm and a transdiagnostic approach to diagnosis and social work practice. These discoveries also demonstrate the validity of other hallmarks of social work theory and ethics, including the perspective that humans are inherently resilient and that, through experience and learning, positive change is possible throughout all stages of human growth and development, even at the neurobiological level.

---

[1]We are adopting the term disorder to represent a higher order category that subsumes various forms of interpersonal and intrapersonal suffering, involving disruptive changes in cognition, emotion, physiology, and social interactions that prevent adaptive functioning. Our use of this term is found on the Merriam-Webster definition of the transitive verb: *v)* meaning to disturb the regular functions of. We wish to distinguish our use of the term form the standard psychiatric definition, which implies the presence of a static disease entity stemming from genetically driven structural brain abnormalities.

Guiding Questions

1. Are there common processes that underlie a broad range of psychosocial problems?
2. Can the practice of positive reappraisal contribute to lasting changes in affective dispositions over time?
3. Can the experience of positive emotions counter self-destructive cycles?
4. Can psychotherapies produce neurobiological effects?
5. What are the mechanisms of mindfulness?
6. Can a shift toward an etiologically focused transdiagnostic process better facilitate targeted treatment plans?

Stress and Coping

The concepts of stress and adaptation are central to the bio-psycho-social model. Life is a dynamic process, characterized by constant change and challenges that necessitate continual adaptation to the social and natural environment in order to meet the demands of day-to-day living. Adaptation to changes or challenges in the environment results in a stress reaction when the individual determines the event to be critical to their well-being and yet to exceed their coping resources (Lazarus and Folkman 1984). This process of interpreting the meaning of an event, called *appraisal*, is central to stress and adaptation in humans.

The Stress Reaction The stress reaction involves a myriad of psychophysiological effects that have been termed the "fight-or-flight" response (Cannon 1939). Biologically, this occurs through an activation of two primary neuroendocrine stress response systems, the sympathetic adrenal–medullary (SAM) axis and the hypothalamic–pituitary–adrenal (HPA) axis (Herman and Cullinan 1997). Both systems are driven by the amygdala and the hippocampus brain regions involved in emotional processing and associations (Rauch et al. 1998). The SAM, in particular, is activated automatically without a conscious appraisal of threat or available resources to respond to that threat, prompting the adrenal glands to release both epinephrine and norepinephrine (Compas 2006). These chemicals result in an increase in heart rate, respiration, blood flow, and blood pressure, as well as a decrease in digestive activity, all of which facilitate improved capacity for self-defense through the marshaling of physical resources (Compas 2006). In more familiar terms, this is the surge of adrenaline that happens within a matter of seconds to provide immediate energy to meet the stressor. Corticosteroids produced through the activation of the HPA axis in response to stress appraisal comprise the second phase of the stress response and will be described in greater detail later on. These biological processes are accompanied by a sequence of cognitive, emotional, and behavioral responses integral to stress and coping (Folkman and Moskowitz 2000; Lazarus and Folkman 1984).

Without an accompanying appraisal of personal relevance to well-being (i.e., whether or not an event is "bad for me"), an encounter with the environment will not be perceived as stressful.

Think, for example, of the difference between running from a grizzly bear and running toward the finish line at a marathon. Both are challenging physically, but there is a distinct difference in the level of actual threat to the individual. Yet, it should be noted that perceived threats have just as much potential to induce a stress response as an actual threat. Referring back to our example, while for most people, finishing a marathon might not be an event that is appraised as a threat, for individuals present when the bomb was detonated at the 2012 Boston marathon, a running race might be stress-inducing. Stress, therefore, is contextual, and is the product of individual appraisal of a mismatch between the demands of the external environment and one's needs, resources, and abilities (Lazarus and Folkman 1984).

Cognitive Stress Appraisal Appraisal itself involves two processes. Lazarus and Folkman (1984) posited that first a primary appraisal of an event initiates the stress process based on evaluation of the event's threat value. When an event is appraised as threatening or harmful, psychological distress and physiological arousal arise. In contrast, if the event is appraised as a challenge, that is, demanding yet surmountable, rather than threatening to well-being, physiological arousal may occur without accompanying psychological distress. Next, a secondary appraisal process ensues in which an individual evaluates their capacity to meet the demands of the threat or stressor, and when a determination is made that the demands exceed personal, familial, or collective resources, a bio-psycho-social stress reaction will result. At this point, an individual may utilize either problem-focused or emotion-focused coping efforts in order to deal with the stressor (Lazarus and Folkman 1984). If the individual appraises the stressor as resolvable, he or she may make a strategic attempt to manage the stressor using problem-solving techniques.

Returning to our grizzly bear example, if you encountered an aggressive grizzly bear in the woods, your first appraisal would be that you were in a threatening situation. If, however, you were carrying bear spray or were able to jump into your SUV and drive away, your secondary appraisal would be that you had the resources to effectively deal with the threat and a subsequent bio-psycho-social stress reaction would be adverted as a problem-solving technique was utilized. If, however, the stressor is appraised to be unresolvable, emotion-focused coping is used to manage the distress. Emotion-focused coping consists of the use of cognitive strategies to regulate one's emotional responses to a stressor.

For instance, one might engage in *positive reappraisal*—reframing the meaning of a stressful event in such a way as to see that event as growth promoting or meaningful. Some individuals who survived the Boston marathon bombing engaged in positive reappraisal when they realized that surviving the horrific event had taught them to cherish their families and feel loved by those who cared for them in the aftermath of the bombing. Positive emotions result from successful problem- or emotion-focused coping, whereas negative emotions intensify when stressors cannot be resolved through either form of coping. While all emotions can serve adaptive functions depending on the circumstances surrounding their occurrence and expression, negative emotions such as anger, fear, and sadness can become a source of dysfunction when they are exacerbated and prolonged by maladaptive cognitive processes, behaviors, and social interactions (Garland et al. 2010).

Socio-environmental Stressors The appraisal process, then, is primarily responsible for resultant experiences of stress. However, environmental factors that multiply the frequency of necessary appraisals and the use of available resources can have a cumulative effect that increases the likelihood of future negative appraisals and subsequent stress. Modern society presents an environment characterized by tremendous advances in technology, urbanization, globalization, and secularization. While there are advantages to these modern developments, at the same time, they also contribute to significant demands on the individual that result in increasing levels of stress. For example, technological advances have enabled near constant multitasking, which has led to relentless pressures and demands on time (Monideepa et al. 2007). Urbanization has largely contributed to profound shifts in social organization and family life that have reduced availability and access to social support (Marsella 1998). Globalization has resulted in catastrophes such as international economic crises, conflicts, wars, pandemic disease, and natural disasters, which are rendered continually present to the individual through 24-hour media coverage and the effects of these events on an economically interdependent world. Secularization has, in many cases, removed a significant source of meaning, purpose, and direction that historically has provided a framework to bolster coping and provide a higher existential purpose in the face of stress and suffering. These modern-day challenges are compounded by an impending ecological crisis, economic recession, and the struggles of daily living that imbue the social environment with ubiquitous and inevitable stressors.

Resilience Fortunately, the deleterious *consequences* of stress are not inevitable. Stressors can be present in an individual's life without accompanying persistent bio-psycho-social stress. When this occurs, we refer to the individual as being *resilient*, that is, having the ability to adapt well to changes or challenges within the environment (Block and Block 1980; Block and Kremen 1996; Lazarus 1993). Being resilient does not imply an absence of stressors or emotional pain. On the contrary, resilient individuals experience stressors but are especially able to "bounce back" from these events and experience psychological growth as a result of encountering them (Tugade et al. 2004). Resilience is developed through a combination of external protective factors such as family functioning, financial resources, and social status, as well as internal traits and processes such as temperament, cognitive coping ability, and emotion regulation skills (Richardon 2002). For resilient persons, stress can have a positive effect on performance and productivity, as well as on personal growth. This type of stress has been termed eustress, which literally means "good stress," which was first named by endocrinologist Selye (1974). Some individuals, however, are more vulnerable to the cumulative effects of stress and are less able to cope due to the inequities of poverty, oppression, and social disparities that they may already face. Some may also lack cognitive–emotional resources in consequence of a myriad of compounding stressors and thereby experience distress, or "bad stress," which can subsequently lead to the development of mental or physical disorders. Natural disasters demonstrate how an event can have dramatically different effects on people depending on the way the event is cognitively appraised and the individual's level of resilience.

During Hurricane Katrina, for example, some of those who were affected were able to recognize the things that mattered most in life in spite of losing their material possessions, drawing closer to their families and friends as a result. Others were devastated by the disaster due to the compounding effect of Katrina on the existing stressors in their lives. Such individuals might not have had the luxury of not worrying as much about basic physical survival and safety and may have had a harder time finding a sense of meaning in the face of adversity, making "bouncing back" from such a tragic event extremely difficult.

Mental Disorder as a Downward Spiral of Stress, Emotion, and Maladaptive Coping

Stress and Emotion The experience of stress is an inevitable part of life due to the continually changing demands that life presents to each individual. However, acute and chronic distress has the potential to negatively influence all levels of emotional well-being (Gottlieb 1997; Connor-Smith et al. 2000). In this way, extreme or prolonged stress can precipitate psychological suffering and manifest in disruptions in functioning that are often labeled as mental disorders. Stress impacts affective traits, moods, and emotions (Rosenberg 1998; Fredrickson 2001). Affective traits are stable predispositions that include personality features such as pessimism, optimism, or neuroticism (Rosenberg 1998; Fredrickson 2001). Moods and emotions are transient affective states, rather than traits. Moods occupy an intermediate level between traits and emotions, and while they fluctuate throughout the day, they last longer than emotions (Lazarus 1991; Rosenberg 1998). Emotions, on the other hand, are the most brief and fleeting of the affective phenomena, but they are also the most acute and intense and are comprised of the interaction of subjective feeling states, patterns of brain activation, changes in autonomic, visceral, and peripheral physiology, facial expressions, body posture, and cognitive and behavioral repertoires (Rosenberg 1998; Fredrickson 2001; Garland et al. 2010). For example, the experience of fear involves neural, cardiovascular, endocrine, and muscular changes that produce the urge to fight, flee, or freeze (Canon 1939). Emotions, as interdependent response patterns, have been naturally selected and evolutionarily conserved over time to support appropriate and efficient responses to recurrent opportunities and threats within the environment.

Downward and Upward Spirals of Emotion The modern science of emotion (or *affective science*) reveals that emotions can develop into self-perpetuating systems that operate to maintain and maximize their own organization through interdependent relationships between cognitive, behavioral, and physiological mechanisms. In other words, emotions are not merely feelings, but also involve thoughts, action tendencies, and bodily responses that influence one another to produce an emotional experience; for example, the emotional experience of fear involves distressing thoughts, emotions, and body sensations. Emotions are both generated and maintained through dynamic interactions between these mechanisms. In this way, emotional systems are characterized by positive feedback loops—in other words, the outputs of the system (e.g., fearful behavior like running away) subsequently become the inputs of the same system (e.g., increased heart rate and the thought "I'm in danger so I've got to get out of here!"), driving the system toward greater and greater intensity (Bateson 1972).

Anxiety, for instance, tends to co-occur with ruminations about the past or worry about the future, coupled with avoidant behavior and somatic symptoms such as tension, nausea, restlessness, sweating, flushing, heart palpitations, and shortness of breath. These various co-occurring components of anxiety can produce subsequent feelings such as fear about the ways in which anxiety interferes with one's ability to function at work or interact appropriately in social situations. This leads to further avoidance, which contributes to the development of emotion-consistent appraisal tendencies that reinforce or increase fears about the future or ruminations about the past by increasing the attention given to external cues that match current emotional states, as well as leading to interpretations of new experiences that fortify negative beliefs about oneself and the world (e.g., the belief "The world is a dangerous place and I am helpless"). This cycle becomes a downward spiral that can become both debilitating and self-destructive, manifesting in patterns of maladaptive thoughts, feeling states, and behaviors that are then labeled "mental disorders" (Garland et al. 2010). Conversely, positive emotions are also self-perpetuating and can increasingly lead to optimal functioning, and therefore may result in upward spirals that increase the likelihood of continued positive emotional experiences (Garland et al. 2010). It is important to note that downward and upward spirals are fundamentally different in several important respects. Downward spirals involve narrowed focus on the self and defensive behaviors that contribute to limited or rigid social interactions. Upward spirals, on the other hand, broaden one's focus beyond the self, increase openness to others, and are characterized by more behavioral flexibility, which will be described in greater detail later in the chapter.

Neurobiological and Neurocognitive Aspects of Downward Spirals At the neurobiological level, negative emotions prompted by acute stress and trauma stimulate the hypothalamic–pituitary–adrenal (HPA) axis, which is the central coordinator of the neuroendocrine stress response system, leading to abnormal regulation of cortisol levels, a key stress hormone implicated in physical illness and mental disorder (Chrousos and Gold 1992; Rosmond 2005). Concurrently, when the HPA axis is stimulated, the hippocampus and prefrontal cortex tend to be inhibited, while the amygdala is activated (Sherin and Nemeroff 2011). These neurobiological adaptations enable ready access to the biological resources neces- sary to respond to an environmental stressor (Talarico et al. 2004; Schmitz et al. 2009). Physiologists refer to this neurobiological process as *allostasis*, or stability through change (McEwan and Wingfield 2003; Sterling and Eyer 1988). However, when stress is chronic or an external stimulus is traumatic, a sustained activation of the HPA and related pathways develops, which can impair necessary executive functions and the capacity to appropriately discriminate threats within the envi- ronment. If stressful stimuli persist, or if allostatic processes fail to disengage, self- regulatory mechanisms are no longer able to continue adapting to the environment, resulting in an allostatic load, a "wear and tear" on brain and body systems that contributes to both the generation and acceleration of disease processes (McEwan and Wingfield 2003; Sterling and Eyer 1988). Sustained cortisol exposure has adverse effects on hippocampal neurogenesis (Sapolsky 2004), or the generation of new neurons which, as studies show, is important for learning, growth, and change (Sherin and Nemeroff 2011). The HPA also communicates with the rest of the body through the autonomic nervous system (ANS), which is divided into two main branches: the sympathetic and the parasympathetic nervous systems. The sympa- thetic nervous system is activated in response to a threat and prepares the body for flight or fight by increasing blood pressure, heart rate, and breathing rate, as well as slowing down digestion (Brading 1999; Jänig 2008). The parasympathetic nervous system, on the other hand, is activated when an individual perceives that he or she is safe, which allows the body to rest and to save energy. The pulse rate slows, blood pressure decreases, and digestion can resume (Brading 1999; Jänig 2008).

The neurobiological adaptations to stress and trauma that have been described disrupt the body's normal functions in an effort to create stability in response to external threats (Bandura 1991). This can lead to increased sensitization to future stressors, which ultimately results in cognitive biases to stress-related cues—that is, to people, places, and things that are related to the stressor (Mathews and MacLeod 2005; Mineka et al. 2002). Cognitive biases are patterns of perception and thinking based on preexisting beliefs, experiences, and emotions. When people become biased toward stress and threat, they find their attention captured by and fixated on signs of future threat such as an angry face on a passerby or the shadow in an alleyway when walking down the street alone at night (e.g., Macleod et al. 1986). Cognitive biases also produce emotionally consistent appraisals that cause a person to interpret new experiences through the lens of past negative experiences and distress (Garland et al. 2010). For example, one might hold the appraisal that other people do not like them, causing feelings of sadness, loneliness, and potentially even anger. As they go about their day, if they pass someone in a hallway who does not acknowledge them, they interpret this as a confirmation that that person does not like them. They then isolate from others, perpetuating their belief and negative emotions, which become increasingly more rigid over time.

This example demonstrates that when repeated over time, negative appraisals gradually develop into long-lasting and even rigid beliefs about oneself and the surrounding world. These negative beliefs increase the likelihood of repeated experiences of distress, as well as socially-isolating tendencies toward thoughts and actions that lead to the weakening or loss of relationships. The resulting isolation increases emotional distress, and in the absence of effective ways of coping, people often turn to maladaptive coping behaviors. Maladaptive coping is rooted in cognitive distortions such as rumination or catastrophizing, in which one repeatedly obsesses over and exaggerates threats while devaluing one's ability to manage that threat (DeLongis and Holtzman 2005). This harmful cognitive process sets the stage for fear-avoidant withdrawal and the use of addictive negative coping behaviors such as substance abuse, self-harm, binge eating, workaholism, compulsive use of internet or social media, and sexual addictions (Hatcher 1989; Weinstein and Lejoyeux 2010).

Taken together, the bio-psycho-social factors described above outline a process whereby acute and chronic stress can initiate and propel a downward spiral of negative emotion and biased cognition, which can disrupt the normal healthy functioning of brain and body and result in maladaptive or self-destructive behavioral patterns. This process likely underpins the bewildering array of psychiatric disorders described by the DSM. Although each disorder may appear distinct on the surface, they are underpinned by a common set of cognitive, affective, and physiological processes. This "deep structure" of transdiagnostic (i.e., cutting across different diagnoses) processes has been studied extensively by modern psychology and neuroscience (Garland and Howard 2014).

Case Conceptualization with an Actionable Treatment Plan and Interventive Techniques

There are five key transdiagnostic processes to be explored in the case conceptualization process, which researchers have discovered through utilizing a wide array of performance-based behavioral tasks, neuroimaging techniques, and neuroendocrine measures paired with subjective self-report tools. These key processes include automaticity, attentional bias, memory bias, interpretation bias, and thought suppression. In order to illustrate the role of these key processes in the development and perpetuation of disorders, we will include examples of each, drawing on a variety of mental health conditions.

Automaticity The first process, automaticity, refers to actions that are executed without conscious volition or often even awareness due to repetitions that have created conditioned responses to environmental stimuli (Bargh and Chartrand 1999; Schneider and Chein 2003). While automaticity is pragmatic in many ways, it can also become the source of dysfunction when it drives negative coping behaviors, addictive cycles, or distorted thinking habits. Automaticity is the default mode in the absence of intentionality and focused awareness, but is also increased when the stress response is activated, due to neurobiological changes that inhibit conscious decision-making (Dias-Ferreira et al. 2009). For soldiers who have experienced repeated indirect fire from mortars or artillery while in combat, automaticity that was once functional in deployed environments can become maladaptive once they return home and without thinking, they seek cover in response to loud noises in their environments. Many veterans who develop posttraumatic stress disorder also develop negative coping behaviors such as alcohol or substance abuse in order to seek relieve from persistent stress responses that are no longer warranted.

Attentional Bias People cannot possibly attend to all the stimuli within their environment; hence, emotionally significant stimuli receive preeminence during information processing and thereby tend to govern behavior (Desimone and Duncan 1995). This is referred to as attentional bias, which creates motivation toward certain objects or behaviors that are pleasurable and away from objects and behaviors that are aversive (MacLeod et al. 1986; Friedman and Förster 2010). Attentional bias, therefore, is associated with craving and is evident in persons with addictive disorders (Field et al. 2009). Research demonstrates that people tend to focus their attention on objects and events that are congruent with their current mood state, resulting in a cycle that reinforces their mood and increasingly biases their attention toward objects and events that are consistent with their mood, which over time can result in changes to stable states or personalities (Mathews and MacLeod 2005). Attentional bias has been identified as a component of a number of addictive cycle disorders. For example, attentional bias has been demonstrated among opioid dependent chronic pain patients whose attention is automatically and involuntarily captured by opioid-related cues, such as photographs of pills (e.g., Oxycontin, Vicodin), pill bottles, and syringes, which is significantly associated with opioid craving and may promote addictive behavior (Garland et al. 2013).

Memory Bias It is obvious to anyone who has discussed childhood memories with siblings that memory is not necessarily an accurate representation of the past. People who share common experiences often remember those experiences very differently. This is primarily due to the fact that memories are shaded by individual perceptions held at the time of the past event, as well as by current emotional states that add retrospective or "backward" shading (Mayer et al. 1995). Events and experiences that are congruent with one's current emotional state are recalled more easily and thus memory may be biased by emotion. For example, individuals in a depressive episode exhibit a memory bias toward loss, pain, and regret and an overgeneralized synopsis of past events rather than specific details (Williams et al. 2000). Memory bias is particularly problematic when memories of past frightening events initiate a stress response that is out of proportion to the current situational context. For example, if an individual was bitten by a dog as a child, phobic anxiety may develop around any dog, even when the dog is not actually a threat.

Interpretation Bias Closely related to memory bias is the transdiagnostic process of interpretation bias, which fuels maladaptive beliefs by leading a person to misconstrue evidence in ways that confirm these beliefs as actual truths. Uncertainty is unavoidable in life, which generates cognitive dissonance or contradictory beliefs or values, which then require appraisal to be resolved. Appraisal, as we have been discussing, is rooted in past experiences that create patterns of interpretation of uncertain or ambiguous events that reinforce beliefs and ways of making meaning. Interpretation bias is exhibited in tendencies to interpret ambiguous events negatively. For example, individuals with social anxiety disorder tend to interpret neutral facial expressions as hostile (Mathews and MacLeod 2005).

Thought Suppression The final key transdiagnostic process is thought suppression, which is an effort to not think about an unwanted experience as a means of coping. Paradoxically efforts to suppress thoughts actually increase the accessibility of the unwanted thought to consciousness (Wegner et al. 1987; Wenzlaff and Wegner 2000) through an unconscious monitoring process that searches for mental content that is inconsistent with the desired state. In this way, thought suppression results in an increase in the number or intensity of unwanted thoughts and feelings (Wegner and Erber 1992). Binge-eating disorder is an example of the paradoxical effect of trying to suppress thoughts related to food, wherein efforts to not think about food result in increased cravings and urges to eat that ultimately lead to binge-eating behavior.

Resilience as a Malleable Phenomenon

Resilience is a malleable phenomenon that can be enhanced through mindfulness and reappraisal. While chronic stress and negative emotions can drive the transdiagnostic processes underpinning psychopathology, positive emotions can serve as a buffer against stress and reduce its deleterious effects. Positive emotional states, although often fleeting, when experienced recurrently can trigger lasting changes in the brain that promote the development of durable positive traits and bolster adaptive thoughts and behaviors central to resilience.

Broaden-and-Build Theory of Positive Emotions To explicate how fleeting positive emotions can accrue into durable psychosocial resources, social psychologist Barbara Fredrickson proposed the broaden-and-build theory of positive emotions (Fredrickson 1998, 2003, 2009). Fredrickson's theory explores the interactions between transient emotional states and the development of enduring affective traits and suggests that positive emotions broaden individuals' repertoires of cognition and behavior and thereby build lasting social, psychological, and physical resources. The theory, in part based on evolutionary psychology, holds that negative emotions that narrow the scope of attention and thought in order to focus on the immediate threat may have aided human ancestors in their survival against predators and were therefore evolutionarily adaptive. Positive emotions, on the other hand, broaden one's scope of attention, enabling greater behavioral flexibility and a wider range of thoughts and ideas, as well as reducing urges to fight or flee.

Over time, this expanded mindset enables the incremental accrual of durable psychosocial resources and the capacity to honor desired actions that lead to enhanced well-being.

For example, increased behavioral flexibility and perspective is conducive to the development of meaningful and supportive relationships. Those who experience positive emotions are less likely to negatively interpret the behavior of others and are more likely to ascribe positive intent to actions. This develops and strengthens relationships, which promote additional positive emotions and positive personality traits over time. Hence, repeated experiences of hedonic well-being, or the experience of pleasurable emotions, can lead to a lasting eudaemonic well-being, or the achievement of meaning and self-realization, which is achieved through valued and purposeful living, social connectedness, and a sense of fulfillment gained through striving to reach one's potential.

Adaptive Neuroplasticity The question, then, is whether or not states and traits that have been developed through these transdiagnostic processes can be changed, even well into adulthood. Previous to 1998, it was widely believed that, unlike the brains of infants and children which are characterized by plasticity (the capacity of being molded or changed), the adult brain was fixed and unalterable due to established neuronal connections. However, neuroscientists have since discovered that neurogenesis, the growth of new neural tissue, continues in the brains of adults throughout their lifetime (Eriksson et al. 1998). Neurogenesis occurs through exposure to novel sensory experiences or by learning new behaviors and skills through physical practice and mental exercises (Eriksson et al. 1998). The genesis of new neural tissue is driven by changes in gene expression (Mundkur 2005). Recent research in psychosocial genomics (Rossi 2002), or what has been more recently termed neuroepigenetics (Sweatt 2013), indicates that psychological and social experiences impact the expression of genes as proteins and neural structures. In this way, novel psychological and social experiences (including stress and learning) are also able to activate or deactivate genes, which then stimulates the development of new or strengthened neural pathways (Garland and Howard 2009; McCutcheon 2006). While the genetic code continues to serve as a "blueprint" during gene expression, signals from the internal and external environments influence and modulate this process, creating substantial variability in psychosocial experience (Eisenberg 2004). The discovery of neuroplasticity thus lends support to the perspective that humans are inherently resilient and can grow and change even in the face of adverse life experiences.

Mindfulness as a Form of Mental Training Just as physical exercise builds muscle tissue, neuroplasticity researchers have demonstrated that brain tissue can be developed through mental training (Pascual-Leone et al. 2005). For instance, taxi drivers in London have been shown to have larger hippocampi, perhaps the result of tens of thousands of hours learning the network of routes throughout the city (Maguire et al. 2000). Mental training focused on challenging negative thinking and strengthening positive emotions, such as that which is provided by psychotherapy, may also foster neuroplasticity (Kandel 1998). As one such example, structural magnetic resonance imaging of the brains of patients with chronic fatigue syndrome indicates that 8 weeks of cognitive–behavioral therapy can increase gray matter concentration in parts of the brain involved in memory and attention (de Lange et al. 2008). One type of mental training that may be capable of stimulating neuroplasticity is mindfulness meditation. Although it has ancient contemplative roots, mindfulness meditation emerged in the Western world as a psychological intervention in the late 1970s and has become an evidence-based treatment as a result of a number of rigorously controlled clinical trials conducted on specific treatments such as mindfulness-based stress reduction (Kabat-Zinn 1994) and mindfulness-based cognitive therapy (Segal et al. 2002). Indeed, a recent meta-analysis of randomized controlled trials demonstrates that mindfulness-based interventions can significantly reduce psychological distress (Goyal et al. 2014).

Mindfulness as State, Trait, and Practice   There are three forms of mindfulness, and it is important to highlight the distinctions between them. Mindfulness can be a state, a trait, or a practice. Mindfulness as a *state* involves metacognition, which is awareness of the process of cognition or thinking rather than just the products and content of that process (Kabat-Zinn 2003). To illustrate this concept, in the mindfulness traditions, thoughts are often metaphorically compared to clouds passing by in a clear blue sky. In this analogy, however, the clouds are the products or content of cognition, while metacognition involves expanded awareness of the space of the sky they are passing through, the space of observing awareness. In other words, mindfulness is a state that allows an individual to "step back" from thoughts and observe them without reaction. In turn, the psychological space afforded by the state of mindfulness allows one to dis-identify from his or her thoughts and recognize that thoughts are merely fleeting mental experiences that are not necessarily valid or true.

Access to the mindful state can be developed through the recurrent practice of mindfulness meditation, which involves intentionally focusing attention on present moment experience in a nonjudgmental way (Kabat-Zinn 2003). With continued intentional practice over time, one can access the state of mindfulness more readily and more deeply (Bishop et al. 2004), such that eventually the individual becomes a more mindful person in everyday life even when not meditating. Thus, the state of mindfulness, when engaged recurrently through mindfulness practice, can accrue into the *trait* of mindfulness (Davidson 2004; Garland et al. 2010), characterized by the tendency to be nonjudgmental, nonreactive, and attentive to sensory and emotional experience and aware of one's automatic tendencies (Baer et al. 2006).

This link between state and trait mindfulness is supported by a host of neuroscientific studies that show that training in mindfulness can lead to lasting changes in brain function (Holzel et al. 2011), and perhaps even more notably, in brain structure. In that regard, research has demonstrated that participation in 8 weeks of mindfulness training is associated with increases in gray matter concentration in brain regions associated with the regulation of attention, emotion, and self-awareness (Holzel et al. 2012). Such neuroplastic changes might underlie the cultivation of trait mindfulness through the *practice* of evoking the state of mindfulness during meditation, a practice that is known to reduce stress and enhance coping.

Mindful Coping with Stress The mechanisms through which mindfulness reduces stress and improves coping capacity have been conceptualized through the Second-Order Cybernetic Model of Stress (Maturana and Varela 1987), which holds that mindfulness enables individuals to extricate themselves from the stress reaction by facilitating cognitive reappraisal of the stressor. Whereas the primary stress response is based on automatic appraisal of threat or harm, mindful reappraisal allows one to consciously reframe and respond to difficult life events with less emotional distortions and cognitive bias. In traditional cognitive–behavioral therapy, reappraisal of stressful events is achieved through confronting and challenging one's distorted, overly negative, or unhelpful ways of thinking (Beck et al. 1979). However, this can be difficult to do in the moment of distress, given that psychophysiological stress reactions limit the executive functioning required to dispute distorted thinking. Mindfulness-based approaches to reappraisal (see Garland 2013) are distinct in that they disrupt habitual ways of thinking while broadening attention and awareness of sensory and perceptual experience (Holzel et al. 2011), which in turn increases access to new information with which a reappraisal can be formulated to reduce emotional suffering (Garland and Fredrickson 2013). This is achieved through a process of psychologically "stepping back" from stress appraisals into an observing state in which negative thoughts and emotions are seen as fleeting and not necessarily accurate reflections of reality. The result of this process is a reduction in catastrophizing, relief from psychological distress, and the realization that meaning is created and ascribed to a situation rather than inherent (Shapiro et al. 2006). In turn, this realization allows the individual to position himself or herself outside their narrative about the stressful event and, in so doing, to reappraise the stressor in a more positive and adaptive way. Ultimately, mindful reappraisal may make possible the selection of new narratives or life stories that engender eudaimonic meaning, resilience, and the sense of purpose in life (Garland and Fredrickson 2013).

Conclusions

As this chapter has indicated, recent advances in neuroscience suggest that there are a number of core processes that underlie a range of psychiatric disorders. Thus, rather than continuing to devote time and resources to refining what is presumably *distinct* about each condition in order to devise an ever-more perfect nosology and find a precise classification for each client, it may be more fruitful to turn in a different direction. The transdiagnostic perspective looks behind and below these apparent differences, illuminating the fundamental processes that give rise to a broad array of clinical presentations. This shift in focus may offer a viable alternative to the DSM that has greater utility for practitioners in the field.

Identifying the key processes that contribute to a client's distress and maladaptive coping behaviors may also offer a more effective means of case conceptualization. Through understanding how these processes are at work in the way an individual responds to stressors, targeted, actionable, and effective interventions can be developed. In that regard, mindfulness, as a transdiagnostic intervention strategy, holds great promise as a means of promoting resilience and adaptive neuroplasticity leading to lasting change and enhanced well-being.

Application to the Case of Ray

With these key transdiagnostic and resilience processes in mind, we must first establish the pathogenic factors underlying Ray's present problems to be able to effectively develop an actionable treatment plan. He has been diagnosed with Bipolar Disorder type II, which suggests a number of broad symptom clusters but does not provide enough precision for targeted treatment of the causal factors. When utilizing the transdiagnostic perspective, clinicians must identify the key processes that are contributing to a client's distress and maladaptive coping behaviors. Based on what we know about Ray from the case study, we can identify a pattern of violence that suggests a conditioned self-protective response to a history of bullying through which Ray has learned to fight when he feels threatened. Previous to his relationship with Cecilia, his fighting had been confined to bar fights, but gradually this pattern has extended into other areas of his life. He describes his violence as "this thing that just comes over me," suggesting a lack of volition and awareness that, together with the frequency of his violent encounters, indicates a problem with automaticity. If his reports of his Tylenol overdoses are truthful and there was no suicidal intent, this automaticity is also suggested by his statement that he "didn't realize" how many pills he was taking.

Attentional bias is also likely to be a problematic process for Ray. He seems to perceive insults where none were intended, which leads to violent reactions. This occurs in bars where he often gets into fights, but he also seems to fix his attention on indicators of negative social feedback in his relationships with women and the world around him. He states, "All I ever see are the worst things about people—mugging, rape, knifings, people hurting each other," suggesting that he attenuates his focus on the negative things that people do. Granted, this can likely be attributed to his line of work, but the result of his life and work history may nonetheless be an attentional bias toward negative or threatening stimuli. This bias has increased the frequency and duration of negative emotions in Ray's life, and has made changes to his disposition over time.

Ray also seems to struggle with memory bias, particularly in his past relationships. He reports that his first marriage ended due to Leslie's "materialism, self-absorption, and coldness," as well as her incapacity or unwillingness to provide emotional support. While all of these things may in fact be true, the way in which they are related, and the fact the Ray did not acknowledge his own role in the dissolution of his first marriage, suggest a biased memory that is focused on ways in which others have wronged him, which he also seems to struggle to let go of. This type of bias also emerges in the way he describes his relationship with Cecilia. Even though here he acknowledges his violence, he feels angry and betrayed by her decision to leave, seeing only disloyalty and filtering out other factors in their shared history that might justify her decision.

In his reports of his trauma history, Ray interprets personal responsibility where there is none on his part. The sexual abuse he received from his priest caused him to wonder or believe that there was something about him that invited the abuse, that it was somehow his fault. Later, he says to his therapist, "I don't know what you think of me now that you know this. You probably never imagined I was one of those kids you read about," indicating again that his history of being sexually abused means something about him as a person, that he is weak and vulnerable. He clearly also feels a great deal of shame regarding these incidents, which almost always indicates an interpretation bias. He has been challenging this shame by opening up about the abuse with his therapist, his father, and a priest at his old parish, which seems to be helping him to reinterpret his trauma history.

Finally, there also may have been some thought suppression related to his trauma history. At one point after weeks of talking about the abuse, he angrily says to his therapist, "Stop making such a big deal out of this. It was a long time ago, I put it behind me, it has nothing to do with why I'm here." His efforts to "put it behind" him may have actually been a form of thought suppression that have paradoxically increased his accessibility to these memories and perpetuated his feelings of shame surrounding these incidents.

We have identified that each of the five key transdiagnostic processes may potentially be problematic for Ray. Once we have a clear conceptualization of the underlying processes that are contributing to Ray's problems, we can develop a targeted treatment plan aimed at positively influencing these specific processes. For example, we might target Ray's attentional bias toward negative or threatening stimuli and automaticity (the movement toward violence) through mindfulness training (De Raedt et al. 2011; Garland et al. 2010; Garland and Howard 2013). His memory bias in his past relationships could be addressed through a historical test of schema, or a review of past objective experiences to verify or challenge his distorted beliefs or perceptions (Padesky 1994). Ray's interpretation bias of his trauma history might be effectively treated through cognitive restructuring, which is the process of learning to identify, dispute, and reappraise cognitive distortions or maladaptive thoughts (Beck et al. 1979). Finally, his thought suppression of his sexual abuse could be altered through acceptance techniques, which involve non-judgmentally observing unwanted thoughts and allowing them to be present, rather than avoiding, suppressing, or distracting from them (Hayes et al. 2006).

The techniques utilized to effect positive changes in these transdiagonistic processes may be grounded in a variety of theoretical orientations to social work practice. A twenty-first century approach to clinical practice truly informed by neuroscience and the biobehavioral paradigm would relinquish fixation on psychiatric taxonomy and, in its place, embrace the transformative value of mindfully cultivating positive emotions, prosocial actions, and meaning in life in the face of adversity.

Practical Exercises

1. Think about a client with whom you have recently worked. Explain that case using the transdiagnostic perspective described above.
2. Consider the bio-psycho-social issues this client is facing. How do stress and coping factor into the case?
3. Recall a recent stressor in your own life. Cognitively reappraise that stressor by asking yourself the following questions: "Is there an alternative way of looking at this situation? Is there a silver lining here? How can I become a stronger person by getting through this experience? What can I learn from this experience?" Notice how the process of cognitive reappraisal changes your emotional reaction and the physiological state of your body.

References

Baer, R. A., Smith, G. T., Hopkins, J., Krietemeyer, J., & Toney, L. (2006). Using self-report assessment methods to explore facets of mindfulness. *Assessment, 13*, 27–45.

Bandura, A. (1991). Social cognitive theory of self-regulation. Organizational Behavior and Human Decision Processes, *50*, 248–287.

Bargh, J. A., & Chartrand, T. L. (1999). The unbearable automaticity of being. *American Psychologist, 54*, 462–479.

Bateson, G. (1972). *Steps to an ecology of mind*. Chicago: The University of Chicago Press.

Beck, A. T., Rush, A. J., Shaw, B. F., & Emery, G. (1979). *Cognitive therapy of depression*. New York, NY: Guilford.

Bishop, S. R., Lau, M., Shapiro, S., Carlson, L., Anderson, N. D., Carmody, J., et al. (2004). Mindfulness: A proposed operational definition. *Clinical Psychology: Science and Practice, 11* (3), 230–241.

Block, J. H., & Block, J. (1980). The role of ego-control and ego-resiliency in the origination of behavior. In W. A. Collings (Ed.), *The Minnesota symposia on child psychology, 13*, 39–101.

Block, J., & Kremen, A. M. (1996). IQ and ego-resiliency: Conceptual and empirical connections and separateness. *Journal of Personality and Social Psychology, 70*, 349–361.

Brading, A. (1999). *The autonomic nervous system and its effectors*. Malden, MA: Blackwell Science.

Cannon, W. B. (1939). *The wisdom of the body* (2nd ed.). New York: Norton (original work published 1932).

Chrousos, G. P., & Gold, P. W. (1992). The concepts of stress and stress system disorders: Overview of physical and behavioral homeostasis. *Journal American Medical Association, 267*, 1244–1252.

Compas, B. E. (2006). Psychological processes of stress and coping. *Annals of the New York Academy of Sciences, 1094*, 226–234.

Connor-Smith, J. K., Compas, B. E., Wadsworth, M. E., Thomsen, A. H., & Saltzman, H. (2000). Responses to stress in adolescence: Measurement of coping and involuntary stress responses. *Journal of Consulting and Clinical Psychology, 68*, 976–992.

Davidson, R. J. (2004). What does the prefrontal cortex "do" in affect: Perspectives on frontal EEG asymmetry research. *Biological Psychology, 67*(1–2), 219–233.

de Lange, F. P., Koers, A., Kalkman, J. S., Bleijenberg, G., Hagoort, P., van der Meer, J. W., et al. (2008). Increase in prefrontal cortical volume following cognitive behavioural therapy in patients with chronic fatigue syndrome. *Brain, 131*, 2172–2180.

DeLongis, A., & Holtzman, S. (2005). Coping in context: The role of stress, social support, and personality in coping. *Journal of Personality, 73*, 1–24.

De Raedt, R., Baert, S., Demeyer, I., Goeleven, E., Raes, A., Visser, A., et al. (2011). Changes in attentional processing of emotional information following mindfulness-based cognitive therapy in people with a history of depression: Towards an open attention for all emotional experiences. *Cognitive Therapy and Research, 36*, 1–9.

Desimone, R., & Duncan, J. (1995). Neural mechanisms of selective visual attention. *Annual Review of Neuroscience, 18*, 193–222.

Dias-Ferreira, E., Sousa, J. C., Melo, I., Morgado, P., Mesquita, A. R., Cerqueira, J. J., et al. (2009). Chronic stress causes frontostriatal reorganization and affects decision-making. *Science, 325*, 621–625.

Eisenberg, L. (2004). Social psychiatry and the human genome: Contextualising heritability. *British Journal of Psychiatry, 184*, 101–103.

Engel, G. L. (1977). The need for a new medical model: A challenge for biomedicine. *Science, 196* (4286), 129–136.

Eriksson, P. S., Perfilieva, E., Bjork-Eriksson, T., Alborn, A. M., Nordborg, C., Peterson, D. A., et al. (1998). Neurogenesis in the adult human hippocampus. *Nature Medicine, 4*(11), 1313–1317.

Field, M., Munafo, M. R., & Franken, I. H. (2009). A meta-analytic investigation of the relationship between attentional bias and subjective craving in substance abuse. *Psychological Bulletin, 135*, 589–607.

Folkman, S., & Moskowitz, J. T. (2000). Positive affect and the other side of coping. *American Psychologist, 55*(6), 647–654.

Fredrickson, B. L. (1998). What good are positive emotions? *Review of General Psychology, 2*(3), 300–319.

Fredrickson, B. L. (2001). The broaden-and-build theory of positive emotions. *American Psychologist, 56*(3), 218–226.

Fredrickson, B. L. (2003). The value of positive emotions: The emerging science of positive psychology is coming to understand why it's good to feel good. *American Scientist, 91*, 330–335.

Fredrickson, B. L. (2009). *Positivity: Groundbreaking research reveals how to embrace the hidden strength of positive emotions, overcome negativity, and thrive.* New York: Crown Publishing Group.

Friedman, R. S., & Förster, J. (2010). Implicit affective cues and attentional tuning: An integrative review. *Psychological Bulletin, 136*(5), 875.

Garland, E. L. (2013). *Mindfulness-oriented recovery enhancement for addiction, stress, and pain.* Washington, DC: NASW Press.

Garland, E. L., Fredrickson, B. L., Kring, A. M., Johnson, D. P., Meyer, P. S., & Penn, D. L. (2010a). Upward spirals of positive emotions counter downward spirals of negativity: Insights from the broaden-and-build theory and affective neuroscience on the treatment of emotion dysfunctions and deficits in psychopathology. *Clinical Psychology Review, 30*, 849–864.

Garland, E. L., Gaylord, S. A., Boettiger, C. A., & Howard, M. O. (2010b). Mindfulness training modifies cognitive, affective, and physiological mechanisms implicated in alcohol dependence: Results from a randomized controlled pilot trial. *Journal of Psychoactive Drugs, 42*, 177–192.

Garland, E. L., & Fredrickson, B. A. (2013). Mindfulness broadens awareness and builds meaning at the attention-emotion interface. In T. B. Kashdan & J. Ciarrochi (Eds.), *Linking acceptance and commitment therapy and positive psychology: A practitioner's guide to a unifying framework* (pp. 30–67). Oakland, CA: New Harbinger Publications, Inc.

Garland, E. L., Froeliger, B. E., Passik, S. D., & Howard, M. O. (2013). Attentional bias for prescription opioid cues among opioid dependent chronic pain patients. *Journal of Behavioral Medicine, 36*, 611–620.

Garland, E. L., & Howard, M. O. (2009). Neuroplasticity, psychosocial genomics, and the biopsychosocial paradigm in the 21st century. *Health and Social Work, 34*(3), 191–200.

Garland, E. L., & Howard, M. O. (2013). Mindfulness-oriented recovery enhancement reduces pain attentional bias in chronic pain patients. *Psychother Psychosomatics, 82*(5), 311–318.

Garland, E. L., & Howard, M. O. (2014). A transdiagnostic perspective on cognitive, affective, and neurobiological processes underlying human suffering. *Research on Social Work Practice, 24*(1), 142–151.

Gottlieb, B. H. (1997). *Coping with chronic stress*. New York: Plenium Press.

Goyal, M., Singh, S., Sibinga, E. M. S., Gould, N. F., Rowland-Seymour, A., Sharma, R., et al. (2014). Meditation programs for psychological stress and well-being: A systematic review and meta-analysis. *JAMA Internal Medicine, 174*(3), 357–368.

Hatcher, A. S. (1989). From one addiction to another: Life after alcohol and drug abuse. *The Nurse Practitioner, 14*(11), 13–20.

Hayes, S. C., Luoma, J. B., Bond, F. W., Masuda, A., & Lillis, J. (2006). Acceptance and commitment therapy: Model, processes and outcomes. *Behavior Research and Therapy, 44*, 1–25.

Herman, J. P., & Cullinan, W. E. (1997). Neurocircuitry of stress: central control of the hypothalamo-pituitary-adrenocortical axis. *Trends in Neurosciences, 20*, 78–84.

Hölzel, B. K., Carmody, J., Vangel, M., Congleton, C., Yerramsetti, S. M., Gard, T., et al. (2012). Mindfulness practice leads to increases in regional brain gray matter density. *Psychiatry Research, 191*(1), 36–43.

Hölzel, B. K., Lazar, S. W., Gard, T., Schuman-Olivier, Z., Vago, D. R., & Ott, U. (2011). How does mindfulness meditation work? Proposing mechanisms of action from a conceptual and neural perspective. *Perspectives on Psychological Science, 6*, 537–559.

Jänig, W. (2008). *Integrative action of the autonomic nervous system neurobiology of homeostasis*. Cambridge: Cambridge University Press.

Kabat-Zinn, J. (1994). *Wherever you go, there you are*. New York: Hyperion.

Kabat-Zinn, J. (2003). Mindfulness-based interventions in context: Past, present, and future. *Clinical Psychology: Science and Practice, 10*(2), 144–156.

Kandel, E. R. (1998). A new intellectual framework for psychiatry. *American Journal of Psychiatry, 155*(4), 457–469.

Lazarus, R. S. (1991). *Emotion and adaptation*. New York: Oxford University Press.

Lazarus, R. S. (1993). From psychological stress to the emotions: A history of changing outlooks. *Annual Review of Psychology, 44*, 1–21.

Lazarus, R. S., & Folkman, S. (1984). *Stress, appraisal, and coping*. New York: Springer.

MacLeod, C., Mathews, A., & Tata, P. (1986). Attentional biases in emotional disorders. *Journal of Abnormal Psychology, 95*, 15–20.

Maguire, E. A., Gadian, D. G., Johnsrude, I. S., Good, C. D., Ashburner, J., Frackowiak, R. S., et al. (2000). Navigation related structural change in the hippocampus of taxi drivers. *Proceedings of the National Academy of Sciences, 97*(8), 4398–4403

Marsella, A. J. (1998). Urbanization, mental health, and social deviancy: A review of issues and research. *American Psychologist, 53*(6), 624–634.

Mathews, A., & MacLeod, C. (2005). Cognitive vulnerability to emotional disorders. *Annual Review of Clinical Psychology, 1*, 167–195.

Maturana, H., & Varela, F. (1987). *The tree of knowledge: The biological roots of human understanding*. Boston: Shambhala.

Mayer, J. D., McCormick, L. J., & Strong, S. E. (1995). Moodcongruent memory and natural mood: New evidence. *Personality and Social Psychology Bulletin, 21*, 736.

McCutcheon, V. (2006). Toward an integration of social and biological research. *The Social Service Review, 80*(1), 159–178.

McEwen, B. S., & Wingfield, J. C. (2003). The concept of allostasis in biology and biomedicine. *Hormones and Behavior, 43*(1), 2–15.

Mineka, S., Rafaeli, E., & Yovel, I. (2002). Cognitive biases in emotional disorders: Information processing and social-cognitive perspectives. In R. J. Davidson (Ed.), *Handbook of affective sciences* (pp. 976–1009). Cary, NC: Oxford University Press.

Monideepa, T., Tu, Q., Ragu-Nathan, B. S., & Ragu-Nathan, T. S. (2007). The impact of technostress on role stress and productivity. *Journal of Management Information Systems, 24*, 301–328.

Mundkur, N. (2005). Neuroplasticity in children. *Indian Journal of Pediatrics, 72*(10), 855–857.

Padesky, C. (1994). Schema change processes in cognitive therapy. *Clinical Psychology and Psychotherapy, 1*, 267–278.

Pascual-Leone, A., Amedi, A., Fregni, F., & Merabet, L. B. (2005). The plastic human brain cortex. *Annual Review of Neuroscience, 28*, 377–401.

Rauch, S. L., Shin, L. M., Whalen, P. J., & Pitman, R. K. (1998). Neuroimaging and the neuroanatomy of PTSD. *CNS Spectrums, 2*, 30–41.

Richardon, G. E. (2002). The metatheory of resilience and resiliency. *Journal of Clinical Psychology, 58*(3), 307–321.

Rosenberg, E. L. (1998). Levels of analysis and the organization of affect. *Review of General Psychology, 2*(3), 247–270.

Rosmond, R. (2005). Role of stress in the pathogenesis of metabolic syndrome. *Psychoneuroendocrinology, 30*, 1–10.

Rossi, E. L. (2002). Psychosocial genomics: Gene expression, neurogenesis, and human experience in mind-body medicine. *Advances in Mind-Body Medicine, 18*(2), 22–30.

Sapolsky, R. M. (2004). Is impaired neurogenesis relevant to the affective symptoms of depression? *Biological Psychology, 56*(3), 137–139.

Schmitz, T. W., De Rosa, E., & Anderson, A. K. (2009). Opposing influences of affective state valence on visual cortical encoding. *Journal of Neuroscience, 29*(22), 7199–7207.

Schneider, W., & Chein, J. M. (2003). Controlled & automatic processing: Behavior, theory, and biological mechanism. *Cognitive Science, 27*, 525–559.

Segal, Z. V., Williams, J. M. G., & Teasdale, J. D. (2002). *Mindfulness-based cognitive therapy for depression: A new approach to relapse prevention.* New York: Guilford.

Selye, H. (1974). *Stress without distress.* Philadelphia, PA: J.B. Lippincott Co.

Shapiro, S. L., Carlson, L. E., Astin, J. A., & Freedman, B. (2006). Mechanisms of mindfulness. *Journal of Clinical Psychology, 62*(3), 373–386.

Sherin, J. E., & Nemeroff, C. B. (2011). Post-traumatic stress disorder: the neurobiological impact of psychological trauma. *Dialogues in Clinical Neuroscience, 13*, 263–278.

Sterling, P., & Eyer, J. (1988). Allostasis: A new paradigm to explain arousal pathology. In S. Fisher, & J. Reason (Eds.), *Handbook of life stress, cognition, and health.* New York: Wiley.

Sweatt, J. D. (2013). The emerging field of neuroepigenetics. *Neuron, 80*(3), 624–632.

Talarico, J. M., LaBar, K. S., & Rubin, D. C. (2004). Emotional intensity predicts autobiographical memory experience. *Memory and Cognition, 32*(7), 1118–1132.

Tugade, M. M., Fredrickson, B. L., & Barrett, L. F. (2004). Psychological resilience and positive emotional granularity: Examining the benefits of positive emotions on coping and health. *Journal of Personality, 72*(6), 1161–1190.

Wegner, D. M., & Erber, R. (1992). The hyperaccessibility of suppressed thoughts. *Journal of Personality and Social Psychology, 63*(6), 903.

Wegner, D. M., Schneider, D. J., Carter, S. R., & White, T. L. (1987). Paradoxical effects of thought suppression. *Journal of Personality and Social Psychology, 53*, 5–13.

Weinstein, A., & Lejoyeux, M. (2010). Internet addiction or excessive internet use. *The American Journal of Drug and Alcohol Abuse, 36*(5), 277–283.

Wenzlaff, R. M., & Wegner, D. M. (2000). Thought suppression. *Annual Review of Psychology, 51*, 59–91.

Williams, J. M., Teasdale, J. D., Segal, Z. V., & Soulsby, J. (2000). Mindfulness-based cognitive therapy reduces overgeneral autobiographical memory in formerly depressed patients. *Journal of Abnormal Psychology, 109*, 150–155.

Chapter 7
The Role of Temperament in Conceptualizations of Mental Disorder

Mary K. Rothbart

Abstract This chapter describes how understanding individual differences in temperament and the role of temperamental traits and variation in human development can shed valuable light on the origins, assessment, and treatment of dysfunction. It begins by defining temperament as enduring, constitutionally based individual differences in reactivity and self-regulation—that is, in how an individual responds to the challenges and opportunities offered by both stressful and promotive environments—and traces the development of these traits during a child's maturation. Aspects of temperament including effortful control, affect modulation, soothability, and stimulation tolerance are thus affected by environment, experience, and parental behavior, as well as by genetic disposition. In addition, the chapter reviews current research on ways of measuring and assessing temperament, including both observational and longitudinal studies, and explores the relationship between temperament and dysfunction. Vulnerability to dysfunction is thus seen as strongly affected by the "goodness of fit" between an individual and his or her environment, rather than as something residing in the individual.

Keywords Adaptability · Constitutional · Effortful control · Executive attention · Surgency · Inhibitory control · Intensity · Over-stimulation · Reactivity · Rhythmicity · Self-regulation · Soothability · Threshold

Introduction: Why This Matters

This chapter addresses individual differences in temperament and ways that an understanding of temperament can promote healthy development. Through the study of temperament and its role in human development, we can gain important insight into the origins and assessment of dysfunction, as well as ways to design and evaluate interventions that take development into account. It is possible, for

M.K. Rothbart (✉)
Department of Psychology, University of Oregon, Eugene, OR, USA
e-mail: maryroth@uoregon.edu

© Springer International Publishing Switzerland 2015
B. Probst (ed.), *Critical Thinking in Clinical Assessment and Diagnosis*,
Essential Clinical Social Work Series, DOI 10.1007/978-3-319-17774-8_7

133

example, that what is seen as a "mental disorder" may be a temperament that does not fit the requirements of society or significant others; thus, it is important to address problems with the popular concept of an inherently "difficult" temperament.

Temperament is part of the broader domain of individual differences in personality, defined by Allport (1937) as traits "that determine his (or her) unique adjustment to his (or her) environment" (p. 48). Personality traits in Allport's view are patterns of thoughts, emotions, and behavior that show consistency across situations and stability over time, and are centered around adjustment, i.e., coping with challenge and taking advantage of opportunity.

Guiding Questions

1. What is temperament, how is it assessed, and how does it differ from other ways of thinking about human variation?
2. What are some of the key dimensions of temperament, and what is the research evidence for considering these to be core components?
3. How do events in early development affect the emergence of temperamental tendencies?
4. What is the relationship between temperament and mental disorder?

Defining Temperament

Temperamental traits and capacities are aspects of human nature that are biologically based, show consistency across situations and stability over time, are present early in life, and form the building blocks of personality and social development. Temperament has been defined more precisely as constitutionally based individual differences in reactivity and self-regulation (Rothbart 2011; Rothbart and Bates 1998, 2006; Rothbart and Derryberry 1981). By *constitutional*, we mean that temperament is biologically based and influenced over time by genes and experience. *Reactivity* refers to the ease of arousal of emotions, attention, and actions, including actions toward, away from, and against objects. *Self-regulation* refers to the temperamental capacities that control reactivity. Temperament traits are often combined with related action tendencies in order to cope with situations that arise. Thus, for example, general tendencies toward keeping levels of stimulation low to avoid overstimulation or high to seek high levels of stimulation are often called introversion–extraversion.

Critical to self-regulation is *attentional* or *effortful control*. In early infancy (the first four months), control by orienting develops. This capacity will be shown throughout life, when we look away from a disturbing stimulus or distract ourselves from information that might lead to distress. There is evidence that some executive attention capacity is present in infancy, at least in the form of detecting error (Berger et al. 2006), although the neural connectivity of this system develops in a way that allows effortful control of action only much later, during the third year of life (Jones et al. 2003). Executive attention develops strongly during the second and third years of life and allows control of thought and behavior at school and home (Rueda 2012). We have observed this capacity in temperament research (Rothbart et al. 2011), linking it to the executive attention network of the human brain, and term it *effortful control*.

Recent temperament research has employed increasingly sophisticated psychometric methods to identify a basic set of temperament dimensions (see reviews by Goldsmith and Gagne 2012; Rothbart 2011) that extends from infancy (Gartstein and Rothbart 2003) to adulthood (Evans and Rothbart 2007). In our research, factors of Fear, Frustration, Overall Negative affect, Extraversion/Surgency, Orienting/Perceptual Sensitivity, and Effortful Control have been extracted (Putnam et al. 2001). Although final consensus on the list has not yet been reached, individual differences in emotionality and attention regulation are understood as the basic components of temperament (Bates 2000; Rothbart and Bates 2006; Rothbart and Derryberry 1981).

Temperament thus describes an individual's tendencies, dispositions, or capacities. These tendencies are not continually expressed; their expression depends on the appropriate eliciting conditions. A fearful person is not continually distressed or inhibited, for example. In fact, a fearful person may choose to live a quiet life or to develop other coping mechanisms that actually make her or him appear less fearful than others. When experiencing novelty, sudden or intense stimulation, or signals of punishment, more fearful individuals are especially prone to distress, inhibition, and avoidance, experiencing these reactions more rapidly and in response to lower intensities of stimulation than other individuals. Irritable children are not continually bothered or angry, but when their intentions are blocked, there is a failure of their expectations, or they are in pain, they are more prone to anger and frustration reactions than other children.

The Relationship of Temperament to Other Aspects of Human Experience

Temperament and Personality Unlike other personality traits, temperament traits do not necessarily include specific thoughts or cognitions about the self and others, e.g., self-concept, life narratives, or paranoid thoughts. Temperament is present in infancy and early childhood, before linguistic and cognitive capacities develop, and is the biologically based core from which personality develops, varying from person to person. In addition to temperament traits, personality includes attitudes, cognitive coping strategies, self-concept, views of others and the physical world, values, morals, and beliefs. Temperament influences the development of these qualities but can be differentiated from them.

Temperament in the Organism Emotions and attention are evolved biological systems that structure feeling, thought, and action in order to deal with environmental challenges and opportunities (Derryberry and Rothbart 1997; LeDoux 1989). We share our emotions and orienting of attention with other animals. These reactions have been adaptive to our ancestors and serve as direct and rapid indicators of the significance of events to us. A general set of temperament characteristics is inherited by all humans, but differs among people based on specific genetic makeup and life experience. Emotional reactions include tendencies toward, away from, and against objects. Even early in life, an object, person, or situation can have a different meaning to a child depending on temperament (Rothbart 2011). Starting with these evaluations of events, individualized experience in situations provides a further elaboration of meaning in our world.

One of the ways that early dysfunction can develop is through problems with overstimulation and soothability. Some children (and some adults) are prone to distress and do not recover easily. In infant temperament, this is seen in the latency, intensity, and duration of distress. To this distress proneness will be added meanings that are only possible as thought and language come online in development. For example, once a concept of self is developed, the emotions of shame and pride are possible, although infants do not yet have these capacities. As thought and language develop, it becomes possible to focus repeatedly on obsessive ideas.

The emotions include motivation and action tendencies. Fear carries with it dispositions toward freezing, withdrawal, or attack; anger carries dispositions toward attack and aggression. In turn, memory of the reaction in the situation can influence the person's future experience. Executive attention and effortful control are more purely self-regulatory systems; they do not specify particular emotions but can serve a diversity of emotion-related goals. Effortful control allows flexible response in the service of values and represents a developing set of skills. We can measure effortful control in the laboratory by using adapted forms of "Simon Says." For instance: "When the elephant tells you to put your finger on your nose, don't do it. When the bear gives an instruction, do it." Or the child pulls back the plunger on a pinball machine and then is asked to hold it for varying periods of time; many of the children do not.

Temperament and Development Not all aspects of temperament are seen in the newborn, but there is reliable development over the first years of life both in temperament and in the mental capacities that allow us to move beyond temperament to the wider domain of personality (Rothbart 2011). Early in development, emotional reactivity and relatively unregulated action characterize the young child, but as motivational and attentional systems develop, greater control over emotion, thought, and action becomes available. In fact, regulation of temperament tendencies can be seen as a major aim of socialization into a group or culture (Olson and Sameroff 2009).

Problems can occur when parents are not able to deal with high distress proneness or low self-regulation during their child's development (Papoušek and von Hofacker 2007). These are often described in terms of child dysfunction, but they may also be due to the parents' taking over the regulation that might otherwise be developed by the child (Papoušek and von Hofacker 2007). When problems arise, these often involve qualities of the child in conjunction with problems in the parents' adaptation to the child; problems in parenting may also go back to the way the parents themselves were parented (Rothbart 2011).

Fear develops across the first year of life, and inhibitory or withdrawal tendencies can oppose previously developed approach tendencies (Rothbart and Sheese 2007). By the time effortful control comes on line with rapid development over years two to four, regulatory tendencies can moderate reactive ones. In a larger sense, both reactivity and self-regulation are adaptive processes and form the basis for the child's earliest patterns of evaluating and coping with the environment.

We have defined effortful control as the ability to inhibit a dominant response in order to perform a subdominant response, to detect errors, and to engage in planning (Rothbart and Bates 2006; Rothbart and Rueda 2005). Effortful control can be seen as the ability to control one's actions by inhibiting and activating action, emotions, and attention. It can be measured through tests of activation and inhibition, such as the bear–elephant task described above, and through measures of higher persistence and non-distractibility. All of these constitute important aspects of self-control. In ours and others' laboratories, effortful control has been found to undergo rapid development in children between the ages of two and seven years, especially in the preschool years (Gerardi-Caulton 2000; Kochanska et al. 2000; Rothbart et al. 2003). These measures of temperament have been linked to laboratory measures of attention that have in turn been linked to an executive attention brain network that has been studied via brain imaging, patterns of neurochemical modulators, and specific genes (Posner and Rothbart 2007).

The executive network is involved in resolving competing actions in tasks where there is conflict. This is done both by enhancing activity in networks related to our goals and by inhibiting activity in conflicting networks. These controls are affected by long neural connections between the nodes of the executive network and cognitive and emotional areas of the frontal and posterior brain. In this way, the executive network is important for voluntary control and self-regulation (Bush et al. 2000; Sheth et al. 2012). Effortful control is a higher order temperament factor assessing self-regulation that is obtained from parent report questionnaires (Rothbart 2011). In childhood, performance on conflict-related cognitive tasks is positively related to measures of children's effortful control (Rueda 2012). During childhood and in adulthood, effortful control is correlated with school performance and with indices of life success, including health, income, and successful human relationships (Checa and Rueda 2011; Moffitt et al. 2011).

The construct of effortful control has enormous theoretical implications for temperament and development. Early theoretical models of temperament emphasize how actions are driven by level of arousal or by positive and negative emotions. Many of our coping methods are shaped by these processes. The trait of effortful control, however, means we are not always at the mercy of our reactions, nor of one emotional system's dominance over another—e.g., approach versus avoidance, or attack versus withdrawal (Rothbart and Sheese 2007).

With effortful control, we can choose to approach situations we fear and to inhibit actions we desire, giving a strong self-regulatory basis for socialized action, conscience, and self-control. Effortful control also brings with it the possibility of change. With the development of executive attention and effortful control, we can observe our own actions and select actions based on our values and goals. Although the effectiveness of effortful control will depend on the strength of the emotional and motivational processes against which it is exerted, it provides the possibility for true flexibility of thought, emotion, and action.

Temperament and Coping Tronick (2007) argues that the nature of a disorder "will be different given the capacities at the time it is developed and will be transformed as later developing processes come into place." (Tronick 2007, pp. 40–41). As capacities are added, an earlier dysfunction can be interpreted through a later developing skill; for example, when a young child developing language labels an intrusive person as "bad" but later revisits the developmental past and re-envisions the possibilities of a self determined future. There will also be more or less favorable requirements of situations over the course of development. For example, an impulsive child may be labeled "out of control" or having Attention Deficit Disorder, but later the same person may use that very temperament to create and run a successful business.

As the child develops, typical responses to stress and challenge and to new environments can be seen. These develop on the basis of what has worked in the past, and may or may not be suited to adjustment to differing situations. Consider the observations of Bridges (1931) of preschool children in the McGill University Nursery School:

> The most striking differences observed … at any time, were individual rather than age differences in behaviour both social and emotional. Some children 'went their own way' and left others alone, while others seemed as if they had to be always in the crowd. Some children 'hung around' the adults for attention, others spoke to the grown-ups only when necessary, and still others opposed almost every suggestion or request made to them by an adult. Some children cried frequently, others scarcely at all. Some children rushed about and laughed with delight, others sat quietly or stood about, making as few movements as possible and smiling only faintly. Some shouted and squealed frequently, others fought, and others whined in a complaining way (Bridges 1931, p. 11).

The practitioner who works with adults will note that the tendencies described by Horney (1945) as moving toward others, moving against others, and moving away from others can be applied to adults as well as children. In the extreme, these tendencies may create problems for parents, teachers, and peers. They are based on temperamental tendencies shaped by experience and, in some cases, linked to specific contexts. For example, there will be children who are active and smiling at home but reserved and quiet at preschool. There will be adults who behave very differently with coworkers than with their families. Fear is important in these adaptations to new settings in that it can oppose approach as well as the expression of anger and aggression. However, these responses may be expressed under conditions of relative safety. Some children who are initially outgoing and active in the preschool may also be rebuked and punished by their peers, leading to their development of withdrawn behavior (Rothbart 2011).

We can observe more specific adaptations, e.g., to life in the family. If the preschool or school age child is a witness to conflict and fighting between the parents, for example, she/he is likely to become distressed and to try to figure out what these events mean for their own welfare (Cummings et al. 2009). The child may think, "this is my fault" or "my mom and dad are going to get a divorce, and what will happen to me?" The child may also try to cope with the distressing situation by intervening in some way—for instance, by trying to act as a family peacemaker and working toward decreasing conflict between the parents (Cummings et al. 2009). If the child "succeeds" as a peacemaker, this strategy may be used and adapted in other situations.

In a second coping pattern, the child may develop active or aggressive behavior problems that will distract the parents from conflicts with each other as they focus on the problem child. In a third coping strategy, the child may try to avoid the conflict situation altogether (Cummings et al. 2009). Each of these patterns of family interaction can be analyzed in terms of social reactivity and regulation; when siblings are added to the mix, there are additional possibilities for conflict and coping (Volling et al. 2009). It is important to remember, however, that a coping strategy that succeeds in the short term or in one situation with one set of people may be nonadaptive in the long-term or in another setting. Thus, each of the children's coping strategies observed by Cummings and his associates—mediating parent conflict, emotional outbursts, and detached avoidance—can lead to future problems (Cummings et al. 2009). In the marital conflict situation, the child is doing the best she/he can, but the child's strategies may or may not be helpful in the future. A similar analysis can be made of adult behavior, although it may involve the performance of many more roles developed over a longer period.

Each person carries a history of experience and learning with similar objects, persons, and situations. The uniqueness of the person is based on their tendencies, capacities, and life history, including their social roles. Temperament rarely changes with a single experience. A particularly intense or neglectful experience, however, may result in problems that are quite person or situation specific. At the psychological level, an individual's thought, emotion, and action will be influenced by both temperamental dispositions and the nature of the environment at any given point. Yet the "environment" is itself strongly influenced by individual temperament and previous experiences. "Individuals respond selectively to the environment, assign meanings to it, change it, and are changed by it" (Hinde 1998). With increasing development, individuals are able to choose the environments they interact with, an activity that has been called "niche picking." At a biological level, temperament refers to the organization and function of the brain's emotion and attentional processing (Posner and Rothbart 2007a, b). As motivations and their offshoots in language develop, the person can hide emotions, project them on other sources and, after the age of four or five years, develop narratives or stories about the self (Rothbart 2011).

Temperament and Dysfunction The term "temperament" is derived from the Latin *temperare* meaning to "mingle in due proportion." In the ancient Greco-Roman fourfold typology, the *melancholic* person is moody, with a tendency to fear and sadness, and is seen as having a predominance of black bile. The *choleric* person is touchy and active, with a predominance of yellow bile. The *sanguine* person, sociable and easygoing, is seen to have a predominance of blood, whereas the *phlegmatic* individual, calm, even-tempered, and slow to emotion, is seen to have a predominance of phlegm (Rothbart 2011). In modern usage, a "temperamental" person is thought to be emotionally extreme, but the ancient view suggested that we *all* are prone to all of the temperaments, differing in the strength and balance of these components.

A number of ideas from the typology remain important to our current thinking. First, the typology reflected consistently observed patterns in others' and one's own emotions and behavior; second, it was linked to the humors that described the human physiology of the time; and third, it was related to problems in adjustment, as in the relation between melancholia and depression, choleric reactions and aggression, and sanguine reactions and extraversion. Previously I reviewed a long history linking temperament with psychopathology, and contributors to this adult (and canine) temperament literature include Pavlov, Burt, Eysenck, Jung, and many others (Rothbart 2011). However, in this chapter, I focus on the groundbreaking clinical contributions of Thomas, Chess, and their colleagues.

The New York Longitudinal Study The pioneering New York Longitudinal Study (NYLS) has served as the most well-known research in temperament and development. Based on a content analysis of parent interview reports of infant reactions, Thomas et al. (1963) identified nine dimensions of temperament in infancy: activity level, approach–withdrawal, intensity, negative mood, adaptability, threshold, rhythmicity, and attention span/persistence. More recent research has modified this list. The use of psychometric methods indicated that: (a) the separability of approach and withdrawal (one can be high or low on both); (b) intensity, threshold, rhythmicity, and adaptability did not show the consistency across situations required for a temperament dimension; (c) negative emotionality could be further differentiated into anger and fear, with the two sometimes acting to oppose each other; and (d) positive emotionality as reflected in smiling and laughter and pleasure was identified as another important aspect of temperament (Rothbart 2011).

Thomas, Chess, and their colleagues also proposed important ideas about the "goodness of fit" between temperament and environment. When temperamental characteristics were seen as positive by important others, the person's positive development was enhanced. This did not mean that there needed to be a perfect match in temperament between child and family or student and teacher, merely the acceptability or cultural desirability of the child's temperamental tendencies. Goodness of fit also provides a template for thinking about adaptation strategies and how well they can be applied in any new situation. The NYLS researchers questioned the "blame the mother" approach of a number of clinicians and instead pointed out that developing problems might be chiefly due to a temperamentally difficult child. This construct will be considered further after a discussion of temperament assessment.

Assessing Temperament

Measures of temperament belong in the clinician's tool kit. Reliable and validated measures have been developed. In the infant and young child, reactive temperament can be measured through parent report questionnaires and often can be directly observed (Goldsmith and Rothbart 1991). Assessment of patterns of reactivity and self-regulation can be used in thinking about the development of problems, the choice of interventions, and the degree to which the person's values and effortful control are directed toward dealing with problems.

As self-regulation develops, reactivity is often moderated or increased through strategies of coping and defense. Thus, temperament can be measured most easily in infants and young children through observation, parent and teacher report, but also through self-report and peer-report into adulthood (Evans and Rothbart 2007). Self-report measures of temperament can be completed in later childhood and adulthood because of people's awareness of their feelings and action tendencies (Ellis et al. 2004).

A number of methods are used to assess temperament including questionnaires, laboratory measures, physiological assays, and behavioral observations. In our review of temperament research (Rothbart and Bates 2006), we noted that each measure is associated with both advantages and potential sources of error, arguing for the use of multiple measures. We also observed that contributions of questionnaires to our understanding of both temperament and personality have been substantial.

Whether we use questionnaires, home observations, or laboratory measures of temperament, multiple items or observations are used to measure each trait or dimension. This is done because no single item can give us a general measure of a given temperament trait or dimension across situations and over time. Another reason for averaging across items is that although an item or observation is expected to reflect temperament, temperament will be only one of many influences on any given reaction.

Consider, for example, a child's fearful reaction to a clown at a birthday party (this is not actually an item; the event does not occur frequently enough in the life of children). In addition to temperamental fearfulness, other contributions to distress may come from a passing negative mood, parental warnings about strange adults, past experiences at the circus, or the fact that the clown was highly intrusive and disturbing and would have frightened almost any child. In some cases, these influences extraneous to temperament will increase the child's fear score; in other cases, they will lower it. We assume that these other influences occur at random, so that some will tend to give the child a higher score on an item, others a lower score.

The child's temporary state, mood, individual history, or other sources of extraneous influence will thus tend to cancel each other out when a number of items are averaged. When we create an overall score on a scale by averaging items, we expect that we will capture a consistent individual difference. Questionnaires created by this method and appropriate statistical analyses are available at http://www.bowdoin.edu/~sputnam/rothbart-temperament-questionnaires/.

In parent report questionnaires, we take advantage of the many observations a parent makes of an infant or a young child by writing multiple items. In self-report questionnaires, we take advantage of the many observations we make of our own thoughts, actions, and feelings, many of which are not available to outside observers. Averaging is also used in laboratory measures. Thus, we repeatedly evoke a heart rate reaction or an electrophysiological (EEG) reaction through many presentations of a given stimulus. We then average over many measurements to remove effects of extraneous influences present in any single observation.

Combining Information on Temperament with Dysfunction An exciting advance in the field is evidence that using temperament assessment in diagnosis allows for meaningful subtyping of a disorder. Karalunas et al. (2014) used the Middle Childhood Questionnaire, developed in our laboratory to identify subgroups of children diagnosed with ADHD in a large sample of children. They identified three novel types of ADHD that they labeled *mild* (average emotion regulation), *surgent* (extreme approach, positive mood and soothability), and *irritable* (extreme negative emotionality, anger and low soothability). These subgroups were relatively stable over time, related to brain connectivity and cardiac response in the children, and connected with clinical outcomes at one year. The irritable group had a doubled risk of development of new comorbid behavior and mood disorders over this period in comparison with the other two groups. This is a new approach to diagnosis, one that appears to improve on current categories used by clinicians; it is now being studied in connection with the diagnosis of autistic children. Attachment and temperament research to date also suggests that neither construct contains the other, but that individual differences in temperament set the stage for the way that difficulties in relationships develop (Rothbart 2011).

In adults, temperament assessment also offers promise. In a study of adult borderline disorder, control participants were matched with borderline patients on the temperament characteristics of negative emotionality and low effortful control (Posner et al. 2002). In laboratory tests, the borderline patients showed problems with attention and inhibition that went beyond those of the controls. In fMRI studies, borderline patients shown negative stimuli had higher activation in emotional areas (amygdala) and lower activity in self-control areas (anterior cingulate). In addition, borderline patients with higher effortful control and better performance on a measure of the efficiency of executive attention responded more positively to therapy (Silbersweig et al. 2007). Hoerman et al. (2005) identified subgroups of borderline patients related to their scores on temperamental effortful control and found it to be related to the severity of the disorder. In addition, measures of rejection sensitivity, trauma, and executive attention all have proven helpful in assessing borderline personality (Ayduk et al. 2008).

The Difficulty of Difficulty We now return to the difficulty construct. The NLYS measure of difficultness was based on high scores for children on intensity and negative mood, and low scores on approach–withdrawal, adaptability, and rhythmicity. Some researchers, however, have criticized the concept and its measurement (Kohnstamm 1989; Plomin 1982; Rothbart 1982). One problem is that a behavior creating difficulty for one adult person may not for another. In addition, a behavior that creates problems in one situation may not be a problem in another, and indeed may even be an asset. A long attention span, for example, may be helpful when the child is busy with play, leaving the parent free to make dinner, but may seen as difficult when the child is called to dinner and is not ready to leave his or her activity.

The case of Roy from the NYLS also illustrates that what is seen as difficult at one age may not be difficult at another: Distractibility may help in soothing the infant yet contribute to the older child's being late for school and not completing homework assignments (Thomas and Chess 1977). Calling a child "difficult" also attaches a negative label on the child, even when most children's behavior is in fact sometimes "difficult" yet often "easy" (Probst 2008).

Further, cultural values influence adults' views of whether a child is "easy" or "difficult" (Korn and Gannon 1983; Rothbart 2011; Super et al. 2008). Although industrialized Western societies usually judge a child's proneness to negative emotion as difficult, difficulty in Taiwan and Brazil is not associated with distress proneness but instead with a weak and unhealthy infant (Wachs 2000).

Some authors have incorporated temperament into discussion of children's disorders to show how temperamental characteristics can lead to behavioral problems that escalate into, or get labeled as, mental disorders such as ADHD, Oppositional Defiant Disorder, and Social Anxiety. Probst (2008), for instance, proposes that features such as perfectionism and inflexibility can play an important role in the genesis of children's difficulties. A child who, by nature, prefers—or even requires—sameness and predictability can become distressed when expectations are not met or plans change without sufficient time to adjust. The child's inability to tolerate frustration and disappointment, combined with a compelling need to fulfill an inner vision of how something "ought" to be, can lead to tantrums, defiance, and reactions that seem disproportionate and disordered to adults—particularly adults whose own responsive style, tempo, or willingness to adapt are quite different from the child's. So too, a child who cannot navigate an excess of choices or stimulation may "melt down," flee, or withdraw because these are the only strategies available in the face of an emotionally intolerable situation. In this way, when there is a temperamental mismatch between the child and the adults who control the parameters and expectations of the child's environment, *traits* that do not fit the setting can develop into *symptoms* of disorder. In another setting, they might not be problematic.

Indeed, certain aspects of "difficultness" per the Thomas and Chess category have been linked to positive characteristics. High withdrawal or fear, part of the "difficult infant" construct, predicts higher levels of conscience in preschool children and lower aggression later in childhood (Kochanska 1991, 1995; Rothbart and Bates 2006), although it also predicts later anxiety. Negative emotionality in adults is related to their ability to detect errors when they are solving problems (Luu et al. 2000). Finally, difficulty is often measured differently from one study to another. This wide range of definitions for what constitutes difficulty causes confusion for those who read the research, and we need to be very careful in understanding how difficulty is measured in a given study.

At the same time, there is agreement that some aspects of a child's temperament create challenges for parents. Several studies have found that children who are high in distress proneness and socially demandingness are more likely to develop behavior problems later in life (Bates 1989). Nevertheless, "difficulty" is a general label, while a more specific approach to the child's temperament and its interactions with child rearing can be much more revealing.

Conclusions

There are alternatives to placing blame on one or another partner in a disturbed relationship. A better approach to the counseling setting may be to simply identify the problems directly, see how they might have been related to their circumstances of development, including influences of temperament and other biologically and risk-based factors (Lengua and Wachs 2012), and work with the person who bears the most responsibility for outcomes. For the child, this is the parent or teacher; for the adult, self-responsibility is an important source of strength for change.

The clinician in the counseling setting can also take advantage of the temperament characteristics we all share, including the potential for joy and discovery, the ability to do careful work, and the exercise of self-control in the pursuit of valued outcomes. By discussing with clients how they remember themselves as children, the concept of a core self can be developed. This provides a grounding point for thinking about the adaptations the person has made over the course of a life and for realizing that these possibilities continue to exist in everyone and can be strengthened. The positive psychologists revisit the adult's childhood with a view not only of recognizing how problems may have developed, but of strengthening capacities that are part of the core self but may have been neglected.

Using temperament as a construct can inspire much additional research and application in social work and related fields. One direction for this research is to develop psychometrically sound measures of dimensions that have to date not been well explored. An example is the set of variables Probst (2008) has identified. By writing more items and testing scales for internal reliability using large samples, we can expand our view of temperamental individual differences. It will also be important to look for meaningful subscales, such as identifying fear and irritability as separable subdimensions of distress proneness.

It is interesting that the study of temperament and the development of dysfunction leads us to real conceptual problems with identifying problems within a single person rather than the person in a setting. One of my postdoctoral students said he had no idea when he came to work with me that much of the time we would be studying learning in a social setting as influenced by temperament, instead of studying only temperament all the time. By taking a developmental view, what was at the first specified biologically must now be seen in environmental context, and the appropriate intervention understood by the developmental status of each person in a troubled relationship. In all, temperamental weaknesses will be strengths and strengths will be weaknesses, depending on coping and context.

Application to the Case of Ray

Temperament refers to constitutionally based dispositions, tendencies or capacities that persist over time and across contexts; temperament shapes the way a person responds to the environment and copes with stress. Underlying temperamental traits include reactivity to stress and reward, stimulation tolerance, and self-regulation. These traits can be adaptive and developmental; that is, they can provide a healthy foundation for a child to learn how to cope, adjust, restrain impulses, and persevere. However, an easy adaptation to one setting may lead to problems in another.

Speculating about Ray's temperament is difficult. We see that as a young child he enjoyed quiet activities, and this appeared to match the calm, reserved environment of his adoptive parents. No one in the household raged or screamed or displayed extreme emotions; confrontation was avoided. Ray "knew" not to ask about his birth family, suggesting sensitivity to the feelings of others that might accompany a more introspective child. This approach to life would not be challenged in a quiet home.

Yet that very reserve no longer served him once he started school. There, the culture of being a boy likely included the ability to fight. He became the object of bullying, and later the victim of a sexual predator who could count on him not to tell. The way to adapt to a bully is frequently to fight back, and Ray was big and sturdy enough to prevail in fights, even though "that went against his nature." If we take the latter statement seriously, we may see a child temperamentally well matched to a quiet life who needs to make an adjustment to an aggressive world. One important aspect of temperament is that we all carry the basic response patterns that can support a variety of adaptations, even if they do not dominate at the outset. Even a person who is initially not inclined to can fight. Moreover, sensitivity to threats to his manhood appeared to lead to a generalization of fighting from aggression to men to aggression to women.

One of the benefits of applying a temperament/coping lens to the development of emotional and behavioral problems is that it allows us to consider the kinds of stressful experiences and challenges the person is subjected to over the course of development. I think of this in terms of Francois Truffaut's film *The 400 Blows*, based on his own experiences growing up. The protagonist, Antoine is a young boy who is badly treated both at home and at school. When he steals a typewriter in an attempt to get enough money to escape both places, his parents turn him over to a juvenile justice system that does not work. In the last scene, the boy is running from a detention center, at each turning point cutting off options for escape. He finally reaches the sea, where he can go no further. The boy turns to face the camera, and Truffaut freezes the frame of the boy's face.

What kinds of stressors was Ray subjected to? The macho attacks of his schoolmates was one; he coped with this by developing fighting capacities. A later experience was that of sexual molestation by a local priest whom he trusted, a major blow for any child. Ray chose a career in law enforcement that added further stresses that tested his ability to remain calm in the stress of threat, danger, and horrific situations. But following the death of his mother, his control of his emotions began to crumble. When he tried to talk about the horrors he witnessed at work, his wife shut him down, saying "Nobody made you become a cop. You chose it."

A further powerful stressor was working in the rubble after 9/11. Indeed Ray's problems might have been at least partially reflected in PTSD related to his work environment and to his sensitivity to stress. Ray says, "All I ever see are the worst things about people—mugging, rape, knifings, people hurting each other." He can no longer suppress his emotional vulnerability, and soon his capacity for attention, concentration, persistence, and restraint becomes greatly diminished. He lashes out at his girlfriend and picks fights with strangers at the slightest provocation, "almost like I was looking for something to fight about." He feels powerless, as if "this thing just comes over me." Now there are two apparent suicide attempts, in each case followed by hospitalization and therapy.

If we can say that Ray is temperamentally reactive to stress, it is clear that his emotions and impulsivity have at this point overpowered his ability for self-regulation. He appears now to lack a mature ability to respond and cope with the stresses in his environment. One reason for this may lie in his early development. His parents' control was indirect, through tacit messages that emotionality and impulsivity were not permitted to which Ray was sensitive. He had little opportunity to learn how to handle his emotions *after* they had been activated. Once used with his schoolmates, aggression became a growing problem, just as the blows he experienced were enough to break down whatever self-regulation had been developed.

In therapy, Ray is letting go of the armor of his aggressive adaptations and quitting the police force while applying for disability benefits. In his early development, the culture of the home, school, and police force differed in the traits they valued. When those are not the traits that are natural to an individual, the person can either "be himself" and accept a status of lesser value, or seek to "be different." Either brings conflict and distress. Ray has done both, but now has a chance to become who he truly is.

Practical Exercises

1. Think about an adult client who has been diagnosed with a mental disorder such as depression or anxiety, and view that client through the lens of temperament. How would you describe this person in terms of features such as reactivity, distress proneness, self-regulation (effortful control), persistence, and flexibility?
2. Review the DSM criteria for ADHD. How might the notion of temperament help you to reframe some of these symptoms? Which symptoms might be understood as representing dimensions of temperament, or as manifestations of a particular kind of temperament within an ill-suited environment?
3. Since developmental stage and the way developmental tasks are met (or not met) are critical for understanding temperament, can you "map" the growth of self-regulation/effortful control onto one of the psychosocial models of child development such as that of Erikson or Piaget? Does this bring any new insight?

References

Allport, G. W. (1937). *Personality: A psychological interpretation*. New York: Holt.
Ayduk, O., Zayas, V., Downey, G., Cole, A. B., Shoda, Y., & Mischel, W. (2008). Rejection sensitivity and executive control: Joint predictors of borderline personality features. *Journal of Research in Personality, 42*(1), 151–168.
Bates, J. E. (2000). Temperament as an emotion construct: Theoretical and practical issues. In M. Lewis & J. M. Haviland-Jones (Eds.), *Handbook of emotions* (2nd ed.). New York: Guilford.
Berger, A., Tzur, G., & Posner, M. I. (2006). Infant babies detect arithmetic error. *Proceedings of the National Academy of Science, 103*, 12649–12553.
Bush, G., Luu, P., & Posner, M. I. (2000). Cognitive and emotional influences in anterior cingulate cortex. *Trends in Cognitive Sciences, 4*, 215–222.
Bridges, K. (1931). *Social and emotional development of the pre-school child*. London: Kegan Paul, Trench, Trubner, & Co.
Checa, P., & Rueda, M. R. (2011). Behavioral and brain measures of executive attention and school competence in late childhood. *Developmental Neuropsychology, 36*(8), 1–15.
Chess, S., Thomas, A., & Birch, H. G. (1985). *Your child is a person*. New York: Penguin Books.
Cummings, E. M., Papp, L. M., & Kouros, C. D. (2009). Regulatory processes in children's coping with exposure to mental conflict. In S. L. Olson & A. J. Sameroff (Eds.), *Biopsychosocial regulatory processes in the development of childhood behavior problems* (pp. 212–237). New York: Cambridge University Press.
Derryberry, D., & Rothbart, M. K. (1997). Reactive and effortful processes in the organization of temperament. *Developmental Psychopathology, 9*(4), 633–652.
Ellis, L. K., Rothbart, M. K., & Posner, M. I. (2004). Individual differences in executive attention predict self-regulation and adolescent psychosocial behaviors. *Annals of the New York Academy of Sciences, 1021*, 337–340.
Evans, D., & Rothbart, M. K. (2007). Developing a model for adult temperament. *Journal of Research in Personality, 41*, 858–888.
Gartstein, M. A., & Rothbart, M. K. (2003). Studying infant temperament via the revised infant behavior questionnaire. *Infant Behavior and Development, 26*(1), 64–86.

Gerardi-Caulton, G. (2000). Sensitivity to spatial conflict and the development of self-regulation in children 24–36 months of age. *Developmental Science, 3*(4), 397–404.

Goldsmith, H. H., & Gagne, J. R. (2012). Behavioral assessment of temperament. In M. Zentner & R. L. Shiner (Eds.), *Handbook of temperament* (pp. 209–228). New York: Guilford.

Goldsmith, H. H., & Rothbart, M. K. (1991). Contemporary instruments for assessing early temperament by questionnaire and in the laboratory. In A. Angleitner & J. Strelau (Eds.), *Explorations in Temperament: International perspectives on theory and measurement* (pp. 249–272). New York: Plenum Press.

Hinde, R. A. (1998). Integrating across levels of complexity. In D. M. Hann, L. C. Huffman, I. I. Lederhendler, & D. Meineke (Eds.), *Advancing research on developmental plasticity* (pp. 165–173). Bethesda, MD: National Institute of Mental Health.

Hoermann, S., Clarkin, J. F., Hull, J. W., & Levy, K. N. (2005). The construct of effortful control: An approach to borderline personality disorder heterogeneity. *Psychopathology, 38*, 82–86.

Horney, K. (1945). *Our inner conflicts*. New York: Norton.

Jones, L. B., Rothbart, M. K., & Posner, M. I. (2003). Development of executive attention in preschool children. *Developmental Science, 6*(5), 498–504.

Karalunas, S. L., Fair, D., Musser, E. D., et al. (2014). Subtyping attention-deficit/hyperactivity disorder using temperament dimensions: Toward biologically based nosologic criteria JAMA. *Psychiatry, 71*(9), 1015–1024.

Kochanska, G. (1991). Socialization and temperament in the development of guilt and conscience. *Child Development, 62*, 1379–1392.

Kochanska, G. (1995). Children's temperament, mothers' discipline, and security of attachment: Multiple pathways to emerging internalizations. *Child Development, 66*, 597–615.

Kochanska, G., Murray, K. T., & Harlan, E. T. (2000). Effortful control in early childhood: Continuity and change, antecedents, and implications for social development. *Developmental Psychology, 36*(2), 220–232.

Kohnstamm, G. A. (1989). Temperament in childhood: Cross-cultural and sex differences. In G. A. Kohnstamm, J. E. Bates, & M. K. Rothbart (Eds.), *Temperament in childhood* (pp. 483–508). Chichester, England: Wiley.

Korn, S. J., & Gannon, S. (1983). Temperament, cultural variation, and behavior disorder in preschool children. *Child Psychiatry and Human Development, 12*(4), 203–212.

LeDoux, J. E. (1989). Cognitive-emotional interactions in the brain. *Cognition and Emotion, 3*, 267–289.

Lengua, L. J., & Wachs, T. D. (2012). Temperament and risk: Resilient and vulnerable responses to adversity. In M. Zentner & R. L. Shiner (Eds.), *Handbook of Temperament* (pp. 519–540). New York: Guilford.

Luu, P., Collins, P., & Tucker, D. M. (2000). Mood, personality, and self–monitoring: Negative affect and emotionality in relation to frontal lobe mechanisms of error monitoring. *Journal of Experimental Psychology: General, 129*, 43–60.

Moffitt, T. E. et al. (2011). A gradient of childhood self-control predicts health, wealth, and public safety. *Proceedings of the National Academy of Sciences, 108*, 2693–2698.

Olson, S. L., & Sameroff, A. J. (Eds.). (2009). *Biopsychosocial regulatory processes in the development of childhood behavior problems*. NY: Cambridge University Press.

Papoušek, M., & von Hofacker, N. (2007). Clinging, romping, throwing tantrums: Disorder of behavioral and emotional regulation in older infants and toddlers. In M. Papousek, M. Schieche, & H. Wurmser (Eds.), *Disorders of behavioral and emotional regulation in the first years of life: Early risk and intervention in the developing parent-infant relationship* (pp. 169–200). Washington, DC: Zero to Three.

Plomin, R. (1982). The concept of temperament: A response to Thomas, Chess, and Korn. *Merrill-Palmer Quarterly, 28*, 25–33.

Posner, M. I., & Rothbart, M. K. (2007a). *Educating the human brain*. Washington, DC: American Psychological Association.

Posner, M. I., & Rothbart, M. K. (2007b). Research on attention networks as a model for the integration of psychological science. *Annual Review of Psychology, 58*, 1–23.

Posner, M. I., Rothbart, M. K., Vizueta, N., Levy, K. N., Evans, D. E., Thomas, K. M., & Clarkin, J. F. (2002). Attentional mechanisms of borderline personality disorder. *Proceedings of the National Academy of Sciences of the United States of America, 99*(25), 16366–16370.

Probst, B. (2008). *When the labels don't fit*. New York: Random House.

Putnam, S. P., Ellis, L. K., & Rothbart, M. K. (2001). The structure of temperament from infancy through adolescence. In A. Eliasz & A. Angleitner (Eds.), *Advances in research on temperament* (pp. 165–182). Lengerich, Germany: Pabst Science.

Rothbart, M. K. (1982). The concept of difficult temperament: A critical analysis of Thomas, Chess, and Korn. *Merrill-Palmer Quarterly, 28*, 35–40.

Rothbart, M. K. (2011). *Becoming who we are: Temperament and personality in development*. New York: Guilford.

Rothbart, M. K., Sheese, B., Rueda, M., & Posner, M. I. (2011). Developing mechanisms of self-regulation in early life. *Emotion Review, 3*(2), 207–213.

Rothbart, M. K., & Bates, J. E. (1998). Temperament. In W. Damon & N. Eisenberg (Eds.), *Handbook of child psychology: Social, emotional and personality development* (5th ed., Vol. 3, pp. 105–176). New York: Wiley.

Rothbart, M. K., & Bates, J. E. (2006). Temperament. In W. Damon, R. Lerner, & N. Eisenberg (Eds.), *Handbook of child psychology, Sixth edition: Social, emotional, and personality development* (Vol. 3, pp. 99–106). New York: Wiley.

Rothbart, M. K., & Derryberry, D. (1981). Development of individual differences in temperament. In M. E. Lamb & A. L. Brown (Eds.), *Advances in developmental psychology* (Vol. 1, pp. 37–86). Hillsdale, NJ: Erlbaum.

Rothbart, M. K., Ellis, L. K., Rueda, M. R., & Posner, M. I. (2003). Developing mechanisms of temperamental effortful control. *Journal of Personality, 71*, 1113–1143.

Rothbart, M. K., & Rueda, M. R. (2005). The development of effortful control. In U. Mayr, E. Awh, & S. W. Keele (Eds.), *Developing individuality in the human brain: A festschrift honoring Michael I. Posner—May 2003* (pp. 167–188). Washington, DC: American Psychological Association.

Rothbart, M. K., & Sheese, B. (2007). Temperament and emotion regulation. In J. J. Gross (Ed.), *Handbook of emotion regulation* (pp. 331–350). New York: Guilford Press.

Rueda, M. R. (2012). Effortful control. In M. Zentner & R. L. Shiner (Eds.), *Handbook of temperament* (pp. 145–167). New York: Guilford.

Sheth, S. A., Mian, M. K., Patel, S. R., Asaad, W. F., Williams, Z. M., Dougherty, D. D., Bush, G., & Eskander, E. N. (2012). Human dorsal anterior cingulate cortex neurons mediate ongoing behavioural adaptation. *Nature, 488*(218). doi:10.1038/nature11239.

Silbersweig, D., Clarkin, J. F., Goldstein, M., Kernberg, O. F., Tuescher, O., Levy, K. N., et al. (2007). Failure of frontolimbic inhibitory function in the context of negative emotion in borderline personality disorder. *American Journal of Psychiatry, 164*, 1832–1841.

Super, C. M., Axia, G., Harkness, S., Welles-Nystrom, B., Zylicz, P. O., Parminder, P., et al. (2008). Culture, temperament, and the "difficult child": A study in seven western cultures. *European Journal of Developmental Science, 2*(1/2), 136–157.

Thomas, A., Chess, S., Birch, H. G., Hertzig, M. E., & Korn, S. (1963). *Behavioral individuality in early childhood*. New York: New York University Press.

Thomas, A., & Chess, S. (1977). *Temperament and Development*. New York: Bruner/Mazel.

Tronick, E. (2007). *The neurobehavioral and social-emotional development of infants and children*. New York: Norton Press.

Volling, B. L., Kolak, A., & Blandon, A. Y. (2009). Family subsystems and the development of self-regulation. In S. L. Olson & A. J. Sameroff (Eds.), *Biopsychosocial regulatory processes in the development of childhood behavioral problems* (pp. 238–257). New York: Cambridge University Press.

Wachs, T. D. (2000). *Necessary but not sufficient: The respective roles of single and multiple influences on individual development*. Washington, DC: American Psychological Association.

Chapter 8
A Psychodynamic Perspective on Assessment and Formulation

Brian Rasmussen

Abstract This chapter explores the scope, depth, and application of contemporary psychodynamic theory to clinical social work. It opens by refuting several commonly held misconceptions about the psychodynamic approach: that it is synonymous with Freudian psychoanalytic treatment, attends only to internal conflicts rather than to person–environment transactions, and has little empirical support. In fact, the guiding assumptions of psychodynamic theory—the importance of attachment and early development on later functioning; the impact of trauma; the need for sustaining relationships, ego integrity, and a sense of agency; the way the external world is taken in and becomes part of us—are critical to clinical practice. In this chapter, the components of a psychodynamic assessment and case formulation are explored, each with specific examples and assessment suggestions: defenses, affect and affect regulation, attachment style and relational patterns, identifications, conflicts, pathogenic beliefs, self-esteem and identity, trauma, strengths, and the interaction between self and aspects of the environment (e.g., how internalized stigma and oppression affect beliefs, motivation, self-efficacy, and expectations about life). Also important in the psychodynamic perspective is the clinician's use of self as an important source of knowledge.

Keywords Psychodynamic · Relational theory · Affect · Attachment · Conflict · Cognitive distortions · Defenses · Ego strengths and weaknesses · Unconscious · Pathogenic beliefs · Psychodynamic Diagnostic Manual (PDM) · Psychodynamic formulation

Introduction: Why This Matters

Psychodynamic theory has exerted a significant influence on clinical social work assessment, formulation, and treatment. However, this theory is often shrouded in misconceptions, confusion, and controversy, intimidating many newcomers who

B. Rasmussen (✉)
School of Social Work, University of British Columbia, Okanagan, BC, Canada
e-mail: brian.rasmussen@ubc.ca

© Springer International Publishing Switzerland 2015
B. Probst (ed.), *Critical Thinking in Clinical Assessment and Diagnosis*,
Essential Clinical Social Work Series, DOI 10.1007/978-3-319-17774-8_8

erroneously assume that it is suitable only for the "worried well," not for the oppressed and vulnerable populations that social work largely serves. Nonetheless, when beginning clinical social workers are exposed to this way of thinking about human development, psychological symptoms, and suffering, they appreciate the depth and complexity the theory provides for understanding both internal and external dynamics impacting the client. The value of a psychodynamic assessment becomes all the more valuable as a clinician begins to work with a client, whether supportively or in change-oriented therapies.

This chapter begins by defining key terms and exploring the scope and meaning of contemporary psychodynamic theory in social work. A review of the empirical support for psychodynamic theory and psychodynamically oriented practice serves to refute the misconception that the approach has little empirical basis. Next, a dynamic perspective is offered on the interaction between individual and environment that informs psychodynamic thinking, challenging the tendency to bifurcate these domains so that etiology and pathology are situated in one *or* the other domain. The chapter's essential point is that the dynamic and reciprocal interaction between individual and environment must be held central in assessment and case formulation. Consistent with a bio-psycho-social framework, psychodynamic thinking offers theoretical speculation about the hyphenations that separate these ontologically distinct domains, as well as their role in both well-being and suffering.

The scope of psychodynamic assessment is broad and includes, among other factors, attachment/relational style, defenses, ego strengths, early development, conflicts, identifications, self-esteem, pathogenic beliefs, the nature and quality of the facilitating environment, class, gender, race, and various forms of oppression. The subjective experience of the practitioner is also utilized as an important source of clinical information.

Guiding Questions

1. What is contemporary psychodynamic theory and what role does it play in assessment and case formulation?
2. What empirical support exists for psychodynamic concepts and practice?
3. What specific aspects of a person's personality, functioning, and life experience are assessed from a psychodynamic perspective?
4. What is the dynamic interaction between the individual and the environment?

What Is Psychodynamic Theory?

New practitioners are understandably puzzled by what, exactly, constitutes psychodynamic theory (Brandell 2004). Very often, psychodynamic theory is mistakenly equated with the classical Freudian theory of a century ago. Critics who fail to keep up with contemporary advances in psychodynamic theory propagate this myth in stereotypic ways, most egregiously in introductory psychology texts. In fact, contemporary psychodynamic theory contains many elements and guiding assumptions from empirically validated theories in various interdisciplinary fields, including social work, although they are rarely appropriately attributed. These guiding assumptions include the importance of early development for later functioning, the impact of psychological trauma, the need for empathic and sustaining environments, the way the external world is taken in and becomes part of us, and the fact that much of our experience in the world has unconscious dimensions. Support for these ideas comes from empirically validated theories such as attachment theory (Shilkret and Shilkret 2011), regulation theory (Schore and Schore 2014), object relations theory (Goldstein 2001), and neuroscience (Cozolino 2014; Miehls and Applegate 2014). The specific contribution of psychodynamic theory is in its hypotheses about the forces and interactions implied by the *hyphenations* in the bio-psycho-social perspective.

Central to psychodynamic theory, therefore, is the idea of a *dynamic interaction*, in contrast to a static or descriptive account of distinctly psychological and social phenomena. A dynamic perspective accounts for human motivational forces (desires, wishes, impulses) that interact with the external world (structures, rules, demands), producing a variety of possible outcomes. It also accounts for our sense of agency (our relative capacity to act freely in and on the world) and the facilitating or limiting aspects of social structures (external patterns of social organization). In addition, a dynamic perspective accounts for the impacts of oppression beyond a linear and unidirectional force.

In effect, it addresses the forces, motivations, and structures that operate both internally and externally, sometimes consciously, at other times beyond conscious awareness. Conceived in this way, psychodynamic theory is far broader than speculating about psychological conflicts in the mind as if they were independent of the external world. For example, psychodynamic theory allows us to talk meaningfully about a concept like internalized racism. Rather than limiting our understanding of this phenomenon to concrete or descriptive terms, a psychodynamic exploration incorporates ideas related to unconscious processes, psychological defenses, and structural forces. In this way, psychodynamic thinking allows us to understand the complex relationships between various processes and their effects.

It is important to distinguish psychodynamic theory from psychoanalytic theory, although as Berzoff et al. (2011) point out this is not easily accomplished, as the terms are often used interchangeably. Psychodynamic theory is considered much broader in its scope than psychoanalytic theory, although the former clearly draws heavily on the latter. Psychoanalytic theory is derived from, and historically linked to, the practice of psychoanalysis, and is comprised of many streams or schools of thought that owe their origin to Freud's earliest theorizing (Palombo et al. 2009). All subsequent psychoanalytic thinking can, in fact, be thought of as an extension, modification, or rejection of these early contributions. The historical development of psychoanalytic thought led to the emergence of drive theory, ego psychology, object relations, and self-psychology (Berzoff et al. 2011). Contemporary developments include attachment theory, relational theory, and intersubjective theory.

While there are important differences among these schools of thought, each offers unique contributions and answers to enduring clinical questions, including the following: What is the role of the unconscious? What is the impact of early development? What are our prime motivators? How is the mind structured? How does the external world become part of us? How do we connect to others? How do we develop a sense of self? How do we protect ourselves from emotional pain? And how do we regulate our internal world?

Empirical Support for Psychodynamic Practice

> Many aspects of Freudian theory are indeed out of date, and they should be: Freud died in 1939, and he has been slow to undertake further revisions (Westen 1998, p. 333).

Tongue in cheek though it may be, Westen's quip suggests a widely held perception that psychoanalytic theory is still equated with Freud's writing from the early twentieth century and perhaps better left as a relic of that generation. Those not versed in contemporary psychoanalytic writing might ask: What value can psychodynamic theory have for contemporary social work assessment and practice? Well, lots actually. For an extensive empirical review of major psychodynamic concepts, readers are referred to Westen's (1998) wide-ranging analysis of the evidence for major theoretical propositions informing psychodynamic practice. These concepts, for which Westen argues there is considerable evidence, include the ideas that much of mental life, including motivation, is unconscious; our mental and emotional life is often bound up in conflict, particularly around important relationships; stable personal patterns are developed in childhood and endure into adulthood; our mental representations of self and others influence behavior; and finally, personality development moves from less mature and dependent states to greater independence and mature self-regulation. Such empirical evidence is important, as psychodynamic practice relies on a foundation of informed interdisciplinary research. The translation of these ideas into psychodynamic therapies then becomes the focus of research aimed at seeking empirical support for these approaches, both in themselves and in comparison with other treatments.

Mishna et al. (2013), in their review of evidence for psychodynamic practice, suggest that it is "social work's best kept secret" (p. 289). They conclude that a "growing body of evidence signifies the need to incorporate psychodynamic understanding into social work education and practice" (p. 299). Shedler (2010) also concludes that "considerable evidence supports the efficacy of psychodynamic psychotherapy" (p. 98). Both articles provide a compelling review of the literature in support of psychodynamic practice. While a full review of such evidence is beyond the scope of this chapter, readers are encouraged to consult Drisko and Grady (2012) and Fonagy et al. (2005) for additional scholarly review.

The Psychodynamic Assessment Process

Perhaps it is easier to start with what a psychodynamic assessment is *not*. It is not a formulaic process. There is no checklist of items to ask each and every client, no lists of five or seven or twelve criteria to meet (as i DSM diagnostic categories). There are no hard and fast timelines, no rigid rules. Moreover, the assessment process is not separate from or independent of the nature and quality of the developing therapeutic relationship. The assessment process from a psychodynamic perspective is just that—*a process*. There is, of course, content to explore and formulations to develop, perhaps theories to apply, but first, it is important to consider the assessment process itself and the clinician's own stance.

The assessment process begins with attention to the therapeutic relationship and establishment of a connection with the client. Clients make decisions early on as to whether the clinician is a person that they can open up to, tell secrets, and trust. And indeed, as Control Mastery Theory suggests (see Silberschatz 2005), clients continue to unconsciously test the clinician for these conditions of safety. Consequently, attending to the client's subjective sense of safety and trust pays huge dividends in the quality of the information gathered. We will return later to the importance of the therapeutic relationship in the assessment process with a discussion of the value of considering transference and countertransference.

Rather than extracting information from the client, like a laboratory attendant drawing blood, the assessment interview is collaborative in nature. The client is an active participant in the process and is encouraged to speculate on the meaning of events and stories told. The clinician might ask: What effect do you think such and such event had on you? Do you see any connections between this and that? How do you make sense of that? Because insight, self-reflection, and self-understanding are valued in a psychodynamic approach, posing such questions helps the clinician understand how the client has generated meaning and encourages a curious attitude toward life experience. Of course, holding curiosity is a highly valued trait in a clinician as well, and an important force in the process.

The reins of a psychodynamic clinician's curiosity are in the hands of theory and intuition. Held gently, the reins steer here and there, responsive to what is taking place, rather than the tight-fisted grasp of a dogmatic practitioner who is certain which paths to go down. Theory helps us know where to explore, what doors should and can be opened, and what aspects of *this* person's history might be examined. For example, the etiological basis of depression is complex and diverse, requiring us to explore questions of trauma, loss, attachment, abandonment, abuse, neglect, genetic vulnerability, oppression, and so on. Holding the possibility of a complex and diverse formulation of a client's situation necessitates a complex and diverse scope of assessment. The purpose of any assessment is to gather information that will lead to a reasonable and therapeutically viable understanding and formulation of a client's presenting problems. In essence, assessment from a psychodynamic perspective is as much process as product.

What Is Assessed?

The suggestion that assessment from a psychodynamic perspective is a process, a collaborative venture, an exercise driven by both theory and curiosity, has not yet answered the question of what exactly is assessed. In this section, we explore what a psychodynamic assessor attends to.

Consistent with a long-held social work practice principle, a psychodynamic perspective "starts where the client is." Opening questions are directed at what has brought the client here today. What kind of help is he/she looking for? Open-ended questions allow the client to further expand on these problem areas. The importance of open-ended questions cannot be over estimated. These are questions (or more accurately, directives) such as: "Can you say more about that?" "Tell me more about what that was like." "It would be helpful if you could share more about your current situation." Open-ended questions provide space for clients to tell their stories as unimpeded as possible. They also allow the clinician time and space to listen. Much has been written about listening from a psychodynamic perspective beyond what space allows for here, but suffice to say that beyond gathering basic information, the primary activity of the clinician is listening deeply to the client. Such listening also attends to the *way* the client tells the story. The clinician listens for overarching themes, dominant metaphors, and recurring patterns. In addition to this broadly focused attention, the clinician listens for specific data that answer important theoretically informed questions that are highly relevant for formulating a treatment plan. Much of what follows owes considerable credit to McWilliams (1999, 2004); although not a social worker, her writing has made an enormous contribution to the application of psychodynamic theory to assessment, formulation, and treatment.

Assessing Defenses An important part of psychodynamic assessment is evaluating the client's defensive structure. Accordingly, we consider what defenses the client uses most frequently and for what purposes. However, assessing defenses is not straightforward and has to be inferred from a range of client information and behavior. That is, the clinician cannot simply ask: "So, can you tell me what kind of defenses you characteristically employ to ward off anxiety and conflict?" Defenses by their very nature operate unconsciously. Thus, skill in assessing defenses comes with time, experience, knowledge, and helpful supervision.

Nonetheless, each person tends to use a cluster of defenses that are often consistent with individual personality style. Still, we must ask whether these defenses are reflective of the client's current situation or indicative of the client's overall personality style, or both. Are the defenses considered lower or higher level defenses? Lower level defenses tend to distort reality more than higher level ones and, when used consistently over time, reflect the nature of one's personality development (Goldstein 1995). For instance, people diagnosed with borderline personality disorder may be prone to use splitting (seeing others or themselves as all good or all bad), denial (of major aspects of reality), projection (consistently blaming others for one's own downfalls), and projective identification (seeing and fixing the problem in others), particularly when under emotional distress. Individuals who have been severely traumatized may make extensive use of dissociation (separating off internal aspects of themselves). People who function at a higher level may be more inclined to use intellectualization (use of ideas disconnected from feelings), rationalization (giving "reasonable" rationales for behavior), undoing (reversing an unacceptable thought, feeling, or behavior), and sublimation (turning an impulse into socially acceptable behavior) to protect themselves from anxiety and emotional distress. Everyone uses a range of defenses, including the so-called higher and lower level defenses, so it is important not to jump to conclusions early on. The important question is whether these defenses are adequate to manage the anxiety and distress, knowing that what is being defended against is a mixture of conscious and unconscious elements. Assessing a client's defenses is an important aspect of assessing overall ego strength and weakness, which will be discussed below, but it cannot be stressed enough how important defenses are to an individual's overall functioning.

Assessing Affect Hand in hand with evaluating a client's use of defenses is assessing affect and affect regulation. Clinical social workers often work with clients who struggle with affect regulation. Some are impulsive or easily trigger to anger and aggressive outbursts. In contrast, others might be highly constricted in their emotional world and unable to name a feeling. Some may struggle to contain overwhelming feelings of sadness and loss. Still others may be overwrought with anxiety to the point of debilitating panic. The question can be considered for each client: What are the dominant affects the client is struggling with? Sadness? Anger? Rage? Envy? Jealousy? Shame? etc. What is fueling these affects? And further, what is the client's capacity to fully feel, regulate, and verbalize these feelings? Answers to these questions are central to developing a treatment plan that might range from supportive interventions to expressive and ego modifying forms of treatment (Goldstein 1995). Data to answer these questions may come from the observation of the client's behavior in the treatment interview or from self-report. But when we link the issue of affect with the idea of defenses, the assessment from a psychodynamic perspective becomes more complex. For instance, because of psychological defenses, it is not uncommon for a client who presents as sad and weepy in early sessions to actually be experiencing and containing a great deal of anger or rage. The opposite can also be true—a client who presents full of anger and rage may be defending against a good deal of sadness and depression underneath.

Consequently, the clinician who is undertaking an assessment from a psychodynamic perspective will be wondering: Can this client withstand the full impact of affect that is not consciously being processed? What is the client's capacity for affect regulation? Answers to these questions are important with respect to a proposed treatment approach.

Assessing Attachment Style and Relational Patterns Contemporary clinical social work practice has a strong relational foundation—putting the therapeutic relationship at the heart of our work (Goldstein et al. 2009). Consequently, central to a psychodynamic assessment is consideration of the client's attachment style and relational patterns (Brandell and Ringel 2007), as there is considerable evidence that attachment difficulties underscore a host of mental and emotional problems (Fonagy 2001). Although not used in a purely diagnostic sense, it is important to assess whether a client is securely or insecurely attached. If insecurely attached, what descriptive terms aptly fit the client's subjective experience and behavior? Is the client preoccupied with other people? Or, on the contrary, dismissive of attachments, preferring to retreat inside when experiencing need? Are the client's relationship patterns "all over the map," suggestive of a disorganized style of attachment? Is this person able to maintain boundaries when connecting with others? How are separations handled? And in the "here and now," how does the client relate to the clinician? Does the client present as passive and dependent, waiting for the clinician to solve the problems, or does the client keep the clinician at a distance, unable to trust the help that is offered?

Again, answering these questions may take time, and one has to be cautious about reaching conclusions too quickly since there are many reasons a client may be reacting to a clinician—reasons that may have to do with differences in class, gender, sexual orientation, and race within the therapeutic dyad, rather than with an attachment problem. Caution is also advised not to arrive at conclusions based on little information or data that are primarily reflective of seeing a client at an especially distressed period.

Assessing Identifications The link between adult attachment patterns and early development has been well established; so too, there is a strong connection between early development and one's later identifications—that is, the people we have *internalized*. Given that we take in the external world, consciously and unconsciously, the good and the bad, it is important to know something about the significant figures in a person's early life (McWilliams 1999).

The clinician might ask: "Who were you closest to growing up? Who was there for you when you needed help or support? Was there anyone you admired or wanted to emulate?" Sadly, it is sometimes very difficult to find even that one person—when the answer to the question was "nobody was there for me"—but it is important to keep searching, even if the answer is perhaps a coach for one season or a baby sitter at another moment. It is also important to assess whether there were significant figures in the client's life with whom they *dis*-identified, perhaps consciously rejecting them. For instance, a young male client might state, "I knew early on that I did not want to grow up to be like my father who was abusive to my mother and us kids." In assessing these identifications and their internalization, the clinician can simply reply: "Tell me about your mother/father—what was she/he like as a person?" The answer to this open-ended question provides a glimpse of how that person was internalized by the narrator. What the clinician is listening for is not some objective truth about this person (as even siblings may have very different perspectives) but, rather, how the person is held in the mind of the client. Frequently, the client captures the internalized experience in a metaphor or a prototypical story.

As is often the case, significant figures in one's life were/are neither all good nor all bad. Consequently, the internalization of these important people may contribute to conflicted internal states in relation to these people. One way of defensively dealing with this conflict is to split off "all the good parts" or split off "all the bad parts." In the latter case, it is not unusual for a client to initially present a parent in idealized terms, only later to share "the other side." Another client might initially portray a parent as all bad, negating the positive qualities and good aspects of this caretaker. The realization that caretakers can be both good and bad leads to what Melanie Klein referred to as the depressive position (Hinshelwood 1989).

Assessing Psychological Conflict Freud believed that living in a modern civilized world contributed to psychological conflict, an idea that seems to have proven true. As Freud also knew, people are conflicted for many reasons: relationships, work, parenting, major life decisions, transitions, and so on. Consistent with psychoanalytic thinking, aspects of these conflicts are usually unconscious.

Moore and Fine (1990) write that "psychic or intrapsychic conflict refers to struggle among incompatible forces within the mind [while] external conflict is that between the individual and aspects of the outside world. (They often go together, however)" (p. 44). Some conflicts may emanate from opposing desires such as independence and dependence, or autonomy and wish to please others. Other conflicts might emerge as a consequence of clashes between sexual and aggressive impulses and one's internalized prohibitions about such behavior. Wrought with conflict about these opposing desires and wishes, the ego is thought to institute compromise formations that may take the form of symptoms (Schamess 2011). For example, a young person might be conflicted about a choice to attend college away from home or to study nearby. Operating outside of awareness is the idea that leaving home will injure one or both parents. The conflict about pursuing independence might result in depressive symptoms that, by default, cause the young person to remain in the home.

Similar to assessing defenses, it is not simply a matter of directly asking the client: "So what are you conflicted about?" Rather, the process requires careful listening to the tension in the narratives, the "push and pull." In many cases, the clinician will hear a tension that can be summarized as a conflict between *wishes and fears*. In the above example, the client's conflict is between the wish for independence and a fear of harming a loved one. The impact is often symptomatically expressed with anxiety or perhaps depressive symptoms. To what degree there is a basis for this particular fear may require further therapeutic exploration.

Assessing Pathogenic Beliefs In addition to grappling with a client's conflicts, it is important to assess pathogenic beliefs, that is, cognitive distortions that may have conscious and/or unconscious dimensions. These pathogenic beliefs may take the forms such as: "I'm just a bad apple"; "Everybody is just there to use and exploit me"; "I can't do anything right"; "If I let someone get close to me they will leave"; "Nobody can be trusted"; or as in the example cited above, "If I pursue my own independence it will harm others."

There are enumerable pathogenic beliefs that can be identified during assessment using cognitive models of practice (Northcut and Heller 1998). What differs in a psychodynamic perspective is the idea that the origin of some of these pathogenic beliefs may remain unconscious (McWilliams 1999). A clinician might curiously explore these beliefs further with questions such as: "When did you first start thinking that you were a bad apple?" Or, "Where do you think that idea came from?" Consequently, exploring the origin and interpersonal history of these beliefs that are outside of the client's awareness becomes part of the work toward changing these cognitions.

Assessing Self-esteem Self-esteem and its regulation are frequently presented as a problem in clinical practice. Chronic low self-esteem can be associated with numerous disorders, particularly mood disorders. Therefore, assessing for healthy self-regard and its maintenance is important. Does the individual have a strong self-regard that is not prone to wild, sporadic fluctuations? For instance, some individuals who are sensitive to criticism can find themselves plunging to depths of despair and self-loathing following a minor insult or psychological injury. Others may have an unrealistic overevaluation of themselves, giving off an air of arrogance and self-centeredness, consistent with a narcissistic personality style. For others, their presentation might secretly conceal a veiled form of narcissism (Kealy and Rasmussen 2012). Like other aspects of a psychodynamic assessment, the clinician must determine whether the presentation of the client is situational and contextually driven, or reflective of longer patterns of self-experience.

Assessing for Trauma Trauma, abuse, and neglect are frequent experiences in the lives of many social work clients (Ringel and Brandell 2012). Psychodynamic theory has made many important contributions to understanding the effects of traumatic experience and their relationship to mental disorder. Indeed, early psychoanalytic theory frequently concerned itself with the effects of psychic trauma, particularly in response to world wars and sexual abuse. Contemporary concerns for the effects of trauma have broadened our conceptualizations to include relational or developmental trauma (e.g., sustained childhood abuse and neglect), in addition to shock trauma (e.g., being robbed at gunpoint). Severe and lasting childhood trauma will affect neurodevelopment and impact, among many things, an individual's capacity for affect regulation (Schore 2012a).

Awareness of trauma and its relationship to mental health alerts the clinician to assess for such experiences. For example, van der Kolk (2005) argues that the origins of borderline personality disorder are related to early childhood traumatic experience. Accordingly, at one mental health clinic where I worked, it was a standard part of the assessment interview to ask "Have you ever had unwanted sexual experiences?" The reasoning was that if you *don't* ask directly, it may be a long time before the client is able to share these potentially traumatic experiences, particularly experiences that generate shame.

Other questions might address specific aspects of the client's potential experience. For people from non-dominant groups: "Have you ever been bullied?" For people of color: "Have you experienced racial hate?" For first responders (police, fire fighters, paramedics, etc.): "Have you ever had your life threatened?" For people living in impoverished neighborhoods: "Have you ever been the victim of violent crime?" In each case, the line of questioning has to be done with tact and timing, always for the purpose of understanding the client's presenting concerns and life story. At the same time, it is important to remember that not everyone who is exposed to a potentially traumatic experience will develop symptoms.

Assessing Strengths Having explored the need to assess for defenses, affects, attachment style and relational patterns, identifications, conflicts, pathogenic beliefs, self-esteem, and trauma, it is equally essential to assess for strengths, assets, and positive aspects of the person's life. The importance of identifying a client's strengths for a balanced assessment and treatment planning ought to be patently obvious; nonetheless, it often remains neglected. In doing so, there is no need to shift paradigms; that is, one can still hold a dynamic perspective. Using the concepts from above with the same line of questioning and listening, a clinician can similarly identify an individual's strengths. For instance, a client could be described as having a secure attachment style, trust for others, strong ego defenses, and healthy self-esteem. From an ego psychology perspective (see Schamess and Shilkret 2011; Goldstein 1995), an individual might be assessed as having good reality testing, clear judgment, and considerable mastery of some of life's essential tasks. The same person might, of course, also show significant impairment in object relations, poor regulation of affects and impulses, and rigid use of defenses. A balanced assessment of a client's relative strengths and weaknesses provides the clinician with greater clarity and specificity moving forward into treatment. Additionally, the clinician assesses strengths in the client's social environment and the impact of these resources for the client's well-being.

Clinician's Use of Self

As objective as we would like to be in conducting a clinical social work assessment, we can never make claims for complete objectivity—nor would we want to. Our subjectivity, or put in psychodynamic terms, our countertransference, provides an additional *way of knowing*. From an interpersonal neurobiological perspective (Schore 2012b), we connect with clients right-brain- to-right-brain, registering nonverbal, non-conscious affect. Our job, from this perspective, is to reflect upon and attempt to sort out what we are feeling and experiencing. This reflective knowledge may suggest important information beyond the client's conscious verbal reports.

For instance, a client may tell a story of loss in a matter-of-fact way that evokes considerable sadness in the clinician. Does this affective experience in the clinician reflect split off or dissociated affect in the client? Possibly. But whatever the answer may be, a clinician must hold a reflective stance about his or her own psychological and emotional experience of being with this person at this time. Further, this view on the clinician's use of self-necessitates that the clinician have a deep awareness of his or her *own* identities, personality, life history, and social location. Given that the assessment interview is a profoundly relational event, understanding our side of the equation becomes essential in the interpretation and formulation of the assessment data.

A Dynamic Perspective on the Role of the Environment

The role of the environment has been a theoretically contentious issue in clinical social work practice. The historic splits in theorizing, what some refer to as the battles between the internal and external (Berzoff et al. 2011) or the micro-and-macro divide (Kondrat 2002; Payne 2005), have plagued social work for more than a hundred years (Haynes 1998). Much of this debate is beyond the scope of this chapter to review. Suffice it to say that psychoanalytic theory has long been criticized for privileging the internal world of the client over external realities. However, contemporary psychodynamic perspectives have witnessed a major shift in recent years, a shift toward the *dynamic interaction* between the individual and the environment. This integrated approach requires that we theoretically incorporate both psychodynamic theories and critical social theories in our assessment and treatment interventions. Again, space here does not allow a full exposition of these ideas but readers are encouraged to explore the work of Berzoff et al. (2011), Rasmussen and Salhani (2008, 2010a, b), Alford (1989), Craib (1989), Elliot (2004), Clarke (2003), Borden (2009), Layton et al. (2006), Oliver (2004), Rustin (1991), Wachtel (2002), and Altman (2010). All are fine examples of work to integrate the social and psyche dimensions in a dynamic fashion.

In assessing the environment, psychodynamic practitioners are interested to know about many aspects of life that are common concerns from a general social work perspective—work, income security, family, access and barriers to resources, housing, supports, spiritual elements, education, and so on. Most particularly, however, a psychodynamic assessment is interested in understanding forms of oppression such as race, class, gender, ability, age, and sexual orientation from both a *descriptive* account of these categories and also as the *dynamic* interaction between these oppressive social forces and their relationship to the presenting problems or symptoms.

For instance, oppressive social forces of homophobia and heterosexism exert a negative force on individuals who do not conform to heteronormative models and thus need to be accounted for. Such understanding must be mindful of conscious and unconscious dimensions of these dynamics, accounting for internalized oppression along with the very real external barriers that prevent one from actualizing a full life, including the effects of external and internalized stigma. This same thinking considers how the practitioner may have also internalized oppressive dynamics at an unconscious level.

The Use of the DSM and Psychodynamic Diagnostic Manual (PDM)

Psychodynamic practitioners, like many other social work clinicians, have an uneasy relationship with the *Diagnostic and Statistic Manual* (DSM). Critiques of the DSM come from many quarters, and certainly this volume captures many of these concerns. Perhaps a central critique of the DSM from a psychodynamic perspective is the fact that it is descriptive and atheoretical. Although describing disorders by clusters of symptoms holds some value and arguably remains an important starting ground for treatment decisions, the diagnosis tells us little about individuals' uniqueness, personal stories, subjectivity, and the experience and meaning of the "symptoms" that have been catalogued. The DSM describes much yet explains little for a particular individual.

Consequently, some psychodynamic practitioners have turned to the Psychodynamic Diagnostic Manual (PDM). This manual was collaboratively developed by several psychoanalytically oriented professional associations representing psychiatry, psychology, and from social work, the National Membership Committee on Psychoanalysis in Clinical Social Work (PDM Task Force 2006). Diagnostically, the framework set forth in the PDM systematically describes "healthy and disordered personality functioning; individual profiles of mental functioning, including patterns of relating, comprehending and expressing feelings, coping with stress and anxiety, observing one's own emotions and behaviors, and forming moral judgments; and symptoms patterns, including differences in each individual's personal subjective experience of symptoms" (PDM Task Force 2006, p. 2).

In this regard, the PDM is argued to better represent the whole person, rather than a cluster of symptoms. Complexity is embraced through a multidimensional approach to capture overall functioning and subjective experience. The PDM is organized along three dimensions or axis; Dimension I includes personality patterns and disorders, Dimension II captures mental functioning, and Dimension III focuses on manifest symptoms and concerns. Integrated into an overall understanding of the individual, the PDM contributes to a more comprehensive diagnostic formulation that captures cognitive, emotional, and behavioral functioning.

The Psychodynamic Formulation

A psychodynamic formulation is thus a theoretically driven exercise in analyzing and synthesizing complex data about a person and his or her life experience. While it is a formulation, it is far from formulaic. It is essentially a tentative hypothesis about psychosocial functioning that attempts to understand symptoms and presenting problems within an indivdiual's life context. It is more than simply recounting or summarizing the client's history. Although a psychodynamic formulation may incorporate a DSM diagnosis, where appropriate, it recognizes that, for example, depression in one person can look considerably different from depression in another. A depressed gay African American adolescent may present with the same symptoms (low mood, poor appetite, poor sleep, suicidal ideation, etc.) as a fifty-year-old white male executive, also diagnosed with depression, but the social and psychodynamics of each case may be significantly different and lead to different formulations. The symptoms are important, but so too are the unique events, life situations, and subjective experiences.

A psychodynamic formulation may be focused around a core issue, particularly if that issue is thought to underscore the client's most pressing concerns. Summers and Barber (2010) organize their thinking around the following core psychodynamic problems: depression, obsessionality, fear of abandonment, low self-esteem, panic anxiety, and trauma. For Luborsky and Crits-Christoph (1998), developers of the Core Conflictual Relationship Theme (CCRT) method, the focus is on three interacting components. The first component has to do with what the client wishes for, the second component with the way other people respond to this wish, and the third with how the client reacts to these reactions. For example, a child may wish to be comforted by a parent when emotionally distressed but is rebuffed, which the child internalizes as "my feelings don't matter." When this experience is repeated many times, the child may develop an internal style of disavowing his or her own feelings, with a concordant interpersonal style of not expecting emotional attunement from others.

From a clinical social work perspective, one that gives credence to the bio-psycho-social perspective, a psychodynamic formulation must also consider a broad range of social forces. In particular, a dynamic formulation must include an understanding of various forms of oppression. This work is speculative and requires thoughtful consideration on the clinician's part, especially in the task of attributing proportional weight to various oppressive factors. To exclude these forces is to deny important aspects of a client's lived experience.

Conclusions

Assessment from a psychodynamic perspective is a complex, unfolding process. Recognition is given to conscious and unconscious forces, present and past, and internal and external dynamics. Held central is the dynamic and reciprocal interaction between the individual and the social world; often, identification of a core issue attempts to explain as much of the person's suffering as possible. As we will see in the case of Ray, the ensuing analysis results in a rich and intricate formulation that attempts to do justice to his lived experience. While trauma and loss will be suggested as core issues for Ray, this is not meant to negate other possible assessments and treatment issues. It is entirely possible that two psychodynamically oriented clinicians might arrive at somewhat different conclusions, given the same data. In the end, however, most would agree that attending to unconscious forces, early development, defenses, attachments, identifications, relational qualities, pathogenic beliefs, personality, oppression, trauma, and one's dynamic interaction with the environment form the basis of assessment for the purpose of providing clinical social work treatment. Nonetheless, any assessment is only the starting point—merely an abstract impression of a real life.

Application to the Case of Ray

The case of Ray is complex. Respecting that complexity, yet succinctly capturing core issues in a way that leads to treatment goals, is the task of a psychodynamic assessment and formulation.

Briefly summarized, Ray's presenting problems involve relational dynamics with his current girlfriend including, most importantly, acts of physical aggression toward her. Aggression is further noted in other settings toward males with little provocation. He presents to therapy reluctantly at first, apparently motivated to save his relationship. Ray is currently faced with the possibility of losing his police job, deemed not stable enough for full duty. He has overdosed twice in the past few months and was diagnosed with a major depression. Following the second overdose, he was diagnosed with bipolar disorder, type II. Ray's history is presented in somewhat idealized ways, although there is a significant history of victimization (bullying and child sexual abuse) and trauma (failure to rescue children, and the events of 9/11). He was adopted shortly after birth, presenting his early environment in positive terms.

To begin, Ray presents with a number of important strengths. He is hard working, determined, loyal, and a committed parent. He completed high school and police academy, suggesting intelligence, ego strength, and the ability to complete goals. In treatment, he appears motivated to change and has deepen a relationship with the clinician.

From a psychodynamic perspective, *core* problem areas appear to arise from the effects of trauma and loss. Trauma has both a significant historical dimension in the form of sexual abuse and a more recent impact through work-related experiences. The repeated sexual abuse occurred at the hands of a highly valued authority figure, at a key developmental period (age 13) for building *relational* intimacy and trust. It is hypothesized that shame and disgust are likely dominant *affects* that Ray must defend against. These affects are, for the most part, *unconscious*. He appears to keep these affects outside of awareness through the *defenses* of denial, dissociation, minimization, and turning against the self. Further, the unresolved effects of trauma include, most prominently, rage. This affect may be displaced and acted out in current life situations, disconnected from its original source. Consequently, affect and its regulation are central therapeutic concerns.

Cognitive distortions in the form of self-blame ("he felt it was his fault") are characteristic for victims of sexual abuse, and function to diminish *self-esteem*. His self-esteem is further negatively impacted by the potential loss of a valued occupation and relationship problems. Indeed, it seems that his whole worldview (loyalty, duty, trust) has been severely challenged by these traumatic life events.

Diagnostically, Ray is thought to suffer from a major depression and bipolar disorder. The evidence for depression seems non-controversial; however, data supporting the diagnosis of bipolar disorder are not evident in the case description and would need further exploration. The Psychodynamic Diagnostic Manual (PDM) describes two different depressive personality disorders as follows: "the introjective (previously called melancholic), characterized by guilt, self-criticism, and perfectionism, and the anaclitic, characterized by shame, high reactivity to loss and rejection, and vague feelings of inadequacy and emptiness" (p. 44). There is some evidence for both forms of this subjective experience of depression for Ray; consequently, further probing in treatment is recommended. Either way, longer-term treatment is recommended by the PDM. The PDM states "…data suggests that interpretation and insight are pivotal to therapeutic progress with introjective patients, while the experience of a reliable relationship seems more central to the improvement of anaclitic ones" (p. 46).

Curiously, the *diagnosis of PTSD* is not mentioned despite considerable evidence for the label (nightmares, helplessness, emotional distress, guilt, intrusive images, etc.) and direct exposure to overwhelming traumatic situations. This traumatic distress was exacerbated with subsequent police duty of watching screens of people being victimized, while immobilized to help. Although trauma does not explain all of Ray's life difficulties, it would seem to be a huge mistake to not fully assess its impact on his functioning. The PDM notes that PTSD impacts affective states, cognitive patterns, somatic states, and relationship patterns. With respect to the latter, the PDM indicates that "relationship patterns may include changes in relating to others, based on decreased trust and increased insecurity, and states of numbness, withdrawal, chronic rage, and guilt" (p. 103–104).

Ray presented for help "distressed over his relationship with his live-in girlfriend Cecilia." What can be said about his *relationship style and attachment patterns*? While further assessment information is required, particularly with respect to details related to the adoption, there is some suggestion of an anxious, preoccupied attachment style. He appears jealous and controlling in his intimate relationships. His current relational difficulties are in contrast to his reports of more idealized early childhood experience, although interestingly, there is no mention in the report of his mother and their relationship—including information about her death and his experience of this loss. However, the case study report does suggest a deepening therapeutic relationship characterized by increase sense of safety and trust, which bodes well for a successful therapeutic outcome.

There are numerous social forces that shape and influence this case study. Being *Caucasian* ordinarily concurs considerable privilege, and likely does for Ray, yet he was bullied as a youth for his different appearance of being "blonde and slight of build." *Gender* dynamics influence the way the Ray experiences his own masculine identity and relationship expectations, giving shape to the way he presents his problems. Ray's violence in his intimate relationship suggests the internalization of patriarchal views of male dominance in such unions. He highly values loyalty ("above all else") and experiences rejection as a complete affront to his sense of self ("once something is broken, it's broken"). His views with respect to intimate relationships require additional exploration and challenge. Further, Ray's middle-*class* upbringing intersects with gender in his expressed values and aspirations. He appears to seek satisfaction and stability in family life and work. His choice of occupation is consistent with traditional gendered identity and middle-class values. Unfortunately, while success in these goals was temporarily attained, it has recently been lost. His income, one important marker of class and status, is at serious risk. A rapid downward shift in his class status has been experienced as a "devastating" loss for Ray and must be incorporated into an understanding of his suicidal depression as well as his relationship losses.

Practical Exercises

1. Select a client from your field placement, or consider a character from a book or film, and try to understand the person in terms of some of the core concepts of psychodynamic assessment. What conflicts, identifications, and defenses can you identify? What do you observe about this person's affect regulation, relational patterns, and self-esteem? What kind of assessment tell you that a psychiatric assessment does not?

2. Now consider this person within his or her environment. First, write a straightforward *description* (economic and cultural factors, oppression, etc.). Then rewrite this description from a *dynamic* perspective, exploring the interaction between social forces and their relationship to the presenting problems or symptoms. What has been internalized? What unconscious processes may be occurring?

3. A psychodynamic formulation revolves around a core issue. Based on your analysis in the first two exercises, what do you believe is the person's core issue? What evidence supports your conclusion? What evidence might be used to argue against this conclusion? What do you need to find out in order to decide whether your conclusion is correct?

References

Alford, F. (1989). *Melanie Klein and critical social theory*. New Haven: Yale University Press.
Altman, N. (2010). *The analyst in the inner city: Race, class, and culture through a psychoanalytic lens* (2nd ed.). Hillsdale: The Analytic Press.
Berzoff, J., Melano Flanagan, L., & Hertz, P. (Eds.). (2011). *Inside out and outside in: Psychodynamic clinical theory and psychopathology in contemporary multicultural contexts* (3rd ed.). Lanham: Jason Aronson.
Borden, W. (2009). *Contemporary psychodynamic theory and practice*. Chicago: Lyceum Books.
Brandell, J. (2004). *Psychodynamic social work*. New York: Columbia University Press.
Brandell, J., & Ringel, S. (2007). *Attachment & dynamic practice. An integrative guide for social workers & other clinicians*. New York: Columbia University Press.
Clarke, S. (2003). *Social theory, psychoanalysis and racism*. New York: Palgrave Macmillan.
Cozolino, L. (2014). *The neuroscience of human relationships* (2nd ed.). New York: W.W. Norton & Company.
Craib, I. (1989). *Psychoanalysis and social theory*. Amherst: University of Massachusetts Press.
Drisko, J., & Grady, M. (2012). *Evidence-based practice in clinical social work*. New York: Springer.
Elliot, A. (2004). *Social theory since freud: Traversing social imaginaries*. London: Routledge.
Fonagy, P. (2001). *Attachment theory and psychoanalysis*. New York: Other Press.
Fonagy, P., Roth, A., & Higgitt, A. (2005). Psychodynamic psychotherapies: Evidence-based practice and clinical wisdom. *Bulletin of the Menniger Clinic, 69*(1), 1–58.
Goldstein, E. (1995). *Ego psychology and social work practice*. New York: Free Press.
Goldstein, E. (2001). *Object relations theory and self psychology in social work practice*. New York: The Free Press.
Goldstein, E., Miehls, D., & Ringel, S. (2009). *Advanced clinical social work practice: Relational principles and techniques*. New York: Columbia University Press.
Haynes, K. (1998). The one-hundred year debate: Social reform versus individual treatment. *Social Work, 43*(6), 501–509.
Hinshelwood, R. D. (1989). *A dictionary of Kleinian thought*. London: Free Association Books.
Kealy, D., & Rasmussen, B. (2012). Veiled and vulnerable: The other side of grandiose narcissism. *Clinical Social Work Journal, 40*(1), 356–365.
Kondrat, M. E. (2002). Actor-centered social work: Re-visioning person-in-environment through a critical theory lens. *Social Work, 47*(4), 435–448.
Layton, L., Hollander, N. C., & Gutwill, S. (Eds.). (2006). *Psychoanalysis, class and politics: Encounters in the clinical setting*. London: Routledge.
Luborsky, L. & Crits-Christoph. (1998). *Understanding transference: The core-conflictual relationship theme method* (2nd ed.). Washington, DC: American Psychological Association.
McWilliams, N. (1999). *Psychoanalytic case formulation*. New York: Guilford Press.
McWilliams, N. (2004). *Psychoanalytic psychotherapy: A practitioner's guide*. New York: Guilford Press.
Miehls, D., & Applegate, J. (2014). Introduction to neurobiology and clinical social work. *Smith College Studies in Social Work, 84*(2–3), 140–143.
Mishna, F., Van Wert, M., & Asakura, K. (2013). The best kept secret in social work: Empirical support for contemporary psychodynamic social work practice. *Journal of Social Work Practice, 27*(3), 289–303.
Moore, B., & Fine, B. (1990). *Psychoanalytic terms and concepts*. New Haven: The American Psychoanalytic Association and Yale University Press.
Northcut, T., & Heller, N. (1998). Assessment of cognitive schemes and attribution in psychodynamic treatment. *Smith College Studies in Social Work, 68*, 185–202.
Oliver, K. (2004). *The colonization of psychic space: A psychoanalytic social theory of oppression*. Minneapolis: University of Minnesota Press.

Palombo, J., Bendicsen, H., & Koch, B. (2009). *Guide to psychoanalytic developmental theories*. New York: Springer.

Payne, M. (2005). *Modern social work theory* (3rd ed.). Chicago: Lyceum Books.

PDM Task Force. (2006). *Psychodynamic diagnostic manual*. Silver Spring, MD: Alliance of Psychoanalytic Organizations.

Rasmussen, B., & Salhani, D. (2008). Resurrecting fromm. *Smith College Studies in Social Work, 78*(2/3), 225–301.

Rasmussen, B., & Salhani, D. (2010a). Some social implications of psychoanalytic theory: A social work perspective. *Journal of Social Work Practice, 24*(2), 209–225.

Rasmussen, B., & Salhani, D. (2010b). A contemporary Kleinian contribution to understanding racism. *Social Service Review, 84*(3), 333–350.

Ringel, S. & Brandell, J. (Eds.). (2012). *Trauma: Contemporary directions in theory, practice, and research*. Los Angeles: Sage.

Rustin, M. (1991). *The good society and the inner world: Psychoanalysis*. Verso, London: Politics and Culture.

Schamess, G. (2011). Structural theory. In J. Berzoff, L. Melano Flanagan, & P. Hertz (Eds.), *Inside out and outside in: Psychodynamic clinical theory and psychopathology in contemporary multicultural contexts* (3rd ed.). Lanham: Jason Aronson.

Schamess, G., & Shilkret, R. (2011). Ego Psychology. In J. Berzoff, L. Melano Flanagan, & P. Hertz (Eds.), *Inside out and outside in: Psychodynamic clinical theory and psychopathology in contemporary multicultural contexts* (3rd ed.). Lanham: Jason Aronson.

Schore, J. (2012a). *The science of the art of psychotherapy*. New York: W.W. Norton & Company.

Schore, J. (2012b). Using concepts from interpersonal neurobiology in revisiting psychodynamic theory. *Smith College Studies in Social Work, 82*, 90–111.

Schore, J., & Schore, A. (2014). Regulation theory and affect regulation psychotherapy: A primer. *Smith College Studies in Social Work, 84*(2–3), 178–195.

Shedler, J. (2010). The efficacy of psychodynamic psychotherapy. *American Psychologist, 65*(2), 98–109.

Shilkret, R., & Shilkret, C. (2011). Attachment theory. In J. Berzoff, L. Melano Flanagan, & P. Hertz (Eds.), *Inside out and outside in Psychodynamic clinical theory and psychopathology in contemporary multicultural contexts* (3rd ed.). Lanham: Jason Aronson.

Silberschatz, G. (2005). An overview of research on control-mastery theory. In G. Silberschatz (Ed.), *Transformative relationships: Control-mastery theory of psychotherapy* (pp. 189–218). New York: Routledge.

Summers, R. F., & Barber, J. P. (2010). *Psychodynamic psychotherapy: A guide to evidence base practice*. New York: Guildford.

Van der Kolk, B. A. (2005). Developmental trauma disorder: Toward a rational diagnosis for children with complex trauma histories. *Psychiatric Annals, 35*(5), 401–408.

Wachtel, P. (2002). Psychoanalysis and the disenfranchised: From therapy to justice. *Psychoanalytic Psychology, 19*(1), 199–215.

Westen, D. (1998). The scientific legacy of Sigmund Freud. *Psychological Bulletin, 125*(3), 333–371.

Chapter 9
Narratives of Illness, Difference, and Personhood

John P. McTighe

Abstract Narratives help us weave the tale of who we are and of how we fit (or don't) into the world around us. Thus, a search for meaning—an enduring "root metaphor" for one's identity and existence, and a way of coping with challenges to that metaphor—is central to the narrative perspective. The question for a clinician is not simply: "Is this client mentally ill" or "With which mental illness should the client be diagnosed." Rather, it is: "What is this person's understanding of the nature of his or her experience, and the meaning of that experience for identity and sense of self? What does it mean, for this person, to be mentally ill? To think of oneself, or be thought of by others, as mentally ill?" Using narrative theory, the chapter examines how ideas and attitudes about mental disorder are shaped by cultural values and stereotypes, and how the experience of trauma can shatter the narrative of self and world. Placing the question of illness, differentness, and personhood within a social justice perspective, it challenges clinicians to consider how the vocabulary of illness is used to frame experience and, in many cases, to minimize, marginalize, or discount the individual's own lived experience.

Keywords Constructivist · Intentionality · Particularity · Phenomenality · Referentiality · Root metaphor · Temporality · Trajectory

Introduction: Why This Matters

Human beings are storied creatures. As we live our lives from start to finish, within the bounds of what both memory and interpretation will allow, we weave the tale of who we are as persons and of how we fit (or do not) into the world around us. These stories both emerge from and serve to craft our sense of ourselves, the world, and ourselves in the world. The term that is commonly used for the construction of these stories and their role in our development and identity is *narrative*. For those who

J.P. McTighe (✉)
School of Social Work, Ramapo College of New Jersey, Mahwah, NJ 07430, USA
e-mail: jmctighe@ramapo.edu

© Springer International Publishing Switzerland 2015
B. Probst (ed.), *Critical Thinking in Clinical Assessment and Diagnosis*,
Essential Clinical Social Work Series, DOI 10.1007/978-3-319-17774-8_9

suffer from what we consensually refer to (though with a good deal of subjectivity and variation, as we shall see) as a "mental disorder," a psychiatric diagnosis can have a significant impact, not only on the course of treatment that is indicated but on the very sense of self—the sense of one's own personhood. What does it mean to be mentally ill? To think of oneself, or be thought of by others, as mentally ill? And how does this impact the story of who I am in the world?

In this chapter, we will consider the nature and function of narrative and the implications of a narrative understanding of mental illness for the social and cultural worlds in which we live. We will explore what this means for the sense of self of persons identified by themselves or others as mentally ill. We will consider the multiple ways that this term may be used by individuals, families, institutions, and society. As social workers are interested in justice for the clients with whom we work, it is essential for us to be aware of the ways in which constructs like "mental illness" may be used, not only to understand and support people who are suffering in a particular kind of way, but also how the term "mental illness" may be used in subtle and not so subtle ways as a weapon of oppression and marginalization (Wakefield 2013). We need to understand that the words we use to frame our own experience or that of others may serve to minimize, marginalize, or, in some other way, further discount the lived experience of the persons with whom we work. We need to understand the responsibility that comes with the role of diagnostician that we take on in our practice.

Guiding Questions

1. What is narrative, and what does it mean to consider the nature of lived experience through a narrative lens?
2. Is mental illness a condition that an individual experiences? Or is it an attribute of the person's self—an aspect of identity?
3. What is the impact of culture (in all its many layers and manifestations) on our understanding of mental illness, and how is the label of mental illness used in the social environment?
4. How can a narrative understanding of the nature of mental illness, and an openness to the ever-unfolding narrative of our clients, inform our approach as social workers?

Background

Narrative and narrative psychology belong under the general rubric of constructivist theory. Constructivist theory is based on the notion that what is observed is conditioned upon the observer and that the development of a sense of identity and self has both psychological and sociological dimensions (Crossley 2003; Kelley 1996). White and Epston (1990) pioneered a particular form of narrative therapy as a means of helping individuals deconstruct and reconstruct the ways in which they crafted the stories of their personal lives by selective attention to certain details along with the subjugation of other details. This approach highlights the central role of language and story (inherently both psychological and sociological) in the constitution of the self in the social world (Crossley 2003).

In other words, when we tell the story of who we are or how some aspect of our lives has unfolded, we invariably craft and interpret that story by selecting certain details of experience that both shape and illustrate our understanding of our experience. This selection is inevitably limited and, as we will see, is influenced by the seemingly countless individuals and happenings that have contributed to our sense of self.

Consider, for example, a client named Robin who tells you, her social worker, that she began a new job a couple of weeks earlier. When you ask Robin how the job is going, she replies that she is miserable! She goes on to say that on that day, she was given a task to complete that was terribly complicated. She had never been asked to do anything like that before. She found it very confusing, was rushing to meet the deadline given to her by her boss, and felt overwhelmed to the point of tears. In fact, she is thinking of quitting her job the next morning, or not even going to work at all. She is certain she will never be able to handle the job. She does not even know why they hired her in the first place. In response, you empathize with how difficult the day was for her, of course, and how overwhelmed she is feeling. You go on to ask Robin how she was feeling about the job prior to the frustrating events of the day. She reports that, generally speaking, she has really liked the work she has been doing. She has a pleasant and supportive boss and friendly coworkers. She actually felt quite proud of herself for getting the job since it is really a step up from her former job, both in responsibilities and salary.

When you ask her to reflect on how she has handled such challenging work assignments in the past, particularly when the work is new to her, Robin reports that she seems to have always found a way to get the job done. She says that she has is a hard worker who can figure things out when she puts her mind to it. And she has never had the experience of a boss being really unhappy with the work she has done. She has asked questions when she needs to and has usually gotten the support she needs to do her work. She even goes on to tell you about a seemingly impossible task in a previous job that she was able to tackle all on her own, and how her boss was so proud of her for what she had done. As you reflect back to her what she has said about her overall positive experience of the job so far, and her history of competence and success in the work place, you begin to see the expression on her face changes. "What might all of this positive experience have to say to you about the kind of day you had today" you ask her? Robin pauses and suggests that maybe it was just a really bad day and that she will likely adjust to the new work and responsibilities as she has done in the past. From a narrative perspective, we might say something like this. In order for the client to tell herself the story that her new job is bad, overwhelming, and beyond her abilities, she has to subjugate or ignore all the positive experiences she has had since starting the job as well as her history of success in the workplace. She does not do this purposefully or consciously, of course. The power of the unpleasant experience and story of the day simply takes over and gets in the way of her telling a more balanced story of the events. The narrative approach helps her to balance out the story in her mind in a way that is richer and more adaptive while still being realistic.

Crossley (2000, 2003) states that narrative is built upon the notion that human consciousness is constructed by the ordering of events in a meaningful way. Two constitutive dimensions of this, he suggests, are time/temporality and relationships/connections. That is to say, the meaning of all human events is structured by their placement in time and over the course of time, as well as by their relationship or connection to other events that make up the life narrative of the subject.

Some social constructivist perspectives are criticized for portraying daily, lived experience as overly disordered, chaotic, and random. In contrast, Crossley states, the narrative approach attends to the more orderly sense of daily existence that we structure along the lines of meaningfulness and anticipated trajectories. To illustrate this, Crossley uses the example of trauma and the disruption it causes to the survivor's sense of self and his or her expected course of experience. This is similar to the notion that trauma shatters the assumptive world of the survivor (Janoff-Bulman 1992). Through the experience of the rupture of trauma, or the development of a mental illness that may change the anticipated course of our life, we realize the profound orderliness that that we had come to expect from the narrative of our experience. But beyond this, it is through the process of narrative and story making that we reconstitute a sense of meaning and order both in ourselves and in the world around us.

Sarbin (1986) introduces his work on narrative with the premise that all human conduct is framed by the structure of a story and that such stories provide the vehicle for the interpretation of inter- and intrapersonal interactions and intentionalities. Calling upon the work of Pepper (1942), Sarbin offers the notion of the *root metaphor* as a framework for understanding the function of narrative.

> [Pepper] demonstrated how the root metaphor provides the framework for the construing of occurrences in the natural and man-made worlds. The root metaphor constrains the kinds of philosophical or scientific models to be applied either to the task of observing and classifying or to the task of interpreting and explaining. (p. 4)

In other words, the root metaphor conditions the way we think about experience and the meaning it has in the overall narrative of our life. To this end, narrative makes use of *emplotment* to organize events and the observations of experience into coherent and relatable units of meaning. It is the way in which human beings "impose structure on the flow of experience" (p. 9).

Narrative, Meaning Making, and the Search for Meaning

Arguably the foremost thinker of the twentieth century with respect to the role of meaning making was Frankl (1946/1984). Based on his experience of life in a Nazi concentration camp, Frankl's development of logotherapy aimed to address what he saw as the existential importance of making meaning of suffering and adversity as a way of accessing inner resources that could lead to survival and transformation. Frankl writes:

> We must never forget that we may also find meaning in life even when confronted with a hopeless situation, when facing a fate that cannot be changed. For what then matters is to bear witness to the uniquely human potential at its best, which is to transform a personal tragedy into a triumph, to turn one's predicament into a human achievement... In some way, suffering ceases to be suffering at the moment it finds a meaning, such as the meaning of sacrifice. (p. 135)

Numerous theoreticians and researchers have since added to the literature regarding meaning making and the search for meaning in human experience, as well as to the understanding of the human person as a meaning-making creature. As far back as the eighteenth century, Kant (1787/1965) argued that the human person seeks to bring order to the world based on distinct criteria that structure our experience. This all has important ramifications for our understanding of what is means to be diagnosed (or to diagnose someone else, for that matter) and to live with a mental illness.

Narrative, Meaning and Trauma As in the case of Frankl (1946/1984), meaning is commonly sought in the context of trauma, loss, and suffering. Indeed, the psychological consequences of trauma can be conditioned by the meaning ascribed to the event by individuals, families, and communities (Fullerton 2004). Neimeyer (2005) notes that human beings understand loss in the context of narratives that are thematized in such ways as to offer us a sense of the *why's* of our experience. Trauma, however, can shatter the themes by which we understand our world and incite us to renegotiate our systems of meaning.

This notion is central to the work of Janoff-Bulman (1992, 2006) who suggests that human beings possess a conceptual system of assumptions about the world and the way it works. These assumptions are hierarchically organized such that our most basic assumptions are also the most general and the least open to change. Janoff-Bulman (1992) proposes that most people share three basic assumptions. First, the world is benevolent. This belief may be held even in the face of contradictory evidence because the fundamental point of reference is one's personal experience of the world and the people in one's life, and most people's experience has been predominantly positive. Second, the world is meaningful. The notion that the world makes sense emerges from our desire to find congruity among ourselves, other people, and the events that happen to us. We tend to look to culturally endorsed rules like justice and personal control, for example, to understand this. Third, the self is worthy. Most of the time, most people perceive themselves as good, capable, and moral, even if this requires some degree of compartmentalization or rationalization.

Janoff-Bulman (1992) suggests that the origins of these assumptions are to be found in the earliest periods of human development in relationship to what has been variously conceived of as our emerging sense of basic trust (Erikson 1968), the sufficiency of the holding environment (Winnicott 1965), the positive nature of our attachment to our primary caregivers (Bowlby 1969, 1973), or the organization of our earliest perceptions and experiences into what Stern (1985) calls representations of interactions that have been generalized (RIGS).

According the Janoff-Bulman's (1985, 1992, 2006; Janoff-Bulman and Frantz 1997) thinking, the experience of trauma shatters the fundamental assumptions on which we have built our sense of the world. Consequently, the process of recovery from trauma requires a renegotiation or rebuilding of our assumptions in order to reestablish our sense of equilibrium. This is an intuitive rather than a deliberate process that allows us to regain our ability to perceive benevolence and meaning in the world, as well as our own sense of self-worth.

Janoff-Bulman (1992) highlights three strategies by which traumatized individuals accomplish this. First, comparison to others allows us to focus on those whom we perceive to be worse off than us, thereby providing us with some sense of reassurance with respect to our own experience and position in the world. Second, the interpretation of one's role in the victimization (often entailing self-blame) allows us to restore the notion that we, in fact, had some sort of control over the situation. This, she notes, may be characterological ("There is something wrong with me, not the world") or behavioral ("I did something I should not have done or misjudged the situation in some way"). Third, individuals search for some benefit from the trauma they have endured or a sense of the purpose for which this might have happened to them. This effort to find deeper meaning in the experience (e.g. lessons that have been learned, a deepened sense of altruism, a validation of justice or fairness) enables us to continue perceiving the world as a place that makes sense.

Utilizing social work's traditional emphasis on the strengths perspective combined with a narrative constructivist view, Norman (2000) encourages clinicians to create a supportive, listening environment in which clients can begin to tell the story of their trauma, all the while listening for and identifying signs of strength, survivorship, and resilience. Whether clients have been traumatically impacted by a single event or prolonged exposure, whether they have been traumatized in adulthood after a history of relatively healthy psychological functioning or bear the enduring scars of a traumatic childhood, helping them to reframe their stories in light of these positive elements can facilitate clients' growth and allow for the creation of useful metaphors that can help them find meaning in past as well as future experience.

Narrative and culture The effort to make meaning of our experience extends beyond the realm of the individual and the interpersonal into the social and cultural worlds in which we are immersed (Neimeyer 2005). Here too, human beings seek validation of their interpretation of experience as they express it in culturally endorsed ways.

Bruner (1986, 1990, 1991, 2004) has been a key contributor to the understanding of the role of narrative in organizing human experience and the recursive relationship between intentionality, action, and interpretation. In a seminal essay on narrative, Bruner (1991) argues that narrative is a cultural product that aids in the organization of our sense of reality. He proposes that narrative has ten features:

- Diachronicity: the unfolding of events over time
- Particularity: the relationship of narrative to *specific* events
- Intentional state entailment: the influence of narrative characters' beliefs, desires, theories, and values
- Hermeneutic composability: the human capacity to tell and interpret stories *as* stories
- Canonicity and breach: the notion that what makes a story worth telling is the way in which it constitutes a break from that which is routinely expected
- Referentiality: the relationship between the contents of the story and its resemblance to our consensual sense of what is possible in reality
- Genericness: the ability of a narrative to be identified with a certain genre
- Normativeness: the implication of the narrative about the way in which one ought to behave or what one ought to do
- Context sensitivity and negotiability: the relationship between the roles of the author or story and the reader/listener with respect to context and interpretation of the narrative
- Narrative accrual: the notion that stories build on one another and flow from one to the other

Bruner further develops his thought about the matrix that gives rise to narrative in his understanding of the reflexive relationship between narrative and culture. Beginning with the premise that life in time is necessarily cast within and described by a narrative structure, Bruner notes that life is not only expressed in narrative form, but that narrative comes to structure the expectations and parameters within which life can be experienced (Bruner 2004). This is importantly and more broadly set on the stage of culture where the relationships between individual and communal narratives are shaped. Thus, Bruner suggests, culture provides us with the canon within which our narratives are formed and so conditions the range of meanings and possible worlds accounted for in our stories (Bruner 1986, 2004). Bruner (1990) writes:

> …by virtue of participation in culture, meaning is rendered *public* and *shared*. Our culturally adapted way of life depends upon shared meanings and shared concepts and depends as well upon shared modes of discourse for negotiating differences in meaning and interpretation. (p. 12–13)

Howard (1991) agrees and suggests that narrative is a way of knowing within the context of culture and cross-cultural society. Culture can be seen as communal consensus regarding a system of meaning that informs the way individuals within groups make sense of lived experience. "Thus, a culture can be thought of as a community of individuals who see the world in a particular manner—who share particular interpretations as central to the meaning of their lives and actions" (p. 190). Such meanings may fall into the domains of science, religion, politics, morality, and others. Furthermore, individuals may participate in any number of subcultures that make up a larger social framework and may take on a variety of roles within these subcultures. It is also possible for there to be conflicting messages that are delivered by the subcultures to which one belongs. All these factors contribute to the way in which people make meaning of their experience in the world.

This is particularly important in the context of social work practice as we attend to the ways in which differences between our clients and us impact our understanding of their experience. We must always maintain a curiosity that wonders how the world, or life, looks and feels from the perspective of the client. This is always shaped by the many aspects of diversity that inform our experience: race, ethnicity, gender, age, socioeconomic status, sexual orientation, ability, family structure, social history, etc.

Saleeby (1994) details the significance of attending to the intersection of the meaning systems of the client, the worker, and the culture in which they are embedded. This perspective takes seriously the impact of the social and political environment, and can provide a vehicle for the client and worker to name and challenge structures that may oppress the client as well as the community. This is particularly important when considering issues of diagnosis and the stigma that, for so many, is attached to the idea of mental illness.

Building on the work of Bruner (1986), Josselson (1995) suggests that Bruner has brought legitimacy to the study of narrative as a means of understanding human knowing. This narrative perspective gives a privileged place to the human experience of the observer or teller who is embedded in the matrix of society and culture. Josselson writes: "Narratives are not records of facts, of how things were, but of a meaning-making system that makes sense out of the chaotic mass of perceptions and experiences of a life" (1995, p. 33). This perspective is essential when we consider the nature of diagnosis. Particularly compared to the exercise of diagnosing according to the fixed criteria of the DSM, the narrative perspective draws our attention to the lived experience of the individual in the context of society and culture, and seeks to understand the meaning of that experience on these multiple levels.

The Impact of Culture and Dimensions of Diversity: A Narrative Tapestry

As we consider social work practice with the mentally ill, these insights compel us to reflect further on the multiple cultures and subcultures to which our clients belong. We must ask ourselves what the multi-layered cultural and social system reflects to the client about the meaning of mental illness and of being mentally ill. Even before receiving a diagnosis, the client has been raised and immersed in a particular cultural milieu and has absorbed its outlook. Following a diagnosis, the client may well find him or herself to be the object of the culture's narrative about mental illness and the mentally ill. Clients are likely to internalize these messages as they strive to make sense of their experience and to reconfigure their sense of self and the narrative of their past and anticipated future in light of a mental illness. This interaction between the individual and the social environment is the birthplace of stigma, both *externalized* stigma projected by others and *internalized* stigma absorbed into the person's sense of self.

We have noted that the nature of narrative development is recursive. That is to say, individual and communal narratives shape, challenge, and reinforce each other. We are influenced by the dominant narratives of the cultures in which we are immersed. We, in turn, to a greater or lesser extent impact the narratives of our culture(s). This may occur in spheres ranging from the closest circle of family and friends, to the broadest social and cultural arenas within which we live. Those who are marginalized and oppressed, however, may experience severe barriers to their ability to influence the narrative of the wider culture, particularly with respect to an experience like mental illness. This may be true, for example, of the homeless, those who do not share the language of the dominant culture, and the poor, as well as racial, ethnic, and sexual minorities. These individuals—who, because of their marginalized status, often feel invisible and unheard—may well find this is only exacerbated by a diagnosis of mental illness.

As was discussed with respect to the work of Bruner (1986, 2004), we frame our experience in the language and constructs that are available to us. In other words, the social and cultural vocabularies that we have learned both shape our understanding of our experience and provide the parameters within which we can communicate about it. A clear example of this phenomenon is found in the cultural concepts of distress discussed in the DSM–5 (American Psychiatric Association 2013). For example, the experience of *ataque de nervios* (an attack of nerves) is encountered among many Latino clients as a culturally understood if upsetting manifestation of anxiety and distress. Similarly, *ghost sickness* may be manifested by members of some Native American communities as a consequence of the work of witches or other evil powers. Within their cultural contexts, these conditions have a significance that would be understood differently (or not at all) by those outside the culture.

Examples of culture-based understandings of mental illness and mental distress abound. In Quechua-speaking rural communities in southern Peru, for example, mental illness, or what is referred to as "madness," is considered a social and family phenomenon that is manifested in a disturbance of behavior around food and eating. Here, where the sharing of food has deep relational significance for the family, a disruption in the ability to partake in the meal is a key sign of mental illness. Similarly, the act of feeding and the provision of food is viewed as an essential aspect of care for the person who is mentally ill (Orr 2013). Additionally, culture has a great bearing on the process of many individuals in their struggle to accept a mental health diagnosis. Culture may serve both as a facilitator and as a barrier to this kind of acceptance (Mizock and Russinova 2013; Sosulski et al. 2010).

In order to work ethically with our clients and to connect empathically with their experience, social workers must always reflect on the meaning of mental illness in cultural context. This requires having a familiarity with the kinds of symptoms or forms of emotional expression that are endorsed and those that are pathologized in a given cultural and social situation. This distinction influences both the experience of the client who internalizes such messages and the way in which the environment responds to the individual.

For example, consider how a phenomenon such as grief is viewed in your culture. Following the death of a loved one, what is considered an "appropriate" amount of time to grieve? What are the common ways that grief is expressed in your culture? How do others respond to those who are grieving? At what point would a person's grief come to be viewed as "dysfunctional" or problematic? All of these questions serve to reflect the notion that grief is both a personal and a social/cultural experience. The meaning of grief is conveyed to us through a social and cultural narrative that helps us make sense of that experience. When an individual's experience or manifestation of grief falls outside of this culturally endorsed narrative, we come to think of this as a "problem"—something that deviates from what is acceptable and thus needs to be addressed.

Members of the mental health community, including social workers, have a unique voice in shaping the social narrative around issues of mental illness and psychopathology. Consider, for example, the origins of the term *hysteria*. The word hysteria comes from the ancient Greek term for *womb* or *uterus*. This reflected the Greek notion that symptoms of hysteria were caused by a medical issue in the uterus. Thus, hysteria was an illness experienced exclusively by women. Over time, this medical connotation gave way to a more psychological understanding of hysteria as a neurotic disorder marked by symptoms of anxiety with somatic manifestations such as fainting and paralysis (Freud and Breuer 1985/2004). It was continued to be viewed, however, as a condition related to the uterus, and thus, diagnosed only in women. In social and cultural narrative, the term has come to take on a negative connotation that led to its use as a gender-biased form of dismissal or marginalization.

Currently, the debate about cultural narratives of mental illness continues. With the publication of the most recent edition of the *Diagnostic and Statistical Manual of Mental Disorders* (American Psychiatric Association 2013), there has been much discussion of the broader significance of changes to a manual that is already a product of a social and cultural discourse about mental illness. Horwitz and Wakefield (2007), for example, have posed the challenging question of whether or not the psychiatric establishment has come to pathologize the experience of ordinary sadness. If this is so, is it a reflection of a culture that has grown increasingly intolerant of the experience of emotional discomfort or of a medical and pharmaceutical industry that is invested in classifying the experience as a disorder for which they can provide costly treatment? In other words, if you are experiencing troubling feelings in your mind and body, and there is a medicine that might allow you not to have to feel those feelings, does this mean you have a disorder? Given what is known about the recursive nature of narrative development, the great likelihood that it is both and that each of these factors serves to reinforce the other.

All of this has clear implications for our understanding of the nature and experience of mental illness as well as for the work of assessment and diagnosis in which we engage as social workers. Social workers are continually "walking the tightrope" between diagnostic and environmental approaches to an understanding of mental illness (Probst 2013). It is imperative for us, at all times, to maintain an awareness of the socially constructed nature of the concept of mental illness—a concept that simultaneously shapes both the ways in which we receive the experience of our clients and our understanding of mental illness itself. Narrative theory is well suited to this approach (Fisher and Freshwater 2014). A narrative perspective must ask not only, "Is my client mentally ill" or "With which mental illness should be client be diagnosed" but "What is my client's understanding, both of the nature of their experience, and the meaning of this for their identity and sense of self?" This is a question to which we now turn our attention.

Diagnosis and the Self: Do I Have a Mental Illness? Or Am I Mentally Ill?

Since narrative both emerges from and continually shapes our appraisal of the meaning of our experience, it has an inevitable relationship to our sense of self and identity. The way in which we tell the story of our life gives dimension to our sense of self, the world, and our self in the world. When considering the nature of mental illness then, the question that arises for those struggling with such conditions is, "Do I have a mental illness? Or am I mentally ill?" As with other chronic and serious conditions affecting the health of our clients (e.g. cancer), individuals with mental illness come to think of their illness and themselves within the framework that society and culture sets for them (Bruner 1991, 2004). This shapes the range of possible versions or meanings available to them and may be quite limiting. It may also mean that these individuals struggle greatly to maintain a sense of self that is broader than the illness with which they live. For many, this entails a process of mourning the loss of the life that they might have imagined for themselves—not necessarily a life marked by any particularly grand accomplishments, but one free of the burdens that a mental illness may impose.

Narrative Practice with Diverse Populations

Social work practice is about encounter—which means encounter with the *other* (Ploesser and Mecherill 2011). This may be construed, of course in many ways, inasmuch as there are perhaps countless ways of being *other*. Narrative approaches to practice perhaps pay particular attention to this kind of encounter with the *other*. Our engagement with clients almost inevitably stands at the intersection of a variety of forms of otherness, since the likelihood of encountering a client who is "like me" in every readily identifiable way is more than remote (and even then there is still more otherness to discover!).

Whether we are focusing on difference in gender, race, ethnicity, sexual identity or preference, religious belief, socioeconomic status, family structure, physical or intellectual ability, or even mental health, we are continually interacting with clients whose otherness may be more or less apparent to us. As often is the case in social work practice, the ways in which a client appears different may be more apparent to us than the ways in which we are similar. This may be particularly true when we work with clients who are marginalized or oppressed. When intersectionality, the compounding effects of the interaction of multiple categories of marginalization or oppression, is at play, our sense of the client's difference may be even greater (Murphy et al. 2009).

Of course, difference or otherness is likely to be a factor not only for us, but for the client as well. Relying on perceptions of our difference from them, clients may question our ability really to hear and understand the story of their experience. Together, clients and social workers may be drawn into the sometimes tempting fantasy that, in order to understand each other, we must be "similar" is some sort of apparent way. This, of course, is deceiving and dividing, and can undermine the development of a productive therapeutic alliance. In fact, both similarity and difference from our clients contain the possibility of many layers of meaning. What is more essential is our ability to convey an openness to the *other* in the experience of their otherness and to demonstrate to our clients the kind of curiosity that was discussed above.

Our encounter with otherness in the social worker/client relationship is an instance of the intersection of unique narrative worlds. For this reason, work with two clients will never be quite the same, even if we do grow through the process of accumulating knowledge as we become more familiar with some of the shared aspects of experience. Like our clients, we come to this work with our own narratives—our stories of ourselves, the world, and ourselves in the world. At its deepest level, our ability to work with our clients in all the many aspects of our mutual diversity is not dependent on the acquisition of the "facts and figures" about this or that client group. It is not about what I have learned about a "category" of person, though this kind of information can be somewhat helpful in a general way. Rather, it depends on our ability to be open to the client and the worlds of human experience, understanding, and even misunderstanding they (and we) bring into the consulting room. It depends on our ability to take seriously on a fundamental level their experience as they experience it, and to make ourselves available with whatever knowledge and skill we have so that together we can help the client come to a deeper, richer, and more life-giving sense of self. While it does not guarantee success with every client in every situation, it can go a long way to helping us bridge those gaps that we imagine keep us so far apart.

Conclusions

Just as Crossley (2000, 2003) suggested that the experience of trauma reveals the profound orderliness that we have come to expect from life, so too the diagnosis and experience of a mental illness calls into question profoundly important, but commonly taken for granted dimensions of our day-to-day existence. These include the clarity of mind and stability of emotion that we associate with mental health. Similarly, the ability to study or work, to organize the business of daily life, and to experience mental and emotional leisure, and even the opportunity to participate in stable and reciprocal relationships may all be adversely impacted by mental illness.

As social workers, we must be attentive to the possible impact of all of this on the client's narrative of the self. "Do I have a mental illness, or am I mentally ill?" It is essential to note that some of these narratives, based solely in psychiatric conceptualizations of pathology, may serve to oppress and obscure rather than to liberate and clarify. Some clients may feel that diagnoses have been used to marginalize and blame them, or to dismiss their experience. I still recall the first time I heard a clinician, frustrated by the challenging and erratic moods and behaviors of a client, say dismissively, "She's just a borderline!" I recall, too, a most helpful supervisor who modeled a stance of compassion when she said, "I wonder what terrible things she has experienced in life that taught her that this is what she needs to do in order to have her needs met?" In all the years since that moment, the voice of that supervisor has reminded me to seek to understand the experience of the client—no matter how difficult that experience may be.

As social workers working to achieve justice with and for our clients, (Wakefield 2013) one of our responsibilities may be to help clients break open and challenge the dominant and dominating narratives that have come to shape their sense of identity—to call into question the cultural "givens" and facilitate a re-storying of clients' experience in a way that is nuanced, life affirming, and liberating. This is not to deny the problematic and disruptive aspects or impact of mental illness. Rather, it is to support mentally ill persons in developing a sense of self that is constituted by more than their mental illness. This is something that narrative is uniquely suited to do.

Application to the Case of Ray

How then, can we apply this narrative approach to the case of Ray? In this section, we will consider a number of aspects of Ray's experience and the ways in which they might impact his narrative of his life and experience. This kind of understanding is essential if one wishes to work with such a client from a narrative perspective.

First, it may be noted that Ray is similar to a great number of men who may be compelled at some point to present for treatment. I say "compelled" here, because often such clients will say that they might not have sought out treatment for themselves if the pain they were experiencing and the circumstances they were enduring had not made the need for help clear to them. So often, these men have been socialized to believe that strength and masculinity require emotional endurance and that they should be able to tolerate without difficulty whatever degree of adversity life may throw their way. For such men (and some women as well, of course), reaching out for help represents some form of weakness. Alternatively, some may feel that requests for support should be confined to a specific group of people who may share a similar experience. (E.g. "A cop should only talk to a cop; a fireman should only talk to a fireman. No one else will understand.") It is important to acknowledge that both of these perspectives are, in fact, narratives. They are the kind of narratives that can exercise tremendous emotional authority in the lives of individuals and may make it difficult for some to receive the help they need.

Nonetheless, Ray does find himself in treatment. The distress he is experiencing in his daily living has prompted him to seek out some assistance. There are a number of aspects of Ray's story to which we might attend from a narrative perspective. Ray has a meaningful relationship to his Catholic identity. This has impacted his story in a number of ways. He is a man who believes that loyalty and trust are qualities of great importance in a person. (Note that although this may not seem like a "narrative," it constitutes part of the "story" that Ray tells himself about what it means to be a good person in the world. This is the narrative way of framing Ray's outlook.)

Ray believes that one must never "rat out" another person. This is part of the conflict that he has with his girlfriend, Cecilia. He feels that she has betrayed him to the priest from whom they sought counseling as a couple (something Ray was reluctant to do and agreed to only because he thought it meant they were going to work things out) by disclosing personal details and then "turning on him". It is also part of his conflict in disclosing the abuse he sustained by a priest when he was a boy. One might consider that this reluctance may also be connected to the kind of narrative about male strength that was discussed above. Ray should be strong enough not to be impacted by these events that, however painful, took place long ago.

Ray's narrative as an Irish Catholic has also informed his sense of guilt and the meaning guilt has for him. Ray continues to feel guilt over the three abortions Cecilia had at his request. Here, there is evidence of conflicting narratives. One lies at the heart of his guilt over the abortions. Another lies at the heart of his belief that they were necessary at the time. It is not uncommon to encounter clients who are struggling with two or more competing narratives in treatment. And it is often powerful and therapeutic to be able to "hear" or pick out those narratives and bring those competing claims to light for further exploration and resolution.

Ray's understanding of guilt has also impacted his feelings about not having been able to save a fourth child from a burning building. In this case, the guilt narrative leads Ray to highlight in his consciousness the loss of one child while subjugating or downplaying his rescue of three others. This was reinforced by the events of 9/11 that led to a shift in his narrative about the meaning of being a police officer. Where he once focused on the satisfaction he derived from "doing some good", he now feels that, "All I ever see are the worst things about people...". To make matters worse, in light of recent events, Ray's gun has been taken away and he has been reassigned to a post where he feels that all he can do is wait and watch while bad things happen—a passive stance that further confirms this shift in his narrative.

We may notice that there are ways in which both narratives contain aspects of "truth", but that many circumstances of life lead us to attend selectively to some details more than others. In narratively base treatment, we work with clients to broaden these filters in order to help them see a broader (and hopefully more adaptive and healthy) array of narrative elements that are "also true" and just as true as the more limiting stories they have been telling themselves.

Another significant narrative that has shaped Ray's experience involves the story of himself as different from others (particularly peers), and as needing to defend himself. As a boy of eight or nine, Ray became aware of himself as smaller than and different in appearance from his neighborhood peers. It is also his understanding that these factors contributed to the bullying he experienced. All of this led to the development of his narrative that it is important for him to be tougher and stronger.

While this story or perspective may have served some adaptive purpose (though there certainly might have been other ways to manage the situation) in helping Ray deal with neighborhood bullies, it is also a narrative that has led to more significant troubles in his life. Ray has found himself getting into bar fights over perceived offenses. It has even led to some physical violence with Cecilia. Here again, we notice a conflict between two competing narratives. On the one hand, Ray has a story that tells of the importance of being tough and standing up for yourself—a story in which fighting becomes a means of self-expression, a language of sorts. On the other hand, Ray also has a story of growing up in a loving and peaceful household and of the prohibition against violence toward women. When these two stories come into conflict, Ray knew he needed help because "for the first time this violence had cost him something that really mattered…"

Powerfully intermingled with all of this is Ray's narrative as a survivor of sexual abuse at the hands of a priest when he was a child. From this experience emerge numerous narrative threads that have become so twisted as to form a knot that Ray has struggled mightily to cope with if not undo. Like that of so many survivors of abuse, Ray's narrative has been shrouded in secrecy born of shame. Like so many others he asks himself, "Why me?" "Was there something I did to bring this on? "Was there something I did to encourage it?" Given what we already know about Ray, it becomes apparent that this experience of great pain stands in conflict with some of the dominant narrative themes we have already touched on—themes of trust and betrayal of trust, the theme of being singled out or targeted for abuse, and the theme of guilt, this time over other victims, he feels he might have saved if he had come forward earlier.

Ray's story is a perfect example of the way in which, in narratively informed treatment, the multiple layers of story and meaning are interwoven to form a complex tapestry. For this reason, as was discussed, narrative treatment relies on our ability to listen carefully in a particular kind of way—to listen for the presence of stories and of systems of meaning. We listen for the ways in which those stories are challenged and reinforced, and for the ways in which our clients attend, unintentionally or unknowingly perhaps, to some aspects of the story while ignoring or downplaying others. We listen with great curiosity, wondering where the narrative unfolding will take us, and how the story may play out as we encourage our client to imagine and explore new plot lines that lead to new capacities and a new sense of self.

In this context of a trusting therapeutic relationship, we have the opportunity to play with and stretch the stories that clients tell themselves and tell us. With some prompting and support, the narrative that emerges from this kind of re-storying can be deeply rich even if is marked by great pain. In the telling and crafting of the story, in the powerful exchange that occurs when the story is not only told but heard, not only shared but received, we open up the possibility of discovering something greater than ourselves. In this, we find the possibility of crafting a narrative that takes us simultaneously beyond and deeper to understand ourselves more fully. That is narrative in practice.

Practical Exercises

Consider journaling about your own narrative with respect to some of these questions. You might wish to discuss your thoughts with someone you trust.

1. What are the dominant aspects of your narrative about yourself, the key aspects of the way you understand yourself?
2. Who and what factors have been most formative in the shaping of your own narrative of the person you are? Consider things like ethnicity, family structure, family expectations, and messages about you and your place in the world, gender, sexuality, and spirituality.
3. What has been your narrative of yourself as a social worker and helping professional? What personal experiences have led you into this profession? What is the story you are telling yourself about who you will be as a social worker, the kind of work that you will do, and the impact you will have on your clients?
4. Are there stories or narratives that you find particularly intriguing or compelling? What are the kinds of narratives you most wish to hear (or at least think you will)? Are there narratives that are (or that you imagine will be) too painful or frightening to hear?
5. Are you aware of any narratives that you have inherited from our culture, family, environment, that may be limiting to you, your clients, or your ability to be helpful to them?
   Try some of these prompts and see what they bring up in you and how you respond to them:

   (a) I think of myself as a person who…
   (b) Those who know me well would say that I…
   (c) I find it most difficult when…
   (d) I am at my best when…
   (e) The thing about myself I find most difficult to embrace is…

6. What did you learn from your culture, environment, or the media as you grew up about the mentally ill?
7. How do you understand the causes of mental illness? What thoughts, feelings, and fantasies do you have about those who suffer from mental illness?

8. If you have had the opportunity to work with clients, think back to your encounters and try "listening" from the vantage point of narrative. (You can, of course, practice this in your sessions going forward as well.) What stories do you hear the client telling about themselves and their experience of the world? Have those stories been helpful or unhelpful to them—or somewhere in between? How might a narrative approach impact the way you work with your client? (This can be done as an in-class exercise in pairs or small groups.)

References

American Psychiatric Association (2013). *Diagnostic and statistical manual of mental disorders* (5th ed.). Washington D.C.: American Psychiatric Association.

Bowlby, J. (1969). *Attachment and loss Vol. 1: Attachment.* London: Hogarth Press and the Institute of Psycho-analysis.

Bowlby, J. (1973). *Attachment and loss, Vol. 2: Separation: Anxiety and anger.* London: Hogarth Press and the Institute of Psycho-analysis.

Bruner, J. (1986). *Actual minds, possible worlds.* Cambridge, MA: Harvard University Press.

Bruner, J. (1990). *Acts of meaning.* Cambridge, MA: Harvard University Press.

Bruner, J. (1991). The narrative construction of reality. *Critical Inquiry, 18*(1), 1–21.

Bruner, J. (2004). Life as narrative. *Social Research, 71*(3), 691–710.

Crossley, M. L. (2000). Narrative psychology, trauma and the study of self/identity. *Theory and Psychology, 10*(4), 527–546.

Crossley, M. L. (2003). Formulating narrative psychology: The limitations of contemporary social constructionism. *Narrative Inquiry, 13*(2), 287–300.

Erikson, E. (1968). *Identity: Youth and crisis.* New York: Norton.

Fisher, P., & Freshwater, D. (2014). Methodology and mental illness: Resistance and restorying. *Journal of Psychiatric and Mental Health Nursing, 21*, 197–205.

Frankl, V. E. (1946/1984). *Man's search for meaning.* New York: Washington Square Press.

Freud, S., & Breuer, J. (1985/2004). *Studies in hysteria.* New York: Penguin Classics.

Fullerton, C. (2004). Shared meaning following trauma: Bridging generations and cultures. *Psychiatry, 67*(1), 61–62.

Horwitz, A. V., & Wakefield, J. C. (2007). *The loss of sadness: How psychiatry has transformed normal sorrow into a depressive disorder.* New York: Oxford University Press.

Howard, G. S. (1991). Culture tales: A narrative approach to thinking, cross-cultural psychology, and psychotherapy. *American Psychologist, 46*(3), 187–197.

Janoff-Bulman, R. (1985). The aftermath of victimization. In C. R. Figley (Ed.), *Trauma and its wake: The study and treatment of posttraumatic stress disorder* (pp. 15–35). New York: Bruner/Mazel.

Janoff-Bulman, R. (1992). *Shattered assumptions: Towards a new psychology of trauma.* New York: The Free Press.

Janoff-Bulman, R. (2006). Schema-change perspectives on posttraumatic growth. In L. G. Calhoun & R. G. Tedeschi (Eds.), *Handbook of posttraumatic growth: Research and practice* (pp. 81–99). New York: Lawrence Erlbaum Associates.

Janoff-Bulman, R., & Frantz, C. M. (1997). The impact of trauma on meaning: From meaningless world to meaningful life. In M. Power & C. R. Brewin (Eds.), *The transformation of meaning in psychological therapies* (pp. 91–106). New York: Wiley.

Josselson, R. (1995). Imagining the real: Empathy, narrative and the dialogic self. In R. Josselson & A. Lieblich (Eds.), *Interpreting experience: The narrative study of lives.* Thousand Oaks, CA: Sage.

Kant, I. (1787/1965). *Critique of pure reason*. New York: St. Martins.

Kelley, P. (1996). Narrative theory and social work treatment. In F. J. Turner (Ed.), *Social work treatment: Interlocking theoretical approaches* (pp. 461–479). New York: The Free Press.

Mizock, L., & Russinova, Z. (2013). Racial and ethnic cultural factors in the process of acceptance of mental illness. *Rehabilitation Counseling Bulletin, 56*(4), 229–239.

Murphy, Y., Hunt, V., Zajicek, A. M., Norris, A. N., & Hamilton, L. (2009). *Incorporating intersectionality in social work practice, research, policy, and education*. Washington, D.C.: NASW Press.

Neimeyer, R. A. (2005). Tragedy and transformation: Meaning reconstruction in the wake of traumatic loss. In S. Heilman (Ed.), *Death, bereavement, and mourning*. New Brunswick, NJ: Transaction Publishers.

Norman, J. (2000). Constructive narrative in arresting the impact of post-traumatic stress disorder. *Clinical Social Work Journal, 28*(3), 303–319.

Orr, D. M. (2013). Now he walks and walks, as if he didn't have a home where he could eat: Food, healing, and hunger in Quechua narratives of madness. *Culture, Medicine and Psychiatry, 37*, 694–710.

Pepper, S. (1942). *World hypotheses*. Berkeley, CA: University of California Press.

Ploesser, M. P., & Mecherill, P. P. (2011). Neglect—recognition—deconstruction: Approaches to otherness in social work. *International Social Work, 55*(6), 794–808.

Probst, B. (2013). "Walking the tightrope": Clinical social workers' use of diagnostic and environmental perspectives. *Clinical Social Work Journal, 41*(2), 184–191.

Saleeby, D. (1994). Culture, theory, and narrative: The intersection of meanings in practice. *Social Work, 39*(4), 351–359.

Sarbin, T. R. (1986). The narrative as a root metaphor for psychology. In T. R. Sarbin (Ed.), *Narrative psychology: The storied nature of human conduct* (pp. 3–21). New York: Praeger.

Sosulski, M. R., Buchanan, N. T., & Donnell, C. M. (2010). Life history and narrative analysis: Feminist methodologies contextualizing black women's experiences with severe mental illness. *Journal of Sociology and Social Welfare, 37*(3), 29–57.

Stern, D. N. (1985). *The interpersonal world of the human infant: A view from psychoanalysis and developmental psychology*. New York: Basic Books.

Wakefield, J. C. (2013). DSM-5 and clinical social work: Mental disorder and psychological justice as goals of clinical intervention. *Clinical Social Work Journal, 41*, 131–138.

White, M., & Epston, D. (1990). *Narrative means to therapeutic ends*. New York: W.W. Norton.

Winnicott, D. W. (1965). *The maturational process and the facilitating environment*. New York: International Universities Press.

Chapter 10
Person-Centered and Contextualized Diagnosis in Mental Health

Juan E. Mezzich and Ada M. Mezzich

Abstract A model for person-centered and contextualized diagnosis of mental health [person-centered integrative diagnosis (PID)] is presented in this chapter within the larger framework of person-centered psychiatry and medicine. As the authors note, this is a departure from the prevalent disease-centered model—a departure predicated on both ethical and scientific grounds—representing a more sophisticated, comprehensive, and diagnostically valid evolution of the multiaxial approach found in DSM-III and IV. Among the cardinal features of PID are: diagnosis of a person's whole health (both ill and positive health); considering diagnosis as both a formulation and an interactive process among clinicians, patients, and families; and the use of categories, dimensions, and narratives as descriptive tools. Its multilevel informational structure encompasses health status, health contributors, and health experience and expectations, integrating standardized and idiographic components. The chapter traces the history and methodological basis for the development of PID, as well as offering an example of the PID approach in the Latin American Guide of Psychiatric Diagnosis. It then shows how this model can be applied to produce a comprehensive diagnostic formulation and discusses the implications of such an approach for advancing effective and interdisciplinary mental health care.

Keywords Person-centered psychiatry, medicine, and health · Person-centered care · Person-centered integrative diagnosis · Comprehensive diagnosis · Contextualized diagnosis · Health status · Illness, disabilities, and positive health · Health contributors, risk factors, protective factors · Health experience, values, and expectations

J.E. Mezzich (✉) · A.M. Mezzich
International Center for Mental Health, Mount Sinai School of Medicine,
New York, NY, USA
e-mail: juanmezzich@aol.com

© Springer International Publishing Switzerland 2015
B. Probst (ed.), *Critical Thinking in Clinical Assessment and Diagnosis*,
Essential Clinical Social Work Series, DOI 10.1007/978-3-319-17774-8_10

Introduction: Why This Matters

A model for person-centered and contextualized diagnosis of mental health is presented here—as developed under the name of person-centered integrative diagnosis (PID)—within the framework of person-centered psychiatry and medicine, and engaging recent and evolving methodological approaches to enhance the reliability and validity of diagnostic systems. Among the cardinal features of the PID model are: the diagnosis of a person's whole health (both ill and positive health); considering diagnosis as both a formulation and an interactive process among clinicians, patients, and families; and the use of categories, dimensions, and narratives as descriptive tools. Its multilevel informational structure encompasses health status, health contributors, and health experience and expectations. On all the above bases, the PID contrasts with the DSM and ICD illness-centered diagnostic models, representing a distinctive departure from the more conventional (and prevalent) disease-centered medical model, a departure that is predicated on both ethical and scientific grounds.

Therefore, the first question to be addressed in this chapter is: what is person-centered medicine? Next, the conceptual and procedural bases and the structure of the PID model developed by the International College of Person-centered Medicine (ICPCM) will be described. Third, the first official guide for person-centered diagnosis (the GLADP-VR), recently published by the Latin American Psychiatric Association (APAL) and implementing the PID model, will be presented. Finally, the chapter will address the question of how such person-centered diagnosis guide can be applied to yield a comprehensive and contextualized diagnostic formulation of an illustrative clinical case and what its implications for interdisciplinary care may be.

Guiding Questions

1. What are person-centered psychiatry, medicine, and health, and how do they differ from the prevalent disease-centered model?
2. What is person-centered integrative and contextualized diagnosis? What does it include?
3. How can it be implemented? What practical guides exist to implement person-centered diagnosis?
4. How can the person-centered diagnosis model and guidelines be applied to an illustrative clinical case?

Development of Person-Centered Psychiatry, Medicine, and Health Care

Historical roots for person-centered care can be found in major Eastern civilizations, particularly Chinese and Ayurvedic, which are still practiced today as forms of traditional medicine. Both systems offer a comprehensive and harmonious framework of health and life and promote a highly personalized approach for the treatment of specific diseases and the enhancement of quality of life (Patwardhan et al. 2005). In the West, the need for holism in medicine has been strongly advocated by ancient Greek philosophers and physicians. Socrates and Plato taught "if the whole is not well, it is impossible for the part to be well" (Christodoulou 1987). This position was enriched by Aristotle, the philosopher and naturalist *par excellence* (Ierodiakonou 2011), and by Hippocrates, who brought theory, emotion, and individuality into the practice of medicine and delineated its ethical and person-centered foundations (Jouanna 1999). Prehispanic American medicine vision was also holistic and integrative in context and in beliefs (Mariátegui 1992) and was consistent with the concepts of medicine and health in the earliest Asian and Hellenic civilizations. Such broad and enlightened concept of health (full well-being and not only the absence of disease) has been incorporated into WHO's (1946) definition of health. This notion has maintained its vitality throughout the vicissitudes of contemporary health care.

Modern medicine has brought a number of important advances in the scientific understanding of diseases and the development of valuable technologies for diagnosis and treatment. At the same time, it has led to a hyperbolic, impersonal, and dehumanizing focus on disease, over-specialization of medical disciplines, fragmentation of health services, weakening of the clinician–patient relationship, and commoditization of medicine (Heath 2005).

In response, proposals for re-prioritizing psychiatry, general medicine, and health care as person-centered are emerging that cover a wide range of concepts, tasks, technologies, and practices that aim to put the whole person in context as a center of clinical practice and public health. Among contemporary antecedents of person-centered medicine, particularly prominent is the seminal work of Tournier (1940), who wrote *Medicine de la Personne* in Switzerland. Also important are the contributions of Rogers' (1961) person-centered approach in education and counseling focused on open communication and empowerment in the United States, McWhinney's (1989) family medicine movement in the UK and Canada, and Alanen's (1997) need-adaptive assessment and treatment approach in Finland.

The World Psychiatric Association (WPA), born from the articulation of science and humanism (Garrabe and Hoff 2011), established at its 2005 General Assembly an Institutional Program on Psychiatry for the Person (Mezzich 2007; Christodoulou et al. 2008). This initiative expanded into general medicine through a series of Geneva Conferences since 2008 in collaboration with the World Medical Association, the World Health Organization, the International Council of Nurses, the International Federation of Social Workers, the International Pharmaceutical

Federation, the European Federation of Families of Persons with Mental Illness, and the International Alliance of Patients' Organizations, among a growing number of other international health institutions (Mezzich 2011a). The process and impact of the Geneva Conferences led to the emergence of the International Network (now International College) of Person-centered Medicine (INPCM, ICPCM) (Mezzich et al. 2009; Mezzich 2011b).

In 2011, the ICPCM launched the *International Journal of Person-centered Medicine* in collaboration with the University of Buckingham Press (Miles and Mezzich 2011) promoting research and scholarship on person-centered medicine across the world. Since 2012, the impact of the Geneva Conferences has been extended through Geneva Declarations, including that on Person-centered Care for Chronic Diseases (ICPCM 2012), Person-centered Health Research (ICPCM 2013; Salvador et al. 2013), and Person- and People-centered Integrated Health Care for All (ICPCM 2014a, b; Cloninger et al. 2014). In November 2013 in order to connect with the field in different areas of the world, a series of annual International Congresses of Person-centered Medicine was initiated in Zagreb, Croatia. As in the case of the Geneva Conferences, a Zagreb Declaration on Person-centered Health Professional Education and an accompanying academic paper have been published (ICPCM 2014a, b; Appleyard et al. 2014).

Methodological Basis for person-centered integrative and contextualized diagnosis Addressing the nature of diagnosis, the eminent historian and philosopher of medicine (Laín-Entralgo 1982) cogently argued that diagnosis goes beyond identifying a disease (*nosological diagnosis*) to involve *understanding* what is going on in the body and mind of the person who presents for care. Understanding an individual's clinical condition also requires a broader assessment of experience and life context. As health may be conceived as a person's capacity to continue to pursue his or her goals in an ever-challenging world (Canguilhem 1991), this encompassing perspective should be incorporated in a thorough diagnosis of health. There are indeed compelling reasons for including health-promoting or *salutogenic* factors (Antonovsky 1987) and positive health (Mezzich 2005) under comprehensive diagnosis, bringing it to consistency with WHO's definition of health. Diagnostic understanding also requires a process of engagement and empowerment that recognizes the agency of patient, family, and health professionals participating in a *trialogical* partnership (Amering 2010).

In connection with the above, one should examine the concept of the *validity* of diagnosis as it denotes its value and usefulness. Traditionally, this validity has been anchored on the faithfulness and accuracy with which a diagnosis reflects and identifies a disorder, its nature, pathophysiology, and other biomedical indicators (Robins and Guze 1970). Recently, *clinical utility* has been proposed as an additional indication of the value of diagnosis for clinical care (Kendell and Jablensky 2003). Schaffner (2009) has delineated further the epistemology of these two forms of diagnostic validity under the terms of *etiopathogenic and clinical validities*. Pointing out the significance of the latter, experienced clinicians suggest that treatment planning is the most important purpose of diagnosis (Adams and Grieder 2005).

Concerning the architecture of diagnostic formulations, there has been a progressive development of diagnostic schemas with increasing levels of informational richness particularly to support treatment planning. These have ranged from a simple, typological *single-label diagnosis* denoting a symptom, problem, syndrome, or illness to a more complex *multiple illness formulation*, listing all identified clinical conditions or disorders, including coexisting psychiatric and general medical diseases. Such schemas intend to provide a fuller portrayal of the nosological condition, as well as other aspects of clinical interest such as disabilities, contextual factors, and quality of life, thus attempting to enhance diagnostic understanding, treatment planning, and prognostic determination (Banzato et al. 2009). Multiaxial diagnostic formulations are key components of most recent diagnostic systems including ICD-10 (World Health Organization 1996, 1997), DSM-IV (American Psychiatric Association 1994), GLADP (APAL 2004), GC-3 (Otero 1998), the French Classification for Child and Adolescent Mental Disorders (Mises et al. 2002), and the Chinese Classification of Mental Disorders (Chinese Society of psychiatry 2001). Of note, a multiaxial system was *not* included in DSM-5 (American Psychiatric Association 2013), despite the fact that a broad APA Committee established to evaluate DSM multiaxial systems documented their usefulness (Mezzich et al. 2005; see also Probst 2013, for discussion of the development, reliability, utility, and demise of the fourth axis, used in DSM-III and DSM-IV to identify psychosocial stressors).

Another approach to comprehensive diagnosis involves both standardized and idiographic components. One such model is at the core of the International Guidelines for Diagnostic Assessment (IGDA), developed by the WPA (Mezzich et al. 2003). Its standardized multiaxial component includes four axes dealing respectively with clinical disorders, disabilities, contextual factors, and quality of life. Its idiographic and narrative component covers the clinician perspective, perspectives of the patient and family, and integration of the perspectives of all the above. Many of the methodological developments highlighted above have been discussed in a WPA psychiatry for the person volume (Salloum and Mezzich 2009).

Development of the PID model PID, as developed under the auspices of the ICPCM, is inscribed within a paradigmatic effort to place the whole person at the center of medicine and health care (Mezzich et al. 2009; Mezzich 2011b). The PID model articulates science and humanism to obtain a diagnosis of the person (of the totality of the person's health, both its ill and positive aspects), by the person (with clinicians extending themselves as full human beings, scientifically competent and with high ethical aspirations), for the person (assisting the fulfillment of the person's health aspirations and life project), and with the person (in respectful and empowering relationship with the person who presents for evaluation and care) (Mezzich et al. 2010). This notion of diagnosis goes beyond the more restricted concepts of nosological and differential diagnoses. The development of this diagnostic model was informed by the methodological considerations summarized in the preceding section.

The suitability of the prospective elements of PID was examined through surveys and consultations. Building on its long experience in developing diagnostic models, the WPA section on classification, diagnostic assessment, and nomenclature conducted a survey among the members of the 43-country Global Network of National Classification and Diagnosis Groups (Salloum and Mezzich 2011). The survey was constructed in consultation with network members and aimed at surveying the most important domains to consider in the development of future diagnostic classification for psychiatric disorders. Seventy-four percent of the groups responded. Treatment planning was most frequently chosen as the key role of diagnosis. Communication among clinicians and diagnosis as a means to enhance illness understanding was also identified as key roles of diagnosis. The survey also highlighted the areas of information judged important to be covered by psychiatric diagnosis. These included disorders (100 %), disabilities (74 %), risk factors (61 %), experience of illness (58 %), protective factors (55 %), and experience of health (52 %). The responses suggested that in addition to the recognized importance of nosological diagnosis, subjective explanatory narratives of illness and health are also quite valuable. The survey responses also highlighted the importance of utilizing a variety of descriptive tools including categories (81 %), dimensions (74 %), and narratives (45 %). It also revealed that 80 % of responders choose clinicians, patients, and caregivers together as key players in the diagnostic evaluation process as compared to clinicians alone (20 %).

A number of focus and discussion groups were organized in 2009 with a variety of health stakeholders (health professionals, patients, family members, and advocates) at international events in Athens (Greece), Uppsala (Sweden), and Timisoara (Romania) (Salloum and Mezzich 2011). In an overwhelming manner, the participants in the three settings considered that diagnosis should go beyond disease. Participants unanimously responded that diagnosis should cover dysfunctions and a great majority felt that it was also important to include positive aspects of health. Over 83 % of the participants endorsed the inclusion of experience of health as part of diagnosis. Furthermore, there was unanimous agreement on incorporating contributing factors (including risk and protective factors) and on the use of descriptive methods, including dimensions and narratives in addition to conventional categories. Participants also emphasized that diagnosis is a process and not only a formulation and highlighted the partnership between caregivers and service users as fundamental.

Structure of the Person-Centered Integrative Diagnosis Model

The structure of the PID takes into account that diagnosis is both a formulation and a process. The presentation of the fundamental elements of the model is made according to three defining conceptual pillars: broad informational domains, pluralistic descriptive procedures, and partnership for diagnostic evaluation.

Fig. 1 Key structural levels covering ill health and positive health in the Person-centered integrative diagnosis model

ILL HEALTH	**POSITIVE HEALTH**

I. Health Status

Illness & its Burden	Well Being
a. Disorders	Recovery/Wellness
b. Disabilities	Functioning

II. Contributors to Health

Contributors to Illness	Contributors to Health
(Intrinsic/Extrinsic: Biological,	(Intrinsic/Extrinsic: Biological,
Psychological, Social)	Psychological, Social)

III. Experience of Health

Experience of Illness	Experience of Health
(e.g. suffering, values, perception,	(e.g. identity, contentment, &
Understanding and meaning of illness)	fulfillment)

The PID framework's first pillar, *Broad Informational Domains*, is depicted in Fig. 1. These domains cover both ill health and positive health along three structural levels: health status, experience of health, and contributors to health.

The broadness of the PID informational domains, including ill and positive health, is intrinsic to holistic person-centered health care. The domain level on *Health Status* includes first illnesses or disorders of both mental and physical forms, which correspond to Laín-Entralgo's (1982) nosological diagnosis. They may be assessed according to the international standard, WHO's International Classification of Diseases or a pertinent national or regional version or adaptation. Disabilities can be assessed through procedures such as those based on the International Classification of Functioning and Health (ICF) (World Health Organization 2001). The assessment of the well-being aspect of health status can be conducted through standard scales such as the WHOQOL instrument (WHOQOL Group 1994).

The domain level on *Experience of Health* appraises the patient's illness- and health-related values and cultural experiences, possibly with a guided narrative procedure built on worldwide experience with the cultural formulation (Mezzich et al. 2009). The third domain level on *Contributors to Health* covers a range of intrinsic and extrinsic biological, psychological, and social factors of both risk and protective types. Their assessment may involve a combination of procedures aimed at assessing healthy and unhealthy lifestyle factors and related health contributors (Seyer 2012).

The PID model's second defining pillar, *Pluralistic Descriptive Procedures*, opens up the opportunity to employ categories, dimensions, and narratives for greater flexibility and effectiveness for the evaluation task at hand (Jablensky 2005; Kirmayer 2000). The third defining pillar of the PID model is *Partnership for Evaluation*. Such partnership is a fundamental element of person-centered care and involves the pursuit of engagement, empathy, and empowerment as well as respect for the autonomy and dignity of the consulting person. In fact, it is crucial for achieving shared understanding for diagnosis and shared decision-making for treatment planning (Adams and Grieder 2005). Additional information on the elements of the PID model can be found in Mezzich et al. (2010).

Application of PID: The Latin American Guide of Psychiatric Diagnosis

An application of the PID model is at the core of the Latin American Guide of Psychiatric Diagnosis, revised version (GLADP-VR) (de América Latina 2012). This guide represents a revised version of the original GLADP edition (de América Latina 2004). The GLADP-VR incorporates the basic elements of the PID model. The main difference between the PID model and the GLADP-VR schema is that the former has health experience as the second informational domain level, while the latter has health experience as the third level. Furthermore, the GLADP-VR third level is enriched in its content with health values and expectations.

The **key information domains or levels** of the GLADP-VR diagnostic schema are summarized below.

Health Status The first component of this model corresponds to health status. This includes standardized coverage of both pathological and positive aspects of health. As shown on the GLADP-VR personalized diagnostic formulation, the health status component starts with a listing of mental and general medical disorders and other significant clinical conditions. These disorders and conditions are to be coded according to the various chapters of ICD-10, including, in addition to standard disease codes, the Z codes for non-disease conditions that require clinical attention.

Next in the health status component comes the evaluation of personal functioning in the areas of personal care, occupational, family, and social activities, each measured with a 10-point scale marked as follows: 0: worst functioning, 2: minimal functioning, 4: marginal functioning, 6: acceptable functioning, 8: substantial functioning, and 10: optimal functioning.

Finally, the health status component assesses degree of the person's well-being, from worst to excellent, by directly marking on the 10-point line displayed on the formulation form, with or without the help of an appropriate standardized instrument. This assessment is principally based on the judgment of the person involved, modulated collaboratively with perceptions by the clinicians and family.

Health Contributing Factors The second component of the GLADP-VR personalized diagnostic formulation corresponds to health contributing factors. These include risk factors as well as protective and health promotion factors. Assessment in each case starts with the identification of relevant factors from the list presented on the form. These factors come from the Health Improvement Card prepared by the World Health Professions Alliance (Seyer 2012), supplemented by some factors particularly relevant to mental health. It continues with a narrative formulation of additional information about the identified factors and others that could also be elicited.

Health Experiences and Expectations The third component of the GLADP-VR personalized diagnostic formulation assesses experience and expectations on health. This is based on the combination of elements from the experientially described cultural formulation (Mezzich et al. 2009) and of patient's needs and preferences (Fulford et al. 2011). This assessment is obtained through narratives on the following three points: (a) personal and cultural identity (self-awareness and its potentials and limitations), (b) suffering (its recognition, idioms of distress, and beliefs on illness), and (c) experiences with and expectations for health care (Mezzich 2012).

Other PID Applications

A full second edition of the Latin American Guide for Psychiatric Diagnosis (GLADP-2) is in the works as a priority project of the Diagnosis and Classification Section of the APAL. For covering mental and general medical disorders, it will be based on the categories and codes of the prospective eleventh revision of the International Classification of Diseases (ICD-11), which is expected to be completed around 2017. Its development will be based on the ongoing experience implementing, teaching, and studying the GLADP-VR.

There are also plans to develop under the auspices of the ICPCM a PID practical guide intended for use in general medicine.

Conclusions

Person-centered psychiatry, medicine, and health care represent an emerging approach to refocus the health field from disease to person with strong ethical and clinical effectiveness bases supported by major global institutions in clinical care and public health.

The PID model is a keystone of person-centered medicine intending to organize and provide a joint understanding of a clinical situation leading to care planning through shared decision-making. All these are found on a common ground established among clinician, patient, and family in an interactive process. Such a diagnostic process would lead to a diagnostic formulation covering three crucial informational levels: health status, health contributors, and health experience and expectations. To maximize descriptive power, the formulation employs categorical, dimensional, and narrative tools.

One of the first practical implementations of the PID model has been the Latin American Guide for Psychiatric Diagnosis (GLADP-VR), published recently by the APAL for the use of health professionals in Latin America and beyond.

The GLADP-VR person-centered diagnostic formulation and care plan have been applied to the illustrative case of Ray. This resulted in statements that appear to show the value of the model and guide to produce a richly informative diagnostic understanding and from this an inter-disciplinary clinical care plan within a person-in-environment framework.

Application to the Case of Ray

The PID model implemented through the Latin American Guide of Psychiatric Diagnosis (GLADP-VR) can be applied to an illustrative clinical case—the case of Ray, a 34-year old Caucasian male of Irish ancestry.

First, the GLADP-VR personalized diagnostic formulation for the case of Ray is presented in Fig. 2. It includes categorical, dimensional, and narrative elements corresponding to the diagnostic formulation's three levels: (1) health status, (2) health contributors, and (3) health experience and expectations. This formulation would have resulted from interviews among clinicians, Ray, and accompanying others such as close relatives. listing problems extracted from the personalized diagnosticunderstanding of the clinical situation.

The main purpose of the personalized diagnostic formulation presented in Fig. 2 is to serve as an informational base for the preparation of a clinical care plan, in addition to serving as the matrix for the establishment of a common ground among clinicians, Ray, and family. Such a common ground is also important for the preparation of a clinical care plan based on shared decision-making. This can be considered a person-centered approach to treatment planning (Adams and Grieder 2005).

An illustrative GLADP-VR Clinical Care Plan for Ray is presented in Fig. 3. This encompassed first listing problems extracted from the personalized diagnostic formulation as targets of care. Then, specific interventions are listed for the identified problems, followed by timeline observations.

The proposed interventions for the identified clinical, psychological, and socio-cultural problems and issues illustrate the participation of pertinent mental health professionals, such as psychiatrists, psychologists, social workers, and nurses in a coordinated manner. A well-articulated team approach is a hallmark of person-centered care (Ghebrehiwet 2013).

Name: Ray   Age: 34   Sex: *Male*   Marital Status: *Divorced*   Occupation: *Police Officer*   Date*: October 10, 2014*

I: HEALTH STATUS

Clinical Disorders and Related Conditions (as classified in CIE-10).

A. Mental Disorders (in general, including personality and developmental disorders, and related conditions):

	ICD-10 Codes:
Recurrent Depressive Disorder	*F33.9*
Bipolar Affective Disorder (tentative)	*F31.0*
Post Traumatic Stress Disorder	*F43.1*

B. General Medical Conditions:

	ICD-10 Codes:
Analgesic overdoses	*X60*

Functioning of the Person (Use the following scale to evaluate each of the functioning areas)

Poorest	Minimal		Marginal		Acceptable		Substantial		Excellent	
0	1	2	3	4	5	6	7	8	9	10

Functioning Areas		Score						
A	Personal care	0	2	4	_6_	8	10	?
B	Occupational (wage earner, student, etc.)	0	2	_4_	6	8	10	?
C	With family	0	2	4	_6_	8	10	?
D	Social in general	0	2	4	_6_	8	10	?

Degree of Well-being (Indicate level perceived by the person on the following scale, optionally using an instrument).

Fig. 2 Case study GLADP-VR personalized diagnostic formulation

Practical Exercises

1. Consider one of the persons with whom you work in light of some of the dimensions of a PID. Focusing on the person's experience of illness and of health, try to formulate how you believe this person experiences "being ill" (What does suffering mean and feel like? What values are evoked? What maintains the illness?). Then, try to formulate how you believe the person experiences "being well" (What does it mean to be content? To be fulfilled? What helps to maintain well-being?).

Poorest   Excellent

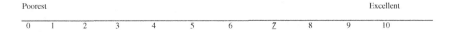

II. HEALTH CONTRIBUTING FACTORS

Risk Factors: [ ]Abnormal weight   [ ]Hyper-cholesterolemia   [ ]Hyperglicemia   [ ]Hypertensión   [ ]Tabacco

[ ]Alcohol   [ ]Family psychiatric problems   [X]Severe child trauma   [X]Prolongued or severe stress

Additional information: *Child abuse; failed relationships with women; family, cultural and economic stresses.*

Protective Factors: [ ] Healthy diet   [X] Physical activity   [ ] Creative activities   [X] Social participation

Additional information*: Loved and well treated by adoptive parents, very involved with his two children and a dog, actively*

participating in outpatient therapy, good athlete, good-looking, socializing with fellow volunteer firefighters.

III. HEALTH EXPERIENCE AND EXPECTATIONS

Personal and cultural identity: *Irish Catholic male who when 8 years of age was violently targeted and ridiculed for looking*

different from the Italian mainstream culture in his elementary school.

Suffering (its recognition, idioms of distress, illness beliefs): *Suffers from being a victim of child abuse by priest (inadvertently*

facilitated by mother's strong religious faith); painful memories from pulling out dead body from WTC rubble; feeling

betrayed, abandoned, helpless, guilty, loss of control with live-in girlfriend and other women; feeling guilty for saving only 3

out of 4 children from a burning home; distress over repeatedly watching violence helplessly on video monitors at work; hiding

ownership for apparent suicidal attempts.

Experiences and expectations on health care: *Positive experience with current outpatient therapy, exercised courage and*

commitment in disclosing his child molestation, open to seeking avenues to heal his painful past.

Fig. 2 (continued)

2. Now, ask the person how he or she would respond to these questions. What differences, if any, were there between your perceptions and the person's perceptions? What steps might you take to achieve a shared understanding of the diagnosis and shared decision-making, in light of PID's principle of partnership (the quest for engagement, empathy, empowerment, as well as respect for the autonomy and dignity of the individual)?
3. What are the person's expectations for care and recovery? Are they explicit or implicit? If you do not know, how can you find out? How well do you think these expectations will be met? What steps might be taken to address any gaps between expectations and the treatment plan currently in place?

Name: *Ray*   Record No.: _____   Date (d/m/y): 10/10/2014

Age: *34*   Sex: *Male*   Marital Status: *Divorced*   Occupation: *Police Officer*

Clinicians involved: *TBD*

Service: *Out Patient Clinic*

Instructions:

Under **Problems,** list important clinical disorders, idioms of distress, disabilities and contextual problems presented. Keep the list as short and simple as possible. Consolidate within an encompassing term all problems that share the same care plan.

Interventions would list diagnostic studies, treatments and health promotion activities pertinent to each problem. Specify as much as possible planned doses and schedules, amounts, and time references as well as clinicians responsible for each intervention.

The space for **Observations** may be used flexibly. It could include expected dates for the resolution of problems, dates for expected re-evaluations, or notes indicating that a specific problem has been resolved or has become inactive.

PROBLEMS	INTERVENTIONS	OBSERVATIONS
1. *Depressive Disorder* 2. *Bipolar Disorder* 3. *PostTraumatic Stress Disorder*	a. *Address dosage and effectiveness of medication* b. *Outpatient Therapy (Individual and subsequent Group Therapy):* • *Role play exercises to heighten awareness/sensitivity on his role in domestic violence towards women,*	*Re-evaluate in 2 weeks* *Re-evaluate in a month*
	• *Cognitive Behavior Therapy, learning coping skills, breathing techniques for feelings of guilt and helplessness when witnessing violence*	
4. *Social and economic contextual issues*	a. *Career counseling to look for jobs other than police work.* b. *Education on obtaining financial assistance* c. *Engaging with social groups to increase positive peer socialization skills* d. *Group sport activities*	*Follow up* *Follow up* *Follow up*

Fig. 3 GLADP-VR clinical care plan for the case of Ray

References

Adams, N., & Grieder, D. M. (2005). *Treatment planning for person-centered care*. Amsterdam: Elsevier.

Alanen, Y. O. (1997). *Schizophrenia: Its origins and need-adaptive treatment*. London: Karnak.

American Psychiatric Association. (1994). *Diagnostic and statistical manual of mental disorders (DSM-IV) (4th ed.)*. Washington DC: Author.

American Psychiatric Association. (2013). *Diagnostic and statistical manual of mental disorders (DSM-5) (5th ed.)*. Arlington, VA: Author

Amering, M. (2010). Trialog—An exercise in communication between consumers, carers, and professional mental health workers beyond role stereotype. In: Conceptual explorations on person-centered medicine. *International Journal of Integrated Care, 10*, Supplement 10.

Antonovsky, A. (1987). *Unraveling the mystery of health*. San Francisco: Jossey-Bass.

Appleyard, J., Ghebrehiwet, T., & Mezzich, J. E. (2014). Development and implications of the Zagreb declaration on person-centered health professional education. *International Journal of Person Centered Medicine, 4*, 8–13.

Banzato, C. E. M., Jorge, M. R., & Kastrup, M. (2009). Multiaxial schemas for psychiatric diagnosis. In I. M. Salloum & J. E. Mezzich (Eds.), *Psychiatric diagnosis: Challenges and prospects*. Chichester, UK: Wiley-Blackwell.

Canguilhem, G. (1991). *The Normal and the Pathological (1966)*. New York: Zone Books.

Chinese Society of Psychiatry. (2001). *Chinese classification of mental disorders, version 3 (CCMD-3)*. Jinan: Author.

Christodoulou, G. N. (Ed.). (1987). *Psychosomatic medicine*. New York: Plenum.

Christodoulou, G. N., Fulford, K. M. W., & Mezzich, J. E. (2008). Conceptual bases of psychiatry for the person. *International Psychiatry, 5*(1), 1–3.

Cloninger, C. R., Salvador-Carulla, L., Kirmayer, L. J., Schwartz, M. A., Appleyard, J., Goodwin, N., et al. (2014). A time for action on health inequities: foundations of the 2014 Geneva declaration on person-and people-centered integrated health care for all. *International Journal of Person Centered Medicine, 4*, 69–89.

de América Latina, A. P. (2004). *Guía Latinoamericana de Diagnóstico Psiquiátrico*. Guadalajara: Asociación Psiquiátrica de América Latina, Sección de Diagnóstico y Clasificación.

de América Latina, A. P. (2012). *Guía Latinoamericana de Diagnóstico Psiquiátrico, Versión Revisada (GLADP-VR)*. Lima: Asociación Psiquiátrica de América Latina, Sección de Diagnóstico y Clasificación.

Fulford, K. W. M., Christodoulou, G. N., & Stein, D. J. (2011). Values and ethics: Perspectives on psychiatry for the person. *International Journal of Person Centered Medicine, 1*, 131–133.

Garrabe, J., & Hoff, P. (2011). Historical views on psychiatry for the person. *International Journal of Person Centered Medicine, 1*, 125–127.

Ghebrehiwet, T. (2013). Effectiveness of team approach in health care: Some research evidence. *International Journal of Person Centered Medicine, 3*, 137–139.

Heath, I. (2005). Promotion of disease and corrosion of medicine. *Canadian Family Physician, 51*, 1320–1322.

Ierodiakonou, C. S. (2011). *The psychology of Aristotle, the philosopher*. London: Karnak.

International College of Person Centered Medicine. (2012). Geneva declaration on person centered care for chronic diseases. *International Journal of Person Centered Medicine, 2*, 153–154.

International College of Person Centered Medicine. (2013). Geneva declaration on person centered health research. *International Journal of Person Centered Medicine, 3*, 107–108.

International College of Person Centered Medicine. (2014a). The Zagreb declaration on person centered health professional education. *International Journal of Person Centered Medicine, 4*, 6–7.

International College of Person Centered Medicine. (2014b). Geneva declaration on person-and people-centered integrated health care for all. *International Journal of Person Centered Medicine, 4*, 67–68.

Jablensky, A. (2005). Categories, dimensions and prototypes: Critical issues for psychiatric classification. *Psychopathology, 38*, 201–205.

Jouanna, J. (1999). *Hippocrates* (M. B. Debevoise, Trans.). Baltimore: Johns Hopkins University Press.

Kendell, R., & Jablensky, A. (2003). Distinguishing between the validity and the utility of psychiatric diagnoses. *American J Psychiatry, 160*, 4–12.

Kirmayer, L. J. (2000). Broken narratives: Clinical encounters and the poetics of illness experience. In C. Mattingly & L. Garro (Eds.), *Narrative and the Cultural Construction of Illness and Healing* (pp. 153–180). Berkeley: University of California Press.

Laín-Entralgo, P. (1982). *El Diagnóstico Médico: Historia y Teoría*. Barcelona: Salvat.

Mariátegui, J. (1992). La concepción del hombre y de la enfermedad en el antiguo Perú. *Revista de Neuropsiquiatría, 55*, 156–166.

McWhinney, I. R. (1989). *A textbook of family medicine*. Oxford: Oxford University Press.

Mezzich, J. E. (2005). Positive health: Conceptual place, dimensions and implications. *Psychopathology, 38*, 177–179.

Mezzich, J. E. (2007). Psychiatry for the person: Articulating medicine's science and humanism. *World Psychiatry, 6*, 65–67.

Mezzich, J. E. (2011a). The Geneva conferences and the emergence of the international network of person-centered medicine. *Journal of Evaluation in Clinical Practice, 17*(333–336), 2011.

Mezzich, J. E. (2011b). The construction of person-centered medicine and the launching of an international college. *International Journal of Person Centered Medicine, 2*, 6–10.

Mezzich, J. E. (2012). Towards a health experience formulation for person-centered integrative diagnosis. *International Journal of Person Centered Medicine, 2*, 188–192.

Mezzich, J. E., Banzato, C. E. M., Cohen, P., Cloninger, C. R., et al. (2005). Report of the American Psychiatric Association Committee to evaluate the DSM multiaxial system. Presented to the APA Assembly, Atlanta, May 21, 2005.

Mezzich, J. E., Berganza, C. E., von Cranach, M., Jorge, M. R., Kastrup, M. C., Murthy, R. C., et al. (2003). Essentials of the WPA international guidelines for diagnostic assessment (IGDA). *British Journal of Psychiatry, 182*(Suppl), 45.

Mezzich, J. E., Caracci, G., Fabrega, H., & Kirmayer, L. J. (2009a). Cultural formulation guidelines. *Transcultural Psychiatry, 46*, 383–405.

Mezzich, J. E., Salloum, I. M., Cloninger, C. R., Salvador-Carulla, L., Kirmayer, L., Banzato, C. E., et al. (2010). Person-centered integrative diagnosis: Conceptual bases and structural model. *Canadian Journal of Psychiatry, 55*, 701–708.

Mezzich, J. E., Snaedal, J., van Weel, C., & Heath, I. (2009b). The international network for person-centered medicine: Background and first steps. *World Medical Journal, 55*, 104–107.

Miles, A., & Mezzich, J. E. (2011). Advancing the global communication of scholarship and research for personalized healthcare: *The International Journal of Person Centered Medicine*. *International Journal of Person Centered Medicine, 1*, 1–5.

Mises, R., Quemada, N., Botbol, M., Burzsteijn, C., Garrabe, J., Golse, B., et al. (2002). French classification for child and adolescent mental disorders (CFTMEA). *Psychopathology, 35*, 176–180.

Otero, A. A. (1998). *Tercer Glosario Cubano de Psiquiatría (GC-3)*. La Habana: Hospital Psiquiátrico de La Habana.

Patwardhan, B., Warude, D., Pushpangadan, P., & Bhatt, N. (2005). Ayurveda and traditional Chinese medicine: A comparative overview. *Evidence-based Complementary and Alternative Medicine, 2*, 465–473.

Probst, B. (2013). The life and death of axis IV: Caught in the quest for a theory of mental disorder. *Research on Social Work Practice, 24*(1), 123–131.

Robins, E., & Guze, S. (1970). Establishment of diagnostic validity in psychiatric illness: Its application to schizophrenia. *American Journal of Psychiatry, 126*(7), 983–987.

Rogers, C. R. (1961). *On becoming a person: A therapist's view of psychotherapy*. Boston: Houghton Mifflin.

Salloum, I. M., & Mezzich, J. E. (2011). Conceptual appraisal of the person-centered integrative diagnosis model. *International Journal of Person Centered Medicine, 1,* 39–42.

Salloum, I. M., & Mezzich, J. E. (2009). *Psychiatric diagnosis: Challenges and prospects.* Chichester, UK: Wiley-Blackwell.

Salvador-Carulla, L., Cloninger, C. R., Thornicroft, A., Mezzich, J. E. & the 2013 Geneva Declaration Consultation Group (2013). Background, structure and priorities of the 2013 Geneva declaration on person-centered health research. *International Journal of Person Centered Medicine, 3,* 109–113.

Schaffner, K. F. (2009). The validity of psychiatric diagnosis: Etiopathogenic and clinical approaches. In I. M. Salloum & J. E. Mezzich (Eds.), *Psychiatric diagnosis: Challenges and prospects.* Chichester, UK: Wiley-Blackwell.

Seyer, J. (2012). *Development of the health improvement card developed by the world health professions alliance.* Paper presented at the 5th Geneva Conference on Person-centered Medicine. International College of Person Centered Medicine, May 2012.

Tournier, P. (1940). *Médicine de la Personne.* Neuchatel: Delachaux et Niestle.

WHOQOL Group. (1994). The development of the World Health Organization quality of life assessment instrument (the WHOQOL). In J. Orly & W. Kuyken (Eds.), *Quality of life assessment: International perspectives.* Heidelberg: Springer.

World Health Organization. (1946). *Constitution of the World Health Organization.* Geneva: Author.

World Health Organization. (1996). *Multiaxial classification of child and adolescent psychiatric disorders.* Cambridge, UK: Cambridge University Press.

World Health Organization. (1997). *Multiaxial presentation of the ICD-10 for use in adult psychiatry.* Cambridge, UK: Cambridge University Press.

World Health Organization. (2001). *International classification of functioning and health (ICF).* Geneva: Author.

Chapter 11
Integrating Practice and Research on Mental Disorder

Mark Hardy

Abstract In this chapter, the question of whether assessment is best seen as 'art' or 'science' is explored in connection with the overarching question of the role that research can or ought to play in clinical practice and what the integration of research evidence into practice actually involves. Exploring the strengths and limitations of each position ('art' and 'science'), the chapter discusses the use of tacit knowledge and reflective practice in the more 'bottom-up' intuitive approach, as well as the use of structured and actuarial approaches in the more 'top-down' analytic approach. It then outlines the basis for a 'knowledge-based' approach to assessment and diagnosis in which evidence is synthesized from multiple sources, and practice-based research is utilized to challenge the limitations of more traditional approaches. It concludes by making the case for critical pluralism, a pragmatic approach to assessment that allows practitioners to assess the relevance and utility of particular forms of knowledge for particular clients and to reconcile some of the tensions between competing, and often polarized, approaches to diagnosis.

Keywords Anti-psychiatry · Critical pluralism · Interpretivism · Pragmatism · Reflective practice · Research mindedness · Scientism · Sociology of knowledge · Structured and actuarial approaches · Tacit knowledge

Introduction: Why This Matters

Diagnosis is a crucial 'sense-making' activity that various professionals within the mental health system engage in, including social workers. It can set the parameters for subsequent stages of the social work process including decision making, planning, and direct intervention. In social work, it represents one component in the broader-based enterprise of assessment. But how practitioners ought to best undertake this key task is not necessarily straightforward. There are ongoing

M. Hardy (✉)
School of Social Policy and Social Work, University of York, York, England
e-mail: mark.hardy@york.ac.uk

© Springer International Publishing Switzerland 2015
B. Probst (ed.), *Critical Thinking in Clinical Assessment and Diagnosis*,
Essential Clinical Social Work Series, DOI 10.1007/978-3-319-17774-8_11

debates regarding whether assessment is best conceived of according to a broadly 'artistic' or 'scientific' logic. Consequently, the role that research evidence might play in assessment can sometimes be unclear.

This chapter will review these issues as they apply to both diagnosis and assessment in mental health care, particularly in those settings where social workers play a key role, including the significant task they fulfill in some contexts of deciding whether or not to detain someone in hospital involuntarily. It will explore what diagnosis and assessment 'are'; differing approaches to them, including both subjective clinical approaches and objective actuarial and structured approaches, their respective strengths and limitations; and their association with evidence-based practice, as well as claims that recent developments in practice have fundamentally affected the nature and function of such judgments, and thus have changed the nature of social work itself.

This chapter will also specify what the integration of research evidence into practice actually involves. Research represents a crucial source of knowledge that practitioners might draw upon in arriving at a clinical judgment. Traditionally, however, formal sources of knowledge, such as research evidence, have been accorded relatively little significance. There is a strong case for encouraging better integration of evidence from research with other important sources of knowledge, and a specific skills base for doing so. However, there are also limits to what social work research can contribute, both generally and in clinical social work in particular. Research findings represent just one of many sources of knowledge that social workers must integrate, alongside service user and practitioner knowledge, as well as knowledge embedded within organizational and policy frameworks. This chapter will therefore outline the basis for a 'knowledge-based' approach to assessment and diagnosis in mental health social work in which evidence and understanding from multiple sources are synthesized and in which practice-based research is utilized to challenge some of the limitations of more traditional research approaches. It will conclude by making the case for critical pluralism, a pragmatic approach to assessment, which offers potential in enabling practitioners to reconcile some of the tensions between competing—and often polarized—approaches to diagnosis.

Guiding Questions

1. What are some of the arguments for an 'artistic' or intuitive approach to social work assessment? On what values and aims is this approach based?
2. What are some of the arguments for a 'scientific' or analytic approach? On what values and aims is it based?
3. Is synthesis possible? What are some challenges to achieving this kind of integrated approach to clinical practice?
4. How can clinicians use 'critical pluralism' or 'pragmatism in practice' for deciding whether, in what ways, and *which* research to utilize? How can they assess the relevance and utility of particular forms of knowledge for particular clients?

Background

Social work is a generic discipline, a broad domain comprised of numerous specialties, each of which has followed a distinctive developmental trajectory. The mental health social work role is closely associated with the post-World War Two trend toward enhanced use of community-based mental health care. Newly available medication meant that continued reliance on institutional care—the asylums— would be much more expensive than community treatment. The expertise of social workers derived from their 'knowledge of the social factors influencing the presentation of mental disorder and knowledge of the facilities available to support patients in the community' (Peay 2003: 17) in conjunction with 'a holistic, humanistic approach with an established commitment to anti-oppressive practice' (Stanley and Manthorpe 2001). Cumulatively, these came to represent the basis for invoking alternative services to avoid hospital admission and so the position of mental health social work as primarily (though by no means exclusively) a community-based alternative to institutionalization was established.

Assessment

Despite the distinctive roles and tasks that mental health social workers fulfill in different settings, the social work process is very similar in these diverse specialties, entailing assessment, planning, intervention, review, and evaluation (Parker and Bradley 2004). Assessment in particular represents a major element of the social work process. In most social work agencies, practitioners are required to formulate assessments of service users. These assessments generally involve the identification and description of key social, individual, and psychological factors at play in a particular situation, as well as analysis of, and an attempt to formulate an explanation for, what is going on and why. In this respect, social work assessments correspond quite closely to the case formulation model used in psychology. They represent attempts to make sense of particular situations and provide a basis for deciding whether and how best to intervene. In clinical mental health settings, assessment may overlap with or contribute to diagnosis, where diagnosis represents confirmation of the presence of a discrete physiological dysfunction—a mental illness—via the observation and identification of symptomatic behavioral traits assumed to correlate with 'internal' functioning. The status of diagnosis as a factual representation of 'reality' is inherently controversial, with debate centering on the subjective nature of the judgments upon which diagnosis depends, widely acknowledged to vary according to time and space and thus rarely meeting the criteria required to differentiate knowledge from opinion or belief (Shaw 2008).

Since its inception, there have been debates within social work about the relationship between 'cause' and 'cure' (Cree 2002; Wilson et al. 2008), with assessment representing the means through which these causal relationships are identified, described, elaborated, and untangled. As well as representing a discrete stage within the social work process, assessment itself comprises a number of elements including information gathering, analysis, judgment, and decision making. When explicitly engaging in assessment, however, there are a number of key issues that practitioners focus upon:

Firstly, what is going on in this particular situation?
Secondly, what should be done about it? And underpinning each of these:
What sources of information must be gathered?
What processes should be followed in arriving at judgments?
And what are the implications of those judgments for decisions regarding if and how to intervene?

These generic issues resonate with the case formulation and diagnostic process and function of the 'psy' disciplines of psychiatry and psychology (Rose 1996).

In social work, then, assessment is the process via which practitioners make sense of people and their environments, including social situations and relationships, and the intersections between them. It is while they are engaged in the analysis of information that practitioners form views and opinions about the situation, character, motivation, responsibility, and—sometimes—blameworthiness of those they are assessing. Consequently, assessment plays a very influential role in framing the extent, nature, and content of future contact between social workers and potential service users, determining—at least temporarily—the basis on which any intervention will be made. It is clearly crucial, then, that the basis on which these judgments and the decisions which flow from them are made are as accurate as possible, if what follows is to be effective. Thus, we need to ask:

What is the nature and status of the knowledge on which these crucial judgments are made?
What information do practitioners gather?
How is (and should) it be filtered, analyzed, and integrated in arriving at a conclusion?
And how should the relationship between symptom and behavior be formulated in the less than straightforward sets of circumstances that mental health assessments seek to make sense of?

Although it is a crude dichotomy, here I will use the recognized distinction between 'artistic' and 'scientific' approaches to assessment (Holland 2011; Hudson 2009) as a framework for illuminating various ways that social workers might address these issues.

The 'Art' of Assessment

The idea that art might function as a useful metaphor for understanding the nature of social work practice is enduring (Gray and Webb 2008; Martinez-Brawley and Zorita 1998). Key to understanding its utility is its emphasis on the creative interaction between worker and service user as a necessary prerequisite for meaningful judgments regarding what is going on in a particular scenario, the possible relationship between cause and cure, and how best to intervene. Priority is attached to the significance of the relationship between worker and client, and the creative intersubjective process they engage in when they interact as the basis for the co-construction of meaning. Here, formal knowledge is accorded secondary status to that derived experientially via contact with, and a developing understanding of, the service user and his or her situation.

Tacit Knowledge Key here is the work of Schon (1983) that represents a significant exposition of the necessity for, and benefits of, tacit knowledge. Contrary to the view that practice is best seen as entailing the application of preexisting knowledge, Schon argues that theory, or knowledge utilized in practice, is only meaningfully articulated through action. This is because much of the reality of practice is far removed from how it is theorized. Indeed, because of this mismatch, practitioners must adapt generalized theory to the concerns of the individualized client or situation. This adaptability should in itself be seen as a central component of what it is to 'be' a practitioner, and it is around the notion of reflective practice that this idea has developed. Because of the unpredictability of the situations that social workers operate within, it is not possible to develop pre-proscribed responses, which is the aim of the 'scientific' approach. The creative capacities of the practitioner are therefore called upon to circumvent the limitations of formal knowledge. Each situation has its own unique character, as determined by the interaction between formal theory, experiential knowledge, intuitive responses, and the particular characteristics of the 'case' in question.

Tacit knowledge is privileged here, on the basis that the problems that practitioners must deal with are of a different nature than those which can be addressed by knowledge generated via empirical methods. This context—the 'swampy lowlands' of practice—is such that practitioners must modify or interpret existing knowledge to make it useful for their immediate purposes. They require different 'forms' of knowledge than that which is generated via empirical methods; although generalized knowledge can guide the development of policy, it has much less significance in individualized scenarios. Consequently, practitioners have little option but to rely on informal, tacit knowledge. Tacit approaches reflect an interpretivist worldview, in that there is a divide between the assumption that formal knowledge produced by positivist means necessarily corresponds with 'reality' and the awareness held by practitioners that the problems they deal with and the solutions that emerge are subjectively constructed rather than objectively determined.

Reflective Practice From this perspective, then, reflective practice is regarded as perhaps the major means through which practitioners can 'make meaning'. This is especially significant in relation to decisions about how to act, as in social work these are not straightforward since they reflect the inherent complexity and ambiguity of the human subjects and situations with which workers are involved. As such, there are many circumstances in which formal knowledge is insufficient.

Although often social workers will draw upon formal types of knowledge, they are also required to make judgments between competing knowledge claims, some of which arise because the accounts of events that they have are either inaccurate or untrue. There are commonplace scenarios in practice where 'evidence' about how best to respond is limited, inconclusive, or contested. Situations are complex, ambiguity is evident, and decisions that need to be made are not technical or instrumental but ethical or moral. Choosing between accounts ultimately has to be a subjective process and is an unavoidable aspect of practice (Taylor and White 2000). Practitioners therefore engage in 'making knowledge' through their subjective judgments and the actions that follow. Thus, it is not feasible to portray decisions and actions by practitioners as being solely or ideally based upon an objective knowledge base derived from the application of the philosophy and methods of empirical science.

The suggestion, then, is that it is right and proper that knowledge be recognized as multiple and contingent, but that this in itself does not mean that knowledge cannot be used selectively in accordance with immediate practical requirements according to criteria of relevance, adequacy, and utility. Decision making by practitioners should therefore include careful appraisal of options and associated outcomes within a wider context in which 'everyday critical practices' are developed to ensure that there is congruence between overall purpose and situated decision making. This reflexivity represents more than some ill-defined reflection. It is a means of bringing professional assumptions, or tacit knowledge, to the fore via critical analysis that makes explicit the links between practice, professional constructions and interpretations, and the wider social and political context.

Reflective practice has a commitment to the value of tacit knowledge such that 'bottom up' inductively produced knowledge is accorded equal, if not greater, status with 'top down' deductively produced knowledge. As a corollary, practitioner intuition and 'artistry' are acknowledged as significant within professional practice, especially via the adaptation of existing knowledge and skills or the generation of new knowledge within novel contexts, and regarded as essential if practitioners are to be able to adapt to changing circumstances. Reflective practice, then, asks that practitioners be reflective about their work and integrate an understanding that the nature of their role and tasks are contextually and contingently constructed, rather than being actual reflections of reality. In meaningful terms, this asks that practitioners do their jobs in an awareness that the knowledge claims that they make in the process—this person is '*this* sort' of person, the best way to deal with this issue is by way of *this* intervention—are not 'facts' but attempts to make meaning. This is well and good, but according to critics, it is a separate challenge from the urgent need to counter the criticisms regarding social work's ability to effectively identify and manage risk and vulnerability and so bolster the standing of the profession.

Anti-psychiatry The idea of diagnosis as a form of subjective interpretation has been influential in critiques of the medical approach to mental health care. The political critique related psychiatric power and the oppression associated with this to its institutional base, evident in the work of Foucault (1961) on the relationship between psychiatric power and knowledge, and Goffman (1961) on the dominion over the lives of mental health patients exercised on behalf of wider society. These perspectives overlapped in the work of the 'anti-psychiatrists' such as Szasz (1961), Scheff (1966), Cooper (1967), and Laing (1960) who focused on the dehumanizing impact of psychiatric treatment, including the perceived inhumanity entailed in strict behaviorism, electroconvulsive therapy, and psychosurgery. Madness was reconstituted as a powerful and stigmatizing label that served social functions, based on normative rather than substantive criteria. Often, psychiatrists miscon-strued particular forms of communication as indicative of individual pathology. Behaviors that are either of no particular consequence or necessary for the func-tioning and healing of an individual who had suffered difficult or unusual experi-ences were seen as dysfunction in need of amelioration. Szasz, for example, suggested that what is referred to as 'schizophrenia' is merely behavior that offends norms or sensibilities. Similarly, Scheff, following labeling theorists, saw the mentally ill as 'rule breakers' who, once categorized in a particular fashion, would inevitably live up to their categorization. Laing, from a psychodynamic viewpoint, saw the symptoms of madness as an elaborate defense against accepting respon-sibility for oneself. In such analyses, practitioners were cast as driven by power, status, and self-interest rather than genuine concern for the health or well-being of others.

Anti-psychiatry thus locates the symptoms of madness not within the patient but in the mental health practitioner whose perceptions of what is being communicated 'make the language of psychosis unintelligible by attributing it to "inhuman pro-cesses"' (Tantam 1991: 338). Critics proposed an alternative approach: assuming that what is being communicated has meaning; recognizing that illness is 'caused' by environmental stimuli, especially social relationships; and acknowledging the positive potential of 'symptoms' for the individual concerned. There was emphasis on the significance of family dynamics including insularity and oppression in the genesis of emotional distress. Laing went as far as to suggest that 'the family is a pathogenic variable in the genesis of schizophrenia' (Laing and Esterton 1970: 12). This theme was extended to 'the social' more generally as the impact of social division on individual capabilities became apparent. There was also a powerful assertion that practitioners within 'the system' were inherently oppressive, 'at best…the policeman of society and at worst…as small part in an extensive system of violence' (Tantam 1991: 341). Overall, such critique pointed to 'the processes through which the frontiers between the normal and the pathological are erected, and once erected, how difficult it is to move from the side of pathology to that of normality' (Miller 1986: 28).

The polemical nature of much 'anti-psychiatry' is emphasized by Tantam, who is critical of the extent to which it rejected even the most fundamental tenets of mental health practice. 'There is something frightening about treating as mad someone who is in fact sane. There is also something very disturbing about treating someone who is mad as if they were responsible' (1991: 337). Castel suggests that anti-psychiatry wrongly treats 'mental health professionals as mere agents of state power' (1991: 293), while Scull (1986) makes the apt point that although labelling theory and social constructionism have contributed much to our understanding *of reactions to* madness, they have not demonstrated that there is *no such thing as* mental illness. Nevertheless, arguably anti-psychiatry has had practical effect in the move from asylums to community.

This 'critical sensibility' regarding the substance of psychiatric knowledge claims dovetails with 'artistic' approaches to judgments and decision making. Both stress the value of self or what the practitioner—and more recently, the service user —brings to this interaction. Creativity is privileged as a basis for the holistic interpretation of individuals and their circumstances and problems. Holism entails attention to all aspects of an individual's circumstances and functioning, both past and present, rather than to discrete elements. Assessments, then, are co-constructed via communication within relationships between practitioner and service users. Rather than representing an incidental add-on, knowledge derived through lived experience is privileged, a necessary precursor for what follows.

Although this is a seductive vision, 'artistic' approaches have inherent limitations. A lack of precision regarding processes of reasoning—how particular judgments are arrived at—leaves decision making 'shrouded in mystery' (Sheppard 2006, p. 170). Logically, judgments that are not founded on transparent processes of reasoning are difficult to justify and so do not lend themselves to defensible decision making (Kemshall 1998). Attempts to specify means by which accurate assessments are formulated are thus hampered, with implications for practitioners if and when something goes wrong, and, as a corollary, the credibility and legitimacy of agencies. As a result, there have been concerted efforts recently to shift social work away from its subjective 'artistic' bearings to approaches to assessment that are more objective, evidence-based and scientific.

The 'Science' of Assessment

Science represents a means of generating knowledge according to a particular method, entailing the generation and testing of theories in the form of hypotheses. The production of knowledge fills gaps and reduces uncertainty. Kirk and Reid (2002) argue that numerous historical innovations in social work can be regarded as low-level efforts to 'scientize' social work by shifting the basis of knowledge claims from informal to formal knowledge sources and therefore reducing uncertainty of prognosis, prediction, and outcome. Examples include the use by nineteenth-century Charities Organization Service caseworkers of home visits and interviews to generate knowledge which would enable them to differentiate between the 'deserving' and 'undeserving' on the basis of an evaluation of moral character (Cree 2002).

Similarly, Mary Richmond's specification of the key principles of casework for practitioners to utilize in their practice represented a move toward the formalization of approaches to practice based on the application of empirical principles—those deemed to have been confirmed by experience as contributing to the achievement of positive outcomes. These were outlined in her influential *Social Diagnosis* (Richmond 1917) which Soydan referred to as 'a scientific manual of methods' (Soydan 1999, p. 90). The integration of psychoanalytic theory into casework, whereby social problems came to be seen as being underlain by the psychological needs of the individual, a contemporary 'acting out' of the enduring effects of experiences in early life which impacted on the establishment of bonds with primary caregivers, can also be regarded as a shift toward ensuring that social work practice is premised upon a 'scientifically' derived knowledge base, albeit according to a formulation of science which is now outmoded.

Approaches to practice that draw on behavioral and cognitive psychology are more overt in their emphasis on the merits of scientific method, namely 'rigor... replicability and transferability' (Sheldon and Macdonald 2008, p. 52). Relatedly, the ascendency of evidence-based practice reflects a belief that the methods of science represent a more appropriate means of determining if and how to intervene than the 'vagaries' of practitioner preference (Shaw 1999).

Structured and Actuarial Approaches Whereas conceiving of assessment as 'art' entails autonomous, individualized, relationship-based meaning making of an inherently subjective nature, scientific approaches involve more objective processes drawing on pre-defined sources of knowledge in accordance with consistent processes rather than individual creativity. Rather than basing judgments on informal forms of knowledge, these more structured approaches privilege objective sources of knowledge. Clinical judgment entails practitioners arriving at a decision regarding what is going on and how to intervene on the basis of their knowledge of this 'case' or 'patient' gleaned from their own involvement and interaction with particular service users. Structured approaches, often utilizing assessment aids and actuarial scoring tools, by contrast, entail assessment according to pre-specified criteria, and the making and using of generalizations based on the accumulation of statistical data regarding other, similarly categorized people. In such circumstances, some believe that the centrality of the relationship between service user and worker is devalued, and in the process that the professional endeavor takes on a wholly different nature. The ability of the practitioner and client to co-construct meaning on the basis of empathy and understanding is inhibited by an emphasis on compliance with pre-proscribed assessment frameworks. These are not professional tasks, properly understood, and so lay the ground for a process of de-skilling in which unqualified staff increasingly undertake roles and responsibilities that previously were firmly within the province of the professional practitioner.

The Sociology of Knowledge This perspective is supported by work in the sociology of science that demonstrates disjuncture between the rhetoric and reality of scientific research. The sociology of knowledge focuses on the ways in which changes in individual experiences, as well as community and institutional practices, reflect society's developing understanding of the world and how it works. Knowledge, of course, is difficult to define and conceptualize but is generally taken to refer to what is *known*, as opposed to what is not known or merely thought of as known, reflecting Plato's distinction between knowledge, belief, and opinion (Shaw 2008). The main foci for the sociology of knowledge, then, are the ways in which social change—broadly defined—affects how knowledge is defined and utilized. Traditionally, post-Enlightenment, and reflecting dominant modernist principles, the assumption was that cumulatively and progressively, the application of scientific method would allow individuals to ascertain knowledge—or truth—regarding the world and their place in it with ever-increasing degrees of certainty. Here, knowledge represents the solution to problems stemming from uncertainties associated with ignorance, or lack of knowledge.

However, over the last 50 years or so, the rise to prominence of postmodern perspectives has challenged the dominance of these assumptions, such that faith and confidence in the modernist ideal has waned. Key theorists have revealed the inherently subjective nature of supposedly objective knowledge claims and so have challenged the authority and legitimacy of foundational truths. Strong claims about the world, and about categories and classifications routinely applied to groups and individuals, are now recognized as social constructions (Berger and Luckman 1967), intimately entwined with the operation of power in society (Foucault 1972), while science itself is recognized as a messy business, often entailing subjective, interpretive judgments, rather than the straightforward specification of objective facts (Lakatos 1978).

As a consequence of more widespread recognition of the subjective nature of supposedly objective knowledge, the uncertain status of knowledge claims routinely made by all decision makers, including social work practitioners, is now widely recognized. This changed understanding of knowledge and its relationship to uncertainty has impacted on the institutions and practices of social work and mental health over the last thirty years or so. The decline of the welfare ideal, a pervasive lack of trust in the effectiveness and veracity of 'social' practices, the shift from welfare to risk, the development of actuarial practices, and the evidence-based agenda—all of these developments relate to some extent to shifts in confidence in the knowledge base which underpins the actions of professionals (Garland 2001).

Critical scholars have emphasized the ways that shifts 'from art to science' have eroded transformative potential in favor of a reliance on managerial systems (e.g., Feeley and Simon 1992; Fitzgibbon 2011a, b), and in some respects, this is true. However, they also overstate the case. It is known that even in a 'risk society', professionals continue to draw on informal, tacit, and clinical knowledge in arriving at judgments regarding complex issues. This should not be surprising. It mirrors what science and technology studies demonstrate regarding science more generally (e.g., Latour and Woolgar 1986). Internally, science is driven by contention, with the knowledge bases of particular specialties much less robust than is ordinarily assumed, and arrived at via processes that are as mundane and everyday as is the case in 'soft' disciplines. The essential role that subjectivity plays in scientific processes is manifest. If even in science, pure objectivism is tempered by evident subjectivism, then the standard positivist critique of interpretivism is weakened. In the practice-based disciplines, this means that professional knowledge claims, whether a diagnosis, case formulation, or risk assessment, and whether based upon formal, informal, or 'hybrid' knowledge sources, also remain best guesses rather than facts.

Of course, proponents of scientific approaches are unconvinced by arguments that assessment either ought or must be a subjective endeavor (Sheldon 2001). They claim that emphasis on social work as art or craft has not served the profession or its users well. Generally, over time, and at the level of general populations, more systematic and procedurally led assessments would be more accurate in their appraisal of need and risk, and crucially, the intersection between the two. As I suggested earlier, this is an enduring debate, which has not, as yet, reached its conclusion.

Notwithstanding the quite significant changes to assessment practice associated with a shift from 'art' to 'science', demands that social workers improve their practice have not receded. Service failures have highlighted the apparent inadequacy of social work decision making and seeming inability of practitioners to get judgments right on some occasions. Cumulatively, such failings suggest a lack of professional competence, with a consensus that further change is required to improve the quality and accuracy of assessment practice. Central to this is renewed emphasis on the ways in which assessors' judgments and decisions might improve if the knowledge on which they were based was more substantive. There are long-standing debates concerning the nature of knowledge (see Evans and Hardy 2010, Chap. 1). Several 'varieties' of knowledge are generally acknowledged, broadly divided into informal and formal, with the latter including research knowledge. The incorporation of research knowledge into judgments and decision making is increasingly seen as a means of potentially enhancing the quality of social work assessment practice. In the UK, both the Munro report (Munro 2011) and curriculum guidance issued by the College of Social Work emphasize the need for social workers to develop and utilize skills in reasoning, making judgments and decisions, and the application of knowledge as a basis for good practice.

Research-minded Assessment

Research mindedness entails practitioners 'informing themselves of research findings and applying them to practice, and undertaking their own research where appropriate' (Humphries 2008: 2). The success of research mindedness as a strategy for improving assessment practice is dependent on various related components.

First, a commitment to embedding both research and evaluation within practice is required (see Shaw 2011 for an account of how individual practitioners might actualize this), which is dependent on rejection of the primacy of the 'decision maker as expert' model.

Second, an awareness of ontological and epistemological perspectives is needed, so that the paradigmatic affiliations underpinning a knowledge claim can be taken into account when making sense of and integrating competing knowledge claims.

Third, critical appraisal skills are required, whereby practitioners actively seek, identify, and integrate research findings during the various stages of assessment (information gathering, judgment, and decision making) based on explicit recognition that research represents one of various sources of knowledge that need to be taken into account in decision making. Critical appraisal 'is about deciding whether or not to use particular research findings to inform decision making within practice' (Newman et al. 2005, p. 56). It is therefore key in determining *whether or not and if so in what way* research is relevant and useful to practice, as the intention is that research findings should inform assessment, rather than determine its outcome.

Additionally, there is also merit in recognizing the potential utility of assessment skills to social work research as the skills that social workers utilize in their day-to-day practice (information collation, interviewing, critical thinking, analysis) parallel those that are important in social inquiry. Gilgun (1994) argues that research and practice fit each other like 'hand and glove' and that consequently social workers themselves are well placed to undertake practice-based research so as to further enhance knowledge and understanding. Practice-based research has a potentially crucial contribution to make here (Dodd and Epstein 2012).

Practitioners who are 'research minded', then, will contribute both to their own professional development by continually engaging with and appraising research literature, but will also ensure that an up-to-date and evolving understanding of how knowledge in their area of practice is developing over time informs the ongoing development of the disciplinary knowledge base. Consequently, 'research minded practitioners are likely to be excellent social workers' (D'Cruz and Jones 2004, p. 81).

There is a clear logic to this account. However, although the potential that research might play in illuminating the causes and consequences of social problems is seductive, this should not be overstated. Research has real limitations, which undermine the ambitions of strong advocates of 'research-based' practice. The knowledge generated via research, particularly research undertaken within the social sciences, including social work research, is rarely definitive and usually contested. In this, it reflects its subject matter, human beings, whose thoughts and feelings differentiate them from the more predictable variables that form the foci of the natural sciences. This applies irrespective of whether data are quantitative or qualitative, as neither is inherently robust enough to render challenges to claims of quality or specificity redundant. Additionally, research criteria vary according to *inter*disciplinary and *intra*disciplinary conventions (Shaw and Norton 2008).

Consequently, when engaging in assessment, social workers concerned to do justice to the complexity of a client's reality, and to complete as accurate an assessment as possible, *of necessity* need to incorporate but also supplement research-based knowledge with that derived from other sources.

Knowledge-Based Assessment

Knowledge-based practice recognizes that research knowledge is one of many 'sources' of knowledge that practitioners need to take into account in practice if they are to arrive at the fullest and therefore potentially most 'accurate' or 'truthful' approximation of a situation as a basis for determining how to intervene, as well as whether an intervention is working. Pawson et al.'s (2003) taxonomy specifies that, when integrated, knowledge from practitioners, service users, organizations, policy, and research enables us to formulate as complete a picture as possible. Although there are sometimes tensions between these various sources, reflecting the various stakeholders, a genuinely knowledge-based approach to practice requires that the value of each of these sources be acknowledged and incorporated within key activities such as diagnosis, assessment, and decision making.

This taxonomy emphasizes that research has a crucial role to play in assessment practice, but also that there are strengths and limitations associated with each of these 'sources', including research. Complexity confounds knowledge because the precise specification of the relationships between multiple variables is by definition a difficult task, which even where successful does not necessarily lend itself to transferability of knowledge beyond the situation in which it was generated. Put another way, it does not tell us 'what works for whom, in what circumstances, and why' (Pawson and Tilley 1997), thus rendering the generalizable application of evidence of possible effectiveness from one setting to another problematic (Kazi 2003). Even high-quality research knowledge acquired via the development and application of well-formulated research design and robust methods, which satisfies conventions and criteria for 'quality' such as validity, rigor, and trustworthiness, cannot be assumed transferable (Hammersley 2013), particularly within what Sheppard (2007) refers to as 'the practice paradigm'. It would therefore be foolish to suggest that research-based approaches, or any other strategy premised on certainty as a prerequisite, will directly impact on outcomes. Consequently, it is apparent that the difficulties assessors face in arriving at accurate judgments and making appropriate decisions have as much to do with the challenges entailed in synthesizing diverse sources of knowledge as the perceived competence of either individual social workers or the profession as a whole.

Aware that research is one of several components of the wider knowledge base of the profession, each of which has strengths and limitations in specific situations or contexts, practitioners need to develop two related skills. *First*, the ability to assess relevance and utility in context, and *second*, to synthesize knowledge generated from alternative sources according to fluid and variable conventions that nevertheless enable judgments and decisions to be both made and substantiated. This is a challenging task, by any standards, and helps us to understand the difficulties that practitioners sometimes face in seeking to undertake assessments that are timely, focused and accurate.

Technical Knowledge In theory, empirical practice represents a means of ensuring that necessary decisions are based on logic and rationality rather than mere opinion, bias, or prejudice, therefore minimizing error and enhancing quality and effectiveness. This shift from 'art' to 'science' has attracted pointed criticism. Parton (2008), for example, has suggested that structured approaches, especially those based on computerized algorithms, herald a shift 'from the social to the informational,' whereby assessments are based upon spurious connections between disjointed fragments of data rather than true knowledge or understanding gained via 'depth-level' engagement with service users and their situations. Similarly, in relation to mental health, Rose (2005) highlights the potential in practice for risk 'factors' to mutate into markers of dangerousness as service users become bearers of immutable pathological dispositions. The work of Pithouse et al. (2012), meanwhile, points to systemic difficulties in work with children and families, where measures introduced to improve the quality of practice paradoxically distract practitioners from their principal tasks. Additionally, and perhaps counterintuitively, however, such initiatives can contribute to a climate in which error is more rather than less likely. This is because practitioners may become over reliant upon formalized knowledge, neglecting skills required to make judgments and decisions where existing knowledge is not relevant or available, via skills such as 'reflection in action.' Despite the efforts of science, much of social work remains uncertain. The nature of knowledge is such that answers to all of the questions that need to be answered are not possible. Consequently, it is worth noting that it has also been suggested that assessment is neither art nor science. Instead, art and science, intuition and analysis, and subjective and objective are best represented as points on a continuum, with 'good enough' practice as a hybrid amalgamation located somewhere toward the midpoint (Corby 2006a, b). This is a helpful way of thinking about these issues, which transcends undue polarization of positions, and is increasingly recognized as a valuable component within assessment practice, particularly where concerns regarding risk are to the fore.

Synthesizing Knowledge Conceiving of assessment as the analysis and synthesis of knowledge from multiple sources to usefully inform judgments and decision making is potentially helpful. It emphasizes that assessment is a complex, imprecise, and difficult endeavor, both in terms of what is entailed in the task and in doing it accurately. There are practical and theoretical challenges to integrating multiple sources of knowledge, particularly regarding how much weight should be attributed to each and on what basis. In social work agencies, there will be disputes at the 'borderlines' in differentiating the sorts of cases—people, situations, needs, risks, and disorders—that ought to be dealt with 'scientifically' from those requiring a more artistic approach. Agencies may respond procedurally where knowledge is relatively certain by virtue of its 'scientific' status. Logically, this would imply that they would privilege 'artistic' approaches where knowledge is relatively uncertain. In reality, however, often they do not. But it is worth stressing that the case for *integrating* art and science is a strong one. This is because both actually rest on the same fundamental assumptions. By this I mean that artistic processes mirror those that science—properly understood—also utilizes. Scientists themselves utilize subjectivity, which arguably is built into scientific method itself. They use it in making decisions, and they use it in theory development (Collins 1985; Collins and Evans 2007).

This understanding of science as something other than the objective production of incontestable knowledge is distant from the assumptions of evidence-based approaches to assessment, but congruent with those of knowledge-based practice. This recognition means that there is little merit in arguing that subjective and objective knowledge are in some way incommensurate, and much to be said for highlighting how reciprocal interaction between art and science necessarily complement each other and contribute to a knowledge base which has real practical impact. As Glasby (2011) puts it, there is:

> …a need to move away from traditional models of 'evidence-based practice'…towards a more inclusive and broader concept of 'knowledge based practice'. Whilst this may be difficult, seeking to combine insights from theoretical, empirical and experiential sources may be one way of making different and better decisions about health and social care in the future. (p. 96)

The dividing line between certainty and uncertainty represents a difficult balancing act, but the integration of art and science might go some way to enabling social workers to better navigate the complex terrain of practice. This might not guarantee certainty, but it increases the likelihood of judgments that are accurate, and thus intervention that is effective.

But How? From Practice to Principles and Back Again

All of which is easier said than done. Independently of her work for government, Eileen Munro has sought to develop a model of social work practice that combines the strengths of both objective and subjective, or analytic and intuitive, approaches to judgment and decision making that are at the heart of assessment practice (Munro 2005; Munro 2008). This broadly systemic model privileges notions of complexity and seeks to specify not how to eliminate uncertainty, but how to manage or engage with it. The assumption is that it is possible to improve and potentially standardize the quality of decision making in practice where the appropriate style of reasoning informs particular judgments. Munro (2010) distinguishes between areas of practice which ought to be proceduralized and those which should be judgment based, but acknowledges the challenges entailed in establishing which areas of practice in which contexts and domains fit into each category and of establishing criteria that might be utilized as the basis for such differentiation. In the absence of definitive guidance regarding how such judgments can or should be made, then, the question arises—are there *principles* which might helpfully inform how practitioners do this? It does seem that the ubiquity of uncertainty helps us to understand why studies of social work practice consistently highlight the *pragmatic* approach that practitioners describe when accounting for the decisions they make. The potential that pragmatism might hold as a philosophy for practice is little discussed in social work, perhaps because of misunderstanding of what it entails, itself related to lay usage of the term as meaning 'unprincipled.' Properly understood, however, pragmatism offers real potential as a framework that practitioners might use to inform assessment practice.

Pragmatic Principles The pragmatic position on perennial philosophical concerns regarding the nature of knowledge and how we might 'know' is distinctive. Rather than being defined as some objective representation of reality, knowledge is primarily regarded as a means of problem solving so as to achieve specific, practical, and ethical ends (see Evans and Hardy 2010, for a more elaborate account of what pragmatic thought entails).

Although philosophy tends to be an abstract discipline, Harvard psychiatrist Brendel has elaborated on its practical implications for mental health services. He specifies four pragmatic principles that ought to inform practice: *practicality, pluralism, participation,* and *provisionalism* (Brendel 2006), suggesting that where these criteria are adhered to, there is real potential to promote an integration of art and science in practice-based disciplines.

Practicality relates to the notion that ideas should be judged according to their capacity to assist people in addressing the challenges they are faced with. As these challenges are diverse, they require responses that are flexible and open-minded, or **plural**. Life is lived interpersonally, and so there is recognition that any approximation of 'truth' will include the views and perspectives of all of those **participating**, albeit with awareness that the uncertain, complex, and ever-changing nature of people and the world they live in is such that knowledge is only ever **provisional** and will alter according to context and circumstances.

Thus, in social work decision making, assessors will need to consider the extent to which their judgments, and the actions that follow from them, will facilitate **practical** effects, rather than whether or not a particular theory or version of reality appeals to us at an abstract level or resonates intellectually or aesthetically. Because pragmatists reject the notion of one single truth or means of establishing it, they regard negotiation between **plural** perspectives as more appropriate than approaches that seek to prove or disprove alternative approaches. Consequently, where knowledge derived from different sources is to some extent contradictory, tensions are addressed through the Hegelian approach known as dialectical reasoning. This involves paying attention to the positions and arguments of varying approaches and attempting to integrate the perspectives of all **participants** in a conciliatory way. It 'does not lead to the triumph of one approach over the other, but instead to a dynamic equilibrium between scientific and humanistic concepts' (Brendel 2006,

p. 13). In this way, assessments are more likely to lead to useful, workable solutions that have potential for achieving practical gains.

Pragmatists, then, are all too aware of the limitations of both aesthetics—its relativity—and reason—its fallibility. Their assumption is that, whatever its source, knowledge is **provisional.** As a corollary, assessors need a provisional sensibility, characterized by open-mindedness and flexibility, whereby the value of a knowledge claim is assessed according to its practical merit. Decisions made according to pragmatic precepts, then, would be integrative rather than based on singular sources. Judgments regarding if and how and when to intervene will be made on the basis of the 'balance of evidence' generated from multiple sources. It is unavoidable that such decisions will involve differentiating between competing claims based on less than full knowledge. This, however, is the reality in social work. As Evans and Hardy (2010) suggest, practitioners have little option but 'to make decisions and act as though these choices are objective, knowing full well that the knowledge upon which they are based is often contested and so their judgments and actions may be "wrong"' (p. 175).

Pragmatism in Practice Pragmatism, then, has real potential as a framework for assessment and diagnosis in social work. This is mainly because its underpinning assumptions correspond closely with those of social work, properly understood. This does mean, however, that its emphasis will differ from those of strong advocates of other, quite particular, approaches. Assessments undertaken according to pragmatic principles would, for example, be nonpartisan. Partisanship—'taking sides'—is incompatible with pluralism, here understood as a commitment to ensuring that assessments incorporate the views of the various stakeholders with a perspective on a case. 'Taking sides' is central to some understandings of the social work task, particularly radical and critical variants, and, to some extent, person-centered models, but pragmatism emphasizes the need to avoid 'taking sides' and instead retain a concern with practical effects.

Additionally, in statutory settings, there are all sorts of judgments and decisions that practitioners make that one or more stakeholders may disagree with, including service users. Service user perspectives have come to the fore in social work in the last couple of decades (Glasby and Beresford 2006; McLaughlin 2010), challenging the substance of clinical decision making, but tensions remain regarding the extent to which, in certain situations, partnership working is practicable, when it might be appropriate for practitioners to override service user views, and on what basis. Although useful work has been undertaken considering the inclusion of service user perspectives in risk assessment (e.g., Langan and Lindow 2004; Ryan 2000), this does not resolve the issue of whether and when the views and perspectives of 'experts by experience' should supplant (rather than inform) the judgments and decisions of practitioners.

One clear benefit of approaches to assessment that are integrative stems from the tendency toward confirmatory bias that Munro (2003) identifies. In social work, this has manifested in, for example, the so-called 'rule of optimism' (Dingwall et al. 1983) in child protection, or an uncritical acceptance of service user perspectives as representing the 'true' account of a situation. Knowledge synthesis has the potential to counter the bias that manifests in partisan decision making by ensuring practitioners take into account sources of knowledge other than those based on gut instinct. As indicated earlier, tacit knowledge is important in social work but requires integration with more formal sources.

Finally, for many, reflection is central to ensuring good practice. Within a pragmatic framework, however, the emphasis would be on suspending undue reflection in favor of situated problem solving and action. Pragmatists are aware of the potential for idealism to limit action and thus the achievement of practical effects. However, and contrary to the caricature of pragmatism as value-free, it is clear that pragmatic method supplements rather than supplants ethical deliberation, in that although its concerns may be situated rather than global, they occur within the context of a commitment to the notion of action as a means to a particular end, which is 'what is best in a particular situation for a particular person' (Polkinghorne 2004, p. 123).

Toward Critical Pluralism

In the absence of certainty, we need to keep our options open, which is what the application of pragmatic principles to assessment enables us to do. It seems unlikely that we will ever be fortunate enough to have anything approaching definitive knowledge regarding 'what works for whom in what circumstances and why,' and so it is essential that practitioners are equipped, and free, to utilize pragmatic principles as a basis for determining how to act to achieve their ends. In its commitment to practical action, pluralism, participation, and provisionalism, pragmatism offers potential to do justice to the 'common place complexity' that characterizes social work, without allowing awareness of the ubiquity of uncertainty to descend into relativism or anti-scientism. Pragmatists regard uncertainty as a starting point rather than an insurmountable difficulty that we have no option but to celebrate. Of course, by definition, a pragmatic framework for practice is unable to offer prescriptive guidance to practitioners regarding how assessment 'ought' to be undertaken. It does, however, encourage practitioners to navigate the tensions between art and science according to criteria that have clear relevance and utility within the practice paradigm. The unavoidable process of *considered but tentative selection of the seemingly most appropriate strategy in a given situation*—critical pluralism—represents a robust defense of the necessity of professionalism to social work practice.

Conclusions

Emphasis on the value of research knowledge as a key element for social workers and its integration, based on shared assumptions and characteristics, offers potential to contribute to the development of approaches to assessment which genuinely integrate art and science. There is no expectation that this approach will lead to infallible decisions in social work practice. But it is my contention that this integrative, pragmatic approach offers a useful framework within which assessment practice can be undertaken. It is worth stressing, however, that this is not to be overly critical of established ways of undertaking assessment. At heart, the pragmatic approach to decision making has both an empirical and a normative basis—it describes how practitioners actually work, and suggests that this is as it should, or perhaps must, be. We do not actually know how accurate social work assessments are. We do know that the number of child deaths per annum remains about constant or is in decline (Corby 2006a, b) and that international reviews indicate high levels of satisfaction with social welfare services. These facts are hardly suggestive of incompetence unless competence is equated with infallibility. Nevertheless, social work will remain a demanding and challenging profession; however it is conducted. Perhaps critics should remember that when social work fails, it is because it is actually very difficult to get right. The fact that 'extreme failures' are so few is testament to the enduring professionalism of its practitioners.

Application to the Case of Ray

How can we think about what is going on for Ray? Thoughts about 'what is going on' are inevitably linked to thoughts about 'what should be done?' Clinical practice is not linear, and assessment cannot be considered apart from its implications for intervention; both are ongoing, recursive, and provisional. Thus, beginning with the case as given, we need to think as much about *what we still need to find out*, and *how* we might find out, as we do about *what we already know*. What kinds and sources of information should be identified and gathered, what processes should be followed in arriving at judgments, and what are the implications of those judgments for intervention decisions? More specifically:

- What sorts of things do we *not* yet know about Ray?
- How might we go about finding out more in order to supplement our existing knowledge?
- How reliable are the various sources of knowledge we might draw upon and what should we do if they offer contradictory claims or accounts?

- What kinds of research and professional knowledge might be helpful for understanding Ray? What do we know about people who, like Ray, have had similar experiences? To what extent should be use this knowledge, if at all?
- What are the potential benefits of applying research knowledge to Ray's case? What are the limitations or caveats?

Each of these questions can be usefully explored through the application of pragmatic principles. Ray's is a complex case, and as indicated above, it is the very complexity of social work that pushes us toward a pragmatic framework for practice. How, then, might the application of the principles of pragmatism help the assessment process?

Provisionalism—perhaps the most straightforward underlying hypothesis in this case is that there is a relationship between Ray's experience of abuse as a child, his subsequent mental illness, and his own abusive violent behavior and functioning in relationships. Although there is a clear logic to this account—it mirrors the well-established 'cycle of violence' (de Zulueta 1993)—nevertheless, it is only useful to the extent that Ray or those working with him find it helpful as a means of understanding and potentially changing his behavior. Nor should it necessarily be assumed to be accurate, however much it helps us to make sense of the situation. Additionally, although based on information from Ray, this information may change, and as such, our assessment of the relationship between these factors, including how past, present and future intersect, would also change. We must always remain open to the possibility of a changed understanding of the nature of the relationship between variables, and thus of what has, is, or will happen in a particular case.

Practicality—it is all very well formulating an elaborate assessment of Ray's functioning and mental health. But in what ways does this formulation practically assist Ray? As a formulation, it may resonate, either logically or by appealing to broadly aesthetic sensibilities, and point in the direction of various therapeutic interventions. However, Ray is not particularly comfortable talking about the past, which might rule out depth-level therapy. What other approaches might assist? Solution-focused approaches might be one useful alternative, but there are many others. Ultimately, it will be the theoretical account (the possible explanation) which is most helpful, rather than one that resonates with other possible criteria, that will be have most validity within 'the practice paradigm'.

Plurality—we have Ray's account, but who else might we usefully consult regarding his behavior, functioning, and actions? What might specific individuals—family, friends, partners, and other professionals—know regarding Ray and his situation that Ray's account alone, or our interpretation of it, might have neglected? Are there other sources of knowledge that we additionally need to consult, either within our own agency or the wider community who have an interest in the issues which are manifesting in the case, whether that be at an organizational, policy, or research level?

Participation—in such a complex situation, how can we ensure that the varying views and perspectives of those people and agencies with a 'stake' in Ray's case are accommodated within our assessments? Importantly, is the conciliatory approach—dialectical reasoning that pragmatists advocate sufficiently flexible but also robust enough to enable potential conflicts to be worked through in ways that are practically meaningful?

Practical Exercises

1. Think of a client who came for help with a specific problem. What strategies came to mind for addressing this problem? Now take a step back to review your own thinking process by explicitly applying the four principles of pragmatism to the problem at hand: *practicality* (ideas need to be evaluated by their capacity to help people address the challenges they are faced with), *pluralism* (the need for flexible responses), *participation* (the client's perspective must be included), and *provisionalism* (all knowledge must be viewed in context).
2. Where do you see yourself on the artistic-to-scientific continuum? How did you come to this position—that is, what influences, experiences, or training may have led you to this stance? What would it take to 'move you' a bit closer to the middle? How open are you to changing your location on this continuum?
3. Which areas of social work practice do you think ought to be proceduralized, and which ought to be more judgment based—that is, up to the 'artistry' of the individual clinician? Think about your own practice setting. Which aspects of your work or expectations of the milieu are based on established evidence and which are left to clinical judgment? How is that working for both staff and clients?

References

Berger, P., & Luckman, T. (1967). *The social construction of reality: A treatise in the sociology of knowledge*. New York: Doubleday.
Brendel, D. H. (2006). *Healing psychiatry: bridging the science/humanism divide*. Cambridge, MA: MIT Press.
Castel, R. (1991) From dangerousness to risk. In G. Burchell, C. Gordon & P. Miller (Eds.), *The foucault effect: Studies in governmentality*. Hemel Hempstead: Harvester Wheatsheaf.
Collins, H. (1985). *Changing order: Replication and induction in scientific practice*. London: Sage.
Collins, H., & Evans, R. (2007). *Rethinking expertise*. Chicago: Chicago University Press.
Cooper, D. G. (1967). *Psychiatry and anti-psychiatry*. London: Tavistock.
Corby, B. (2006). *Applying research in social work practice*. Maidenhead: Open University Press.
Corby, B. (2006b). *Child abuse: Towards a knowledge base*. Maidenhead: Berkshire.
Cree, V. (2002). The changing nature of social work. In R. Adams, L. Dominelli & M. Payne (Eds.), *Social work: Themes, issues and critical debates*. Basingstoke: Palgrave Macmillan.
D'Cruz, H., & Jones, M. (2004). *Social work research: Ethical and political contexts*. London: Sage.

de Zulueta, F. (1993). *From pain to violence: the traumatic roots of destructiveness*, London: Whurr.

Dingwall, R., Eekalaar, J., & Murray, T. (1983). *The protection of children: state, intervention and family life*. Oxford: Blackwell.

Dodd, S.-J., & Epstein, I. (2012). *Practice-based research in social work: a guide for reluctant students*. Abingdon: Routledge.

Evans, T., & Hardy, M. (2010) *Evidence and knowledge for practice*. Cambridge: Polity.

Feeley, M., & Simon, J. (1992). The new penology: Notes on the emerging strategy for corrections. *Criminology, 30*(4), 449–75.

Fitzgibbon, W, (2011), *Probation and social work on trial: Violent offenders and child abusers*. Basingstoke: Palgrave Macmillan.

Fitzgibbon, W. (2011b). *Probation and social work on trial*. Basingstoke. Palgrave Macmillan.

Foucault, M. (1961) *Madness and civilisation: A history of insanity in the age of reason*. London: Allen Unwin.

Foucault, M. (1972). *The archaeology of knowledge*. London: Tavistock.

Garland, D. (2001). *The culture of control*. Oxford: Oxford University Press.

Gilgun, J. (1994). Hand into glove. The grounded theory approach and social work practice research. In E. Sherman & W. J. Reid (Eds.), *Qualitative research in social work* (pp. 115–125). New York: Columbia University Press.

Glasby, J. (2011). From evidence based to knowledge based policy and practice. In Glasby, J. (Ed.), *Evidence, policy and practice: critical perspectives in health and social care*. Bristol: Policy Press.

Glasby, J. & Beresford, P. (2006) Commentary and issues: Who knows best? Evidence-based practice and the service user contribution. *Critical Social Policy, 26*, 268–284.

Goffman, E. (1961). *Asylums: Essays on the social situation of mental patients and other inmates*. New York: Doubleday.

Gray, M., & Webb, S. (2008). Social work as art revisited. *International Journal of Social Welfare, 17*, 182–193.

Hammersley, M. (2013). *The myth of research based policy and practice*. London: Sage.

Holland, S. (2011). *Child and family assessment in social work practice* (2nd ed.). London: Sage.

Hudson, C. G. (2009). Decision making in evidence based practice: Science and art, *Smith College Studies in Social Work, 79*, 155–174.

Humphries, B. (2008). *Social work research and social justice*. Basingstoke: Palgrave Macmillan.

Kazi, M. (2003). *Realist evaluation in practice*. London: Sage.

Kemshall, H. (1998). Defensible decisions for risk: Or 'it's the doers wot get the blame. *Probation Journal, 45*(6), 67–72.

Kirk, S. A., & Reid, W. J. (2002). *Science and social work: A critical appraisal*. New York: Columbia University Press.

Laing, R. D. (1960). *The divided self*. London: Tavistock.

Laing, R. D., & Esterton, A. (1970). *Sanity, madness and the family*. Harmondsworth: Penguin.

Lakatos, I. (1978). *The methodology of scientific research programmes*. Cambridge: Cambridge University Press.

Langan, J., & Lindow, V. (2004). *Living with risk. Mental health service user involvement in risk assessment and management*. Bristol: Policy Press/Joseph Rowntree Foundation.

Latour, B., & Woolgar, S. (1986). Laboratory life: The construction of scientific facts. Princeton, NJ: Princeton University Press.

Martinez-Brawley, E. E., & Zorita, P. M. B. (1998) At the edge of the frame: Beyond science and art in social work. *British Journal of Social Work, 28*(2), 197–212.

McLaughlin, H. (2010). Keeping service user involvement in research honest. *British Journal of Social Work, 40*(5), 1591–1608.

Miller, P. (1986). Critiques of psychiatry and critical sociologies of madness. In P. Miller & N. Rose (Eds.), *The power of psychiatry*. Cambridge: Polity.

Munro, E. (2003). *Formal risk assessment instruments or intuitive knowledge?* Houten, The Netherlands: Bohn Stafleu Van Loghum.

Munro, E. (2005). Improving practice: Child protection as a systems problem. *Children and Youth Services Review, 27*(4), 375–391.

Munro, E. (2008). *Effective child protection* (2nd ed.). CA, Sage: Los Angeles.

Munro, E. (2010). Learning to reduce risk in child protection. *British Journal of Social Work*, (4), 1135–1151.

Munro, E. (2011) *The munro review of child protection: Final report. A child-centred system.* London: Department for Education.

Newman, T., Moseley, A., Tierney, S., & Ellis, A. (2005). *Evidence-based social work: A guide for the perplexed.* Lyme Regis: Russell House).

Parker, J., & Bradley, G. (2004). *Social work practice: Assessment, planning, intervention and review.* Exeter: Learning Matters.

Parton, N. (2008). Changes in the form of knowledge in social work: From the 'social' to the 'informational'. *British Journal of Social Work, 38*(2), 253–269.

Pawson, R., Boaz, A., Grayson, L., Long, A., & Barnes, C. (2003). *Types and quality of knowledge in social care. Knowledge review 3.* London/Bristol: Social Care Institute for Excellence/Policy Press.

Pawson, R., & Tilley, N. (1997). *Realistic evaluation.* London: Sage.

Peay, J. (2003). *Decisions and dilemmas: Working with mental health law.* Oxford: Hart.

Pithouse, A., Broadhurst, K., Hall, C., Peckover, S., Wastell, D., & White, S. (2012). Trust, risk and the (Mis)management of contingency and discretion through new information technologies in children's services. *Journal of Social Work, 12*(2), 158–178.

Polkinghorne, D. E. (2004). *Practice and the human sciences: The case for a judgment-based practice of care.* Albany: State University of New York Press.

Richmond, M. E. (1917). *Social diagnosis.* New York: Russell Sage Foundation.

Rose, N. (1996). Psychiatry as a political science: Advanced liberalism and the administration of risk. *History of the Human Sciences, 2*, 1–23.

Rose, N. (2005). In search of certainty: Risk management in a biological age. *Journal of Public Health, 4*(3), 14–22.

Ryan, T. (2000). Exploring the risk management strategies of mental health service users. *Health, Risk and Society, 2*(3), 267–282.

Scheff, T. J. (1966). *Being mentally ill.* London: Weidenfeld and Nicolson.

Schon, D. (1983). *The Reflective Practitioner: How professionals think in action.* New York: Basic Books.

Scull, A. (1986). Mental patients and the community: A critical note. *International Journal of Law and Psychiatry, 9*, 383–392.

Shaw, I. (1999). *Qualitative evaluation.* London: Sage.

Shaw, I. (2008). Ways of knowing. In M. Gray & S. A. Webb (Eds.), *Social work theories and methods,* London: Sage.

Shaw, I. (2011). *Evaluating in practice* (2nd ed.). Aldershot: Ashgate.

Shaw, I., & Norton, M. (2008). Kinds and quality of social work research. *British Journal of Social Work, 38*(5), 953–970.

Sheldon, B. (2001). The validity of evidence-based practice in social work: A reply to Stephen Webb. *British Journal of Social Work, 31*(5), 801–809.

Sheldon, B., & Macdonald, G. (2008). *A textbook of social work.* London: Routledge.

Sheppard, M. (2006). *Social work and social exclusion.* Aldershot: Ashgate.

Sheppard, M. (2007). Assessment: From reflexivity to process knowledge. In Lishman, J. (Ed.), *Handbook for practice learning in social work and social care* (2nd ed.). London: Jessica Kingsley Publishers.

Soydan, H. (1999). *The history of ideas in social work.* Birmingham: Venture Press.

Stanley, N., & Manthorpe, J. (2001). Reading mental health inquiries: Messages for Social Work. *Journal of Social Work, 1*(1), 77–99.

Szasz, T. S. (1961). *The myth of mental illness: Foundations of a theory of personal conduct.* New York: Deel.

Tantam, D. (1991). The anti-psychiatry movement. In G. E. Berrios & H. Freeman (Eds.), *One hundred and fifty years of British psychiatry 1841–1991*. London: Gaskell.

Taylor, C., & White, S. (2000). *Practicing reflexivity in health and welfare: making knowledge*. Buckingham: Open University Press.

Wilson, K., Ruch, G., Lymbery, M., & Cooper, A. (2008). *Social work: An introduction to contemporary practice*. Harlow: Pearson.

Chapter 12
Meeting the Challenge of Teaching Integrated Assessment

Howard Robinson

Abstract In this chapter, the focus shifts to an exploration of how the flexible, multilayered approach to assessment set forth in previous chapters can actually be taught to students. Like clients, teachers and students have different styles, needs, and preferences, and thus, different approaches will resonate under different conditions and with different groups of learners. The skillful and effective instructor must be able to shift and adapt among a diverse pedagogical repertoire in order to convey how ideas, concepts, and models are actualized and rendered useful in real-world practice. Three approaches are described that foster this kind of knowledge-for-use: cognitive apprenticeship, problem-based learning (PBL), and experiential teaching. Principles, examples, and specific teaching strategies are provided for each model, with discussion of caveats and potential challenges. Exemplars of classroom activities and assignments are then analyzed to show how they embody or elicit the pedagogical principles of these three models. The chapter concludes with a list of ten essential teaching heuristics.

Keyword Cognitive apprenticeship · Content knowledge and process knowledge · Divergent thinking · Experiential teaching · Knowledge domains · Modeling · Praxis · Problem-based learning · Recontextualization · Scaffolding · Transformative learning

Introduction: Why This Matters

During the course of this book's development, Dr. Probst and I met frequently for coffee and entered into absorbing talk about the nature of clinical assessment. We propelled each other into avenues of inquiry that seemed inexhaustible and overwhelming, yet remained excited by the challenges of defining what constitutes a

H. Robinson (✉)
Graduate School of Social Service, Fordham University, New York, NY, USA
e-mail: hrobinson@fordham.edu

© Springer International Publishing Switzerland 2015
B. Probst (ed.), *Critical Thinking in Clinical Assessment and Diagnosis*,
Essential Clinical Social Work Series, DOI 10.1007/978-3-319-17774-8_12

clinical assessment, how we can incorporate intuition and tacit knowledge, how we tailor ideas to each individual, and how we organize assessment information into useful clinical formulations. As a professor of clinical practice, I peppered Barbara with questions of pedagogy: How can we teach students in the mental health professions about the diversity of assessment models without creating cognitive dissonance and facilitate, instead, their capacity to integrate multiple perspectives effectively? How do we teach the process of making a clinical assessment while also teaching complex content? How do we teach the value and skills of being evidence based while supporting a student's mindfulness of interpersonal dynamics? How do we help students to access knowledge encapsulated in metaphor and to use right brain thinking processes? And so, with my focus on teaching, I continued to press Barbara: "Yes, all of this assessment talk is well and good, *but how do we teach it?*" At this point, Barbara, like an Aikido master, deftly sidestepped and replied, "Well, why don't you write about this and see what you come up with?" I accepted Barbara's invitation with trepidation, but viewed it as my professional responsibility to answer my own questions. This chapter, written specifically for teachers, is my response.

Guiding Questions

1. What are the essential features of each of the three approaches to teaching presented in this chapter? How are the approaches similar and how do they differ?
2. Specific uses and caveats are offered for each approach. Are there others? How might you decide which approach to use with a particular group of students or for a particular topic?
3. Learning goals are also suggested for each approach. How can you know if your students have achieved a specified goal?
4. What principles are illustrated for teaching that promotes critical thinking and multiple perspectives on assessment?

The Challenge: How Do We Teach Clinical Assessment?

Teaching students how to make useful clinical assessments is often mystifying. Beginning professionals collect abundant information when interviewing, but their ability to sift, connect, and integrate what they harvest into a relevant clinical formulation is geometrically more challenging; yet, as we know, an accurate assessment that "fits" the person and the situation is essential for treatment planning. Some magic exists in both teaching and learning that, like an egg in baking, binds the ingredients into a whole.

As with clients, students are different from one another and unique in their life paths and worldviews. Learning styles differ; clinical experience, sensitivity, and sophistication at the point of entry into graduate school may vary widely. Past learning experiences, sense of competence and comfort in learning, motivation to achieve, cultural viewpoints and expectations, and the priority given to one's educational endeavor in the context of the competing demands of work and family, will affect the teacher–student relationship and mediate the learning process. Teaching is not a "one size fits all" activity. Methods proposed in this chapter, like assessment methods outlined in this book, will also require "tailoring" to the population served. Adapting teaching to the diverse group of learners seated before us is a continual challenge.

What wizardry, then, do teachers possess to impart content, process, and purpose when teaching about clinical assessment to adult learners from diverse backgrounds? I maintain one essential principle in my exploration of teaching in this chapter: Clinical knowledge is *knowledge for use* and needs to be taught in a manner that helps students *to apply understanding with purpose*. Teaching needs to communicate the "what" and "how" of practice while clarifying the "why" of the worker–client collaboration. Content, process, and purpose must be served as we teach clinical practice. Mezirow, speaking about transformative learning, describes action as "praxis," "the creative implementation of a purpose" (1990, p. 12). Clinical assessment has a purpose, and it is as much an "action" as it is a set of intellectual ideas. Teaching students what assessment is and how to do it are combined in praxis (Mezirow et al. 2009). The assumption in this chapter is that teaching clinical assessment moves beyond content; teachers have a responsibility to find creative ways to demonstrate how ideas, concepts, and models are actualized, rendered useful, and are, in fact, inseparable from praxis.

This chapter is an exploration of the magic that nudges students one step forward in the acquisition and application of clinical assessment. It begins with a discussion of a cognitive teaching approach that is widespread but perhaps not used with full clarity about its components and its requirements. Next, a contrasting model is offered that begins from a different set of assumptions about what learning is and how learning is achieved. Finally, experiential methods are explored that draw on right brain capacities for imagination and creativity. These methods are not exhaustive but have been chosen to illustrate some of the ways that assessment can be taught; both teachers and students have different styles and preferences, and thus different approaches will resonate under different conditions and with different groups of students.

Cognitive Apprenticeship

The authors in this book have brilliantly described, questioned, and explored multiple facets of assessment. In addition, they have applied their ideas to a common case. Applying concepts to a case is a necessary component of learning but not an easy one; moving from concept to case involves multiple cognitive steps that, when identified, help one to "roll out" information in carefully sequenced steps. When using a model of pedagogy called "cognitive apprenticeship," the teacher defines a domain of knowledge to be learned, models the process of application, coaches the student in the task, gives corrective feedback, and finally has the student reflect on what was learned (Mirriam et al. 2007). Cognitive apprenticeship takes into consideration the transfer of knowledge from classroom to client, a step that is critical in transforming knowledge into praxis. Teachers can help students to transfer what they learn by using the case of Ray in this book as a transitional step toward the direct application of their knowledge with clients

Preparation is key in cognitive apprenticeship; the learning process is based on step-by-step scaffolding provided by the teacher. For example, to teach an ego psychology approach (a subset of psychodynamic theory; see Chap. 8) to the assessment of Ray, the knowledge domain might include concepts such as adaptive ego, reality testing, object relations, impulse control, affect regulation, cause-and-effect thinking, regression in service of the ego, and defenses. These, and other basic ideas used in ego psychology, would be specified as the "set of concepts" essential to understanding the theory and its application. Students, viewed as "novice" learners in this model, need to master the foundation content before proceeding to application. Evaluation of learning is also important, and the teacher must develop a tool to assess the readiness of students to take the next step. Typically, teachers use quizzes to test mastery of content. Following evaluation of content knowledge, the teacher *demonstrates* how concepts are applied in order to model the approach of the "expert."

Modeling in cognitive apprenticeship includes sharing with students the thinking behind the action. In Ray's case, for example, the teacher might reflect upon Ray's statement regarding fighting in which he says, "This thing just comes over me." Ray's quickness to harm others without forethought may be analyzed as an example of poor impulse control, fragile defenses, and poor judgment in moments of emotional dys-regulation. The teacher might tease apart how multiple concepts from ego psychology and psychodynamic assessment can be used to understand Ray's maladaptive acting-out, a behavior that has "cost him something that really mattered." The teacher might also use this last statement to explain how Ray presents his behavior to the social worker as dystonic and explain why this is an important step toward change.

Cognitive apprenticeship is distinctive in that it explicitly requires teachers to be transparent about their "cognitive and metacognitive processes that comprise expertise…to bring these tacit processes into the open where students can observe, enact, and practice them (Collins et al. 1989, p. 458)." Brinknell and Muldoon (2013) call for teachers to make their "disciplinary thinking and expert performance visible" as they work. "Learners are guided to perform authentic activities that practitioners and experts engage in during real problem solving situations. This enables expert cognitive processes to be visible and accessible to novice learners" (p. 36).

While modeling application, the teacher may voice questions, cautions, and doubts that coexist when assessing Ray's ego capacities. For example, the instructor might say: "At this point in the case, I need to keep in mind that I still have limited information. I do not yet know, for example, if the rapid escalation of affect, the loss of rational thinking, and the impulsive aggressive behavior demonstrated by Ray is typical in every situation. As far as we know, Ray has maintained control on the job as a policeman, so he also demonstrates ego strengths that include regulation of affect, rational thinking, and impulse control, strengths that he does not exercise in the bar. We cannot make a blanket statement about his ego functioning but need to recognize that our assessment of his functioning is limited to his presenting problem of getting into fights with men, particularly in bars where alcohol use may also play a role, and with women in relationships. We can assess Ray's ego capacities but must determine when he employs them and when he does not. I am not sure yet why he loses the capacities he has at particular moments, and I say to myself that context and circumstance are important, and I need to understand what is different about situations where he loses control and situations where he does not. There must be a meaningful difference."

The instructor models critical thinking by making the reasoning process transparent, cautioning about assumptions, demonstrating openness to new information, and revising hypotheses. For example, the teacher might say: "As I begin to understand Ray's personal sense of betrayal by others, his emotional invisibility to his first wife, and his experiences of trauma, I need to expand my thinking and include in my assessment that his loss of control may be driven by his past emotional wounds and trauma memories. The legacy of these experiences compromises his ego and puts enormous stress on ego capacities that are present but not strong enough to manage the emotional force of shameful rejection and the activation of traumatic stress." In doing this, the expert reveals how she builds and integrates her thinking about what explains Ray's presenting problems. The teacher demonstrates the process knowledge (the "how to" of assessment) that students need to construct their own assessments.

After the assessment process is modeled, the teacher facilitates skill building with focused exercises, and students practice for themselves. Separately, or in groups, students are given small "pieces" of the Ray case to analyze, followed by class report. The teacher then gives corrective feedback that shapes and reinforces student learning: "Fighting is not the only example of Ray using poor judgment. What are other examples?" Ideally, the teacher develops exercises graduated in levels of difficulty from least to most complex so that students build confidence while gaining mastery.

To attain summative "conceptual knowledge" from which students can generalize to new and diverse situations—the final step of cognitive apprenticeship—the teacher gives students complex clinical cases to solve. Students reflect on their analytic process and articulate their thinking. By doing so, they construct their own working model for assessment. Teachers often shift at this point to actual experiences that students have with clients, moving from the virtual world of planned classroom exercises to the real-world practice. Using clients from internship for analysis helps to bridge class and field so that each serves the other. Students appreciate that academic learning is directly relevant to practice and prepares them for clinical tasks within their internships as well as for future professional practice.

Using Cognitive Apprenticeship to Teach the "Case of Ray" To present the "case of Ray" using cognitive apprenticeship, the teacher deconstructs the case into parts for students to analyze. If, for example, the teacher wants students to assess Ray for post-traumatic stress disorder (PTSD), then symptom criteria are taught first, practice exercises specific to PTSD created, and then case material presented for student practice. A "snippet" from the Ray case involving his fighting, for example, can be analyzed as behavior arising from PTSD. The teacher selects other vignettes from the case where PTSD symptoms are identifiable and asks students to analyze the case data from a PTSD perspective. Students must reorganize their thinking and hunt for PTSD indicators: evidence of previous trauma, numbing and dissociation, intrusion such as flashbacks and nightmares, etc. What was previously defined as deficits in ego or loss of ego capacities (ego psychology lens) may now be assessed as a form of emotional and behavioral dysregulation driven by traumatic stress (a neurobiological and PTSD approach). A transdiagnostic approach, as discussed in Chap. 6, might be considered here to link assessment of how Ray regulates stimuli with ideas about temperament such as effortful control (Chap. 7). Well-defined learning goals are key, with case vignettes that will help students achieve them.

What strategy can a teacher use to design this kind of structured learning? In cognitive apprenticeship, a direct connection between domain knowledge, procedural knowledge, and summative knowledge is created through "backward design." Learning goals (student outcomes) are established first, and steps to the goals are crafted to ensure logical connection and sequence. In the design process, the teacher reflects on the following questions: "What knowledge base is required to achieve the defined learning outcomes? What procedural knowledge must be taught and activities planned for students to turn knowledge into skills? What evaluation measures will demonstrate student mastery of learning goals?" Outcome goals are developed first, and the knowledge and procedures required to achieve them are designed afterward, hence the name "backward design."

Learning goals that teachers might choose to teach the case of Ray include specifying that students will demonstrate ability to:

- assess Ray's presenting situation cogently using one assessment model
- compare and contrast models as they apply to the Ray case
- interpret facts within the case of Ray from two or more perspectives of assessment
- form a clinical opinion as to which assessment model provides the "best fit" to help Ray move toward change
- transfer learning from the case of Ray to clients in one's own caseload

The authors in this book offer different philosophical and theoretical lenses for assessment, and a variety of learning goals can be constructed using them. For example, using the narrative approach (Chap. 8), a relevant outcome goal might be: "Students can elicit the dominant 'story' of the client and frame the story elements in a way that is explanatory and accepted by the client as meaningful and true."

Working backwards, the teacher maps the learning path that leads to this goal. Domain knowledge such as "story," "saturated narrative," "externalizing," and "re-authoring" needs to be understood. Procedures in how to invite clients to narrate their experiences with textural richness must be taught. The teacher models how to take an "investigator" role using narrative techniques such as story expansion and re-authoring. Following this process, students practice and are then evaluated using summative questions such as: "What is Ray's dominant narrative?" "What events inform his narrative?" "How does Ray envision himself and others in his narrative plot?" "What message does Ray's story communicate to him?" "How might Ray 're-author' or re-tell his narrative to promote change?"

Teachers using this book are encouraged to think of one major learning outcome for each chapter and to identify data from the case of Ray to provide illustration. Authors of each chapter have already applied their model to the Ray case, and this provides scaffolding to construct learning exercises in class.

In summary, the teacher using cognitive apprenticeship systematically leads students in a developmental learning process that moves from concrete information to complex application involving higher order thinking. The teacher designs the learning pathway with careful attention to sequence, provides a model for its application, and voices ways of thinking while doing so. Critical reflection on the learning process can also develop an awareness in students of the internalized assessment schemas that they construct for themselves (Collins et al. 1989; Dennen 2008; Dennen and Burner 2007; Mirriam and Caffarella 1999; see also the research summarized in Appendix D by Probst et al. 2015).

Caveats to Using Cognitive Apprenticeship During a semester, multiple models of assessment can be taught sequentially with one class devoted to a psychodynamic perspective, another to temperament, a third to the narrative approach, and so on. Different assessment models can be compared and contrasted in their assumptions, values, concepts, procedures, and purposes. This kind of straightforward, cognitively based presentation of content is a typical learning approach. However, presenting multiple models also requires students to shift cognitive frame and "recontextualize" the data using new explanatory structures, i.e., new paradigms. Shifting between and among different cognitive frameworks can be challenging, even daunting to the novice learner. Anxiety often occurs when learning something new. This is a challenge because students need to feel secure in what they know—to feel earth below their feet, certainty, and confidence. Most students need a lot of practice to cement their understanding and to feel competent about what they know. Shifting the presentation of models quickly may create self-doubt and cloud learning. Juggling concepts from different models may be easy for some but difficult for others. And students who are more engaged by self-directed and experiential learning approaches may "tune out" to cognitive ones.

Problem-Based Learning

As previously discussed, cognitive apprenticeship is characterized by several features: It is teacher driven, prescribes learning, moves step by step, and views the student as a novice who is dependent upon the expert as the model. In many ways, problem-based learning (PBL) turns cognitive pedagogy on its head. PBL promotes self-directed learning at the outset, draws upon the innate problem-solving skills of the adult learner, and uses group collaboration to construct knowledge (Hmelo-Silver 2004; Wood 2003). Students using PBL identify for themselves what they need to learn, how to proceed, and what resources to use. The power differential between teacher and student is diminished, encouraging learning from student peers.

The PBL teacher does not dispense expert knowledge but supports student inquiry by challenging thinking, encouraging reflection, pointing out implications, and facilitating student problem-solving when needed. The teacher is responsible for framing the task and managing teams of students to promote the greatest potential for their mutual learning.

In PBL, teachers need to attend to group process and be aware that time is needed for students to "gel" as a cohesive learning group. To hasten team building, teachers can model the PBL process with a small group of students so that others can learn how to engage in collaborative team learning. Teachers should not assume that students know how to do this despite previous experience doing group projects. Often what students have learned from group assignments is that one or two people "carry" the team while others tag along (a group process known as "social loafing."). Students may resist group learning for this reason. Therefore, the teacher must communicate clearly at the outset the expectation that everyone within the team will participate.

Using PBL to Teach the "Case of Ray" To use PBL, the instructor can create teams of five to seven students and assign each team a complex real-world scenario for them to problem-solve. Students may use any number of resources including textbooks, articles, and databases to help each other. For example, a paragraph describing Ray's presenting problems may be given to students with the task of constructing multiple hypotheses explaining his situation. PBL is used extensively to teach physicians medical diagnosis in the United States, with an emphasis on using evidence-based data to evaluate hypotheses. PBL teaches students evidence-based practice by adhering to four central questions when examining case material:

1. What are the "facts"?
2. What hypotheses (explanatory guesses) fit the known facts?
3. What do you need to know to validate or invalidate your hypothesis?
4. What are next steps?

These four questions train students to think rationally using research-based evidence. The third question, for example, calls for students to examine the research literature for evidence relating to their clinical hypothesis. If Ray, for example, were a Moslem refugee from Syria, what does current research tell us about the cultural beliefs, the plight of refugees, and the social structure of the Moslem–Syrian community that needs to be taken into account in order to assess Ray's behaviors and his mental health? Students are encouraged to research clinical literature, discover knowledge new to them, and use the strongest empirical evidence available to evaluate their hypotheses. Students also construct questions that might illuminate their assessment; class time must be provided for them to find answers through research. In this way, students develop skill defining their learning, being self-directing, and researching.

In determining the facts of the case, students learn to distinguish fact from inference, an eye-opening activity for many. In the case of Ray, for example, teachers might present the first four or five paragraphs giving the Ray's background:

> Ray came to the clinic for therapy because of distress over his deteriorating relationship with his live-in girlfriend Cecilia. He described a history of violence, primarily fist fights with men, but also several instances of physical violence toward Cecilia and other women … He denied any violence in his marriage to Leslie, his ex-wife, and said the marriage had ended because of her materialism, self-absorption and coldness. When his mother died a prolonged and painful death from cancer, Leslie had not provided any emotional support. When he came home distraught over incidents he'd witnessed as a police officer, she merely replied, "Nobody made you become a cop. You chose it." After his mother's funeral, which she did not attend, he moved out.

At this beginning juncture, students often draw inferences or present "explanations" before they have established what facts are truly known. When questioned about the facts, a student may answer, "Ray is in denial about his anger toward women and is rationalizing about the end of his marriage to Leslie." This response, however, moves beyond what is actually presented in the excerpt, allowing teachers to make students aware of how quickly they close inquiry by jumping to conclusions without establishing the facts first. Another may argue that the facts within the excerpt do not fit the student's hypothesis because Ray explicitly states that the reason for his marriage ending relates to his wife's behavior ("her materialism, self-absorption, and coldness"). The teacher might then ask students what they think about Ray; why do some students believe what Ray says and others do not? This provides opportunity for students to reflect on their own biases and attitudes toward Ray, the client, just as one would (or should) in "real-world" practice. Students gain clarity about the difference between facts and inferences, both of which are important. In addition, teachers can guide students in discovering the relationship of facts to hypotheses.

Teachers can also use PBL to expand domains of assessment considered by students simply by asking new questions. Although chapters in this book focus on individual assessment, PBL can be used to augment what is here by exploring other important client systems such as couple, family, and community. This can be accomplished by directing students into new avenues of discovery:

1. If Ray and Cecilia came to therapy as a couple, what models of couple assessment might be relevant?
2. In what ways would a couple's assessment be different from an individual assessment?
3. What facts about the couple and the relationship would be important to ascertain in order to make a useful couple's assessment?
4. Using a couple's assessment, how would treatment goals be constructed, and how would assessment and treatment goals relate to one another?

Similarly, teachers can raise family assessment questions about Ray's role relationships with his children and extended family members. The teacher can insert important community and psychosocial assessment variables into the conversation such as oppression and racism, poverty, impingements on human rights, and social stigma. In these ways, teachers can use the PBL method to broaden the assessment landscape.

The PBL method promotes critical thinking by challenging students to identify what they need to know when case data are missing—as so frequently happens at points of intake, initial assessment, and assignment for treatment. For teaching purposes, cases *lacking* information help students think about *what* they need to know, *why* they need to know, and *what they can do* to find out. This leads students into the realities of case assessment where mental health professionals, particularly in social work, treat clients within a web of mediating social systems, including the child welfare system, medical systems, and the judicial system. Case exploration requires procedural knowledge to work within these systems. Real-world problem-solving also brings professional ethics into play such as concerns about privacy and confidentiality when seeking information. Students who have practice experience in these areas are a valuable resource for collaborative peer learning.

Caveats to Using Problem-Based Learning The individual characteristics and capacities of students most suited to benefitting from self-directed learning has been the subject of extensive research (Mirriam et al. 2007). A principal concern in PBL is the readiness of students to be self-directed. PBL assumes that students are reflective, comfortable within a group environment, and learn well from interaction with others. For students habituated to receiving lectures, PBL can be disconcerting. Classroom time is often needed to prepare students—to teach the method, to clarify the responsibility of the students, and to manage teams where intra-group dynamics may allow one or two people to dominate. Teaching the *method of learning* to students may require as much attention as providing time for students to achieve the goals of the learning itself. Teachers also need to resist taking the "expert" role, and instead, help students to reflect on their discoveries and deepen their insights. The PBL method takes practice—both by students and by teachers.

Experiential Teaching

Another form of learning is experiential. Teachers provide opportunity for students to assume the roles of the client and the mental health worker while enacting the assessment interview. Students benefit by trying on these roles and reflecting upon what the experience is like for each. They learn "in action" and "through action" in real time. What occurs is spontaneous and often parallels what actually happens between the worker and the client. Thus, students practice skills, rehearse the worker role, and learn what the client may feel when being interviewed. Role-play teaches students how clients experience the worker; it tunes them into feelings that clients may not verbalize; and it helps them learn how assessment may be engaging or off-putting. Ideally, role-play will help students learn how to perform an assessment in a collaborative, empathically attuned, and engaging way.

Just as students can play different roles, they can also experiment using different assessment models and procedures. Students, for example, might practice interviewing Ray using a narrative approach and then replay the interview to surface information about temperament or internal conflict, for example. One advantage to role-play is that the actor can share afterward what the experience was like. In this way, students playing the worker can receive feedback on specific aspects of their interaction and identify where they felt stuck or unable to adhere to the model.

Role-play exercises can be assigned in groups of three where two people enact the interview and one observes. The role of the observer is to give feedback to the players on what he or she noticed. Each student within the group takes the turn of client, worker, and observer. This gives everyone in the class opportunity to practice. A variation is the "fishbowl" technique, in which two people enact a role-play surrounded by their peers. Those who silently observe on the outside can be given specific tasks relating to assessment criteria: When and how does the client express shame? Employ psychological defenses? Give evidence of distortion in cognitive schema? Appear dysregulated? Show a transferential dynamic? After the role-play, students report back from their assigned task only. It is very important that students do not critique the performers, who should be thanked and respected for their work and the contribution they have made to class learning. Role players also need to "de-role," i.e., be explicitly removed from their role by stating who, in fact, they really are: "I am Shaniqua and not the client Sarah." They also need to be given opportunity to say what it was like for them in their role and to process any reactions they may have had. The fishbowl exercise needs to be carefully planned so that tasks for students are clear, for both those who role-play and those who watch. The teacher is responsible for the learning tasks of everyone in the class, and there is as much focus on the observers as on those observed.

Using Experiential Learning to Teach the "Case of Ray" Role-play is a beginning step in engaging the imagination and creativity of students, who make their roles "real" by bringing their own experiences to bear in creating the role. Learning can become even more imaginative by enacting "parts" of the client in a psychodramatic way. Intrapsychic "parts" of Ray can be embodied in a role, be it

Ray's superego or ego, the force that compels him to fight, the part of him that feels rejected by his wife, his anger at Cecilia, his guilt over abortions, his fear of upsetting his parents. Physical aspects of Ray can be embodied in a role: the eyes that have seen "the worst things about people," the fists that hit others, the suppressed voice that was unable to say "No!" to the abusing priest. Central ideas that Ray holds can be turned into roles, such as "betrayal" and "disloyalty."

Students can play these various parts of Ray, feeling their way into them as the role-play unfolds—the guilt, rejection, shame, intimidation, anger, and so on. The teacher can say, "If these roles could speak, what would they say? What message does each part give to Ray? In what ways do these different parts enable Ray to live in the world?" Through imagination and intuition, students can explore the varieties of forces and feelings that Ray contends with in his life and, in the process, feel viscerally what that might be like for Ray. Depending upon a teacher's comfort and skill in staging such psychodramatic roles, other scenarios can be created in which these parts interact (e.g., how Ray's guilt about abuse and father's acceptance interact). By embodying the stressful feelings within Ray, students might understand better what drives Ray to make suicide attempts as well as what drives him to seek help.

Use of creativity and imagination engages students and makes learning fun. Several examples of experiential learning activities and exercises are offered in Appendix F. For instance, to promote skill in assessing some of the unique developmental and diagnostic issues of childhood and adolescence, Keith Cuniffe has students view the film *Tangled* (Walt Disney Pictures 2010). The fairy tale story of Rapunzel makes the serious act of assessment feel like a form of play and lessens students' performance anxieties. The animation and cartoon-like figures also symbolize, as dreaming does, while tapping into functions of the right hemisphere of the brain that apprehend through metaphor and analogy. Cinematic story telling mobilizes deep emotion in the viewer, more so than a clinically written case presentation may do. This strengthens engagement and motivation in learning.

After students watch *Tangled*, Cuniffe asks them to reflect on developmental aspects of Rapunzel's life and to identify themes within the characters' lives that are salient for assessment. Cuniffe adds open-ended reflective questions that include diagnostic categories as well as assessment perspectives that reach beyond the DSM, as this book does. He ends his assignment by moving from cinematic case material to internship practice, allowing students to link class learning with field practice. It is edifying how Cuniffe designs the learning task: he provides an experience to students that is engaging and evokes emotion (the film), then has students shift to cognitive processing (reflection and analysis), and finally encourages knowledge transfer and praxis (linking to real cases and developing assessment questions).

Another example of the use of film is Probst's suggestion to have students select from a list of films that depict people with mental disorder, such as *Boys Don't Cry* (1999), *Don Juan de Marco* (1995), and *The Three Faces of Eve* (1957). Using a critical theory lens, she guides student reflections and invites them to consider social work values and positionality. For example, she asks students to identify the socioeconomic circumstance of characters and to appraise its differential effects on minority social groups, raising awareness of the cultural dimensions of commercial cinema that explicitly or implicitly reflect social mores, biases, and stereotypes. As a result, students grasp at a feeling level the power that social attitudes and social stigma can exert on human suffering.

The assignment can be augmented by asking students to reflect on their own reactions to the film and to identify personal biases toward characters and their behaviors. Acute self-reflection illuminates the deeper meaning-making structures of one's own thinking and leads to a reorganization one's own lived experiences. This kind of critical self-reflection is the basis for transformative learning (Mezirow 1990); it challenges the meaning-making perspectives that inform what and how we know, and promotes adult learning that is more "inclusive, discriminating, permeable, and integrative" (Mezirow 1990, p. 14).

Many other excellent films are available for teachers to choose from, including *Antwone Fisher, Prince of Tides, A Beautiful Mind,* and *Ordinary People.* The book *Movies and mental illness: Using films to understand psychopathology* (Wedding and Niemiec 2014) is a useful resource in preparing classes using commercial films.

Caveats to Using Experiential Learning Participating in role-play can be anxiety provoking, and students most often require warm-up exercises to engage spontaneously and playfully in a role. Students can be organized into small groups for short preparatory exercises before role-plays are enacted in class. Exercises should serve the role-play that the teacher has decided upon. If, for example, a role-play of a first meeting with Ray was planned, students might first talk together in small groups about what it would be like for Ray to meet the therapist:

- What fears and anxieties might Ray have?
- What hopes and dreams?
- What might be easiest for him to talk about?
- What most difficult?
- How might Ray think the therapist will view him?
- How might Ray want to be viewed?
- What kinds of things would Ray say to introduce himself?
- How might he talk about parts of his history?
- What are the hopes and fears of the therapist?
- How might the therapist begin the conversation?
- What might the therapist ask Ray?

The exercise is similar to the way that clinicians "tune-in" before meeting a client and is a good warm-up before enacting a role-play. Without warm-ups, students are unlikely to volunteer and be spontaneous in action.

Experiential learning may improve sensitivity and help students to "tune-in" more fully, but without verbal processing, students may not actually be aware of what they learned and what they know. Having all students role-play in one class may not be possible, so that those who actively participate often benefit the most. It is also difficult to assess what students have learned when using experiential methods. Reflective journaling after class, however, is one way for students to capture more consciously what they have learned through the experience and its relevance to their work (Hubbs and Brand 2005).

Exemplars of Assignments and Classroom Exercises

In addition to the assignments of Cuniffe and Probst discussed above, this book contains five other exemplars of class exercises presented in Appendix F that illustrate how various pedagogical techniques can be integrated into one's teaching.

Considering and Reconsidering Arlo's assignment is an excellent example of a PBL approach: presentation of open-ended case material followed by instructions to identify facts, construct a guess as to what might explain those facts (preliminary diagnosis), identify salient information that is lacking in order to reconsider one's initial assessment, and then to investigate further sources of information to test the reliability of the assessment hypotheses considered. Arlo's exercise teaches students a critical thinking framework that underlies evidence-based practice and is especially good at teaching social workers and other mental health professionals to remain open to alternate explanations of case material. By practicing the method of analysis presented by Arlo, students learn to invite complexity into their thinking, sustain contradictions and ambiguity without foreclosing decision-making, and explore new domains of knowledge to arrive at a well-considered professional assessment.

Case Analysis in Successive Layers Rasmussen's assignment, like Arlo's, fits well with a PBL approach by asking for facts separate from inference, hypothesis, or clinical formulation. Students then proceed to organize and interpret the facts of the case through a choice of theoretical lenses relating to relational and psychodynamic theory using a variety of class resources. As adult learners, students use their own capacities to investigate theoretical ideas, think critically about them, and create multiple levels of understanding that is preparatory to linking assessment with intervention. Overlaid upon the student's theoretical analysis is the further challenge of integrating dynamics of race, class, gender, and oppression. Rasmussen's directions implicitly teach students a method for analysis consistent with PBL. His set of questions deepens critical thinking about features of assessment and mirrors what the seasoned practitioner would consider salient. The author's prompts surface his expert way of thinking, as one would do in cognitive apprenticeship.

Rasmussen's assignment can be expanded to include collaborative learning among students, who could share their work in groups, reflect on what they have learned, and report new understandings to everyone in the class. Adding retrospective reflection on learning creates another "layer" of knowledge that would fit well with Rasmussen's assignment.

Different Opinions, Different Reasons Karaban's class exercise is an exemplar of action-based, experiential learning that is highly engaging, calls for critical thinking, and surfaces the diversity of attitudes that people hold about mental health issues. Karaban constructs a cognitively based, individual warm-up exercise that attunes students to their own thoughts and opinions about common attitudes toward mental disorders. He transforms this warm-up into a group activity using action strategies that engage students nonverbally to illustrate the spectrum of opinions on specific topics. Karaban cleverly designs the exercise to maintain the anonymity of student responses and to have students construct and defend answers that they may, in fact, not actually agree with. This surprise directive makes students potentially shift their own thinking and examine a point of view that is contrary to their own. At the least, this promotes appreciation for differences in worldview that students will encounter in their professional work and helps to develop more fluid ability to shift between different cognitive frames. To complete the exercise, students reflect openly with the group on what they have experienced. Karaban demonstrates how to use action strategies to access the personhood of adult learners and the worldviews they carry into the learning environment. Hearing what others think helps students to challenge the habitual assumptions, values, and biases they make toward mental health conditions. The next exemplar by Hanson explores the influences of tacit worldviews of students more extensively.

How Theory Shapes Assessment Hanson clearly states the purpose of his first assignment: "To help students make their individual worldviews ("master narratives") explicit (transparent) so that they can critically appraise them, see how they influence our practice and see what type of "evidence" supports them." Students review a previously completed assessment and reflect critically on their work by answering the question, "Knowing what you know now, what do you think influenced your decision-making?" This part of Hanson's teaching creates a transformative learning experience for students. Hanson systematically guides students to surface their assumptive paradigms of knowledge, appraise the strengths and limitations of their working model, examine how they have applied their master narratives, and reflect critically on the results of their self-appraisals.

Hanson supplies a case example for students to analyze through group collaboration after assigning resource reading that serves to give domain knowledge on contrasting theories of assessment and to model how to compare and contrast theory. This portion of his assignment has elements of cognitive apprenticeship as well as PBL. Through in-class group work, students examine how different theories and practice models highlight different aspects of the case, with the learning goal of defining "what theories are and what functions they serve and to understand the difference between practice theories and practice models." Hanson implements this multidimensional learning task over several class sessions that encompass an ambitious but indispensible learning agenda.

Case Analysis from Multiple Perspectives One of Probst's goals in writing this book is to provide students, teachers, and professionals with models of assessment that explain human struggles and suffering in more complex ways than simply by assigning a DSM diagnosis. She understands, however, that social workers also need skill in using the DSM, since the DSM is a required part of mental health assessment and treatment planning in most contemporary settings. Her assignment thus reflects these two learning goals.

She first asks students to exercise critical judgment by using "salient" information to construct a bio-psycho-social assessment while maintaining a focus on strengths rather than pathology. She underscores social work values by directing students to compare the client's view with the worker's. This step encourages client-centered practice where people are viewed as the true experts on their lives. Students must then provide two plausible DSM diagnoses and exercise critical thinking by arguing *against* assigning each. Probst recognizes that, too often, students (and professionals) identify only information that fits a diagnosis rather than what is inconsistent with it. Finally, she directs students to apply one assessment approach that is not DSM based as a lens for viewing case material. This is a cognitive approach that maps theory to case. Students use domain knowledge of the theory—bolstered by course readings—and they practice critical thinking in applying it to a case. Teachers might consider Probst's assignment as a first stage to learning assessment models. Stage two, and perhaps a summative assignment, would be to have students apply *multiple* models to one case.

Conclusions

This chapter has explored three approaches to teaching: cognitive apprenticeship, PBL, and experiential pedagogy. These methods can be combined to provide variety and to address the spectrum of learning styles of students. Research can also be integrated directly into the classroom as a way of assessing and monitoring what they students are learning and experiencing "in real time."

As Weimer (2002) writes, "In order to facilitate learning that changes how students think and understand, teachers must begin by discovering students' existing conceptions and then design instruction that changes those conceptions (p. 11)." Weimer's insight speaks to the study summarized in Appendix D in which graduate social work students responded to questions about what they think mental disorder is and how a clinician can discern its existence. These two simple questions, like those in Dr. Hanson's learning assignment, surface tacit understandings that students carry into the learning environment. Gathering this information from students takes very little time yet offers rich revelation of "where the student is" at the beginning of the course; students often have wisdom to share from their lived experiences, as well as misconceptions and learning needs. Teachers can use information gleaned from these two survey questions to construct a knowledge profile of students and tailor their instruction. They can also adopt this survey to prompt discussion about similarities and differences in conceptualizations that students hold. Teachers can assign further reflective journaling so that students can document how their thinking has evolved during the course.

We conclude with ten core heuristics for teaching that flow from the pedagogical ideas presented above:

1. Teach students "how to learn" by demonstration and modeling
2. Be generous sharing your own seasoned thinking
3. Create learning goals with class activities that match
4. Teach students to identify what *they don't know* and strategies to find out
5. Encourage critical reflection to appraise assumptions about thinking
6. Use the wisdom of students as a learning resource
7. Use challenge, emotion, and imagination to engage and motivate
8. Provide ample warm-up before role-play activities
9. Invoke left brain (rational/cognitive) and right brain (imaginative/intuitive) functions to enhance learning
10. Move aside and allow peer learning.

References

Brinknell, L., & Muldoon, N. (2013). Rethinking online teaching and learning: A case study of an approach to designing an online learning environment. *The International Journal of Technology, Knowledge, and Society, 8*(4), 1832–3669.

Collins, A., Brown, J. S., & Newman, S. (1989). Cognitive apprenticeship: Teaching students the craft of reading, writing, and mathematics. In L. Resnick (Ed.), *Knowing, learning, and instruction: Essays in honor of Robert Glaser* (pp. 453–493). Hillsdale: Erlbaum.

Dennen, V. (2008). Cognitive apprenticeship in educational practice: Research on scaffolding, modeling, mentoring, and coaching as instructional strategies. In D. Jonassen (Ed.), *Handbook of research on educational communications and technology* (2nd ed., pp. 813–828).

Dennen, V., & Burner, K. (2007). The cognitive apprenticeship model in educational practice. *Handbook of research on educational communications and technology* (pp. 425–439).

Hmelo-Silver, C. E. (2004). Problem-based learning: What and how do students learn? *Educational Psychology Review, 16*(3), 235–266.

Hubbs, D. L., & Brand, C. F. (2005). The paper mirror: Understanding reflective journaling. *Journal of Experiential Education, 28*(1), 60–71.

Mezirow, J. (1990). How critical reflection triggers transformative learning. In J. Mezirow and Associates (Eds.), *Fostering critical reflection in adulthood: A guide to transformative and emancipatory learning* (pp. 1–20). San Francisco: Jossey-Bass.

Mezirow, J., Taylor, E., & Associates. (2009). *Transformative learning in practice: Insights from community, workplace, and higher education*. San Francisco: Jossey-Bass.

Mirriam, S., Caffarella, R., & Baumgartner, L. (2007). *Learning in adulthood: A comprehensive guide* (3rd ed.). San Francisco: Jossey-Bass.

Mirriam, S., & Caffarella, R. (1999). *Learning in adulthood: A comprehensive guide* (2nd ed.). San Francisco: Jossey-Bass.

Probst, B., Balletto, C., & Wofford, N. (2015). What they bring: How MSW students think about mental disorder and clinical knowledge. *Clinical Social Work Journal*. doi:10.1007/s10615-015-0517-6.

Wedding, D., & Niemiec, R. (2014). *Movies and mental illness: Using films to understand psychopathology* (4th ed.). Toronto: Hogrefe Publishing.

Weimer, M. (2002). *Learner-centered teaching: Five key changes to practice*. San Francisco: Jossey-Bass.

Wood, D. F. (2003). ABC of learning and teaching in medicine: Problem based learning. *British Medical Journal, 326*(7384), 328–330.

Chapter 13
Assessment and Diagnosis in Action

Barbara Probst

Abstract The book's final chapter reiterates the key point that all knowledge is partial, provisional, and subject to review as new evidence comes to light. Thus, to guard against tunnel vision and premature closure, clinicians need to avail themselves of *many* forms of knowledge, from *many* domains, that can complement psychiatric categories and offer essential insight for understanding a client's suffering and illuminating pathways for recovery. A discussion of the role and use of the DSM in real-world practice draws on both research and theory to highlight its benefits and limitations, including the challenges of distinguishing primary and secondary conditions, and of responding to subthreshold presentations. The chapter then provides a comprehensive overview of multiple ways of collecting, organizing, and interpreting information—biological, social, psychological, and spiritual—within a framework of therapist–client collaboration. Emergent integrative directions in clinical assessment are reviewed (epigenetics, diathesis–stress theory, the transdiagnostic model, etc.) that consider people in flexible relationship to elements of their environment and suggest how specific aspects of environment can contribute to mental disorder, a connection that has been lacking in previous theoretical models. The chapter concludes with a call for social workers to face the challenge of insuring that culture, spirituality, and the impact of poverty and oppression are not forgotten and that the idea of internal flaw, failure, and deficit does not overwhelm and obscure our commitment to social justice. Our ability to respond to this challenge rests on how well the next generation is taught to think critically, compassionately, and holistically—the very aim of this book.

Keywords Co-morbidity · Coping and adaptation · Diathesis-stress theory · Enactments · Epigenetics · Etiology · Interaction effects · Nominal and ordinal measures · Psychological justice · Resilience · Salience · Spiritual assessment · Tacit knowledge · Technical knowledge

B. Probst (✉)
School for Social Work, Smith College, Northampton, MA, USA
e-mail: Barbara.H.Probst@gmail.com

© Springer International Publishing Switzerland 2015   247
B. Probst (ed.), *Critical Thinking in Clinical Assessment and Diagnosis*,
Essential Clinical Social Work Series, DOI 10.1007/978-3-319-17774-8_13

Introduction: Why This Matters

As these chapters have indicated, all knowledge is partial, provisional, and subject to review as new evidence comes to light. What seems to be "known" can be modified or discarded if fresh or different evidence indicates that another viewpoint is closer to the mark. To guard against tunnel vision and premature closure, social workers need to avail themselves of many forms of knowledge and to consider each in light of what it contributes and what it omits, what evidence and assumptions it rests on, who endorses it, whom it serves, and how well it upholds the values of our profession.

Although psychiatric knowledge dominates in contemporary clinical practice, for many clients other information may be equally or even more salient. Other forms of knowledge—information about temperament, ego defenses, attachment, affective style, somatic experience, beliefs about life, sense of agency, identity, trauma, loss, flexibility of coping strategies, role or value conflict, hope, and motivation for change—may be essential for understanding a client's suffering and illuminating pathways for recovery. These "ways of knowing" provide valuable insight that complements knowledge of psychiatric categories, helping the clinician understand the subjective experience of a disorder—how a generic category is experienced by a specific person. In addition to determining an appropriate diagnosis, the clinician must understand what it means and feels like *to that individual* to be "depressed" or "anxious."

Taking a client's perception seriously while questioning one's assumption of expertise is a fundamental principle of ethical practice and a key to the deep understanding on which skillful assessment depends. It is through questioning and letting-go of presumed knowledge that perception grows. Considering knowledge, once it has been acquired, to be clear and certain may be comforting, but it can impede the growth of understanding as trust develops and moments of insight shed new light on "known facts." Being open-minded does not mean being empty-minded, discarding all prior thoughts and theories, but it *does* mean being willing to accept that one's assessment may have missed the point and needs to be reconsidered. The more sensitive one's understanding of clinical assessment, the greater one's tolerance for ambiguity and uncertainty may need to be. As Berzoff (2011) reminds us, the challenge is to "become knowledgeable and still remain open to ambiguity and the unknown" (p. 133).

Thus, the idea that clinical practice is a linear movement from assessment to treatment plan to intervention to evaluation needs to be replaced with a recursive model in which *re*-assessment occurs periodically as the therapeutic relationship develops and more nuanced understanding emerges. This can be difficult when treatment plans and billing records are organized around a DSM diagnosis given early in the process. There may be resistance to "having to change everything," a complicated endeavor when all documentation needs to match and all codes need to be justified. It may seem simpler to leave the existing diagnosis in place, especially when it seems to have little bearing on the actual work. Yet allowing an incorrect, potentially stigmatizing label to remain attached to a client—particularly when records are available to courts and employers—raises serious ethical concerns.

Clinical assessment calls, in short, for an integration of science, ethics, and art. For professional knowledge to be utilized skillfully and sensitively, the clinician needs to be able to intuit what symptoms mean for real individuals in the fullness of their sociocultural and relational contexts. In this final chapter, we will explore how to do that.

Guiding Questions

1. What challenges do social workers encounter when using the DSM, and how do they deal with them?
2. What kinds of information ought to be included in a comprehensive clinical assessment?
3. What new trends have emerged for integrating the wide range of data gathered during clinical assessment?
4. What is, or might be, social work's unique role among the helping professions?

The DSM in Real-World Practice

Social workers in a wide range of practice settings are expected to be familiar with the DSM and able to use it to make accurate diagnoses; in most states, they must also pass a licensing exam heavily weighted toward DSM nosology in order to advance from basic to advanced practice. "Clinical social work is a master's level profession. In fact, professionals must complete a period of supervised practice before they are allowed to go into private practice or otherwise exercise independent judgment with regard to treating and diagnosing mental illness" (http://www.socialworklicensure.org).

Although requirements for licensure vary from state to state, mastery of the DSM is usually the standard by which advanced competency is determined. In New York, for example, "while an applicant for licensure as an LCSW may provide a range of services that are defined in the Education Law, the only acceptable experience is in diagnosis, psychotherapy, and assessment-based treatment planning" (http://www.op.nysed.gov/prof/sw/lcsw.htm). The DSM is not referred to by name, but diagnosis "in the context of licensed clinical social work practice" is defined as "the process of distinguishing, beyond general social work assessment, between similar mental, emotional, behavioral, developmental and addictive disorders, impairments, and disabilities within a psychosocial framework on the basis of their similar and unique characteristics *consistent with accepted classification systems*"—italics added (http://www.op.nysed.gov/prof/sw/lcsw.htm). This is revealing language: To be at the height of the social work profession, one must demonstrate mastery of a *non*social work system. The difficulties that poses for professional identity, status, and ethics have been well documented (e.g., Probst 2012), and many social workers have expressed acute ambivalence about the role of the DSM in their work.

McQuaide (1999) summarizes the manual's advantages and disadvantages. On the one hand, naming a problem gives a sense of control, provides boundaries, reduces anxiety and blame, helps to organize information, provides a common language among disciplines, suggests appropriate questions and types of help, and links clients to a wealth of research and resources. The label legitimizes a person's suffering and opens a path to recovery. On the other hand, DSM categories provide no information about the dynamics or etiology of a condition and thus no guidance about intervention or realistic goals. By tacitly assuming that categories are universal, it promotes stereotypes and over-generalization. Beyond its purview are many of the problems that clients are actually concerned about such as family relationships, work, loss, marginalization, and oppression; moreover, by classifying problems in living as mental diseases residing in the person, it ignores or minimizes strengths, resilience, and other potential sources of healing and growth. McQuaide does not suggest eliminating the DSM but, rather, urges social workers to use the taxonomy, a "potentially useful and potentially dangerous tool," from a perspective compatible with social work values (p. 410).

Research findings Several studies have examined social workers' attitudes and use of the DSM. A survey by Frazer et al. (2009), sent to a random sample of 558 of the 7000 professionals in the Register of Clinical Social Workers, looked at frequency, purpose, and perceived importance. While 79 % of respondents said they used the manual often or always and 86 % gave a DSM diagnosis often or always, only half said they would do so if not required. Their primary reason for using the DSM was for insurance billing (nearly 93 %) and secondarily as a tool for assessment (78 %). A limitation of the study was the questionnaire's low response rate (56 %); in addition, a high percentage of respondents were in private practice and not necessarily representative of social workers throughout the country. Nonetheless, the findings are striking.

Probst's qualitative study (2013) had the somewhat different aim of understanding how clinical social workers think about, utilize, and navigate two seemingly incompatible worldviews: the psychiatric perspective of the DSM, a requirement for service in nearly every clinical setting, and the contextual perspective of person-in-environment. Findings from in-depth interviews with 30 clinical social workers in a range of practice settings revealed an array of ethical and practical issues centered on the "tightrope" of balancing the need to "ramp-up" problem formulation in order to provide access and justification for service with a desire to "damp down" in order to minimize stigma and avoid pathologizing problems in living.

Findings from these two studies, one quantitative and the other qualitative, indicate that little has changed in the quarter century since Kutchins and Kirk

(1988) explored social workers' attitudes toward DSM-III, the edition in use at the time. The most frequently cited reasons for using DSM III, according to respondents in their national cross-sectional survey, were insurance reimbursement (80 %), agency requirement (45 %), and Medicaid requirement (45 %). Clinical usefulness for understanding client behavior and for determining treatment was rated much lower, at 31 % each. Half the respondents stated that the DSM did *not* serve the purposes of clinical social work, and were concerned about how it shaped and inhibited their understanding of client problems. Overall, they viewed the DSM as a business tool, not a clinical one.

A related study of clinical mental health counselors (Mead et al. 1997) yielded similar results. While those surveyed were counselors rather than social workers, findings echoed social workers' views. Respondents stated that they used the manual for billing and insurance, case conceptualization, communication with other professionals, and meeting requirements of employers and external entities such as courts. Disadvantages included bias, labeling, and difficulty applying the DSM in marriage and family counseling. Many also believed that clients were deliberately misdiagnosed by use of the system.

Frazer et al. (2009) conclude their report with a call for further research on questions including: What happens when social workers select non-billable diagnoses (such as family system issues, represented by V-codes), and how much "fake" or skewed diagnosis occurs to ensure agency survival or private practice income? Does the requirement for a DSM diagnosis de-emphasize attention to contextual issues such as culture, economics, oppression, and social justice? What alternative assessment tools might be developed, and how might clinicians effectively blend them with the DSM? And finally, what price are we, as a profession, paying for "buying into the DSM system and its firm allegiance with the insurance industry?" (p. 336).

"Real-world" use of the DSM These are important questions, yet it is not a matter of being "against" the DSM. The DSM is a tool. It would make as little sense to be "against" the DSM as it would to be "against" a shovel. Like any tool, the system needs to be used with discrimination and intelligence. As McQuaide (1999) points out, a diagnostic system can facilitate the appropriate screening of clients, since "failure to recognize a serious mental illness in a client and an insistence on seeing such a client as having merely a problem with living would be irresponsible" (p. 412). There can be false negatives as well as false positives; both can be harmful to clients.

McQuaide goes on to offer a postmodern approach based on the notion of multiple serves, each elicited under different conditions and in response to particular stressors.

> This vulnerable self, whose symptoms may fit into a DSM category, is just one of many of the individual's selves. It should not be ignored because of a bias against the medical model, nor should it become the dominant discourse of the client's life just because it fits a category described in the DSM (p. 413).

A DSM category, by depicting a generic "type," enables the clinician to understand clients in terms of how they fit the category and how they deviate.

> By providing a first approximation, a prototype, a set of rules, [the DSM] permits us to see a particular client's uniqueness. In the absence of categories, all we have is a client's particular set of difficulties. With it, we have a clearer sense both of how this client is like others and how she or he is unlike others (p. 413).

This "bifocal" view of the client, integrating elements that refer to generic prototypes with elements that are idiosyncratic and particular, suggests a way to go beyond the argument about which perspective is best. Universalism and localism are both needed (Berganza et al. 2005). At one moment, knowledge of the category may be useful for suggesting effective treatments and resources; at another moment, knowledge of the individual's distance from the category or how the category is affected by local circumstances may be more useful.

In fact, many clients are hybrids, with some features that seem to match one category and some features that seem to match another. When more than one issue is present, the clinician may be inclined to give two diagnoses—that is, to identify comorbid conditions. A double label (comorbidity) means the client has more than one mental illness, each with an independent pathogenesis. In many cases, however, one of the conditions is primary, the other a secondary result. For instance, a child with ADHD who is continually chastised for not listening, not sitting still, who cannot seem to make a friend, never gets picked for teams, and always seems to be in trouble may start to feel worthless or angry. It would not be surprising if that child *also* began to show signs of depression, anxiety, rage, or defiance. But these are not independent diagnoses with independent origins; they are results. If the ADHD can be managed, the hostility will abate. Interventions to make the child less defiant without addressing the source of that defiance are like addressing a leaking roof by mopping the floor.

Distinguishing between primary and secondary conditions is essential for correct treatment. A client may appear to be both anxious and depressed, for example. In one case, anxiety prevents the person from venturing into life and having the experiences he longs for; he *then* becomes depressed about how anxious he is and how that is spoiling his life. In another case, depression is keeping someone from experiencing pleasure and finding meaning in life experiences; she cannot seem to escape this oppressive cloud and *then* begins to worry about what is wrong with her. In the first case, anxiety is primary; in the second, depression is primary. Without sensitive assessment, the clinician may treat wrong problem—and thus fail to be helpful or even do potential harm.

Sometimes a client does meet criteria for a DSM diagnosis, yet has other problems that do not map onto a DSM template. In these instances, the task is to determine whether the mental disorder (the diagnosable condition) is the *cause* or the *result* of these other issues—that is, if life problems developed because of an internal dysfunction that led to impairment in functioning (in which case the mental disorder can be viewed as primary), or if internal dysfunction developed because of overwhelming external stressors (in which case the life problem is likely to be primary). For example, a young man who cannot sustain a romantic relationship may indeed meet DSM criteria for depression. Treating the depression—with the expectation that he will be more successful in relationships if he feels and acts less depressed—assumes that depression is the cause of his problems and thus offers an appropriate target of work. On the other hand, one might consider depression to be the result of his failure at relationships. In that case, work would focus on social skills, with the expectation that he will be less depressed if he can have a successful romantic experience. It may be a bit of both, of course, requiring a double-tiered approach that moves recursively between the two goals.

At other times, a client may not quite meet the DSM criteria for *any* diagnosis. Since a specified number of symptoms are required for inclusion in each category, if the minimum number of symptoms is not present, then the disorder is not present either. But what happens when a child meets only five of the required six criteria for ADHD? Does the clinician conclude that ADHD is ruled out and therefore these symptoms are not important? Of course not! The child still has five issues that need to be addressed. What, then, is the point of setting minimums—or, for that matter, of worrying so much about how to define categories, rather than simply addressing their components? Who decided that the category, rather than the issue, had to be the unit of focus?

It all gets back to the assumption, discussed in Chap. 2, that symptoms coalesce into syndromes—even though there is no evidence that this is the most useful way to think about human suffering. What we call "mental disorder" may simply be a collection of experiences, struggles, and "diverse conditions … bound together by little more than psychiatric tradition, shifting cultural value judgments, and the pragmatics of need for treatment" (Haslam and Giosan 2002, p. 479.) At the same time, we cannot simply resort to denialism and dismiss mental disorder as a myth, social construction, or invention of those in power. Mental disorder, no matter how imprecise a construct, still needs to be taken seriously, for several important reasons.

First, it seems clear that there *are,* and probably always will be, individuals for whom the term is appropriate. The debate has always been about where to draw the line, not about the line's existence. Second, whether we like it or not, diagnostic categories are the entrée to services that many of our clients truly need—disability benefits (SSI or Supplemental Security Income), Section Eight housing, educational accommodations under the Individuals with Disabilities Educational Act, low-cost counseling, and case management services. Refusing to use a DSM label because we believe mental disorders are not "real" is more likely to harm than benefit the most vulnerable among those we serve. It may feel good to proclaim that no one can judge another person to be qualitatively different (disordered), but that may be a sentiment of the privileged. Disadvantaged clients may not have the option of throwing away the labels—not if they need services. Disavowing labels may be a way to avoid the uncomfortable truth that difference *does* exist, just as proclaiming not to "see race" may deny the reality of those for whom "being seen" is not a choice (Probst et al., in press). Here again, what may seem *most* ethical (avoiding pejorative labels) may, in fact, be *least* ethical (restricting clients' access to service because it is the clinician, not the client, who is uncomfortable with labeling).

And third, as long as licensing requirements and agency procedures continue to rely on DSM terminology, social work educators need to make sure that students enter the work force fully equipped for professional life. What Epple (2007) calls "traditional" MSW curricula, centered on ecological or systems approaches, "are no longer adequate to prepare students for practice in the current era" (p. 276) in which managed care and state licensure rely heavily on competence in the use of DSM concepts. It would be naïve, unprofessional, and unhelpful for instructors to refuse to teach their students about the DSM just because they do not like it or resent its power to define mental health: It is no more ethical to use personal aversion to justify withholding important professional training than it is to use it to withhold access to services.

The question, then, is how to master the psychiatric paradigm without losing our roots and hearts. How to master the DSM without allowing it dictate the way we do our work, regardless of pressure from funding sources, the media, and the impulse to adopt psychiatric language as the hallmark of professional expertise? That is one of the core tasks of contemporary social work education.

Putting It All Together

As stated again and again throughout this book, sound assessment depends on seeking, connecting, and reflecting critically on multiple forms of knowledge. The challenge is to integrate this potentially disparate evidence into a meaningful whole. Without an organizing principle, we risk amassing information that has no structure or hierarchy, a mere "laundry list" of isolated facts. As Mattaini and Kirk (1991) observed, a framework and process are needed for "assessing the assessment" and determining *which* data are relevant for a specific individual at a specific moment.

They compare approaches to assessment in terms of purpose, scope, level of measurement, theoretical base, connection to intervention, and limitations. The assessment models of early casework theorists, they remind us, emphasized the systematic gathering of evidence about a client's inner and outer life for the purpose of devising effective interventions. Diagnosis was seen, "not as a decision about the placement of an individual or problem into a category, but rather as a complex process of gathering information, making careful inferences from that information, and developing a plan of intervention" (p. 260). As Mattaini and Kirk note, "diagnostic categorization does not add information; it removes information available to clinicians" (pp. 261–262), *paring down* to what is taxonomically significant. Social work assessment, on the other hand, means *opening up* to any source of knowledge that can shed light on a person's experience, yet without amassing information indiscriminately. Thus, we need to carefully consider how we collect, organize, and interpret clinical data.

Collecting clinical information Many agencies have intake protocols for gathering demographic, historical, and other background data; additional tools may also be used to assess for specific conditions and risks. So too, social workers in private practice collect information through a range of means, formal, and informal. There are questionnaires, scales, and checklists to assess for drug use, trauma, suicide risk, mental functioning, and so on. Many of these instruments have been empirically validated, translated into other languages, and adjusted for multicultural use. The Beck Depression Inventory, for example, is widely accepted as a valid screening tool for depression; there is also a Children's Depression Inventory, adapted for use with children. The Connor's Rating Scale assesses ADHD, with versions for teachers and parents as well as a new version for adult ADHD. These checklists are directly linked to DSM criteria and used to supplement observational data and self-report.

Other instruments such as the Behavior Assessment System for Children (BASC) target children's behavior and emotions without being tied to a specific diagnosis. A functional behavioral assessment (FBA) identifies the purpose or function that problematic behavior serves, with the aim of developing healthier replacement behavior (see Chap. 2). The Behavioral and Emotional Rating Scale (BERS) measures strengths and competencies; parent, teacher, and youth versions identify child strengths in relation to school, family, peers, and affective capacities. The ASEBA (Achenbach System of Empirically Based Assessment), with versions for use with preschoolers through older adults, "offers a comprehensive approach to assessing adaptive and maladaptive functioning, developed through decades of research and practical experience to identify actual patterns of functioning" (http://www.aseba.org). It offers a way to relate scores directly to various DSM-5 categories through special scoring scales that link items to DSM criteria.

Face-to-face observation also provides a wealth of information about speech, gesture, posture, affect, and ways of interacting. Is the client open and forthcoming, or hesitant and guarded? Are responses quick or pensive, direct or tangential, defensive, flippant, hostile, or self-effacing? What is the client's presentation style in light of gendered, generational, and cultural conditioning? For a skilled clinician, listening is a primary assessment tool—attending to *what* is said and *how* it is said. Data can also be collected through nonverbal methods. Some clinicians use dreams, poetry, art, or role-play, or ask clients to bring in favorite song lyrics or photographs as a way to learn about their values and aspirations. Some seek information from people who know the client in settings such as school, work, or family. Staged role-plays or enactments can reveal patterns of engagement and response; journals can monitor targeted behaviors or offer opportunity for reflection and insight.

Organizing clinical information There are various ways to structure this information and "connect the pieces" into a meaningful clinical portrait. *Time*, for example, can be used to structure assessment: by organizing material chronologically or developmentally, along the life course, to indicate an issue's roots and consequences; by using ordinal or graded measures to track changes in severity, frequency, or duration of symptoms, thus indicating whether a person is getting better or worse; and by noting themes that are stable and enduring in order to identify shifts, disruptions, or reversals in the person's life narrative. *Functionality*, another organizing principle, focuses on the purpose of behavior as well as the contingencies that maintain it and the social roles it requires, promotes, or suppresses. *Psychodynamic* principles such as defenses and ego strengths can also be used to organize clinical data. Yet another principle is the *ecological,* where the individual is seen in relation to resources, stressors, networks, barriers, social capital, and other elements in the proximal and distal environment; assessment focuses on how a person is connected—or disconnected—to social systems such as family, community, and culture.

A more comprehensive framework—probably the one used most often by social workers—is the bio-psycho-social. In bio-psycho-social assessment, elements from all three domains are considered. The *biological* aspect includes information about genetic predispositions, neurobiology, health, diet, sleep, exercise, substance use, exposure to toxins, as well as access to adequate nutrition, sanitation, and health care. All of these factors can affect mental health. For instance, a lack of sunlight can make some people experience a form of depression known as seasonal affective disorder—a so-called mental illness with a physical cause. Specific foods, food additives, or medical conditions such as eczema can make other people irritable, edgy, and unable to concentrate. Chronic sleep deprivation, as little as one hour a night, can produce symptoms that mimic ADHD, just as medication prescribed for a physical condition can have psychological side effects. The impact of exposure to lead paint in cognitive impairment is well documented, as are the psychiatric reactions associated with Lyme disease including paranoia, dementia, schizophrenia, panic attacks, and major depression. There are many other examples. Clearly, a medical history is an essential part of assessment.

At the same time, clinicians need to be careful about bio-reductionism, attributing more to biology than is really warranted. The well-documented force of neuroplasticity, for example, casts doubt on the assumption that faulty "brain wiring" or malfunctioning neurochemicals are the cause of emotional distress and impaired functioning. Since brain circuits and cortical maps are continually reshaped by experience, it makes no sense to say that someone is "wired" for a particular kind of dysfunction. It may be equally true that experience and behavior determine a person's brain. Similarly, while research indicates that the mothers of toddlers with depression are likely to have depression themselves, thus seeming to reinforce the idea that depression has a genetic basis, it is also possible that these toddlers are depressed because their mothers are not providing adequate attention, nurturing, and loving care. A careful clinician thus needs to think about systems of reciprocal influence, rather than one-directional causality.

The *psychological* aspect focuses on elements of the interior life such as temperament, attachment, affective style and affect tolerance, resilience, coping strategies, humor, values, sense of agency, ego stability or fragility, internal conflict, and beliefs about life, reality, duty, and one's own worth. The *social* aspect includes family dynamics, peer relationships, economic resources and stressors, social location, cultural affiliation, occupation and leisure, immigration history, the impact of cumulative privilege or disadvantage.

It is difficult, of course, to separate the inner and the outer, the psychic and the physical, social identity, and psychological identity; indeed, such a separation may be artificial and of limited use. As Berzoff (2011) points out, external factors become internalized, particularly for members of vulnerable and oppressed populations who may have fewer possibilities for rejecting the social identities imposed on them by others. We need, she suggests, to understand how a client has "metabolized the social world" (p. 133). Through understanding the internalized effects of oppressive social forces such as discrimination, microaggression, marginalization, and stigma, we can better understand why a client may be "self-defeating, repeatedly victimized, or cannot take what we have to offer" (p. 162).

Some social work theorists have suggested a fourth element, the *spiritual*. Spiritual assessment includes personal (values, beliefs, practices) and interpersonal elements (rituals and celebrations carried out within the family or community). A number of spiritual assessment protocols have been developed, often focusing on patient wishes in connection with illness or death. Other instruments address spiritual distress or the course of spirituality over the life span using spiritual histories, lifemaps, and family ecomaps (Hodge 2001, 2005; Hodge and Bushfield 2006). The Joint Commission on Accreditation of Healthcare Organizations (JCAHO), the largest health care accrediting entity in the USA, now requires a spiritual assessment as part of an overall health care plan and provides guidelines for physicians and other helping professionals (Hodge and Bushfield 2006). Many social workers use spiritual assessment to gain deeper insight into a client's sense of meaning and purpose—important avenues for healing and growth.

Interpreting clinical information After gathering and organizing this information, the clinician must face the question of what it all means—what it means to the client, and what it may indicate based on well-developed, empirically grounded theories of human behavior. Theories offer explanations for the processes that lie behind observed symptoms and verbal reports; they help us to go deeper than mere description. There are many theories to choose from: theories about identity development, attachment, socialization, acculturation, aging, and so on. Although one might ask why any theory is needed, it is difficult to imagine a clinician whose mind is empty of all ideas and prior conditioning: assumptions and tendencies toward interpretation are there whether we acknowledge them or not. (For a discussion of theory-free versus theory-driven scholarship, see the 2001 debate between Bruce Thyer and Tomi Gomory in the *Journal of Social Work Education*.)

The theory must fit the data, however, and not the other way around. It is not a matter of "applying" a theory to a particular client, but of seeing what illumination it might offer; theories are suggestive, not restrictive. As social psychologist Kurt Lewin is famous for declaring, "There is nothing so practical as a good theory." One might add, " … unless it's *several* good theories."

Unlike deductive interpretation, where an a priori framework is applied to new data (top down), skillful assessment is inductive, with meaning emerging from the data themselves (bottom up). Schoen, writing about reflective professional practice, speaks to this important difference when he cautions educators and practitioners about the danger of "mere application." He cites Glazer's observation that schools of social work have fallen prey to the trap of substituting a formulaic application of "scientific" or "technical" knowledge for the artistry of practice wisdom. There is, of course, a danger in leaning too far in either direction—all "science" or all "art," as

Hardy discusses at length in Chap. 10. In social work, as in other disciplines, the pendulum has shifted back and forth over the years in response to changing attitudes toward mental disorder, changing beliefs about what science can "do," and the need to maintain professional status and expertise in a competitive environment. This is reflected in practice standards as well as in approaches to professional education.

In the so-called scientific approach, Schoen goes on to say, "rigorous professional practice is conceived as essentially technical. Its rigor depends on the use of describable, testable, replicable techniques derived from scientific research, based on knowledge that is objective" (Schoen 1992, p. 52) While appropriate for some disciplines, this paradigm cannot be transported to disciplines that deal with human behavior. "By defining rigor only in terms of technical rationality, we exclude as non-rigorous much of what competent practitioners actually do" (p. 54). That is, we dismiss and devalue the very thing that makes these practitioners good at what they do—the artful use of practice wisdom, also called "tacit knowledge" (Schoen 1984).

The problems that people are actually concerned about, Schoen reminds us, are messy, indeterminate, complex, and incapable of technical resolution, requiring different skills in the practitioner. If we confine ourselves to the kinds of problems that can be solved by technical means, we may find "solutions," but they are not solutions to the problems that our clients actually experience and care about. When we think of our work in that way, we are likely to limit the scope of assessment, becoming selectively inattentive to certain kinds of data offered by our clients since we have decided in advance that they are not relevant. As an alternative to the "technical" approach, Schoen argues for an "intelligence in action" that is open, reflective, creative, and adaptive to the immediate situation (1984).

This reflective, adaptive, and emergent "way of knowing" fits well with the contemporary idea of clinical practice as a co-constructed collaboration between therapist and client. Both require an attunement to what is actually taking place, a collaborative willingness to learn from the person we are presumably trying to help. Indeed, the client's view of the situation is at least as important as the clinician's. It may be that clinician and client have different perceptions of the problem. If there are discrepancies between their views about what is wrong or what sort of change is indicated, these discrepancies need to be explored—not necessarily "resolved," but honored and incorporated.

When asked how they see their problems and goals, clients may be more likely to frame perceptions in personal, subjective language rather than using the "technical" language of the DSM. Some may use DSM language, however, given how the lexicon of mental disorder has permeated public discourse and the ease with which people now self-diagnose. It is no longer uncommon for a client to announce, "I really think I'm bipolar" or "Everyone tells me I must be bipolar." The client is, in effect, choosing technical language over personal expression.

When that occurs, the clinician must be respectful but cautious, neither dismissing nor accepting the client's statement. Some find it helpful to open the DSM and review criteria together for the diagnosis that the client believes is appropriate. "Does this sound like your experience?" If not, other diagnoses can be explored. For clients who welcome this kind of partnership, this is a respectful and validating alternative to top-down diagnosis. It allows for verification and feedback, providing a shared basis for work. For other clients, the language of diagnosis may be alien and unwelcome. Receiving a label can bring shame, denial, or simply feel irrelevant to the issues of acute concern—the pain of isolation, rejection, betrayal, doubt, fear; the struggle for identity, intimacy, or a sense of belonging and purpose. There may be a theme to the client's distress and dysfunction for which the DSM has no category.

It is important to remember that the client may not share the clinician's fundamental notions about mental disorder—its cause, purpose, nature, or cure. For the client, what the clinician calls a "symptom" may be a sign of spiritual imbalance, social disharmony, or punishment for misdeeds, knowable through channels other than the rational mind. Genuine respect for intuitive and somatic ways of knowing is critical in these instances; without it, the clinician may miss valuable sources of information as well as the possibility of forging an enduring therapeutic alliance.

Looking Forward: New Directions in Clinical Assessment

Social work's capacity to draw on multiple theoretical orientations has been viewed as both strength and liability. On the one hand, this flexibility and eclecticism allows social workers to make use of different systems of knowledge, depending on the needs of the situation. On the other hand, the fact that there is no distinct "social work theory" has been cited as evidence that social work is not a true profession. The call for a distinctly "social work" assessment system has been sounded many times over the years, yet has not led to the development of a viable alternative to the DSM. As Kirk et al. (1989) noted a quarter-century ago, "In order for the profession to develop a valid assessment system [of its own], research should be directed toward identifying the information that practitioners need. An empirical approach to assessment, grounded in the mission of social work, should be undertaken" (p. 304). Without a research agenda developed and carried out by social workers, the authors conclude the prognosis for a system of "social work diagnosis" is bleak.

The challenge remains. While there is a vast body of research on mental health, much of it conducted by social workers, this research has continued to be organized around DSM categories, rather than toward developing and testing an alternative framework that would reflect social work values and embody the broad contextual domains that social workers actually incorporate into clinical assessment. It could be argued that there is no need for a special "social work system" that would isolate social workers from other helping professions, since social workers can always add dimensions to a DSM-based assessment. That is, in fact, what they do. And, as this book has argued, that is what they need to do—especially if the only alternative is to center assessment on the DSM.

There are, however, some new trends that indicate a growing interest in a more integrative approach to assessment. Recent scholarship has focused on integrating knowledge across disciplines, seeking ways to balance social context and neurobiology, universalism and localism, nomothetic evidence, and idiographic experience.

These efforts have taken several forms. Among these is the development of models such as person-centered integrative diagnosis (see Chap. 9) that "integrates the perspectives of the clinician, the patient, and his/her family into a jointly understood narrative description of clinical problems, the patient's positive factors, and expectations about restoration and promotion of health" (Berganza et al. 2005, p. 39). This transdisciplinary approach incorporates strengths, deficits, culture, and context into a comprehensive matrix in which all elements have equal weight, rather than serving as secondary factors or specifiers organized around a hub of core pathology.

Another integrative approach focuses on the interaction of genetic and environmental factors, or epigenetics. Epigenetics is the study of how factors external to a person's DNA sequence determine which genes are switched on or off, thus determining the protein sequences that activate certain diseases. In developmental psychology, the term is used to describe variation in gene expression and psychological development that result from an ongoing, bidirectional interchange between heredity and experience—the way nature and nurture interact at the neurobiological level. A disorder is thus one possible form of expression of an underlying neurobiological tendency.

Similarly, diathesis–stress theory proposes that stress activates a latent diathesis or genetic predisposition to psychopathology. Each diathesis or predisposing condition has a threshold below which pathology will not be expressed; if stress does not reach this level, behavior will remain within "normal" limits. In this model, stress is non-specific and continuous, occurring at different levels of intensity but undifferentiated by type of stressor (McCutcheon 2006). Originally, the theory only considered events occurring within the year prior to the onset of disorder as stressors, but this has now been broadened to include adverse experience in early childhood that can exert lifetime effects. Under this broader interpretation, "early, temporally distant adverse experiences would be classified as diatheses, and recent adverse events would be classified as stressors" (McCutcheon 2006, p. 165). That is, the former would constitute vulnerabilities—for instance, a lack of early nurturing—while the latter would be seen as precipitating events that trigger a predisposition. While the diathesis–stress model emphasizes negative influences, it can also be applied to environmental factors that prevent or delay the emergence of disorder and promote resilience.

A third approach is identification of the core processes that underlie and cut across diagnostic categories—e.g., difficulty processing stimuli or a bias toward negative perceptions. These underlying mechanisms lead to different types of maladaptive behavior depending on context, temperament, and specific vulnerability. It is not a matter of "carving nature at its joints," per Plato's metaphor, in order to distinguish ever more accurately between discrete problematic conditions. Rather, it is about identifying fundamental processes and the different pathways each can take, depending on risk and protective factors, cultural preferences, and available forms of expression.

As Garland and Howard (2014) note, although taxonomic systems like the DSM classify mental distress on the basis of symptom profiles that are, presumably, distinct from one another, "a growing consensus is emerging that the descriptive taxonomic approach to psychiatric classification may have reached the limits of its clinical and research utility" (p. 142). They offer another perspective, a "transdiagnostic" approach that focuses on the underlying processes that disorders have in common rather than on their purported differences (see Chap. 5).

> Instead of categorizing putative psychiatric taxons by their distinguishing features, the transdiagnostic perspective attends to the common processes underlying the full panoply of psychological distress and manifold forms of suffering. This view is derived from a mature body of empirical research that has identified a common set of cognitive, affective, and psychophysiological processes across a wide array of diagnoses and conditions (p. 144).

In a transdiagnostic perspective, states, traits, and psychological mechanisms exist on a continuum, activated or intensified in an "attempt to adapt to a challenging environmental context" (p. 144), de-activated when the context is less stressful. Garland and Howard's view of the plasticity of these processes reflects the ideas of Oldham and Morris (1995), who proposed that each psychiatric disorder represents a type of adaptive functioning and exists along a situationally embedded continuum, manifesting in mild and functional ways at times of low stress, intensifying at times of high stress until it becomes maladaptive. These approaches, considering people in flexible relationship to elements of their environment, suggest a model of person-in-environment that can begin to show how specific aspects of environment contribute to mental disorder. As such, they offer a response to the concern of Wakefield (1996) and others that "person-in-environment" is merely a perspective, not a theory, because it fails to specify the activities, experiences, mechanisms, or pathways through which dysfunction develops and change can take place.

Garland and Howard (2014) identify several transdiagnostic processes and provided evidence of how they underlie a range of mental disorders. Automaticity, attentional bias, memory bias, interpretation bias, and thought suppression—discussed in Chap. 5—represent ways that people selectively notice or interpret stimuli, thoughts, and information. Like the cognitive heuristics described in Chap. 1, these processes illuminate how people select and make sense of material in their inner and outer worlds to confirm to what they already believe. As Garland and Howard note, this is often biased toward negative memories and cognitions, thus fostering a self-perpetuating cycle in which negative beliefs are reaffirmed.

There may be other processes that cut across DSM diagnoses—for example, breakdown in the face of overload. When confronted with an excess of choices or stimuli, a person may freeze (the "analysis paralysis" associated with OCD), shut down protectively (as in autism and sensory processing disorders), or dissolve into chaotic disorganization, unable to sort or prioritize (as in ADHD). These processes suggest a link with aspects of temperament such as reactivity and effortful control (see Chap. 6).

Resilience Transecting all these processes and predispositions is the protective counterweight of resilience. Resilience has been a topic of extensive study, with recent research indicating that it may be more biologically based than previously believed. On the one hand, scholars maintain that "resilience is not a genetic trait that only a few "superkids" possess, as some journalistic accounts (and even several researchers) would have us believe. Rather, it is our inborn capacity for self-righting" (http://www. resiliency.com/free-articles-resources/the-foundations-of-the-resiliency-framework/). Summarizing 25 years of research on environmental factors that foster children's natural resiliency, Benard (2004) asserts that protective factors in family and community can enable children to resist or even reverse the potentially negative outcomes of high-risk conditions and transform adversity into strength.

On the other hand, as Belsky (2014) reports, new evidence indicates that resilience may have a genetic basis, predisposing some children to be more resilient than others. Reviewing longitudinal studies comparing children who benefitted from intensive interventions with those who did not, researchers are now wondering: why do some children come out of intervention efforts with enhanced capabilities and fewer behavioral problems, while others scarcely seem to be affected? What distinguishes the children who appear to be more susceptible to developmental experiences from those who are less deeply affected? New research seems to point to the role of genetics in children's differential susceptibility to the impact of environment. Children who carry certain alleles or "risk genes" seem to be most adversely affected by negative experiences and most positively affected by supportive ones, while children without these genes may be relatively immune to the effects of both supportive *and* unsupportive environments.

Belsky (2014) goes on to suggest that through genetic testing we may be able to identify those children who will benefit most from special interventions and thus target intervention dollars where they will have the greatest result. This is a disturbing conclusion. Does it mean that children who lack the preferred alleles will be dismissed as unworthy of help, since they are presumed to be unlikely to benefit? Can we really be certain? And even if there *were* a foolproof way to screen every child, can retrospective correlations be used to predict future outcomes in others, given the plethora of variables that may also play a role? Genetic differences may offer appealing "answers" because they are easier to measure and compare than differences in attachment, motivation, acceptance, perseverance, a sense of belonging, and all the other intrapersonal and interpersonal variables that affect individual lives—but that does not prove they are the critical differences.

Biology, responsibility, and empathy In fact, genetic tendencies do not "breed true." What is transmitted genetically are complex patterns of genetic risk that may manifest as one or more DSM disorders within a related cluster, depending on individual circumstances (Hyman 2010). "A given set of genetic risks may produce different symptoms depending on broad genetic background, early developmental influences, life stage, or diverse environmental factors" (http://www.scientificamerican. com/article.cfm?id=dsm-psychiatric-genetics&page=3). Each small variation in DNA sequence may carry only a minor incremental risk, but in "infelicitous combinations" and under unsupportive conditions can lead to the manifestation of mental illness.

In other words, the emergence of a particular mental disorder may be due to complex combinations of genes, epigenetic (variation in gene expression), and non-genetic factors.

Hyman (2010) suggests that there may be "families" of related mental disorders, based on common underlying genetic risk factors—e.g., abnormalities in the neural circuits that determine various aspects of brain functioning, from cognition to emotion to behavioral control, that do not necessarily correspond to DSM symptom checklists. This is, in fact, what the architects of DSM-5 hoped to achieve: If biomarkers can be identified to link specific disorders to specific brain anomalies, then mental disorder can finally be "explained," and people with the bad luck to inherit "dysfunctional brains" can receive targeted treatment without having to feel that they, their parents, or the society they live in are to blame.

It is commonly assumed that a biological approach to mental disorder will benefit clients because it will decrease blame, including self-blame, while fostering empathy and compassion. A recent study challenges this assumption, however. Lebowitz and Ahn (2014) asked 343 mental health clinicians in the USA—psychiatrists, psychologists, and social workers—to read short fictional vignettes about mental health patients, some with explanations of their symptoms based on genetics or neurobiology, others with explanations based on childhood experience and stressful life circumstances. The aim of the study was to see whether biological explanations would affect clinicians' empathy as well as their clinical recommendations. Their findings are striking: *All* clinicians in the sample, across disciplines, responded with less empathy to biological explanations and with more empathy to psychological explanations.

Lebowitz and Ahn's study did not involve actual clients, only simplified vignettes about fictitious cases, so it is possible that clinicians would react differently to real clients with whom they had direct contact. Nevertheless, the study raises an important question about the possibility of unintended negative consequences of the biomedical approach. By promoting the perception of patients as fundamentally different from "normal" people—lacking personal agency and responsibility, at the mercy of their bad "wiring" and deficient neurotransmitters—biological explanations can lead to an increase in dehumanization and social exclusion.

Conclusions

Where, then, does clinical social work fit within these emergent approaches to knowledge? What are social work's specific expertise, theoretical contribution, and domain of clinical knowledge? Should its hallmark continue to be the flexible use of multiple theories, regardless of their origin, or is something more needed?

Dewees (2002) calls for social workers to "contest the landscape of mental health practice" dominated by the DSM in order to provide alternative practice frameworks that are more syntonic with social work's distinctive mission. Social work's commitment to human rights, social justice, and client empowerment impels us to embrace a consumer-led recovery model and a professional identity from which we can live our values and "affirm an autonomous social work orientation, rather than one of ancillary service to psychiatry" (p. 84). He cautions that this approach "will not appeal to some social workers who don't have the inclination to question the power politics of the mental health system or whose source of professional pride rests in the exercise of acute diagnostic skills" (p. 88).

Establishing an "alternative practice framework" is not so easy, as the authors of PIE discovered. Rather than trying to develop an alternative, many social workers simply ignore the DSM, other than for billing, and focus on a client's specific symptoms without necessarily clustering them into a clinical syndrome (Probst 2013). After all, without evidence of shared pathogenesis, there is no real reason why certain traits are grouped under a common heading; most often, it is convention rather than science. There are advantages to focusing on individual symptoms rather than the labels given to groups of symptoms. In addition to offering greater flexibility, this approach mitigates the problem of overlap and "crossover" symptoms (e.g., difficulty sleeping) found among the criteria for more than one DSM disorder. Crossover confounds rather than clarifies differential diagnosis and leads to high levels of comorbidity that weaken the conceptual integrity of the system. Still, it is more like circumventing a flawed system than proposing a better one.

Wakefield (2013) frames the question of a social work practice model in ethical terms, proposing "psychological justice" as the goal of clinical social work. He defines psychological justice as "equipping individuals with a fair complement of the psychological features that our society demands" (p. 133) and urges social workers to provide help for "normal but non-disordered human variation" that does not happen to match the requirements or preferences of contemporary society, yet leads to suffering and reduces opportunity for participation, contribution, and fulfillment. Of all the mental health professions, he asserts, "social work is unique in conceiving its mission as going beyond treatment of mental disorder to seeking social justice through a proper fit between individuals' psychological capacities and the social environment" (p. 133).

In challenging social work to assume a leadership role, Wakefield has shifted from his earlier call for a collaborative relationship between social work and psychiatry. Writing in 2005, he proposed an interdisciplinary approach to assessment:

> There is no alternative but for patients to be routinely assessed for both internal dysfunctions and person-in-environment problems ... The future of psychiatric diagnosis and treatment will have to involve teams of psychiatrists and social workers sorting out the social and internal factors that determine the individual's problem (pp. 91–92).

Instead of "teams of psychiatrists and social workers," social workers tend to assume responsibility for *both* roles (Probst 2012). Straddling two roles is no small task; it means conforming to the requirements of the psychiatric establishment and insurance industry, while striving to uphold core social work values.

> Social work must face the challenge of how we will honor our unique perspective and take care that a client's right to be seen as a whole person is not compromised. How will we

insure that culture, spirituality, gender, the impact of poverty and oppression, and everything we've learned about person-in-environment are not forgotten, and that the idea of internal dysfunction, flaw, failure and deficit does not overwhelm and obscure our commitment to social justice? (Probst 2014, p. 130).

Our ability to respond to this challenge rests on how well the next generation is taught to think critically, compassionately, and holistically. Kutchins and Kirk offer a cogent description of how this might occur. Critiquing the centrality of the DSM in social work curricula and suggesting guidelines for what might take its place, they write as follows:

A comprehensive educational tool in mental health should provide information about the various theoretical approaches to mental disorder and its treatment, and it should review the strengths and weakness of each ... Social work students should be informed of the controversies and should be encouraged to think critically about them (Kutchins and Kirk 1995, p. 163).

That has been the aim of this book.

References

Belsky, J. (2014). The downside of resilience. *The New York Times*, November 28, 2014. http:// www.nytimes.com/2014/11/30/opinion/sunday/the-downside-of-resilience.html?mabReward= RI%3A8&action=click&pgtype=Homepage&region=CColumn&module= Recommendation&src=rechp&WT.nav=RecEngine&_r=0.

Benard, B. (2004). *Resiliency: What we have learned.* San Francisco CA: WestEd.

Berganza, C. E., Mezzich, J. E., & Pouncey, C. (2005). Concepts of disease: Their relevance for psychiatric diagnosis and classification. *Psychopathology, 38*(4), 166–170.

Berzoff, J. (2011). Why we need a biopsychosocial perspective with vulnerable, oppressed, and at-risk clients. *Smith College Studies in Social Work, 81*(2–3), 132–166.

Dewees, M. (2002). Contested landscape: The role of critical dialogue for social workers in mental health practice. *Journal of Progressive Human Services, 13*(1), 73–91.

Epple, D. M. (2007). Inter and intra professional social work differences: Social work's challenge. *Clinical Social Work Journal, 35*, 267–276.

Frazer, P., Westhuis, D., Daley, J. G., & Phillips, I. (2009). How clinical social workers are using the DSM-IV: A national study. *Social Work in Mental Health, 7*(4), 325–339.

Garland, E. L., & Howard, M. O. (2014). A transdiagnostic perspective on cognitive, affective, and neurobiological processes underlying human suffering. *Research on Social Work Practice, 24* (1), 142–151.

Haslam, N., & Giosan, C. (2002). The lay concept of "mental disorder" among American undergraduates. *Journal of Clinical Psychology, 58*(4), 479–485.

Hodge, D. R. (2001). Spiritual assessment: A review of major qualitative methods and a new framework for assessing spirituality. *Social Work, 46*(3), 203–214.

Hodge, D. R. (2005). Developing a spiritual assessment toolbox: A discussion of the strengths and limitations of five different assessment methods. *Health and Social Work, 30*(4), 314–323.

Hodge, D. F. & Bushfield, S. (2006). Developing spiritual competence in practice. *Journal of Ethnic and Cultural Diversity in Social Work, 15*(3/4), 101–127.

Hyman, S. E. (2010). Slipping the 'cognitive straitjacket' of psychiatric diagnosis. *Scientific American* (December 28, 2010). http://www.scientificamerican.com/article.cfm?id=dsm-psychiatric-genetics&page=3.

Kirk, S. A.; Siporin, M., & Kutchins, H. (1989). The prognosis for social work diagnosis. *Social Casework: The Journal of Contemporary Social Work*, 295–304.

Kutchins, H., & Kirk, S. A. (1988). The business of diagnosis: DSM-III and clinical social work. *Social Work*, 215–220.

Kutchins, H., & Kirk, S. A. (1995). Should DSM be the basis for teaching social work practice in mental health? No! *Journal of Social Work Education, 31*(2), 159–165.

Lebowitz, M. S., & Ahn, W. (2014). Effects of biological explanations for mental disorders on clinicians' empathy. In *Proceedings of the National Academy of Sciences.* doi:10.1073/pnas. 1414058111.

Mattaini, M. A., & Kirk, S. A. (1991). Assessing assessment in social work. *Social Work, 36*(3), 260–266.

McCutcheon, V. V. (2006). Toward an integration of social and biological research. *Social Service Review, 80*(1), 159–178.

McQuaide, S. (1999). A social worker's use of the diagnostic and statistical manual. *Families in Society, 80*(4), 410–417.

Mead, M. A., Hohenshil, T. H., & Singh, K. (1997). How the DSM system is used by clinical counselors: A national study. *Journal of Mental Health Counseling, 19*(4).

Oldham, J. M., & Morris, L. B. (1995). *The new personality self-portrait: Why you think, work, love, and act the way you do.* New York: Bantam.

Probst, B. (2012). Not quite colleagues: Issues of power and purview between social work and psychiatry. *Social Work in Mental Health, 10,* 367–383.

Probst, B. (2013). Walking the tightrope: Clinical social workers' use of diagnostic and environmental perspectives. *Clinical Social Work Journal, 41*(2), 184–191.

Probst, B. (2014). The life and death of axis IV: Caught in the quest for a theory of mental disorder. *Research on Social Work Practice, 24*(1), 123–131.

Probst, B., Balletto, C., & Wofford, N. What they bring: How MSW students think about mental disorder. *Clinical Social Work Journal* (doi:10.1007/s10615-015-0517-6).

Schoen, D. A. (1984). *The reflective practitioner: How professionals think in action.* New York: Basic Books.

Schoen, D. A. (1992). The crisis of professional knowledge and the pursuit of an epistemology of practice. *Journal of Interprofessional Care, 6,* 49–63.

Wakefield, J.C. (1996). Does social work need the eco-systems perspective? *Social Service Review* (March 1996). 1–30.

Wakefield, J. C. (2005). Disorders versus problems of living in DSM: Rethinking social work's relationship to psychiatry. In S. A. Kirk (Ed.), *Mental disorders in the social environment: Critical perspectives* (pp. 83–95). New York City: Columbia University Press.

Wakefield, J. C. (2013). DSM-5 and clinical social work: Mental disorder and psychological justice as goals of clinical intervention. *Clinical Social Work Journal, 41*(2), 131–138.

Chapter 14
Supplementary Materials

Abstract This chapter consists of seven appendices to the main text. The first is the case study that is used throughout the book, with each chapter offering an interpretation based on its particular lens. The second appendix provides a brief historical overview of the various editions of the DSM. The third explores the evidence challenging the notion that mental disorder is a matter of chemical imbalance, with particular emphasis on the "deficient serotonin" theory of depression. The fourth appendix summarizes a research study on what MSW students think mental disorder is and how they believe a clinician can know that someone "has" one, and the fifth explores some special considerations in the clinical assessment of children and families. The sixth and seventh appendices are specifically related to teaching: the former consists of seven different assignments and classroom activities that illustrate the approach to learning set forth in this book, and the latter consists of a sample 15-week syllabus to show how this book can be used as a primary text for clinical assessment and diagnosis courses, weaving DSM categories into the chapters rather than organizing chapters around the DSM.

© Springer International Publishing Switzerland 2015   267
B. Probst (ed.), *Critical Thinking in Clinical Assessment and Diagnosis*,
Essential Clinical Social Work Series, DOI 10.1007/978-3-319-17774-8_14

Appendix A: Case Study: The Case of Ray

Ray is a 34-year-old Caucasian male of Irish Catholic background. Divorced for four years, he has two children (a 5-year-old boy and a 7-year-old daughter). He is currently on medical leave for psychological reasons from his job as a police officer, a position he has had for the past twelve years.

Ray came to the clinic for therapy because of distress over his deteriorating relationship with his live-in girlfriend Cecilia. He reported a history of violence, primarily fist fights with men but also several instances of physical violence toward Cecilia and other women. After the last incident, Cecilia told him they needed time apart to rethink their relationship and work on their individual issues. Previously she had urged Ray to seek therapy, but he had refused. This time he agreed to couples counseling with their local priest, but felt "double-crossed" and angry when she decided to move out after their first session. For him, counseling meant they were going to work things out; for her, it provided the courage to leave.

Ray expressed anger with Cecilia and swore he would never forgive her for disclosing personal details and then "turning on him." What he valued above all else, he said, was loyalty—the sense of solidarity he felt with his buddies at the precinct and at the firehouse where he volunteered. "You just don't rat on someone," he declared, "no matter what."

Midway through the first session with his new therapist at the clinic, after explaining his background in a matter-of-fact manner, he became very emotional and said he knew he had to put an end to the violence. He confessed to getting into fights in bars over the slightest insult, real or perceived, "almost like I was looking for something to fight about." Now, for the first time, this violence had cost him something that mattered, and he wanted to put a stop to "this thing that just comes over me."

He denied any violence in his marriage to Leslie, his ex-wife, and said the marriage had ended because of her materialism, self-absorption, and coldness. When his mother died a prolonged and painful death from cancer, Leslie had not provided any emotional support. When he came home distraught over incidents he had witnessed as a police officer, she merely replied, "Nobody made you become a cop. You chose it." After his mother's funeral, which she did not attend, he moved out.

Ray said that he is devoted to his children and spends as much time with them as he can. He feels intense guilt over the three abortions Cecilia had during their four years together, all of which were at his request. "You don't think I'm good enough to have kids with," she told him bitterly, despite his protests. Although he knew they were not in a position to have a child, he remains upset about the abortions—in part because of his Catholicism, and in part because of an incident that continues to give him nightmares—when he was able to rescue three young children from a burning building but could not save the fourth.

Ray's early years on the police force gave him great satisfaction. "I liked feeling that I was doing some good, and I always felt really close to my friends in the precinct. When you go through stuff together like we did—there's a trust there, I can't describe the feeling, it's like nothing else in the world."

The nightmares began after 9/11. He spent weeks pulling body parts out of the rubble; grief and helplessness overwhelmed him. The incident with the child in the fire came shortly afterward. Since then, he has found his job more and more difficult. "All I ever see are the worst things about people—mugging, rape, knifings, people hurting each other."

In contrast, Ray describes his early years as happy and secure. The only child of older parents who adopted him through a Catholic agency shortly after birth, he was told, "God answered our prayers. It was worth the long wait because He brought you to us. You were our gift." Ray does not remember ever being explicitly told that he was adopted; "it was just something I always knew." He wondered about his birth family from time to time but did not feel that his parents wanted to talk about it and thus never asked.

He remembers the household as calm and loving. His parents did not argue, at least not in front of him, and spent quiet evenings reading, while he drew or built complicated structures out of Legos. They were proud of him, he remembers, and he remains extremely close to his widowed father. Difficulty came when he was eight or nine and became the victim of school bullies. Blonde and slight of build, he looked different from everyone in the Italian neighborhood where he grew up. He decided that the only way to survive was to become a tougher, better fighter than his peers, even though that went against his nature. He did not tell his parents about his fights, knowing how much it would upset them.

Ray attended Catholic school and became an altar boy. The church was important to his family, especially to his mother who often went on religious retreats and whose sister was a nun. When he was thirteen, he was sexually abused by a priest who had befriended him. Trusting the priest, he had gone to his private room "for a talk." The abuse was repeated on a number of other occasions over the course of six months. Afraid to say anything for fear of upsetting his parents, afraid of causing trouble, afraid no one would believe him anyway, Ray did not know how to say no to the priest's insistence that he "come and talk." He felt, too, that somehow it was his fault for inviting the abuse. "What was it about me? Why me? Why did he pick me, out of everyone?" Eventually the priest left the parish for another city. At the time Ray did not question the reason for the move—he only felt relief—but now he wonders if the priest was transferred because his habits were discovered, as such things were usually handled in those days. In any event, he told no one.

He went on to become a gifted athlete and was accepted into the police academy after graduation from high school. Good-looking, he had many girlfriends, often juggling several relationships despite what he described as a feeling of emptiness. He married Leslie partly because she had become pregnant and partly because he wanted a family and a home of his own. He states that he was faithful to her during their marriage.

Loyalty and fidelity are important to Ray. He states that the first time he hit Cecilia was when she was unfaithful to him. Even though she apologized and promised it would never happen again, "I just never felt the same after that. Once something is broken, it's broken."

Presenting Situation

In the past six months, Ray has twice taken large doses of Tylenol and ended up in the hospital's psychiatric unit. The first time occurred shortly before he came to the clinic for therapy. When asked about the overdose, he stated that he was just "trying to get some sleep," worry over Cecilia had kept him from sleeping, and he was so tired and had such an intense headache that he "didn't realize" how many pills he had swallowed. While in the hospital, he was diagnosed with major depression and prescribed 50 mg of Zoloft; this was his first experience with psychotropic medication. He reported that it made him a bit dizzy and nauseous, but otherwise, "I didn't really feel that different." Weekly therapy was recommended as part of his discharge plan. Although Ray had never considered therapy before, he said he was open to it and hoped it might help him deal with his distress over the breakup with Cecilia.

Ray engaged easily with the therapist and expressed his eagerness to "get a handle on things and make some changes." While he talked readily about the violence he had engaged in, he stuttered and became agitated when speaking about the violence he had witnessed. He did not reveal his early sexual abuse until after two months of therapy, stating that this was the first time he had ever spoken about it. Details came slowly over a period of several weeks. At one point, he became angry with the therapist, snapping, "Stop making such a big deal out of this. It was a long time ago, I put it behind me, it has nothing to do with why I'm here." Later, he apologized for the outburst, adding, "I don't know what you think of me now that you know this. You probably never imagined I was one of those kids you read about."

The second hospitalization occurred after several months of therapy, when many issues had been opened for the first time. Ray was in a vulnerable and fragile state, having worked hard to strip away layers of armor, knowing he could no longer live the life he had been leading but not knowing what lay ahead. He had been on restricted duty on the police force, his guns taken away after the first hospitalization, and had been assigned to monitor video cameras in the stairwell of a housing project.

"In a way that was even worse," he said, "just staring at these screens and seeing these things happen, people getting beat up, but not being able to do anything to stop it." His job was to continuously scan 24 monitors, never knowing where violence might erupt. "I couldn't take it," he said. "I just wanted to escape. I just wanted to get away from everything."

After the second overdose, which he again claimed was an accident, he was diagnosed with bipolar disorder, type II, and prescribed 750 mg of Depakote. He has taken the medication faithfully, despite feeling "kind of passive" and having begun to gain weight. He was placed on medical leave from his job, pending a hearing to determine his fitness to resume duty. At first, the idea of not being a police officer was devastating—"it's all I've ever known"—but during the course of therapy, Ray has come to feel that it may not be the right job for him anymore. The police psychiatrist, whom he also sees on a regular basis, feels that continuing any kind of active duty places him at considerable risk. Ray is currently awaiting a date for a formal hearing and hopes to be dismissed with pension and benefits.

He remains active as a volunteer fireman, which provides a connection with a network of friends whom he sees frequently at the local firehouse. He plays softball, has dated a couple of women casually although has not become sexually involved, and spends most of his time with his children, father, and dog; he has had no further contact with Cecilia. He commented that this is the first time in his life that he is ever lived alone, "but it's not so bad."

After several months in therapy and at the therapist's suggestion, Ray told his father about the early sexual abuse. Although he had longed to tell him, he had been afraid. His father proved to be supportive and loving. "He just said he wished I could have told him back then, when it was happening." A few weeks later, Ray went to the local priest and told him about the abuse, which had happened in the same parish. Though ambivalent about "ratting on someone," he found it a great relief to enter the same building and finally tell. A report was filed with the diocese, and Ray discovered that criminal charges had been brought against the priest in question several years later in California for sexual abuse of an adolescent boy. It made Ray wish he had told much sooner "so other kids wouldn't have had to suffer," but he admitted that it was a tremendous relief to know that he was not the only one.

Ray was given information about a national support group called SNAP (Survivors Network for Those Abused by Priests). After weeks of hesitation, he called but stated that he is not comfortable going to a meeting and "sitting in a room with a bunch of other guys talking about this stuff. I'd rather just talk about it privately, like we've been doing."

Appendix B: Historical Overview of the DSM

1952: The first DSM was simply a list of disorders prepared for the veterans administration hospital to assist with record keeping. Strongly influenced by psychoanalytic theory, many disorders were classified as "neuroses" resulting from unconscious conflict. The slim manual—106 disorders in 130 pages—never had a major role in research or clinical practice.

1968: DSM-II still reflected psychoanalytic theory, with disorders defined in descriptive paragraphs rather than by lists of criteria as in later editions; reliability was not a concern, since the purpose of the manual was simply to describe, not to predict or guide treatment. Only four pages were added to the original volume, but the number of disorders increased to 182.

1980: DSM-III ushered in a major revolution in the way mental illness was conceived, abandoning psychoanalytic theory in favor of criterion-based taxonomy. The new manual grew out of psychiatry's need to overcome its isolation from the rest of medicine and become more "scientific;" DSM-II had been based on unproven theories and had categories that looked nothing like medical diseases and thus was not taken seriously by the rest of the medical profession.

Two principles governed this new paradigm. The first was psychometrics, the notion that the only valid concepts are those that can be quantified and measured; symptoms, too, ought to be measurable. The second was a category-based or "neo-Kraepelin" approach to disorder, named after Emil Kraepelin, a German psychiatrist, who was the first to separate psychosis into two distinct categories, schizophrenia and manic depression. Kraepelin proposed that mental illnesses are real entities, distinct from one another, based on biological processes and markers that can be discovered. If those processes and markers are not yet known, in the interim categories can be based on observable signs, progression of the disorder, and treatment response. Eventually, however, underlying mechanisms and markers are knowable—or so the neo-Kraepelians maintained. In the absence of validity ("proven" criteria and boundaries), DSM-III prioritized reliability, since it was considered useful to have categories that everyone can agree on. (Of course, we can all agree and all be wrong, but that was not a concern of the editors of the new manual.)

The third edition swelled to 494 pages describing 265 different disorders. It also included, for the first time, a multi-axial system for assessing and recording different kinds of information. In a multi-axial approach, "an individual is evaluated in terms of several different domains of information that are assumed to be of high clinical value. Each of these domains is assessed quasi-independently of the others, but together they represent a view of the patient's condition that is more comprehensive than an evaluation that is limited to one or more mental disorder diagnoses" (Williams 1985, p. 175). Despite the increased demand this kind of evaluation places on a clinician's time, multi-axial assessment is generally considered to be worthwhile because of its ability to capture the complexity of the interrelationships between bio psycho-social factors.

Axis IV, the so-called social work axis, was conceived as way to rate and rank the role of particular psychosocial stressors in the genesis of mental disorder. Clinicians were asked to rate the severity of each stressor on a seven-point scale ranging from "none" to "catastrophic," with severity determined by comparison with what an "average" person would experience under similar conditions, given the amount of undesirable change attributable to the specific event or enduring condition (Probst 2014).

1987: DSM-III-R, a revised version of DSM-III, was published. Only 22 disorders and 73 pages were added, representing only minor changes.

1994: DSM-IV, though nearly doubling in size to 886 pages, preserved the approach to mental disorder presented in DSM-III. There were now 297 disorders, with new categories added but relatively little change in the way they were conceived and organized.

Axis IV underwent a major change, however. Critics had raised concerns about its "inappropriately etiologic" formulation within an allegedly atheoretical manual (Williams 1985, p. 179), since it required the clinician to determine the extent to which stressors, individually and in aggregate, contributed to a person's mental disorder. Many also objected to the requirement to combine all stressors, both chronic and acute, into a unified rating implying a single causal mechanism. There was no empirical evidence for the construct validity of this assumption, nor did many clinicians feel comfortable making judgments about etiologic significance (Probst 2014).

Thus, Axis IV was reformulated for DSM-IV. Because of the difficulty in reliably quantifying the etiologic contribution of specific stressors to mental disorder, it was simplified into a list from which the clinician could select and note salient elements without trying to rate their severity or precise contribution.

2000: DSM-IV-TR, an updated version of DSM-IV, included additional information on each diagnosis, with changes in some of the diagnostic codes to maintain consistency with the ICD. The diagnostic categories and the vast majority of the specific criteria for diagnosis were unchanged.

2013: DSM-5, representing the most significant change since DSM-III, had several aims. Among them were

- A new focus on neurobiological etiology. Attempting to link mental disorder to brain disorder, the editors hoped there could eventually be genetic or laboratory tests for each disorder as a way to (finally) establish the validity of diagnostic categories.
- Elimination of the multi-axial system, including replacement of Axis IV with an expanded list of V codes. Although Axes III–V had always been optional, moving psychosocial stressors out of one of five (supposedly) "equal" axes into an Appendix was a way of signalizing the centrality of a neurological approach.

- A dimensional or continuum approach with severity scales to allow clinicians to differentiate milder, even subclinical variations of a disorder from more severe forms.
- Organizing chapters to reflect the life cycle, with disorders grouped into "families" as part of the search for a common genetic etiology for related conditions. Some disorders, such as trauma-related disorders and obsessive-compulsive disorders, were now given their own chapters; others, like Asperger's syndrome, were subsumed under broader categories.

Unlike other editions, the number of disorders was reduced, yielding only 212 diagnoses, but the book weighed in at 947 pages.

References

Probst, B. (2014). The life and death of axis IV: Caught in the quest for a theory of mental disorder. *Research on Social Work Practice, 24*(1), 123–131.
Williams, J. (1985). The multiaxial system of DSM-III: Where did it come from and where should it go? Its origins and critiques. *Archives of General Psychiatry, 42*(2), 175–180.

Appendix C: Challenging the Narrative of Chemical Imbalance: A Look at the Evidence

Jeffrey Lacasse and Jonathan Leo

The idea of a "chemical imbalance" underlying mental disorder is pervasive in our society. In particular, the idea that clinical depression is caused by an imbalance of the neurotransmitter serotonin (which can be corrected through use of antidepressant medication) has been popularized since the introduction of the modern antidepressants in the late 1980s (Lacasse 2005). This message has also been disseminated in the media, in direct-to-consumer advertising, and in educational materials for mental health clients (Lacasse and Leo 2005; Leo and Lacasse 2008; Hess et al. 2014). The serotonin theory of depression has been a crucial piece of the ascendance of biological psychiatry, the viewpoint asserting that DSM-defined mental disorders are diseases of the brain (a biological organ), in the same way that diabetes or cancer are diseases of other biological organs (Whitaker 2010).

Clinical social workers who diagnose will often also play a psychoeducational role, informing clients about the cause, course, and prognosis of their diagnosis. In this situation, the clinical social worker carries significant power in the clinician–client relationship. The social worker will be seen as the expert, and clients are likely to believe that what they are told is scientifically valid information. Thus, telling depressed clients that it is known that they have a chemical imbalance in their brain—that they have a brain disease—could have major effects on how clients see themselves, their condition, and their treatment needs (Hess et al. 2014). For instance, Kemp et al. (2014) found that when participants with a history of depression were told they had a serotonin imbalance, this had negative effects including a more pessimistic prognosis and the impression that drug treatment was more effective than psychotherapy (see also Deacon and Baird 2009).

Thus, it is clear that bioreductionistic explanations have the potential to cause harm to clients and that this issue should be carefully considered by practicing social workers. This raises two crucially important issues. First, do we know that social workers are in fact telling depressed clients that they suffer from serotonin imbalance? This research question has not yet received the extensive attention that it deserves, but there is evidence that this is beginning to occur. In a small study, Acker (2013) found that 92 % of clinical social workers at least "sometimes" explain to their clients that depression is caused by a chemical imbalance. Other research demonstrates that it is common for clients to be informed of this within mental health treatment more generally (Cohen and Hughes 2011; Johnston et al. 2007), and there is little evidence that clinical social workers in general take a contrarian position as compared to psychiatry or psychology (Gomory et al. 2011).

The second and more important question is whether or not the serotonin theory of depression is *true*. Social workers have an ethical mandate to "critically examine and keep current with emerging knowledge relevant to social work" (National Association of Social Workers 2008). Therefore, the scientific veracity of the serotonin theory is important. If social workers are informing clients of well-tested, accurate neuroscience research to help them better understand their condition, this makes good sense. However, if the serotonin theory has been scientifically falsified and social workers continue to use this explanation nonetheless, this would be deeply problematic.

Below, we make the case that the latter is unfortunately true. The serotonin theory of depression was falsified many years ago. Its current popularity can be attributed to a number of factors: relentless pharmaceutical marketing of antidepressant drugs, the influence of biological psychiatry on the field of social work, deficits in the education of aspiring mental health professionals, and the intuitive appeal of reducing complex human behavior to simple explanations rather than the application of critical thinking (Kirk et al. 2013; Lacasse and Gomory 2003; Valenstein 1998). However, what is well established is that the serotonin theory of depression no longer holds the status of even a viable scientific theory—let alone information that should be passed on to social work clients. Given how easy it is (see below) to build the scientific case against the serotonin theory, its continuing popularity and use in clinical practice could be seen as astonishing.

The Serotonin Theory

In 1965, Joseph Schildkraut put forth the hypothesis that depression was associated with low levels of norepinephrine (Shildkraut 1965), and later researchers theorized that serotonin was the neurotransmitter of interest (Coppen 1967). In subsequent years, there were numerous attempts to identify reproducible neurochemical alterations in the nervous systems of patients diagnosed with depression. For instance, researchers compared levels of serotonin metabolites in the cerebrospinal fluid of clinically depressed suicidal patients to controls, but the primary literature is mixed and plagued with methodological difficulties such as very small sample sizes and uncontrolled confounding variables. In a review of these studies, the chairman of the German Medical Board and his colleagues stated, "Reported associations of subgroups of suicidal behavior (e.g., violent suicide attempts) with low CSF–5HIAA [serotonin] concentrations are likely to represent somewhat premature translations of findings from studies that have flaws in methodology" (Roggenbach et al. 2002). Attempts were also made to induce depression by depleting serotonin levels, but these experiments reaped no consistent results (Heninger et al. 1996). Likewise, researchers found that huge increases in brain serotonin, arrived at by administering high-dose L-tryptophan, were ineffective at relieving depression (Mendels et al. 1975). This and other research led many to conclude that the serotonin theory of depression was not a viable scientific theory—for instance, in 1990, Astra pharmaceutical company research scientist John Evenden stated, "The simplistic idea of 'the 5-HT [serotonin] neurone does not bear any relationship to reality" (Shorter 2008).

Contemporary neuroscience research has also failed to confirm any serotonergic lesion in any mental disorder and has in fact provided significant counterevidence to the explanation of a simple neurotransmitter deficiency. Modern neuroscience has instead shown that the brain is vastly complex and poorly understood (Horgan 1999). While neuroscience is a rapidly advancing field, to propose that researchers can objectively identify a "chemical imbalance" at the molecular level is not compatible with the extant science. In fact, there is no scientifically established ideal "chemical balance" of serotonin, let alone an identifiable pathological imbalance. To equate the impressive recent achievements of neuroscience with support for the serotonin hypothesis is a mistake.

With direct proof of serotonin deficiency in any mental disorder lacking, the claimed efficacy of SSRIs is often cited as indirect support for the serotonin hypothesis. Yet, this *ex juvantibus* line of reasoning (i.e., reasoning "backwards" to make assumptions about disease *causation* based on the response of the disease to a *treatment*) is logically problematic—the fact that aspirin cures headaches does not prove that headaches are due to low levels of aspirin in the brain. Serotonin researchers from the US National Institute of Mental Health Laboratory of Clinical Science clearly state, "[T]he demonstrated efficacy of selective serotonin reuptake inhibitors...cannot be used as primary evidence for serotonergic dysfunction in the pathophysiology of these disorders" (Murphy et al. 1998).

Reasoning backwards, from SSRI efficacy to presumed serotonin deficiency, is thus highly contested. The validity of this reasoning becomes even more unlikely when one considers recent studies that call into question the efficacy of the SSRIs. A series of studies finds only a small, clinically insignificant difference between the effectiveness of placebo and antidepressants (Kirsch et al. 2008). This modest efficacy and extremely high rate of placebo response are not seen in the treatment of well-studied imbalances such as insulin deficiency, and casts doubt on the serotonin hypothesis.

Also problematic for the serotonin hypothesis is the growing body of research comparing SSRIs to interventions that do not target serotonin specifically. For instance, a Cochrane systematic review found no major difference in efficacy between SSRIs and tricyclic antidepressants (Geddes et al. 2005). In addition, in randomized controlled trials, bupropion and reboxetine are just as effective as the SSRIs in the treatment of depression, yet neither affects serotonin to any significant degree. The over-the-counter supplement St. John's wort (Szegedi et al. 2005) and placebo (Hypericum Depression Trial Study Group 2002) have both outperformed SSRIs in randomized controlled trials. Exercise was found to be as effective as the SSRI sertraline in a randomized controlled trial, and more effective at preventing relapse (Blumenthal et al. 1999). Perhaps most interestingly, tianeptine, an antidepressant which *lowers* serotonin levels of the brain (but which is not available in the United States) has comparable efficacy to the SSRI drugs (Kasper and Olie 2002). This alone might be enough for some to dismiss the serotonin theory—since the theory is that lower serotonin causes depression and raising serotonin remedies depression.

Although SSRIs are considered "antidepressants," they are FDA-approved treatments for many different psychiatric diagnoses, ranging from social anxiety disorder to obsessive-compulsive disorder to premenstrual dysphoric disorder. Some consumer advertisements (such as the Zoloft and Paxil Web sites) have in the past promoted the serotonin hypothesis, not just for depression, but also for some of these other diagnostic categories. Thus, for the serotonin hypothesis to be correct as currently presented, serotonin regulation would need to be the cause (and remedy) of each of these disorders (Healy 2002). This is improbable, and no one has yet proposed a cogent theory explaining how a singular putative neurochemical abnormality could result in so many wildly differing behavioral manifestations.

However, in addition to these critiques, it is also important to look at what is *not* said in the scientific literature. To our knowledge, there is not a single peer-reviewed article that can be accurately cited to directly support claims of serotonin deficiency in any mental disorder, while there are many articles that present counterevidence. Furthermore, the diagnostic and statistical manual of mental disorders (DSM), which is published by the American Psychiatric Association and contains the definitions of all psychiatric diagnoses, does not list serotonin as a cause of any mental disorder. The *American Psychiatric Press Textbook of Clinical Psychiatry* addresses serotonin deficiency as an unconfirmed hypothesis, stating, "Additional experience has not confirmed the monoamine depletion hypothesis" (Dubovsky et al. 2003).

In conclusion, there exists no rigorous corroboration of the serotonin theory, and a significant body of contradictory evidence. Far from being a radical line of thought, doubts about the serotonin hypothesis are well acknowledged by many researchers, including frank statements from prominent psychiatrists, some of whom are even enthusiastic proponents of SSRI medications. For instance, in 2006, Wayne Goodman, chair of the FDA Psychopharmacological Advisory Committee, admitted that the serotonin theory of depression is but "a useful metaphor"—and one that he never uses within his own psychiatric practice (Lacasse and Leo 2006). And in 2011, psychiatrist Ronald Pies, editor of *Psychiatric Times*, wrote: "In truth, the 'chemical imbalance' notion was always kind of an urban legend—never a theory seriously propounded by well-informed psychiatrists" (Pies 2011).

It seems clear, then, that informing clients that their depression is due to a serotonin imbalance is a serious empirical error. The psychiatric textbooks do not make this claim, and drug companies no longer run advertisements claiming that serotonin imbalance causes depression (Lacasse and Leo 2005). Prominent psychiatrists have in fact abandoned this theory in response to the data that contradicts it, which is what good science looks like. It has been decades since serious doubts emerged about the serotonin theory and arguably, psychiatry gave up on this theory a decade ago. As social workers, we need to respond to empirical evidence and tell our clients the best-tested information that is out there—and this means jettisoning the chemical imbalance/serotonin theory.

Other Mental Disorders

We have focused here on the serotonin theory of depression because it is clearly the most popular bioreductionistic theory of mental disorder. However, a similar case could be made for claimed chemical imbalances in many other mental disorders.

As previously mentioned, serotonin imbalance has been claimed not just for depression, but for a half-dozen mental disorders such as premenstrual dysphoric disorder and post-traumatic stress disorder. Advertisements for psychostimulants have made claims that attention-deficit–hyperactivity disorder (ADHD) is due to a chemical imbalance remedied by medication (Leo and Lacasse 2009). An advertisement for aripiprazole claimed that the drug would adjust the level of neurotransmitters in the patient's brain like a thermostat (Lacasse and Leo 2006).

ADHD indeed provides another example of the widely held assumption that mental disorders are due to one or another kind of chemical imbalance. Medications have been given to children diagnosed with ADHD for more than half a century, beginning with Ritalin, first licensed by the FDA in 1955 for treating what was known at the time as hyperactivity. At present, 11 % of American children have been diagnosed with ADHD (http://www.cdc.gov/ncbddd/adhd/data.html), a 41 % increase in the past decade, with two-thirds receiving prescriptions for psychostimulants (http://www.nytimes.com/2013/04/01/health/more-diagnoses-of-hyperactivity-causing-concern.html?pagewanted=all). These stimulants target the neurotransmitters dopamine and norepinephrine, purportedly to increase focus and self-control by increasing the availability of these chemical messengers. Many parents have been concerned about the effects of these powerful drugs on developing brains, fearing that there may turn out to be unforeseen harmful consequences. On the contrary, some researchers now assert. Not only are these drugs *not* neurotoxic, nor simply neurochemically neutral, but they are actually "neuroprotective."

In a 2014 interview with Psych Congress Network, Timothy Wilens, professor of psychiatry at Harvard Medical School, stated that meta-analysis of 30 studies of children who have taken ADHD medication show that, over the years, the brains of these children turn out to look more like the brains of non-ADHD youngsters, thus indicating that there is a normalization in both function and structure of the brain following prolonged use of medication (http://www.psychcongress.com/video/are-adhd-medications-neurotoxic-or-neuroprotective-16223). A *New York Times* report from 2015 (http://well.blogs.nytimes.com/2015/02/02/can-attention-deficit-drugs-normalize-a-childs-brain/?hpw&rref=health&action=click&pgtype=Homepage&module=well-region&region=bottom-well&WT.nav=bottom-well) includes a further argument from Dr. Wilens that these medications "normalize" children's brains, rewiring neural connections over time so the child feels more focused and in control.

It is not quite so simple, of course. When asked by the interviewer if these changes occur because the medication is directly altering the brain or because it allows these youngsters to have more normal interactions with the world, which in turn rewires the brain through the reciprocal action of neuroplasticity, Wilens admits that we really don't know. That is a significant gap in the causal chain. If it is *experience* that leads to changes in the brain, there is no inherent reason that pharmaceuticals are the sole or necessary agent for a child to have different experiences. How about changing the environment? (*There's* a novel idea!) Why assume that medication is the active, necessary, or only link between experience and brain? Not surprisingly, Wilens, as well as other authors of the 2013 report that the article cites, have received financial support over the years from pharmaceutical firms. In an email to the *Times* reporter, Dr. Wilens said he had not received "any personal income" from the pharmaceutical industry since 2009. The question of influence aside, the ADHD–dopamine link is far from proven. Just because stimulant medication "works" to make children calmer does not mean that hyperactivity is caused by a lack of the neurotransmitter that the medication activates—no matter how comforting or convenient it might be to think so.

Thus, it is critical for social work students, clients, and prescribers alike to realize what psychiatry diagnosis and treatment represents. Currently, by definition, almost every mental disorder in the DSM-5 is listed as a "mental" disorder because we do not actually know its nature or etiology; this is true whether it is ADHD, depression, schizophrenia, or anxiety. Medical tests and examinations should be performed to ensure that the client's mental distress is not a "downstream" effect of a known medical disease (e.g., thyroid disease causing depression). But the reason that clinical assessment and person-in-environment approaches are so important— the entire reason that social workers and psychiatrists are dealing with mental health clients rather than neurologists—is that these conditions are somewhat mysterious (Lacasse 2014) and we are largely ignorant of the pathophysiology that may be involved.

This uncertainty may be disturbing, but social workers should think twice about "solving" the uncertainty by telling clients that they have a chemical imbalance. This is particularly true in modern age of the World Wide Web, where any client can simply Google "serotonin imbalance" and find many resources explaining that chemical imbalances are lay myths largely disseminated by pharmaceutical companies. Telling clients that they have a chemical imbalance when there is not scientific evidence or tests to confirm this is troubling on an ethical level, but given the wide array of information available to clients, it could also create deep problems in therapeutic alliance.

Conclusion

The question of what to tell clients in lieu of the outdated chemical imbalance theory is a good one, if difficult to answer. It is important to point out that while there has been a huge problem in information dissemination, we have noted accurate portrayals of the chemical imbalance theory. The following statement, previously published on the Web site of the Mental Health Service at McGill University, is perhaps a good place to start:

> The term 'chemical imbalance is thrown around a lot these days. True conditions caused by chemical imbalances are relatively rare. All thoughts, feelings and motions in the brain are mediated by the release of chemicals in brain pathways. Every person's brain is unique, leading each of us to have different traits and abilities. Just because your brain works in a particular way does not mean that you have a chemical imbalance. A certain amount of

sadness, anxiety or other emotional upset is normal, and though we may be able to block these feelings by chemicals, this would tend to dehumanize us. Even when we use medication to help an individual with overwhelming emotions, most of the time this is not to repair a 'chemical imbalance' but simply to help contain symptoms.

References

Acker, J. (2013). *Influences on social workers' approach to informed consent regarding antidepressant medication.* (Unpublished doctoral dissertation). SUNY-Albany, Albany, NY.

Blumenthal, J. A., Babyak, M. A., Moore, K. A., Craighead, W. E., Herman, S., Khatri, P., et al. (1999). Effects of exercise training on older patients with major depression. *Archives of Internal Medicine, 159*(19), 2349–2356.

Cohen, D., & Hughes, S. (2011). How do people taking psychiatric drugs explain their "chemical imbalance?". *Ethical Human Psychology and Psychiatry, 13*(3), 176–189.

Coppen, A. (1967). The biochemistry of affective disorders. *British Journal of Psychiatry, 113,* 1237–1264.

Deacon, B. J., & Baird, G. L. (2009). The chemical imbalance explanation of depression: reducing blame at what cost? *Journal of Social and Clinical Psychology, 28*(4), 415–435.

Gomory, T., Wong, S. E., Cohen, D., & Lacasse, J. R. (2011). Clinical social work and the biomedical industrial complex. *Journal of Sociology and Social Welfare, 38*(4), 135–165.

Healy, D. (2002). *The creation of psychopharmacology.*

Heninger, G. R., Delgado, P. L., & Charney, D. S. (1996). The revised monoamine theory of depression: a modulatory role for monoamines, based on new findings from monoamine depletion experiments in humans. *Pharmacopsychiatry, 29*(01), 2–11.

Hess, J. Z., Gantt, E., Lacasse, J. R., & Vierling-Claassen, N. (2014). Narrating the brain: Investigating competing portrayals of the embodiment of mental disorder. *Journal of Phenomenological Psychology, 45,* 168–208

Hess, J. Z., Lacasse, J. R., Harmon, J., Williams, D., & Vierling-Claasen, N. (2014). 'Is there a getting better from this, or not?' Examining the meaning and possibility of recovery from mental disorder. *Child and Youth Services, 35*(2), 116–136.

Horgan, J. (1999). *The undiscovered mind: How the human brain defies replication, medication, and explanation.*

Hypericum Depression Trial Study Group. (2002). Effect of Hypericum perforatum (St John's wort) in major depressive disorder: a randomized controlled trial. *Jama, 287*(14), 1807–1814.

Johnston, O., Kumar, S., Kendall, K., Peveler, R., Gabbay, J., & Kendrick, T. (2007). Qualitative study of depression management in primary care: GP and patient goals, and the value of listening. *British Journal of General Practice, 57*(544), e1–e14.

Kasper, S., & Olie, J. P. (2002). A meta-analysis of randomized controlled trials of tianeptine versus SSRI in the short-term treatment of depression. *European Psychiatry, 17,* 331–340.

Kemp, J. J., Lickel, J. J., & Deacon, B. J. (2014). Effects of a chemical imbalance causal explanation on individuals' perception of their depressive symptoms. *Behaviour Research and Therapy.* doi: 10.106/j.brat.2014.02.009

Kirk, S. A., Gomory, T., & Cohen, D. (2013). *Mad science: Psychiatric coercion, diagnosis, and drugs.* New Brunswick, NJ: Transaction.

Kirsch, I., Deacon, B. J., Huedo-Medina, T. B., Scoboria, A., Moore, T. J., & Johnson, B. T. (2008). Initial severity and antidepressant benefits: a meta-analysis of data submitted to the Food and Drug Administration. *PLoS Medicine, 5*(2), e45.

Lacasse, J. R. (2014). After DSM-5: A critical mental health research agenda for the 21st century. *Research on Social Work Practice, 24*(1), 5–10.

Lacasse, J. R. (2005). Consumer advertising of psychiatric medications biases the public against non-pharmacological treatment. *Ethical Human Psychology and Psychiatry, 7*(3), 175–179.

Lacasse, J. R., & Gomory, T. (2003). Is graduate social work education promoting a critical approach to mental health practice? *Journal of Social Work Education, 39*(3), 383–408.

Lacasse, J. R, & Leo, J. (2005). Serotonin and depression: A disconnect between the advertisements and the scientific literature. *PLoS Medicine, 2*(12), 101–106.

Lacasse, J. R., & Leo, J. (2006). Questionable advertising of psychotropic medications and disease mongering. *PLoS Medicine, 3*(7), 1192.

Leo, J., & Lacasse, J. R. (2008). The media and the chemical imbalance theory of depression. *Society, 45*, 35–45.

Mendels, J., Stinnett, J. L., Burns, D., & Frazer, A. (1975). Amine precursors and depression. *Archives of general psychiatry, 32*(1), 22–30.

Murphy, D. L., Andrews, A. M., Wichems, C. H., Li, Q., Tohda, M., & Greenberg, B. (1998). Brain serotonin neurotransmission: An overview and update with an emphasis on serotonin subsystem heterogeneity, multiple receptors, interactions with other neurotransmitter systems, and consequent implications for understanding the actions of serotonergic drugs. *Journal of Clinical Psychiatry.*

National Association of Social Workers (2008). *Code of Ethics.*

Pies, R. W. (2011). Psychiatry's new brain-mind and the legend of the "chemical imbalance." *Psychiatric Times.*

Roggenbach, J., Müller-Oerlinghausen, B., & Franke, L. (2002). Suicidality, impulsivity and aggression—is there a link to 5HIAA concentration in the cerebrospinal fluid? *Psychiatry research, 113*(1), 193–206.

Schildkraut, J. J. (1965). The catecholamine hypothesis of affective disorders: a review of supporting evidence. *American Journal of Psychiatry, 122*(5), 509–522.

Szegedi, A., Kohnen, R., Dienel, A., & Kieser, M. (2005). Acute treatment of moderate to severe depression with hypericum extract WS 5570 (St John's wort): randomised controlled double blind non-inferiority trial versus paroxetine. *Bmj, 330*(7490), 503.

Shorter, E. (2008). *Before Prozac: the trouble history of mood disorders in psychiatry.*

Valenstein, E. S. (1998). *Blaming the brain: The truth about drugs and mental health.*

Whitaker, R. (2010). *Anatomy of an epidemic.* New York: Random House.

Appendix D: Results of a Survey: MSW Students' Views About Mental Disorder

Barbara Probst, Catherine Balletto and Nichole Wofford

In order to understand how social work students think tend to about mental disorder, a survey was conducted of MSW students (N = 388) at three campuses in the northeastern United States. Demographically (gender, age, race, ethnicity), the sample resembled the population of MSW students across the USA, using figures from CSWE's 2010 survey of 197 master's-level programs as an indication of MSW students nationwide.

Students were asked to respond to two questions: What is a mental disorder, and how can a clinician know if someone has one? These questions corresponded to the two questions posed at the beginning of Chap. 1 of this book. Inquiry was open-ended, allowing participants to write as much or as little as they wished. A three-person team coded the responses through an iterative inductive process; codes were identified directly from the data, rather than developed in advance and deductively applied. Since most responses incorporated elements from several codes, different codes could be assigned to different portions of a person's response. The unit of analysis was the code, not the person; frequencies reported below are non-exclusive.

What is a mental disorder? Responses to this question pointed to five distinct models or mental schemas, each reflecting a different way of arriving at a definition, as well as a sixth residual category for those who felt that mental disorder was too complex, varied, and subjective to be defined. Disorder was defined by its consequence, by its cause, by society, by the disordered person him/herself, or by reference to official criteria (see Table 14.1).

Impaired external functioning The most frequent response was to equate mental disorder with impairment or disruption in the ability to function in daily life. This might represent a loss of capacity relative to the person's prior level of functioning, or behavior outside the "normal" range in frequency, duration, and/or severity. In this schema, disorder is defined by what a person *does* (or does not do).

Impaired internal functioning Next in frequency were definitions based on distorted or disrupted internal functioning—cognitions, responses, and perceptions that are not reality-based or are outside the "normal" range in nature, severity, or persistence. Here, disorder is defined by how a person *perceives*.

Subjective distress at the inability to thrive Notions of disorder as the subjective experience of distress and suffering—how a person *feels*—were less frequent. Emotional suffering was not, for student respondents, a necessary or sufficient hallmark of mental disorder. Rather, they saw mental disorder as leading to a particular kind of suffering: the pain of being unable to live the life one aspires to, a sense of limited autonomy or efficacy, the gap between the desired and the possible.

Table 14.1 Student schemas: What is a mental disorder?

Schema	Number of references in the data (non-exclusive)
Schema #1: Breakdown: disruption, malfunction in brain or psyche (defined by its cause)	
1-A. Deficient nurturing/development	5
1-B. Environmental stress/trauma beyond ability to cope	22
1-C. Neurobiological abnormality or deficiency	66
Schema #2: Impaired functioning (defined by its consequences)	
2-A. In cognitions/perceptions and/or emotions/responses	93
2-B. In behavior/daily life	139
2-C. In interpersonal relationships	41
Schema #3: Social construction: deviance from social norms (defined by society)	72
Schema #4: Subjective experience: internal distress, suffering (defined by self)	47
Schema #5: Meeting formal criteria (defined by accepted classification systems)	40
Schema #6: Beyond definition, too complex and varied (cannot be defined)	26

In these responses, disorder is defined by its consequences: abnormal behavior and verbal statements are *signs* that disorder is present. We know something's existence because we can observe it, if not directly, then through its manifestation; in the case of mental disorder, observation is indirect since internal states cannot be observed.

Neurological abnormality/chemical imbalance Other definitions were based on cause, rather than consequence: the nature of mental disorder lies in its origin. Most of those who defined disorder by its source offered a genetic, neuroanatomical, or neurochemical explanation. To them, mental disorder is a neurochemical abnormality, a "chemical imbalance in the brain," resulting in a "neurological malfunction." This "deviation from the normal structure of the brain" leads to an abnormal way of processing impressions, which in turn leads to deviant behavior; thus, it is not the behavior, but its origin in the brain that constitutes the disorder.

Social construction The third most frequent response was that mental disorder is a socially constructed notion, either as its primary definition or as an element to be included in a contextual understanding of the experience of being "different." Mental disorder, from this perspective, is little more than a "social construction that pathologizes a set of psychological experiences and behavior due to their deviation from perceived norms."

Fulfillment of official criteria Many respondents also noted that a mental disorder is a condition that meets DSM criteria.

How can a clinician know if someone has a mental disorder? Responses to this question, reflecting forms of evidence, included five schemas plus a default category (when all else is ruled out) and a residual category for those who felt there was no way to really know (see Table 14.2).

Language as evidence The presence of disorder can be established through conversation, formal and informal, to gather information about past and present experience. The reports of others can also help a clinician to know whether a client, who may not be seen as a reliable source of information, is manifesting in ways that indicate disorder.

Observation as evidence The clinician can also observe the way a person acts and responds: behavior, mannerisms, speech patterns, body language, appearance, demeanor, affect. Here, both verbal and nonverbal information is considered.

Expert knowledge as evidence Another way to decide whether disorder is present is by referring to official manuals and standards (like the DSM) to see whether symptoms match established criteria. Tests and psychometric instruments can also be used. A number of students also noted the importance of conferring with other professionals. Interdisciplinary collaboration, consultation with psychiatrists or

Table 14.2 Student schemas: How can a clinician know if mental disorder is present?

Schema	Number of references in the data (non-exclusive)
Schema #1: By talking (language as evidence)	
1-A. Formally: collecting information	51
1-B. Informally: getting to know client over time	50
1-C. Client disclosure, self-identification	45
1-D. Collaterally: speaking with family, friends	19
Schema #2: By observing (behavior as evidence)	
2-A. Client's actions: behavior/responses outside normal range	85
2-B. Client's affect: evidence of distress	61
Schema #3: By matching to DSM criteria (standards as evidence)	76
Schema #4: By forms of expert knowledge (authority as evidence)	
4-A. Testing: standardized scales, instruments	39
4-B. Conferring with experts/official records	11
4-C. Using practice wisdom	10
Schema #5: By bio-psycho-social assessment/ generic	72
Schema #6: By ruling out other causes	13
Schema #7: Unknowable (too complex, variable, subjective)	48

therapists who had treated the client in the past, and review of official records or treatment history were seen as ways to enhance one's own observations.

Interestingly, practice wisdom—the clinician's professional training and experience, "using your clinical eye"—was not a common response. There were only 10 references to clinician expertise (2.5 % of those surveyed), although a number of students mentioned "skillful interviewing." Perhaps this is because, as students and novice clinicians, these respondents had not yet come to understand how clinical knowledge grows with experience.

Generic assessment Generic bio-psycho-social assessment/evaluation combined with observation was the chief means cited for deciding if a disorder is present. Interestingly, impaired functioning was not selected as a means for *ascertaining* the presence of disorder nearly as often it was selected as a primary way of *defining* mental disorder. This is an odd discrepancy. If impaired functioning is a hallmark of disorder, it would seem reasonable that observation of that impairment would be a way to know whether disorder was present. But that is not reflected in students' responses.

The second question, unlike the first, revealed clear differences among the campuses. For students at campus A, a residential program drawing students from all over the country, the most frequent response was that one *cannot* actually "know" if someone else is mentally disordered. One-third of these students expressed this idea; for 60 %, this was the *only* point they made. The notion of mental disorder, for them, is variable, complex, fluid, approximate, intangible, subject to bias and personal interpretation. A clinician might make an informed "guess" based on patterns, hunches, speculation, and culturally constructed categories, but only the individual in question can truly know his or her own lived experience. "Nothing is a disorder until someone defines it" because "disorders are made, not found" based on the "mental health community's collective definition of disorder." Those with power and privilege "agree that certain behaviors constitute disorder," even though "we all probably have some degree of disorder." At best, the labels are approximate; at worst, they are a form of social control.

In contrast, students at the other two campuses—non-residential programs in urban settings—were far less likely to say, "you can't really know." Less than 4 % expressed the idea, with none stating this as the sole response, although several noted that disorder is "not always obvious" or "can go unrecognized" because individuals may "hide their symptoms" or "not see their experience as abnormal because it is normal for them."

If the clinician cannot truly "know" the presence of mental disorder in another person, who can? Who is a reliable source of knowledge? Many students noted the importance of a client's self-report or self-disclosure, although not many cited this as the sole means of knowing. Most included observation of the person's actions by the clinician or by family and friends to corroborate verbal statements, and/or the clinician's interpretation of a client's words. Overall, students at campus A were more likely to mention client self-report, with 27 % citing this as a key source of knowledge. In contrast, less than 5 % of the students at campus B did so. At the same time, since responses were open-ended, there is no way to know whether *any* student would have endorsed additional ideas, had they been offered as pre-determined "select all that apply" options. All that can be known is what they chose to write.

Note. These views of mental disorder do not include all possible views that people might hold, only those that appear to be held by MSW students prior to formal instruction in assessment and diagnosis. Other people might define mental disorder as spirit possession or spiritual imbalance, punishment for past sins, weakness of character, the result of toxins or diet, and so on. The purpose of this survey was not to provide a map of all possible beliefs but, rather, to offer a portrait of the beliefs of social work students before instruction in clinical assessment.

Although students were not asked *why* or *how* they came to the beliefs they chose to articulate, several factors may have contributed to their views. As noted above, evidence indicates that students choosing careers in social work are likely to have had personal exposure to mental disorder, an experience that can leave a powerful impression of mental illness as dysfunctional behavior. In addition, graduate students may have encountered people with mental disorders in their prior work experience, since master's degree students are often returning to school after a period of time in the work force or attending school while working. Past observations of ill people and how they act—or past experience with agency, clinic or hospital protocols—may call to mind the idea of disorder as impaired behavior. The emphasis on behavior may also relate to the dominant model in current clinical practice of problem definition, treatment goals, and evaluation organized around measurement of behavioral change.

This summary is based on an article in the Clinical Social Work Journal of the same name. (DOI: 10.1007/s10615-015-0517-6)

Appendix E: Special Issues in the Assessment of Children and Families

Barbara Probst

In addition to the concerns and caveats noted throughout this book, there are special challenges when assessing children, beginning with the whole question of entrance into the assessment process. Children are rarely voluntary clients, and it is often the adults who have decided that something is "wrong." Even when children are able to put their experience into words, assessment still tends to rely heavily on the report of adults such as parents and teachers, whose judgment about impaired functioning and internal distress—the two hallmarks of disorder—is indirect and inevitably filtered through their own expectations and preferences. This does not mean that their observations and conclusions have no value, but they constitute only one form of evidence. The child's self-report—verbal, or obtained through nonverbal channels such as art, doll, or puppet play—should be accorded equal significance.

There are developmental considerations in the assessment of children, who are still growing and changing. For most disorders, the DSM does not distinguish between developmental stages, even though distress manifests quite differently in 5-year-olds, 10-year-olds, and 15-year-olds. In many cases, diagnostic criteria developed for adults are applied to children, which can be misleading since children may express internal experience differently than adults do and thus their symptoms can be quite different from those of adults. For instance, a child who is depressed may act irritable, defiant, and angry rather than sad.

In addition, children's symptoms are more likely to be context-dependent than the symptoms of adults, who have more choice and control over the environments they find themselves in and can alter or self-select environments that offer a better fit. Children thus need to be assessed in different settings, at different times, and by different people. An assessment conducted in a clinician's office, or by someone who does not know the child well, may not provide an accurate picture. Clinicians also vary in the way they approach the assessment of children and may be constrained by the agenda of the host setting, such as a school, in which the assessment takes place. Indeed, there are numerous sources of error in children's diagnoses: from the person making the diagnosis (lack of training, bias, selective attention, pressure from the expectations of others) to the conditions under which the diagnosis is made (artificial, limited, intimidating) to the ambiguity of the diagnostic criteria themselves.

As Kirk and others have noted, the vagueness and inconsistency of many DSM criteria tend to be especially pronounced in children's diagnoses. Words such as "often" or "frequently" abound in the criteria for behavioral disorders such as ADHD and oppositional defiant disorder (ODD), but are not defined. ADHD is diagnosed when a child *often* has trouble paying attention or following through on tasks, *often* fidgets and squirms, loses or forgets things, blurts out responses, interrupts, has trouble waiting his or her turn and avoids schoolwork. ODD is diagnosed when a child *often* argues with adults, refuses to comply with adults' rules or requests, blames others for his or her mistakes or misbehavior, and is touchy, angry, resentful, or spiteful. But how often is "often," and who decides that the behavior occurs *too often* to be "normal?"

Disruptive mood dysregulation disorder, a new diagnosis in DSM-5, is characterized by severe temper outbursts "that are grossly out of proportion in intensity or duration to the situation or provocation"—as determined by the adults, of course, who have decided that the initial disappointment, frustration, or provocation did not warrant the child's reaction. There are, however, no objective standards for a deciding whether a reaction is "out of proportion" or "in proportion." Nor is there consideration for the role of temperament–environment fit, a significant factor for children who tend to have little control over their environment and may be struggling—perhaps unskillfully—to handle environments that are too inconsistent, rigid, over- or under-stimulating for their natures. There is also wide variation in both the number and percentage of symptoms needed to meet diagnostic thresholds. To be diagnosed with conduct disorder, for example, the child must have met at least three of the 15 criteria over the past 12 months and one criterion over the past 6 months; that is, only 20 % of the criteria need to be met, half the requirement for a diagnosis of panic disorder.

Many social workers include a family assessment in order to understand the context of a child's problems and how they affect, or result from, relational dynamics among other members of the family. Family assessment can also be useful for adults who report difficulty in relationships with partners, siblings, or parents. It can be utilized at any point, even if the focus of work is primarily on the individual.

There are three major avenues for assessing a family. One is through written instruments such as the Family Systems Stressor-Strength Inventory or The McMaster Family Assessment Device (FAD). The FAD, based on the McMaster Model of Family Functioning, is a validated set of six scales that assess structural, organizational, and transactional characteristics of families by measuring dimensions of affective involvement, affective responsiveness, behavioral control, communication, problem solving, and roles, as well as a seventh scale for general family functioning (http://www.nctsnet.org/content/family-assessment-device).

Other assessment tools include pictorial representations such as genograms, ecomaps, social network maps, and family portraits or timelines that depict how the family sees itself. These can be useful for revealing patterns of communication, roles, and alliances, as well as the impact on different people of significant events in the family's history. In addition, the clinician can observe how the family interacts when they are together: who speaks and who is silent; who dominates, interrupts, speaks for someone else, complains, criticizes, or tries to defuse conflict; who is the scapegoat, clown, peacekeeper, outsider; how family members arrange themselves in the space of the room. Known as enactments, these may be spontaneous representations or snapshots of how the family typically behaves, or intentional scenarios set up by the clinician to reveal patterns of interaction under conditions that simulate or exaggerate real life. Depending on the clinician's theoretical orientation, the focus may be on roles, alliances, boundaries, triangles (when conflict between two family members is detoured through a third person), or intergenerational patterns.

Appendix F: Sample Assignments and Exercises for Students

Fordham University, Graduate School of Social Service

Case Analysis from Multiple Perspectives—**Barbara Probst**

Purpose To provide an opportunity to explore assessment from multiple points of view.

Choose a client, preferably from your current field placement, but if that is problematic, you may select someone you work(ed) with in another context. If you cannot identify someone suitable, please see me and we will find a case for you to use.

Organize your paper into three sections, plus a reference list.

1. Provide a concise bio-psycho-social assessment, including *only* the salient information about relevant history, strengths, and stresses. What is the problem, from the client's perspective? What is your assessment of the problem? Are there discrepancies between the two perspectives? If so, why do you think that is?

2. Assuming that you need to give this person a DSM diagnosis for agency or insurance purposes, *select two* plausible diagnoses that might be appropriate and make a case *for* each. Then provide an argument *against* each (why you might not want to choose that diagnosis). Be sure to refer specifically to DSM criteria and to what you know about your client: how do facts about the client match up with specific DSM criteria?

3. Think about another perspective that might shed light on this person's struggles, suffering, and behavior. For example:

   - *Cultural* and/or *spiritual perspective* including cultural factors such as values/value clashes, models of illness and wellness, the impact of immigration
   - *Ecological perspective*: the impact of poverty, class, economic stressors, and/or other elements in both the immediate and macro-environment
   - *Family theory*: influences from the lens of family systems theory, family dynamics, and/or family life stages
   - *Psychodynamic perspective*: ego defenses, attachment/object relations, developmental transitions, or arrests

Select *one* such perspective, other than the psychiatric lens of the DSM, and use it to unpack and understand this person's experience. What is gained by using this lens? What does it add to your understanding, beyond what DSM criteria offer?

Please *reference* at least *four* course readings *in addition to* DSM-5 criteria to support your ideas and analysis.

Case Analysis in Successive Layers—Brian Rasmussen

Purpose The aim of these three sequential assignments is to analyze, synthesize, and integrate theory with problems faced in clinical practice. The challenge is to remain at a "high" theoretical level while grounding your ideas in real-life practice problems.

Task #1: Descriptive Case Study

The case study is a *descriptive* account of an individual, family, or group that has presented for help. It requires **no** theoretical analysis at this point.

The case should be no longer than *3 pages*, double-spaced, and should include basic information about the presenting problem(s), history of presenting problem(s), relevant personal and contextual information. Ideally, the case should be complex (but not bizarre), and representative of work with this client population.

Task #2: Case Analysis Using Relational/Psychodynamic Theory

Explore the ways in which relational/psychodynamic theory contributes to an understanding of the client(s) presenting problem(s). This analysis does not prescribe a single theoretical approach, but rather asks that the student considers the theories presented in the text and other assigned readings to suggest ways in which these theories inform an understanding with respect to the case study. Please attach the case study from Task #1 as an appendix.

Task #3: Case Analysis Integrating Dynamics of Race, Class, Gender, and Other Forms of Oppression

Explore the ways in which your understanding of the dynamics of oppression inform the case study, including analysis of social factors that contribute to the conditions as presented and ways these conditions might be operating on the client. This analysis should be *integrated* into the psychodynamic analysis from the previous assignment. In this sense, the previous submission is reworked to include an integrated perspective of these two broad theoretical frameworks. Outline the practice implications of such an analysis.

Questions to ask from a psychodynamic/relational perspective (Task 2):

1. Is there evidence of recent or past trauma?
2. Are there lasting effects of trauma? What are these effects?
3. Is the client able to regulate their internal world, especially affect and impulses?
4. What psychological symptoms do the client experience?

5. Are there symptoms of anxiety and/or depression? How do you understand the origin of these symptoms?
6. Does the client experience psychological conflict? What are these conflicts?
7. In what ways might the client's early life and early relationships effect current functioning.
8. How does the client think about themselves and others? Are they trusting of others?
9. Describe the client's self-esteem.
10. Does the client hold faulty beliefs about themselves and others?
11. Is the client psychologically minded and reflective?
12. What is the quality of the client's attachments? Are there dysfunctional patterns to their relational functioning?
13. How does the client relate to helping professionals?
14. How supportive is the client's social environment?
15. What are the client's strengths?

Questions to ask from a social theory perspective (Task 3):

1. What appear to be the client's core values? Where do these values originate?
2. What ideas or ideology has the client bought into that may be related to their problems or symptoms? Are there external forms of ideology that oppress them?
3. To what extent is the client free to choose his/her own course of action?
4. To what extent are basic economic needs preoccupying the client?
5. What class does the client belong to? How does membership in this class impact their well-being?
6. In what way, to what extent, and how, is the client experiencing oppression? And social exclusion?
7. How does the client respond to this oppression?
8. What meaning does the client make of their symptoms and/or life problems?
9. How does power factor into your case analysis? Who has power in this story?
10. What discourses does the public hold about these client problems?
11. What stigma is attached to these problems?
12. How does gender play a role in these problems?
13. How does race play a role in these problems?
14. To what extent is oppression internalized by the client?
15. To what extent do social factors contribute to the client's problems?

Case Formulation: Considering and Reconsidering—Claudia Arlo

Consider This Case

Francisco is a 50-year-old engineer, married, living with his wife and three teenage children. He reports that he has been "over-productive" for the past three weeks, sleeping two or three hours per night, feeling very energized by his great plan to start a revolutionary new business in Asia. His reason for coming in for a consultation is that his wife is jealous of his talent and does not believe in the business plan he is preparing which will require that they invest their life savings and children's college funds. This is causing him great distress. In addition, he has been acting out sexually with a neighbor, and his wife is suspicious. He states, "I've never done this sort of thing before but I can't stop myself." His speech is rapid and pressured, and he is sweating profusely. "My mind is going faster than I can speak," he says.

Assessment

What do you know about Francisco and his situation? State the factual information you have.

Based on what you know, what preliminary diagnosis would you give Francisco?

- How did you arrive at that diagnosis?
- Which DSM-5 criteria do Francisco meet?

What information are you lacking?

- What additional information might cause you to change your initial diagnosis?
- What would you change it to, and why?
- What might cause you to rule out your initial diagnosis?

Now think about sources of information.

- Where or from whom might you get the information you are lacking?
- What is the primary source(s) of information in the vignette? What do you think of those source(s) of information?
- What contradictory evidence might prompt you to reconsider your initial diagnosis?

Different Opinions, Different Reasons—Jeffrey Karaban

Purpose To provide a safe, open context for debate about issues that impact diagnosis, including beliefs and opinions other than one's own.

Instructor preparation Develop 10 or 12 controversial statements that reflect attitudes, biases, and beliefs about people with various diagnoses and how those disorders arose or should be managed, for example, "Women living with bipolar disorder should avoid pregnancy." Next to each statement, place 5 boxes for Agree Strongly to Disagree Strongly. Prepare and place signs on the walls around the room that correspond to the five rating categories.

The exercise Give each student a copy and ask them to place an x in the boxes that best match their level of agreement with each statement. This is done anonymously.

Collect, shuffle, and redistribute the sheets so each person gets one. Then, read each statement aloud and have everyone move to the sign that corresponds to the level of agreement on their sheet. In this way, they can graphically see the distribution of answers without having to disclose their own. Then, each group defends the level they selected, for example, the group defends their choice of "Disagree Strongly" to the statement "The sky is blue."

Follow-up debriefing can offer students an opportunity discuss their feelings of surprise at the answer arrays or their experience as a member of a minority answer group.

Understanding How Theory Shapes Assessment—Meredith Hanson

Purpose To help students make their worldviews or master narratives explicit (transparent) so that they can critically appraise them, see how they influence our practice and see what type of "evidence" supports them. This is a multi-step process, spanning several class sessions.

Introductory class discussion I introduce the idea that we all have worldviews (master narratives) that are generally implicit and taken-for-granted. These worldviews or perspectives include our values, knowledge structures, experiences. This opens up a discussion of practice theories (formal knowledge structures) and other factors that clinicians "bring into" the clinical encounter that shape their work.

Ungraded mini-assignment This is a 3–5 page assignment (due class 3) in which students select an "assessment" interview from their field placement and identify the practice theories, perspectives, knowledge sources, and values that informed the assessment. They do this in retrospect, identifying the strengths and limitations of their orientation to practice. ("Knowing what you know now, what do you think influenced your decision making?")

(While one's perspective may help to focus and understand what's going on, it may also minimize other factors that affect what is going on and which may help us to understand more fully. All perspectives give us partial and incomplete understanding. As professionals, we must be aware of this and try to maximize our understanding as much as possible.)

Follow-up reading I assign a 1990 paper by Karasu [see reference below] to help students see how practice theories shape the assessment and intervention process. While the paper is dated, it provides a useful comparison of how three theories/models approach depression (psychoanalytic, interpersonal, cognitive).

Analysis of sample case in teams To the discussion of clinical theories, we introduce the idea of what the client brings into the clinical encounter, and how clinical and community settings shape our work and expectations. I bring a case that anchors the discussion. This is a case involving an older man who has a drinking problem but is seeking help for physical health problems that may be secondary to the drinking; the case includes community elements, family history. Each instructor can bring a case, as desired.[1]

I break students into groups, each group approaching the case using a different practice theory. They compare and contrast the influence of the different theories on their decision making. (Typically, different groups come up with different action strategies, which we discuss. Students see how different theories highlight and downplay different factors in our understanding.) This also helps students to define what theories are and what functions they serve, and to understand the difference between practice theories and practice models.

Mental Disorder in the Media—Barbara Probst

Purpose To increase awareness of how mental disorder is depicted in the media and how this depiction affects public perception

Select one of these films:

- *I Never Promised You a Rose Garden* (1977)
- *Girl, Interrupted* (1999)
- *Boys Don't Cry* (1999)
- *Don Juan de Marco* (1995)
- *Away From Her* (2007)
- *The Three Faces of Eve* (1957)

Reflect on the film in light of each of these issues. Each reflection should make reference to specific scenes in the film, as well as to DSM-5 criteria for the disorder depicted.

1. What model of mental illness underlies the portrayal in this film? Is it obvious or tacit? What evidence did you use to come to this conclusion?
2. How does socioeconomic context effect the development and trajectory of the disorder? How would the main character's story be different if he/she were a

---

[1]Karasu, T. B. (1990) Toward a clinical model of psychotherapy for depression: Systematic comparison of three psychotherapies. *The American Journal of Psychiatry, 147*(2), 133–147.

member of a different demographic group—e.g., a different gender, race, or social class?

3. How did family dynamics and family issues contribute to the story? Do you think the role of family was underplayed, overplayed, or fairly accurate?
4. What do you think about the treatment offered? Did it seem realistic?
5. What messages do you think viewers might take away about people struggling with this condition? What are some positive aspects, and some negative aspects, of the messages conveyed by the film? Consider both explicit and implicit messages.

Reflective Exercise—Keith Cunniffe

Purpose To increase awareness and skill in assessing, identifying, and addressing the unique developmental and diagnostic issues of childhood and adolescence.

Goals:

- To increase skill at identifying developmental concerns of youth and their relevance to clinical assessment and diagnosis.
- To identify symptoms and behavioral indicators that may be important assessment and diagnostic data.
- To practice gathering complex clinical data and formulating this data into a coherent clinical summary.
- To effectively ascertain psychosocial/environmental stressors and how they affect youth in diverse ways.
- To integrate psychosocial history, current functioning, and the mental status exam into a cogent assessment of youth well-being and illness.

Method We will view the film, *Tangled* (Walt Disney Pictures 2010). We will then have a class discussion using the questions below to guide our discussion. Please note that these questions are only a guide; additional questions are encouraged.

Questions to Reflect on:

- What kinds of developmental challenges or barrier is Rapunzel confronted with?
- What might the variety of assessment perspectives say about Rapunzel's psychosocial functioning and coping skills?
- How does Rapunzel's situation impact her family and loved ones?
- What themes or motifs run through the lives of the film's characters that might be important for clinical assessment?
- What relevant clinical data does Rapunzel's relationships with the other characters give us?

- What are some diagnostic categories that might be relevant to Rapunzel and some of the other characters?
- How does Rapunzel's relationship with her stepmother affect her psychosocial development and functioning?
- If you met Rapunzel and were doing an assessment, what kinds of questions would you ask her?
- What aspects of this film are reflected in some of the work you are doing in your internships or in some of the work we have done in class?

Appendix G: Sample Syllabus Using This Book as a Course Text

Below is an outline for a 15-week (single semester) syllabus using this book as a primary course text. Each week includes a chapter from the book focusing on a specific conceptual lens; additional readings taken from the reference list at the end of the chapter; and material on a DSM disorder to be used as an illustration of how the conceptual lens could be applied. Chapter 12 and Appendix E, written for instructors, are not included in this prototype.

Note: The pairings suggested below could easily be rearranged or other disorders could be used instead (e.g., autism, Alzheimer's disorder, gender dysphoria). For a two-semester course, additional DSM categories not covered below (neurodevelopmental disorders such as autism; schizophrenia and psychotic disorders; sexual dysfunction and paraphilic disorders; neurocognitive disorders including Alzheimer's and dementia) could be integrated into longer units. But the point is the same: there is no inherent reason why social work courses on clinical assessment and diagnosis need to be organized by DSM disorders. This syllabus offers an alternative.

Clinical Assessment and Diagnosis Course Syllabus

Organized by Conceptual Lenses

Week 1: Introduction to the course
Overview; introduction to the Case of Ray (Appendix A)
"Many ways of knowing," expectations, and course requirements

Week 2: Thinking about thinking: Epistemological issues in diagnosis and assessment
Chapter 2; Appendix D
Other readings about cognitive heuristics and labeling theory
Illustration: Obsessive-compulsive disorder

Week 3: Using the DSM: The DSM, critiques, and alternatives
Chapter 3; Appendix B; DSM Desk reference and overview
Other readings about validity, reliability, and classification
Illustration: ADHD, impulse control, and conduct disorders

Week 4: Making assessment decisions: Macro-, mezzo, and micro-perspectives
Chapter 4
Other readings about clinical decision making
Illustration: Bipolar disorder

Week 5: Situating disorder: Mental disorder in context
Chapter 5
Other readings about culture, bias, social context, and relationship disorders
Illustration: PTSD, trauma and stress-related disorders

Week 6: Neuroscience, resilience, and the embodiment of "mental" disorder
Chapter 6
Other readings about neuroplasticity, adaptation, coping, mindfulness, and resilience
Illustration: Anxiety disorders

Week 7: The role of temperament in conceptualizations of mental disorder
Chapter 7
Other readings about temperament
Illustration: Personality disorders

Week 8: A psychodynamic perspective on assessment and diagnosis
Chapter 8
Other readings about psychodynamic case formulation, defenses, and ego psychology
Illustration: Attachment and mood disorders in children

Week 9: Narratives of illness, difference, and personhood
Chapter 9
Other readings about narrative theory, recovery, and strength-based assessment
Illustration: Dissociative disorders

Week 10: Person-centered integrative diagnosis
Chapter 10
Other readings about person-centered models and holistic assessment
Illustration: Eating disorders

Week 11: Challenging the narrative of chemical imbalance
Appendix C; source material on psychopharmacology
Other readings on social work and medication
Illustration: Depressive disorders

Week 12: Integrating practice and research on mental disorder
Chapter 11
Other readings about pragmatism and practice wisdom
Illustration: Somatic symptom disorders

Week 13: Assessment and diagnosis in a social justice perspective
Chapter 12
Other readings about bio-psycho-social-spiritual assessment
Illustration: Substance use and addictive disorders

Week 14: Application
Student presentations: in pairs or small teams, students apply one of the perspectives to another case of their choice

Week 15: Final exam/evaluation; course review

Index

A
Adaptability, 140, 143, 209
ADHD, 17, 20, 27, 37, 142, 147, 252, 253, 279, 280
Afrocentric, 87
Analogue studies, 98
Anchoring, 28, 42, 89
Anxiety, 5, 16, 22, 35, 52, 56, 99, 117, 147, 157, 180, 252, 281
Astro-turfing, 74, 75
Attachment, 104, 105, 142, 153, 154, 158, 161, 166, 176

B
Big pharma, 74
Biomarkers, 21, 263
Biomedical industrial complex, 75, 77, 80
Bio-psycho-social assessment, 86, 244, 256, 290
Bio-reductionism, 256
Bipolar disorder, 28, 37, 41, 62, 63, 81, 82, 88, 125, 166, 270
Brain, 17–20, 35, 49, 50, 62, 74, 88, 113, 118, 119, 122, 123, 137, 142, 231, 256, 273, 275, 277, 280

C
Category, 3, 7, 9, 24, 27, 36, 37, 88, 248, 254, 285
Categorical models, 9
Causality, 19, 71, 87, 256
Children, 5, 18, 30, 59, 75, 88, 101, 104, 107, 122, 135–137, 139, 141, 142, 144, 262, 268, 280, 288, 289
Chronicity, 90
Circular reasoning, 20, 51, 61
Class, 22, 36, 95, 101, 152, 162, 167, 233, 235, 239, 241–243

Classification, 3, 26, 36, 37, 39, 71, 103, 124, 195, 261
Cognitive apprenticeship, 231–236, 243
Cognitive distortions, 119, 126, 159, 166
Collaboration, 192, 231, 243, 285
Co-morbidity, 252, 264
Comprehensive, 7, 11, 55
Confirmation bias, 28, 42
Constructional, 72
Constructivist, 172, 174, 176
Content knowledge and process knowledge, 232, 233
Continuum, 24, 37, 225, 261, 274
Correlation, 17, 262
Cortex, 118
Crazy checks, 75
Criteria, 3, 5, 9, 12, 20, 22, 26, 28, 36, 37, 40, 50, 55, 56, 63, 64, 70, 71, 81, 89, 93, 95, 99, 100, 102, 105, 147, 175, 207, 211, 216, 219, 220, 224, 239, 252, 255, 258, 272, 273, 284, 288, 290, 295
Culture, 3, 5, 10, 22, 86, 89, 94–97, 112, 136, 146, 176–179, 181, 251, 265

D
Defenses, 25, 106, 152, 153, 156, 157, 161, 165, 232, 248
Denialism, 20, 53, 62, 253
Depression, 5, 17, 21, 23, 26, 35, 38, 41, 52, 53, 64, 70, 74, 82, 101, 140, 164, 165, 167, 252, 255, 256, 275–278, 280
Deviance, 33, 35, 36, 47, 94
Diagnostic, 2–4, 8, 20, 24, 27–29, 31, 32, 36, 41, 46, 53, 58, 63, 86, 88, 89, 93, 95, 97, 99, 101, 104, 158, 166, 190, 192, 194, 198, 240, 288
Diathesis-stress theory, 260
Dimensional models, 9, 24

© Springer International Publishing Switzerland 2015
B. Probst (ed.), *Critical Thinking in Clinical Assessment and Diagnosis*,
Essential Clinical Social Work Series, DOI 10.1007/978-3-319-17774-8

Dimensions, 7, 9, 12, 58, 103, 104, 134, 140,
    144, 147, 153, 162, 172, 178, 190, 195,
    199, 241, 289
Disability, 19, 35, 47, 60, 75, 107, 253
Disease, 1, 7, 17, 23, 48–50, 52, 54–56, 60, 64,
    71, 75, 86, 89, 118, 191, 192, 194, 256,
    272, 275, 280
Disorder, 3–6, 11, 15–20, 23–25, 27, 29, 31,
    33, 35, 36, 38, 40, 46–54, 56, 58,
    62–65, 77, 82, 86, 88, 89, 93, 94,
    99–103, 105, 106, 112, 116, 119, 120,
    124, 134, 142, 156, 160, 163, 166, 180,
    193, 194, 207, 243, 253, 258, 260, 263,
    264, 272, 275, 277–279, 283, 284, 286,
    288, 289, 298
Distress, 4, 9, 16, 18, 23–25, 34–36, 47, 80, 87,
    94, 97, 101, 114, 116, 118, 123–125,
    135, 136, 143, 147, 166, 179, 184, 197,
    211, 256, 260, 268, 280, 288, 293
Divergent thinking, 243
Domains, 47, 72, 152, 177, 194, 219, 237, 256,
    259, 272
DSM, 3–6, 8, 10, 11, 21, 23, 24, 26, 31, 37, 38,
    40, 41, 46, 47, 50, 53, 60, 61, 63, 75,
    78, 88, 93, 95, 102, 119, 163, 244,
    249–251, 254, 259, 261, 263, 265, 278,
    288
Dysfunction, 4, 7, 17–19, 35, 36, 38, 47, 48,
    50, 93, 94, 103, 115, 119, 136, 138,
    142, 194, 252, 259, 264, 277, 298
Dysphoria, 298

E
Ecological, 29, 86, 90, 93, 107, 115, 254, 290
Effortful control, 134–138, 142, 234, 261
Ego strengths, 152, 233, 255
Emotions, 52, 113, 114, 116–118, 121, 122,
    124, 127, 134, 136, 137, 145, 146, 163,
    281
Empirical, 3, 5, 11, 19, 24, 29, 57, 60, 71, 99,
    103, 112, 152, 154, 209, 213, 219, 237,
    259, 273, 278
Enactments, 255, 289
Epigenetics, 25, 122, 260
Epistemology, 4, 19, 22, 40, 41, 192
Equifinality, 93
Errors, 5, 16, 21, 26, 32, 46, 51, 70–72, 88, 144
Etiology, 20, 47–50, 52, 62, 65, 104, 250, 273,
    280
Eudaimonic meaning, 124
Eurocentric, 87, 95
Evidence, 3–6, 11, 19, 21, 26, 29, 33, 40, 41,
    51, 59, 61, 64, 79–81, 99, 104, 121,
    142, 154, 158, 184, 206, 210, 214, 221,
    234, 243, 253, 261, 273, 277, 278, 285,
    288
Evidence-based, 4, 57, 70, 73, 80, 123, 212,
    230, 236, 242
Executive attention, 135–138, 142
Experiential teaching, 239

F
Family assessment, 238, 289
Family dynamics, 9, 211, 256, 296
Field trials, 78
Functional assessment of behavior, 62, 65

G
Gender, 5, 8, 22, 36, 97, 98, 100, 106,
    158, 162, 167, 181, 186, 242,
    265, 283, 298
Genetics, 18, 21, 25, 39, 262, 263
Ghostwriting, 78

H
Heuristic, 26–29, 42, 89, 261, 298

I
ICD, 3, 190, 273
Idiographic, 39, 85, 193, 259
Impairment, 24, 34, 35, 47, 48, 88, 90, 105,
    112, 161, 249, 256, 286
Inhibitory control, 137
Insurance, 3, 8, 9, 17, 31, 60, 73, 75, 76, 92,
    102, 250, 251, 264, 290
Integrative, 4, 59, 60, 112, 190–194, 196, 198,
    199, 221, 223, 241, 260
Intensity, 3, 5, 52, 57, 58, 96, 117, 121, 136,
    140, 143, 260, 289
Intentionality, 120, 176
Intersectionality, 97, 101, 182

K
Knowledge domains, 232

L
Labeling theory, 33, 212
Labels, 8, 16, 30, 33, 34, 41, 71, 98, 100, 253,
    286
Licensure, 7, 249, 254
Longitudinal, 140, 262

M
Managed care, 75, 254
Medicalization, 70
Medical model, 7, 52, 74, 75, 92, 112, 251
Medication, 8, 19, 20, 41, 52, 55, 56, 62, 63,
    76–78, 81, 207, 270, 275, 279

Mental disorder, 4, 5, 10, 16, 18–20, 24, 25,
    31, 34–36, 40, 46–48, 50, 52, 53, 55,
    61, 62, 75, 76, 81, 88, 93, 96, 103, 116,
    143, 172, 193, 240, 252, 258, 261, 265,
    273, 275, 278, 283, 284, 286, 287
Minimization, 98, 166
Modeling, 232
Motivation, 8, 9, 120, 136, 153, 154, 231, 240,
    248, 262
Multi-axial, 86, 272, 273

N

Narrative, 4, 16, 19, 25, 39, 62, 107, 124, 139,
    159, 171, 172, 174, 176–181, 183–187,
    193, 195, 197, 235, 243, 260
Neuroanatomy, 18
Neurobiology, 4, 259, 263
Neurochemistry, 19
Neuroplasticity, 17, 75, 112, 122, 123, 256,
    299
Nominal and ordinal measures, 255
Nomothetic, 32, 39, 259
Nosology, 22, 61, 124, 249

O

Observation, 6, 41, 58, 59, 86, 100, 105, 141,
    142, 255, 284, 286, 288
Over-confidence, 32, 80
Overlap, 24, 27, 37, 82, 93, 207, 264
Over-stimulation, 134, 136

P

Paradigm, 4, 12, 31, 39, 82, 87, 88, 127, 161,
    217, 224, 243, 258, 272
Particularity, 177
Pathogenic beliefs, 152, 159, 161, 165
Pathologizing, 38, 62, 250
Pattern recognition, 26, 27
Peer relations, 256
Person-centered, 4, 54, 60, 190–193, 195, 197,
    198
PIE, 61, 92, 264
Positive health status, 190, 192, 195
Practice wisdom, 41, 257, 286, 299
Pragmatic principles, 220–222, 224
Praxis, 231, 232, 240
Primary, 5, 6, 55, 75, 92, 104, 114, 156, 213,
    250, 252, 276, 284, 298
Priming, 29, 30, 41, 89
Problem-based learning, 236, 238, 242–244
Problems in living, 90, 92, 93, 103, 250
Protocol, 2, 81, 88, 96, 254, 287
Prototype, 27, 31, 252, 298

Proxy, 21, 32, 101
Psychiatric diagnosis, 17, 21, 46, 55, 93, 102,
    172, 197, 264
Psychoanalytic, 91, 103, 153, 159, 162, 272
Psychodynamic, 4, 11, 18, 24, 57, 152–157,
    160, 162–167, 232, 255
Psychodynamic Diagnostic Manual (PDM), 60,
    163
Psychodynamic formulation, 164
Psychopathology, 54, 63, 91, 98, 121, 140,
    180, 241, 260
Psychopharmacology, 299

R

Racial bias, 99
Randomized clinical trial, 123
Reactivity, 5, 134, 137, 139, 141, 166, 261
Reductionism, 112
Referentiality, 177
Reification, 21, 51, 61
Reimbursement, 3, 10, 73, 75, 76, 86, 251
Relational disorders, 101–103
Relational theory, 154
Research domain, 50
Root metaphor, 174

S

Scaffolding, 232, 235
Secondary, 95, 114, 209, 252, 260
Selective attention, 31, 173, 288
Selective reporting, 79
Self-regulation, 134, 141, 145, 147
Self-report, 41, 102, 141, 142, 286, 288
Sensitivity, 37, 94, 143, 145, 177, 241
Severity, 9, 23, 38, 92, 102, 104, 273, 274
Situational, 29, 31, 52, 53, 120, 160
Social constructivism, 174, 212
Social context, 34, 94, 106, 259
Soothability, 5, 136
Specificity, 37, 38, 216
Spiritual assessment, 257
Standardized tests, 64
Stressors, 19, 86, 93, 94, 106, 115, 116, 118,
    146, 251, 256, 260, 273
Subjectivity, 86, 161, 163, 172, 215
Surgency, 135
Syllogistic reasoning, 49
Symptom, 20, 22–25, 27, 31, 34, 36, 41,
    47, 50, 51, 56, 57, 64, 70, 86, 90,
    93, 94, 100, 117, 143, 152, 163,
    164, 179, 193, 211, 234, 251, 256,
    260, 263, 264, 272, 285, 288,
    289

T

Taxonomy, 36, 40, 217, 250, 272

Temperament, 4, 5, 12, 25, 105, 115, 133–142, 144, 145, 147, 235, 256, 289

Template, 2, 3, 8, 31, 36, 39, 87, 140, 252

Temporality, 174

Third party providers, 10

Threshold, 24, 28, 89, 100, 140, 260, 289

Transactional, 4, 8, 19, 86, 105, 289

Transformative learning, 231, 241, 243

Trauma, 9, 19, 41, 54, 81, 105, 118, 126, 143, 155, 160, 161, 165, 174, 182

U

Unconscious, 17, 30, 57, 88, 99, 153, 157, 159, 160, 165, 167, 272

V

Variation, 17, 88, 95, 97, 105, 239, 262, 289

V codes, 86, 92, 102, 273

Vignettes, 234, 263

Vulnerability, 12, 146, 155, 211, 260

W

Wiring, 18, 263

Made in the USA
Middletown, DE
20 September 2021